'The book seeks to strategically fill a void in the representation of South Asian constitutions and constitutionalism in international discourse. Although parts of South Asia have remained obscure and unstable on the fine balance of constitutional stability and constitutionalism, an appreciable number of countries have successfully operated constitutional schemes that are based on systems developed in the West, through a process of trial and error. A study of the successes and failures of constitutionalism in this extremely diverse region is overdue. This volume's well-researched essays address diverse and crucial issues affecting South Asian constitutionalism. It bears the potential of bringing this subject to the centre-stage of constitutional discourse globally, as well as within the South Asian region. This book will inspire more expansive and critical studies that will benefit the region and other similarly situated regions of the global society. A compelling read, it offers a sturdy platform for follow-up studies.'

—**Professor Mahendra P. Singh**
Chairperson, Delhi Judicial Academy; Vice-Chancellor, The West Bengal National University of Juridical Sciences, Kolkata (2006–11)

'This volume presents rich and excellent perspectives on comparative constitutionalism in South Asia. It reflects on the perennial problems of constitutionalism and explores the utility of cross-pollination of laws and practices as a means of responding to local needs. The essays provide deep insights into the historical, political, legislative, and judicial evolution of constitutionalism in the South Asian states. An important contribution of this volume is an examination of the interpretative models courts can adapt, that not only incorporate valuable lessons from their regional counterparts, but also reflect their unique domestic values. As a whole, the essays will inspire more vibrant debate on comparative constitutionalism in South Asia and provide an excellent foundation for research to follow.'

—**Justice András Sajó**
Judge, European Court of Human Rights; University Professor, Central European University, Budapest

'Is a comparative study of constitutional law merely of academic interest to be dismissed as an esoteric exercise that serves no practical purpose? Given that those involved in the processes of framing, interpretation, and application of constitutional principles and provisions resort to transnational 'borrowing', an analytical justification of the processes is required. A comparative study of constitutional law provides that justification. Constitutional 'borrowing' is perhaps inevitable given the increasing political, economic, and social interaction, and the endorsement by countries of common values and standards as members of the UN. The present study of constitutional developments in South Asian countries by eminent scholars is quite relevant. The articles are brilliantly crafted, informative, critically analytical, and thought-provoking, making for serious and compelling reading for academics and practitioners alike.'

—Justice **Ruma Pal**
Judge, the Supreme Court of India (2000–6)

'This volume pays tribute to two brilliant South Asian thinkers, Neelan Tiruchelvam and Upendra Baxi, by taking their ideas and moving forward into the twenty-first century. The essays are diverse but, like Tiruchelevam and Baxi, have a moral core aimed at securing justice and resolving intractable conflict. It is a thoughtful, provocative collection of essays that will be a must-read for all those interested in constitutional development in South Asia.'

—**Radhika Coomaraswamy**
Special Representative of the UN Secretary General
for Children and Armed Conflict (2006–12);
Chairperson, Sri Lanka Human Rights Commission (2003–6)

Comparative Constitutionalism in South Asia

Comparative Constitutionalism in South Asia

Edited by

Sunil Khilnani
Vikram Raghavan
Arun K. Thiruvengadam

OXFORD
UNIVERSITY PRESS

OXFORD
UNIVERSITY PRESS

Oxford University Press is a department of the University of Oxford.
It furthers the University's objective of excellence in research, scholarship,
and education by publishing worldwide. Oxford is a registered trademark of
Oxford University Press in the UK and in certain other countries

Published in India by
Oxford University Press
22 Workspace, 2nd Floor, 1/22 Asaf Ali Road, New Delhi 110002, India

First Edition published in 2013
Oxford India Paperbacks 2016

ISBN-13: 978-0-19-946660-3
ISBN-10: 0-19-946660-2

Typeset in Adobe Garamond Pro 11/13
by MAP Systems, Bengaluru 560 082, India
Printed in India by Replika Press Pvt. Ltd.

For
Neelan Tiruchelvam and Upendra Baxi

Contents

Preface   xi

Introduction: Reviving South Asian Comparative
Constitutionalism   1

Sunil Khilnani, Vikram Raghavan, and Arun K. Thiruvengadam

1 Modelling 'Optimal' Constitutional Design
   for Government Structures: Some Debutant Remarks   23

   Upendra Baxi

2 How to Do Comparative Constitutional Law in
   India: *Naz Foundation*, Same Sex Rights, and Dialogical
   Interpretation   45

   Sujit Choudhry

3 Constitutional Developments in a Himalayan Kingdom:
   The Experience of Nepal   86

   Mara Malagodi

4 Separating Religion and Politics? Buddhism and
   the Bhutanese Constitution   116

   Richard W. Whitecross

5 The Democratic State and Religious Pluralism:
   Comparative Constitutionalism and
   Constitutional Experiences of Sri Lanka   145

   Deepika Udagama

6   Constitutional Borrowing in South Asia: India,
    Sri Lanka, and Secular Constitutional Identity   180

    Gary J. Jacobsohn and Shylashri Shankar

7   Inheritance Unbound: The Politics of Personal
    Law Reform in Pakistan and India   219

    Matthew J. Nelson

8   Religious Freedom in India and Pakistan:
    The Matter of Conversion   247

    John H. Mansfield

9   Pilate's Paramount Duty: Constitutional Reasonableness
    and the Restriction of Freedom of Expression and
    Assembly   267

    T. John O'Dowd

10 Constitutionalism and the Judiciary in Bangladesh   303

    Ridwanul Hoque

11 Revisiting *The Role of the Judiciary in Plural Societies
    (1987)*: A Quarter-Century Retrospective on Public
    Interest Litigation in India and the Global South   341

    Arun K. Thiruvengadam

Afterword by Michael Kirby   370
Index   379
About the Editors and Contributors   397

Preface

This book is the product of two workshops on South Asian constitutionalism. The first was held in November 2006 at the School of Oriental and African Studies (SOAS) in London. This event was generously supported by the Johns Hopkins School of Advanced International Studies (SAIS) and the General Electric Foundation, and was hosted by SOAS's Law Department. Professors Werner Menski and Alex Fischer at SOAS and Jenika Kaul at SAIS were enormously helpful in planning and executing the event.

Our second workshop took place at the Faculty of Law, National University of Singapore (NUS), in June 2009. It was jointly financed by the Asian Law Institute, the Faculty of Law at NUS, and SAIS. Generous financial support was also provided through a grant (Grant No. R-241-000-070-112) from the Singapore Ministry of Education's Academic Research Fund administered by the National University of Singapore. We thank our NUS colleagues—Kumaralingam Amirthalingam, Michael Hor, and Victor Ramraj—for moderating the sessions at the workshop. We would like to acknowledge the superb administrative support provided by Elizabeth Chua and Wendy Wee. Abhik Majumdar, who was then a graduate student at NUS, also helped in organizing the workshop. Taberez Neyazi, Juliette Duara, Teo Lee Ken, and Lau Si Min Jannelle performed valuable service as research assistants on the overall project.

We thank Praveen Dev at the Oxford University Press (OUP) India for his initial support to our project and his patience through the inevitable delays that arise from putting together an edited volume of contributions. Barun Kumar Sarkar and Manish Kumar of OUP India provided vital assistance during the final stages of the editorial work.

In writing our introduction and during the overall editorial process, we were greatly assisted by the efforts of Matthew Moorhead and Badrinarayan Seetharaman. We are also grateful for the stellar assistance provided to us by Elizabeth Hassan in proofreading the manuscript.

Finally, we dedicate this volume to Neelan Tiruchelvam and Upendra Baxi, who were two early pioneers in the field of South Asian comparative constitutionalism. Tiruchelvam's work and legacy are commemorated in the Introduction, while Baxi's opening essay in the volume is a testament to the importance of this much neglected subject.

SUNIL KHILNANI
VIKRAM RAGHAVAN
ARUN K. THIRUVENGADAM

Reviving South Asian Comparative Constitutionalism

❧❧

Sunil Khilnani, Vikram Raghavan,
*and Arun K. Thiruvengadam**

INTRODUCTION AND BRIEF OVERVIEW OF EXISTING SCHOLARSHIP

South Asia, at once a civilizational as well as a geopolitical entity, consists of nine countries: Afghanistan, Bangladesh, Bhutan, India, the Maldives, Myanmar, Nepal, Pakistan, and Sri Lanka. Together, this region is home to one-and-a-half billion people. Geographically, the region is contained by mountain ranges in the north and by the Indian Ocean in the south. The different people of South Asia reflect the diversity of their surroundings, but despite the array of cultures, thousands of years of shared history have tied South Asia's traditions and people together in complex ways. The search for a common foundation beneath the cultures of South Asia has attracted waves of scholarship, occurring in several distinct phases.

What began as exotic Orientalist accounts of the subcontinent's ancient and spiritual moorings later transformed into strategic and foreign policy area studies fuelled by the Cold War. More recently, Western observers have come to view the region as the singular source of extremist ideology and terrorism, especially after the 9/11 (11 September 2001) attacks on the United States. At the same time, in the economic sphere, South Asia has been influenced by the

* We are grateful to Matthew Moorhead and Badrinarayan Seetharaman for their research support to this essay.

same globalizing forces that have driven a worldwide liberalization of trade and investment flows. Mirroring developments elsewhere in the world,[1] there have been efforts to build regional institutional architecture in South Asia, notably, the creation of the South Asian Association for Regional Cooperation (SAARC) in 1985. Generally, however, regional economic integration has lagged in this part of the world. After more than twenty-five years of the formation of SAARC, the region has been characterized as 'one of the least integrated regions in the world…mired in mutual mistrust and conflict'.[2]

South Asia's economic integration is vital to the region's own prosperity and peace, and it has global implications too. Economic integration in South Asia will be a slow process, and it will require increasing dialogue and interconnection between the legal and governance structures present in the region. Yet such dialogue has rarely been engaged in. This is ironic, for despite their divergent recent histories and political experiences, South Asian countries in fact display a remarkable degree of constitutional and legal kinship. There are several common elements among the region's constitutions, political structures, and legal systems. These elements are drawn from the region's colonial past and from its many diverse indigenous legal traditions. The potential for intra-regional borrowing and comparative study is considerable. Such potential is not restricted only to countries with established constitutional and legal traditions; it also extends to those States that find themselves at an early stage of constitutionalism. Yet this rich potential for comparative study—for the development of a comparative South Asian constitutionalism—has been a relatively unexplored area in the region's jurisprudence and in the social sciences. This neglect is all the more glaring when compared with the thriving field of scholarship on East and Southeast Asian constitutions.[3]

---

[1] Attempts to erect institutional architecture are nowhere new, and have taken place across the world since World War II. For an interesting study of early attempts to understand regionalism in a postcolonial constitutional setting, see, Thomas M. Franck, *East African Unity Through Law* (Yale University Press: New Haven, 1964).

[2] Ramesh Chandra and Rajiv Kumar, 'South Asian Integration: Prospects and Lessons from East Asia', in Masahiro Kawai, Jong-Wha Lee, and Peter A. Petri (eds), *Asian Regionalism and the World Economy* (Edward Elgar: Cheltenham, 2010), p. 415.

[3] See, for example, Tom Ginsburg and Albert H.Y. Chen (eds), *Administrative Law and Governance in Asia: Comparative Perspectives* (Routledge: London, 2009)

There are several reasons why South Asian constitutionalism, with the possible exception of Indian constitutionalism, has either been largely ignored or has not received the attention it deserves. First, exemplifying a certain 'silo mentality', South Asian scholars of public law have on the whole been reticent about undertaking regional studies. Most of their work is focused primarily on their own constitutional law and jurisprudence. Those who do indulge in comparative studies invariably use Western democracies as their reference points. As Radhika Coomaraswamy argues, this situation has contributed to South Asian nations being regarded as 'the illegitimate children of the Anglo-American legal/political tradition'.[4] This sense of illegitimacy, in turn, 'breeds an elusive dependence on the part of the former colonies and an awkward condescension on the part of the patron'.[5] Second, most South Asian law faculties and political science departments face a severe shortage of funds and resources. This constrains their ability to attract and retain academic talent or to finance any meaningful regional research. Third, many scholars perceive little academic recognition or incentive in surveying regional developments. Despite these constraints, there have been some notable attempts to study and analyse South Asian constitutionalism, in the period since decolonization. In what follows, we provide a brief overview of notable individuals and institutions that made significant contributions.

For understandable historical reasons, some of the earliest of such scholars were of British origin. One of the first to write about South Asian law in the post-Independence era was Ivor Jennings, a noted English public law academic who taught for some years at the University of Ceylon and was involved in the drafting of the Dominion of Ceylon's 1948 'Soulbury' Constitution.[6] In his Waynflete Lectures, published as *The Commonwealth in Asia*, Jennings considered the fledging constitutional structures in India and Ceylon.[7] In Ceylon's

---

and Tom Ginsburg, *Judicial Review in New Democracies: Constitutional Courts in Asian Cases* (Cambridge University Press: Cambridge and New York, 2003).

[4] Radhika Coomaraswamy, *Sri Lanka: The Crisis of the Anglo-American Constitutional Traditions in a Developing Society* (Vikas: New Delhi, 1984), p. 1.

[5] Ibid.

[6] See, *The Constitution of Ceylon* (1949).

[7] Ivor Jennings, *The Commonwealth in Asia* (Oxford University Press: London, 1951).

case, Jennings identified the dangers of communalism as the chief obstacle in establishing constitutional government. Compared to India, however, Jennings felt that Ceylon's problems were 'on smaller scale and more easily handled'.[8] The greatest threat to fledgling Indian constitutionalism was the vast emergency power given to the central government to 'suspend fundamental liberties just when they are most needed'.[9] Jennings was also wary of the Indian Constitution's articulation of negative liberties, which was pointedly omitted by the Soulbury Constitution.[10]

This focus on South Asian law was to some extent developed in the Department of Law at the School of Oriental and African Studies (SOAS), established in 1947–8 as a part of the University of London.[11] One of the founding members of the School was Alan Gledhill, who had served on the high court bench in Burma, specialized in constitutional and criminal law, and wrote comprehensive volumes on the constitutional laws of India and Pakistan.[12] Gledhill's colleague at SOAS, Duncan Derrett, reputed as an authority on Hindu law, was also the author of *Introduction to Legal Systems*, which canvassed South Asian law more generally.[13] After Derrett's departure from SOAS in 1980, Werner Menski took up the mantle of writing on Hindu law, while also maintaining a South Asian perspective through a number of other works that analysed aspects of law in India, Pakistan, and Bangladesh more generally.[14]

[8] Ibid., p. 70.

[9] Ibid., p. 108.

[10] The Soulbury Constitution emerged from the workings of the 1944 Soulbury Commission, and largely adopted the recommendations of Don Stephen Senanayake, who became Ceylon's first prime minister.

[11] The details about SOAS mentioned here are drawn from an edited volume that marked the celebration of the fiftieth anniversary of the founding of the SOAS law department. See, Ian Edge (ed.), *Comparative Law in a Global Perspective* (Transnational Publishers: New York, 2000).

[12] Alan Gledhill, *The Republic of India: The Development of Its Law and Constitution* (Stevens: London, 1951); Alan Gledhill, *Pakistan: The Development of Its Laws and Constitution*, 2nd Ed. (Stevens: London, 1967).

[13] J.D.M. Derrett, *Introduction to Legal Systems* (Sweet & Maxwell: London, 1968).

[14] See for example, Werner Menski, Ahmad Rafay Alam, and Mehrin Kasuri Raza, *Public Interest Litigation in Pakistan* (Platinum: London, 2000); Werner

Within South Asia itself, one institution that helped to advance scholarship on South Asian law was the Indian Law Institute. Founded in 1956, it quickly became a dynamic centre for research and publications on comparative law in India, South Asia, and Southeast Asia, and its house publication, *The Journal of the Indian Law Institute*, established a reputation as one of the leading scholarly journals in and about the region. It is striking that the initial issues of the journal featured several pieces by scholars exhorting the need for comparative lessons on various aspects of the law.[15] In addition to South Asian scholars, scholars from other regions who focused on South Asian law also published in the journal; Gledhill, for instance, was a regular international contributor to its pages.[16]

In 1960, the Australian National University organized a seminar on Asian constitutionalism. The objective was to consider how constitutional government was faring in postcolonial Asia. Participants included lawyers and judges from Burma, India, and Pakistan, scholars of Ceylon and Indonesia, and the retired Chief Justice of Australia, John Latham. Their papers were later published in an edited volume called *Constitutionalism in Asia*.[17] The participants at the seminar noted the prevailing challenges: Pakistan and Indonesia had abandoned parliamentary government, Burma had just returned to it, and some scepticism surrounded the long-term survival of constitutional democracy in Ceylon and India. Nevertheless, the seminar participants

---

Menski, *Comparative Law in a Global Context: The Legal Systems of Asia and Africa* (Cambridge University Press: Cambridge, 2006).

[15] See, for example, K. Narayana Rao, 'Public Discipline Service Rules in Pakistan', *Journal of the Indian Law Institute*, (1963), 5: 287–95 (analysing civil service regulations in Pakistan and recommending that the Indian counterpart law be reformed along similar lines); Syed Jaffer Hussain, 'Legal Modernism in Islam', *Journal of the Indian Law Institute*, (1965), 7: 389–98 (analysing legal reforms of Muslim personal laws in Pakistan and India); and Tahir Mahmood, 'Personal Laws in Bangladesh: A Comparative Perspective', *Journal of the Indian Law Institute*, (1972), 14: 583–9 (focusing on progressive reforms of Muslim personal law with respect to rights of women in Bangladesh and encouraging their emulation in India and Pakistan).

[16] See, for example, Alan Gledhill, 'Fundamental Rights in Pakistan', *Journal of the Indian Law Institute*, (1965), 7: 70 (comparing the development of constitutional rights in Pakistan and drawing contrasts to their development in India).

[17] R.N. Spann (ed.), *Constitutionalism in Asia* (Asia Publishing House: London, 1963).

shared an attitude of 'sober optimism',[18] based on a shared conviction that Asia's ruling elites were committed, more or less, to upholding constitutionalism. The five decades since have, in varying ways and degrees, both vindicated and disproved this assessment.

German scholar Dieter Conrad was another important contributor to South Asian comparative constitutional scholarship. Based at Heidelberg's South Asia Institute, Conrad lectured in February 1965 at Banaras Hindu University's Law Faculty on the topic of constitutional amendments. Bearing Germany's experience with the Weimar Constitution in mind, Conrad forcefully argued that there ought to be implied limitations on the Indian Parliament's power to amend the Constitution.[19] Conrad's thesis was later used by lawyers to persuade the Supreme Court of India to restrict Parliament's amending powers under the basic structure doctrine.[20] This doctrine later had a significant influence on constitutional developments in other South Asian jurisdictions.[21]

In later years, scholars of South Asian origin began undertaking comparative studies or analyses that focused on single jurisdictional studies that had implications beyond that jurisdiction. Upendra Baxi emerged as one such voice, and has consistently sought, over the course of the last four decades, to draw attention to developments in other parts of South Asia in the realm of public law.[22] Baxi's essay in this volume (Chapter 1) draws upon that long experience of writing

---

[18] Ibid., p. xii.

[19] Dieter Conrad, 'Limitation of Amendment Procedures and the Constituent Power', *Indian Year Book of International Affairs* (University of Madras: Madras, 1966–7), pp. 375–430.

[20] A.G. Noorani, 'Behind the Basic Structure Doctrine', *Frontline*, (28 April–11 May 2001), 18(09). In addition to Conrad's writings, the doctrine was apparently influenced by a Dhaka High Court judgment.

[21] For a discussion of the Pakistan and Bangladesh cases, see, Dieter Conrad, 'Basic Structure of the Constitution and Constitutional Principles', *Law and Justice*, (1996), 3(1–4): 99–114. The Sri Lankan use of basic structure is analysed in G.L. Peiris, 'Provincial Autonomy within a Unitary Constitutional Framework: The Sri Lankan Crisis', *Comparative and International Law Journal of South Africa*, (1989), 165.

[22] See for example, Upendra Baxi, 'Constitutional Interpretation and State Formative Practices in Pakistan: A Preliminary Exploration', in Mahendra P. Singh (ed.), *Comparative Constitutional Law* (Eastern Book Company: New Delhi, 1989).

on South Asian law to ask some foundational questions about comparative constitutional law in South Asia.

Neelan Tiruchelvam, another notable pioneer in the field of South Asian comparative constitutionalism, deserves special acknowledgment. He was a Sri Lankan lawyer, parliamentarian, and peace activist, remembered around the world for his efforts to find a peaceful resolution to Sri Lanka's civil war through constitutionalism. Through his work and writing, he advanced regional constitutionalism as a means to ensure greater political and economic integration and harmony in South Asia generally, and Sri Lanka in particular.[23]

Tiruchelvam's deep insights into the theory and practice of comparative constitutionalism were respected and valued by scholars and practitioners. He served as a consultant or advisor to constitution-making processes in Nepal, Kazakhstan, and South Africa. In that role, he rejected the form of constitution-making that legitimized the authority of political elites in favour of a consensual form of constitution-making that sought to empower all citizens. A proper constitutional system, he asserted, ought to represent the ideals of the 'different components of the body politic',[24] and provide a means to individual political self-determination. Tiruchelvam's commitment to South Asian constitutionalism is displayed in his final act before his untimely death—a draft constitution for Sri Lanka that ambitiously sought to heal its ethnic divisions and civil war scars by a process of devolution. Tiruchelvam also inspired a future generation of Sri Lankan scholars to undertake genuinely comparative research on South Asian law. These include scholars such as Radhika Coomaraswamy, Rohan Edrsinha, and Deepika Udagama (a contributor to this volume).

Sadly, much of this early impetus towards a more comparative and regional approach to constitutional issues was lost in more recent years. There are, however, some notable exceptions. An important precursor to our volume is a monograph titled *Public Interest Litigation in South*

---

[23] See for example, Neelan Tiruchelvam, 'The Making and Unmaking of Constitutions: Some Reflections on the Process', *The Ceylon Journal of Historical and Social Studies*, (1977). For an assessment of Tiruchelvam's legacy, see, Roberto Unger, *A Fighter for Peace* (Harvard Law School: Cambridge, MA, 1999) and V. Suryanarayan, 'A Great Force for Good', *Frontline*, (5–18 August 2000), 17(16).

[24] Ibid.

Asia.[25] Featuring contributions by prominent judges and scholars from across South Asia—the volume includes essays by Rajeev Dhavan, Kamal Hossain, Soli Sorabjee, and NeelanTiruchelvam—it provides a description of the evolution of public interest litigation in Bangladesh, Nepal, and India, laments its absence in Sri Lanka, and identifies pressing issues for practitioners and judges in the region to consider. Other examples of such scholarship include book-length studies of the availability of state-sponsored criminal legal aid in comparative law by S. Muralidhar,[26] and of the advances made in environmental protection by judiciaries across South Asia by Jona Razzaque.[27]

Recent developments from across the globe demonstrate that people who were once bitter enemies can coexist peacefully and integrate under a common regional legal and regulatory framework. The most remarkable example is of course the history of Europe over the past seven decades. In this spirit, an awareness of the benefits of an open, regional outlook is becoming more evident in the decisions, opinions, and speeches of South Asian judges and lawyers, many of whom have already recognized the value of studying and citing other constitutional and legal systems in the region.[28] Appellate judges and lawyers are emboldened to embark upon regional borrowings by their seemingly apolitical mandate, relative familiarity with the underlying constitutional terrain, and the regular similarity of questions and issues

[25] Sara Hossain, Shahdeen Malik and Bushra Musa (eds), *Public Interest Litigation in South Asia: Rights in Search of Remedies* (University Press: Dhaka, 1997).

[26] S. Muralidhar, *Law, Poverty and Legal Aid: Access to Criminal Justice* (LexisNexis Butterworths: New Delhi, 2004).

[27] Jona Razzaque, *Public Interest Environmental Litigation in India, Pakistan and Bangladesh* (Kluwer: New York, 2004). See also, G.L. Peiris, 'Public Interest Litigation in the Indian Subcontinent: Current Dimensions', *International and Comparative Law Quarterly*, (1991), 40(66), and Ananda Mohan Bhattarai and Vikram Raghavan, 'Judicial Scrutiny of the Dissolution of the Legislatures: Notes from the Indian Subcontinent', *Lawasia*, (1996–7), pp. 21–40.

[28] The South Asian Association for Regional Co-operation in Law ('SAARCLAW') has also been instrumental in promoting regional exchanges among lawyers and judges. SAARCLAW is an association of South Asian judges, lawyers, academics, law teachers, and public officers with national chapters in virtually all member countries. It was established in Colombo in 1991 as an association to share legal information and concerns throughout the region. Its objectives are to promote cooperation and engagement between South Asian legal communities to use and develop law as a source and an instrument for social change.

presented. Yet, the scope for regional osmosis is not confined only to the Judiciary or the legal profession. Elected officials, policy makers, legislators, regulators, and members of civil society can also engage in comparative exercises and simulations.[29] Thereby, something like a South Asian 'constitutional common sense' might be created, which could serve as a valuable resource for achieving more successful and mutually advantageous integration within the region.[30]

THE GENERAL FIELD OF COMPARATIVE CONSTITUTIONAL LAW

A paradox of comparative constitutionalism is that it is simultaneously old and new. Aristotle's *Politics* is arguably one of the earliest works in this field, with its focus on the constitutions of Greek city-states in order to obtain normative insights on democratic design. Similarly, intellectuals in ancient societies in Iraq, China, India, and Egypt speculated about the principles of governance in ways that scholars of constitutionalism would instantly recognize as similar to what they do in relation to contemporary developments.[31] Nevertheless, there is something distinctive about the way the modern discipline has developed.

[29] This potential exists not only for constitutional issues, but also for other legal and policy matters. For instance, Indian and Pakistani telecom regulators have sought each others' inputs on certain regulatory decisions. See, Vikram Raghavan, 'The Global Implications of India's Telecom Regulatory Authority of India', paper presented at Centre for Policy Research and New York University School of Law's Seminar on Global Regulatory Governance, 5–6 January 2008.Other substantive legal areas have also received episodic regional comparative analysis. See, for example, Mark Sidel, *Philanthrophy and Law in South Asia* (University of Iowa: Iowa, 2008)(surveying legal frameworks for philanthrophy in Bangladesh, India, Sri Lanka, Nepal, and Pakistan).

[30] Even so, there are many 'missed opportunities' in South Asia where regional perspectives appear to have been inexplicably neglected for transplants from more distant horizons. See, Kanak Mani Dixit, 'The Life and Death of the Constituent Assembly of Nepal', *Economic and Political Weekly*, 47(31): 35, 40 (noting that even as members of the recently dissolved Constituent Assembly 'trooped to South Africa and Switzerland, the constitutional experience of the [S]outh Asian neighbourhood—India, Pakistan, Bangladesh, [and] Sri Lanka—was scarcely considered').

[31] Rosalind Dixon and Tom Ginsburg, 'Introduction', in Tom Ginsburg and Rosalind Dixon (eds), *Comparative Constitutional Law* (Edward Elgar: Northampton, 2011), p. 1.

Many scholars attribute the rise of modern comparative constitutionalism as a distinct field of study to the explosion of constitutional documents across the world since World War II, and the more recent waves of constitutional reforms that occurred in the 1980s and 1990s.[32] As one scholar notes, '[o]ver 150 countries as well as supra-national entities (for example, the European Union) covering approximately three quarters of the world population have gone through major constitutionalization processes over the last few decades'.[33] Influenced by international human rights treaties, many of these countries adopted bills of rights and established some form of judicial review.[34] In recent years, several governmental institutions, regulators, and constitutional courts around the world have come to rely on comparative constitutional law to carve out solutions for their own domestic contexts. Thus, knowledge of comparative constitutional law has become a vital tool for judges, lawyers, regulators, legislators, and students of domestic constitutional law.

These historical and practical developments have created a corresponding demand for teaching and scholarship in the area of comparative constitutional law. A number of law schools around the world now offer courses on the subject; several specialized centres in the field have emerged across the globe; professional associations of comparative constitutional scholars have seen a substantial rise in membership; and just in the last decade, at least three basic textbooks and a vast number of edited collections and periodicals in the field have emerged.[35] Even as scholars have termed this era 'the heyday for scholars of comparative constitutional law and politics', they

---

[32] Vicki C. Jackson and Mark Tushnet, 'Introduction', in Vicki C. Jackson and Mark Tushnet (eds), *Defining the Field of Comparative Constitutional Law* (Praeger Publishers: Santa Barbara, CA, 2002), p. xiii.

[33] Ran Hirschl, 'The Continued Renaissance of Comparative Constitutional Law', *Tulsa Law Review*, (2011), 45: 771.

[34] Thomas M. Franck and Arun K. Thiruvengadam, 'International Law and Constitution-Making', *Chinese Journal of International Law*, (2003), 2(2): 467–518.

[35] The study of comparative constitutionalism is also expanding online. The website http://constitutionmaking.org is a joint project of the Comparative Constitutions Project and the United States Institute of Peace. Its goal is to provide designers with systematic information on design options and constitutional text, drawing on the Comparative Constitutions Project's comprehensive dataset on the features of national constitutions since 1789.

are quick to acknowledge that certain 'foundational, ontological, epistemological and methodological questions concerning the field's purpose, scope and nature'[36] still need to be addressed. In what follows, we provide a brief overview of debates about how contemporary scholarship should address these unanswered questions.

One of the important contemporary debates within the field is in relation to its overall purpose and function. To an extent, this parallels debates within the older discipline of comparative law, which has been perceived as a distinct body of law since at least the nineteenth century.[37] However, much of the focus there was on private law, and its early exponents focused on concepts and purposes that were more suited to private law.[38] The dominant players in the field of comparative law extolled the virtues of a 'functionalist' approach which would use comparative models and examples to solve problems and arrive at practical solutions.[39] It was therefore natural that comparative constitutional law would also be affected by this overall approach. Subsequently, comparative law also developed a more 'universalist' rationale, which posits that a community's conceptions of law, politics, and justice could be enriched by studying foreign experiences.[40] The latter claim is controversial among those comparative constitutional law scholars who see a 'neo-imperialist' agenda lurking behind the facade of universalist values. There is thus a strain within comparative constitutional law scholarship that emphasizes the problems of

[36] Hirschl, 'Continued Renaissance', p. 772.

[37] This occurred through much of the nineteenth century, culminating in the establishment of the International Congress of Comparative Law in 1900. See generally, David S. Clark, 'Comparative Law in 1900 and Today', *Tulane Law Review*, (2001), 75: 871–912.

[38] Konrad Zweigert and Hein Kotz, *Introduction to Comparative Law* (Clarendon Press: Oxford, 1978).

[39] Ibid., pp. 15–21.

[40] In an early article on the subject, Donald Kommers advocated increased interaction between German and American constitutional law in functionalist terms, emphasizing the potential benefits to both discourses. See, Donald P. Kommers, 'The Value of Comparative Constitutional Law', *Marshall Journal of Practice and Procedure*, (1976), 9: 685. At other points in the piece, Kommers emphasized the possibility of discovering universal truths about 'principles of justice and political obligation that transcend the culture bound opinions and conventions of a particular political community'. Kommers can be understood as providing both 'functionalist' and 'universalist' justifications for comparative constitutional law.

adopting a universalist view, and suggests instead that the methods of critical legal theory (which challenges the possibility of transcultural comparisons) be employed to analyse subjects within the discipline.[41]

Another perspective on this foundational debate focuses on the difficulty in contrasting systems with very different historical traditions, political structures, legal culture, and constitutional language. For some scholars, these and other factors—such as the distinctiveness of public law because of its dependence on historical and institutional contingencies—raise serious questions about the viability of functionalism as the principal purpose of comparative constitutional law.[42] Such scholars emphasize the importance of comparative constitutional law, not only for understanding 'the affinities of comparative legal phenomena' but also for understanding the differences between them.[43]

There is also considerable debate over the relationship between the field of comparative constitutional law and allied disciplines (some of which have a longer historical pedigree and a greater degree of methodological sophistication) and the amount of learning that should occur across such fields. This debate also extends to introspection over the methodology employed by scholars engaged in comparative constitutionalism and their perceived deficiencies and virtues. To provide an overview of these issues, we focus here on views expressed by three leading scholars of contemporary comparative constitutional law.

Sujit Choudhry has criticized the emerging field of constitutional scholarship for its excessive focus on 'comparative approaches to the protection of universal human rights within a liberal democratic constitutional order' that has resulted in a 'literature oriented

---

[41] Ruti Teitel argues that this is approach was adopted by Vicki Jackson and Mark Tushnet in their leading casebook on comparative constitutional law. See, Ruti Teitel, 'Comparative Constitutional Law in a Global Age', *Harvard Law Review*, (2004), 11: 2578.

[42] John Bell, 'Comparing Public Law', in Andrew Harding and Esin Örücü (eds), *Comparative Law in the 21st Century* (Institute of Advanced Legal Studies: London, 2002); Gunther Frankenburg, 'Critical Comparisons: Re-thinking Comparative Law', *Harvard International Law Journal*, (1985), 26: 411. For these scholars, the problem with functionalist approaches is that they do not focus adequately on the extent to which constitutional problems are informed by local politics and culture.

[43] Ruti Teitel, 'Comparative Constitutional Law in a Global Age', *Harvard Law Review*, 11: 2584–7.

around a standard and relatively limited set of cases: South Africa, Israel, Germany, Canada, the United Kingdom, New Zealand, the United States, and to a lesser extent, India'.[44] Choudhry asserts that this may have happened because the field 'has taken its cues from the American literature, and framed its questions around it'.[45] His proffered solution to this problem lies in turning to the field of comparative politics, which has focused on issues beyond rights-based constitutionalism for decades and has developed a vast body of literature that is increasingly relevant for scholars of constitutional law. Choudhry therefore calls for 'bridg[ing] comparative politics and comparative constitutional law through a genuinely interdisciplinary conversation'.[46]

Ran Hirschl is strongly critical of the lack of methodological rigour in much of contemporary comparative constitutional law scholarship.[47] He laments the failure, in many such studies, of the adoption of social scientific research methods of controlled comparison, research design, and case selection which enable the making of proper causal inferences. Hirschl's remedy, like that of Choudhry's, is that scholars of comparative constitutional law learn from their peers in comparative politics. This suggestion is contested by Mark Tushnet, who takes a more favourable view of contemporary literature in the field, and notes the many intellectual accomplishments that have been reached. He argues that many comparative constitutional law scholars adopt the well-established methods used in the study of comparative law, and sets out examples of new insights that have been added as a result.[48]

A very recent trend in comparative constitutional scholarship is towards the use of empirical methods involving large datasets. A good

---

[44] Sujit Choudhry, 'Introduction', in Sujit Choudhry (ed.), *Constitutional Design for Divided Societies: Integration or Accommodation?* (Oxford University Press: Oxford, 2008), pp. 8–9.

[45] Ibid., p. 10.

[46] Ibid., p. 13.

[47] Ran Hirschl, 'On the Blurred Methodological Matrix of Comparative Constitutional Law', in Sujit Choudhry (ed.), *The Migration of Constitutional Ideas* (Cambridge University Press: Cambridge, 2007).

[48] Mark Tushnet, 'Some Reflections on Method in Comparative Constitutional Law', in Choudhry (ed.), *The Migration of Constitutional Ideas*, pp. 67–83.

example is the recent title, *The Endurance of National Constitutions*, by Elkins, Ginsburg and Melton.[49] Using a comprehensive dataset of the constitutions of the world from 1789 to 2005, the authors make several empirical and normative claims that challenge some of the conventional wisdom around constitutionalism, including those related to constitutions in South Asia.

THE THEMES AND CONTENT OF THIS VOLUME

Spurred by our belief that South Asian comparative constitutionalism needs greater scholarly attention, in December 2006 we convened a meeting in London to explore how the region's constitutional and legal traditions had certain similarities, points of intersection, or influences upon each other. Our discussions centred on the themes of constitutional design, federalism, free speech and equality, and emergency regulation. Given the richness of this initial exploration, we organized a sequel conference in Singapore in July 2009. The Singapore discussions brought together judges, practitioners, scholars, and researchers to consolidate our understanding of emerging patterns in South Asian constitutionalism, and to open up other aspects of legal and regulatory integration within the region. Some of the essays in this volume are based on presentations made and discussions held at the London and Singapore conferences. Other contributors were not present at either meeting, but their ideas and scholarship form part of the shaping context of this emerging area of research and debate.

Our collection opens with a challenging essay by Upendra Baxi, that raises foundational questions for anyone interested in the project of resuscitating South Asian comparative constitutionalism. He warns against scholarly tendencies to treat constitutions as governance machines, and to venerate 'efficiency' in constitutional design. The consequences of such an approach can be 'lethal forms of Holocaustian governance'. Baxi challenges the very idea of South Asia, which he believes to be a 'colonial invention', and calls for 'a new postcolonial nomenclature'. In different degrees, the colonial legacy lingers in South Asian constitutions as an 'obnoxious' and

---

[49] Zachary Elkins, Tom Ginsburg, and James Melton, *The Endurance of National Constitutions* (Cambridge University Press: Cambridge, 2009).

unjust inheritance. Although this legacy is uneven, nevertheless, different forms of constitutional nihilism stalk all of South Asia's constitutions. While offering critical views on strains of constitutional scholarship that focus on 'optimal constitutional design', Baxi does recognize that such studies bear the potential 'for a more empirically-based and comparatively-informed public discussion'.

Sujit Choudhry's contribution asks fundamental questions about the meaning, purpose, and value of comparative constitutional law. He seeks answers to these questions in the landmark judgment of the Delhi High Court in *Naz Foundation*.[50] In that historic decision, a comparative constitutional analysis did real work. The application of Section 377 of the Indian Penal Code to consensual sexual acts of adults in private was found to be unconstitutional, as impinging constitutional guarantees to life, liberty, and equality. In reaching its decision, the Court relied on comparative materials, and considered whether the holdings and reasoning of foreign courts were analogically applicable in the Indian context. These materials served, according to Choudhry, as an interpretative tool with which to draw an analogy between the rights of sexual minorities and the uniquely Indian judicial experience with untouchability. Choudhry identifies what he terms a 'dialogic' model of comparative constitutional interpretation in the *Naz* decision, and he compares this model favourably with two other approaches that he terms as universalist and genealogical approaches to comparative constitutionalism. Choudhry argues that the judges in *Naz Foundation* used comparative materials not only to acknowledge, but also affirm, a distinct constitutional identity. This 'identity-affirming' character of the dialogical mode of comparative constitutional interpretation should, in Choudhry's analysis, persuade judges who are wary of using foreign law to be less sceptical about its dangers.

The drafting of a written constitution involves, in part, a process of adapting international standards to indigenous requirements. Close textual similarities exist between many constitutions, but each constitution invariably acquires unique characteristics as it stretches to respond to local needs.[51] Mara Malagodi and Richard W. Whitecross,

---

[50] *Naz Foundation* v. *Union of India*, Delhi Law Times, 160 (277).
[51] Peter Leyland and Andrew Harding (eds), *Constitutional Courts: A Comparative Study* (Wildy, Simmonds and Hill: London, 2009).

in separate essays, examine the efforts of Nepal and Bhutan to balance foreign and national experiences when constructing their respective constitutions. The two accounts assess the success of attempts to assimilate values borrowed from elsewhere.

In a wide-ranging historical survey of constitutional government in Nepal, Malagodi examines a distinctly plural legal system. At various times and reflecting various aspirations of different actors, a range of external legal concepts have been imported by Nepal. These concepts have been received by, or grafted onto, existing institutions and traditions. This centuries-old process has resulted in a synthesized constitutional tradition that is distinctly Nepalese. The demise of the 1990 Constitution has been the most recent and dramatic development in this changing tradition. Malagodi argues that it was a flawed constitution that reflected an unstable political compromise and failed to adequately accommodate the aspirations of the people. She attributes its failure to constitutional abuses by the ruling elite, acquiescence to those abuses by a cowed and compromised Judiciary, and the endurance of long-established divisive tensions in Nepalese society. If the new, as yet unfinalized, constitution is to succeed where its predecessor failed, it must address these challenges. Malagodi concludes that success for the new constitution requires the abandonment of established identities and the development of a new Nepalese identity rooted in a sense of citizenship and shared national purpose, supported by a commitment to constitutional government by politicians and the Judiciary.

While Nepal has operated under several now-discarded constitutions, its neighbour Bhutan provides an interesting contrast, having adopted a written constitution for the first time in 2008. Never colonized by the British and predominantly Buddhist, the story of tiny Bhutan also stands in contrast to the traditions and experiences of its giant southern neighbour. Richard W. Whitecross focuses on these peculiarities to draw unique lessons for South Asia as he examines Bhutan's constitutional history up to the 2008 Constitution. The constitutional system in Bhutan has shifted from theocracy to monarchy, and with the new constitution, has taken a turn towards secular democracy. The Western legal concept of the separation of organized religion from the state has played a role in this development, but church–state separation needs to be reinterpreted in the context of Bhutan. Buddhism is intrinsic to every part of public and private life in Bhutan, and will continue to be linked to law and authority. The newly written constitution has sought to find a role for Buddhism while preserving the secular character of the new Bhutanese State.

Religion may play a unique role in the law and governance of Bhutan, but its influence is also felt in other South Asian states. Deepika Udagama considers the case of Sri Lanka, a state where a consistent jurisprudence on the constitutional protection of religious pluralism is yet to emerge. Contrary to certain popular perceptions, Udagama argues, the main divisions in Sri Lankan society are between ethnicities and language groups, not religions. Religion has been an indicator of ethnicity and language, but not a primary driver of violence. Yet the Sri Lankan Supreme Court's contradictory opinions on the level of protection that the Constitution affords to religious minorities, hold lessons applicable to the language and ethnicity debates. The Court's confusing treatment of religious diversity is indicative of the challenge of maintaining stable pluralism in a divided society. In the case law on the incorporation of Christian institutions, the Supreme Court has engaged in a form of comparative constitutionalism that amounts to borrowing selectively and cynically—and without elaboration—law from abroad. Udagama believes that a rigorous and transparent approach to comparative constitutionalism has the promise to correct this damage. She views the practice of comparative constitutionalism as a judicial tool, or opportunity, to access and import international human rights norms. These norms, it is hoped, will buttress the rights and protections of Sri Lanka's minorities.

Gary Jeffrey Jacobsohn and Shylashri Shankar continue with the focus on Sri Lanka. The connections between the courts of India and Sri Lanka are considered as an example of constitutional comparisons and cross-connections within the South Asian region itself. The authors contend that intra-regional comparative constitutional practices require special attention, for while the 'proximity [of South Asian nation states] may suggest—particularly to the distant observer—greater incentives for cross-national constitutional appropriation, those closer to the scene and possessing a more refined sense of relevant political and cultural differences may, in contrast, find themselves impressed by the obstacles to successful legal transplantation'.

The 'constitutional appropriation' in question is the application of Indian secularism jurisprudence to Sri Lankan constitutional controversies. The authors acknowledge that transmission of constitutional knowledge and experience on such topics does not take place in a sealed academic world. When the State, which is the potential source of borrowed knowledge and experience, is vastly larger than the borrower, as is the case with India and Sri Lanka, sensitive political issues related to constitutional sovereignty and autonomous statehood arise. Given the uniqueness of the constitutional treatment of religion in India, and the traditional pre-eminence of Buddhism in Sri Lanka, extra care must be taken when considering Indian principles of secularism in the Sri Lankan context. Jacobsohn and Shankar examine the combined impact of these considerations in their study of the *Thirteenth Amendment* case. In that case, secularism came into play alongside other subjects of significant interest from a comparative perspective, including federalism and popular sovereignty. Contrasting the 'equal distance' treatment in the Indian framework with a majoritarian impulse to maintain the hegemony of Sinhalese Buddhists in Sri Lanka, the judgment in this case affirmed a constitutional amendment that sought to address the dual demands of the Tamil minority—equal language rights and greater autonomy. A defence of the State's Buddhist identity lies in sharp contrast to the protection of minorities that drove the 'basic structure' doctrine in India. Jacobsohn and Shankar make out a case for an opportunistic borrowing of Indian constitutional law materials, estranged from considerations of its constitutional identity, which reveal a self-awareness that maintains allegiance to Sri Lankan constitutional premises.

Personal laws have long held a special place in comparative studies. Such laws exemplify cultural differences and are often at the edge of a legislature's law-making power.[52] In an empirical analysis of alterations to personal laws from a legal and political framework, Matthew J. Nelson throws up some counter-intuitive conclusions in a comparison between vastly differing 'equal status' Indian and

---

[52] Fernanda Nicola, 'Family Law Exceptionalism in Comparative Law', *Am. J. Comp. L.*, (2011), 58: 777.

'Islamic' Pakistani systems. Despite the lack of a constitution-imposed proscription against reform of personal laws in both India and Pakistan, his study illustrates that in both these nations, substantive religious-cum-legal reform was taken up and put into practice only in two contexts—military/non-military authoritarianism and one-party dominant regimes where the ruling party held more than 60 per cent of the seats in Parliament. His findings raise the question of whether the political unpopularity of such reforms make them too challenging to be addressed in most democratic, multi-party scenarios.

Looking past differences in the trend of pronouncements on the freedom of religion in matters of conversion in the context of marriage, John H. Mansfield examines the two leading judgments of the Indian Supreme Court and the Pakistan Federal Shariat Court—one liberal and the other seemingly conservative—to explore the ideology that drove the judges' interpretations in each case. Moving beyond the text of the judgments, Mansfield observes a trend of growing Islamization in Pakistan over the last six decades, culminating in its status as the fundamental law of the land. In contrast, the Supreme Court of India may yet be influenced by supervening policy considerations such as the protection of vulnerable women, concern for the proselytizing effect of Islam and Christianity, and hostility towards practising polygamy by conversion.

T. John O'Dowd moves the focus of enquiry to constitutional influences originating outside South Asia, particularly to those which engage in human rights issues. The application of international human rights norms is bound up in the comparative study of constitutions. O'Dowd examines the freedom of speech and expression as understood in the subcontinent as against the United States. He considers the arguments for imposing censorship in a combustible, postcolonial society and the libertarian argument that harm is an essential pre-condition to the restriction of the right to expression. He does so by focusing on the similarities between these debates in contemporary South Asia, and the classic nineteenth-century debates on these issues between John Stuart Mill and James Fitzjames Stephen. (O'Dowd's purpose in making these connections is also to draw attention to the deep involvement of Stephen in colonial law-making in British India, and to how that affected his broader thinking.) After outlining the gap in judicial sentiment separating the Indian stance from the American abhorrence of prior restraints, he explores criminal provisions for the application of these philosophical positions. O'Dowd concludes by initiating a conversation on reasonable restrictions between subcontinental legal systems and the European Court of Human Rights and the Canadian courts.

The last two chapters focus on the role of two South Asian judiciaries—those of Bangladesh and India—in upholding the public interest and basic values of constitutionalism. The contribution of Ridwanul Hoque draws attention to the challenges faced by the courts in South Asian states in establishing and maintaining a standard of constitutionalism. Hoque describes the role of the Judiciary in Bangladesh in promoting and enforcing principles of constitutionalism. Against a political background characterized by occasional instability, the courts of Bangladesh have worked to restore faith in the Constitution. The Supreme Court of Bangladesh has sought to construe and enforce the Constitution as a fundamental charter of social and political values in the wake of the Emergency of 2007. Hoque argues that more recently the Bangladesh Judiciary has been adopting a robust conception of constitutionalism to undergird its actions. This is to be welcomed because, he maintains, 'in the context of prevalent socio-political situations and the chances of imbalance of state powers in Bangladesh, the need for judicial vigilance for the protection of justice and good governance is...ever-present'.

The last chapter, by Arun K. Thiruvengadam, revisits one of the classic works in the young field of South Asian comparative constitutionalism. In 1987, Neelan Tiruchelvam and another noted Sri Lankan academic, Radhika Coomaraswamy, co-edited a significant volume titled *The Role of the Judiciary in Plural Societies (ROJ)*,[53] that serves as an excellent example of early comparative constitutional scholarship in Asia and Africa. The final recommendation of *ROJ* sums up the consensus among the various contributors, all of whom could be described as progressives: 'Judicial activism, encouraged by social action litigation [or public interest litigation (PIL)], inspired by constitutional values, may be regarded as a vital human technology

---

[53] Neelan Tiruchelvam and Radhika Coomaraswamy (eds), *The Role of the Judiciary in Plural Societies* (Frances Pinter: London, 1987).

for social change in impoverished societies.' In his contribution, Thiruvengadam revisits this thesis by providing a descriptive and a normative argument. Descriptively, he notes that in the ensuing years, the character and nature of PIL in India changed, attracting criticism from the very constituency that lauded its origins: progressive lawyers and activists. Thiruvengadam notes that contemporary progressives in all South Asian judiciaries today would be far less convinced about the unalloyed benefits of judicial activism. Normatively, he calls for substituting the relatively clear-cut vision offered by the contributors to *ROJ* with a more complex account of the role that judiciaries can play towards achieving social justice in contemporary South Asian societies.

As will be clear from this brief survey, the individual contributions to the present volume generate a rich collective and comparative dialogue on constitutional debate and practice in South Asia. The issue of religion and law has attracted, perhaps understandably, given the region's traits, the scholarly interest and attention of several essays. Others, though, have focused on the processes of constitution-making in some of the smaller and less accessible South Asian nations, while several essays tackle the nature and role of judicial behaviour in disparate contexts.

The various essays also address, either directly or indirectly, several themes that we covered briefly in the second section of this Introduction, that in turn relate to contemporary debates within the field of comparative constitutional law. In common with a number of contemporary constitutional law scholars, the essays by Sujit Choudhry, and Jacobsohn and Shankar also emphasize the importance of focusing on differences in constitutional law, in order to enhance overall understanding of constitutional systems and particular domestic orders. The essays by Malagodi and Whitecross provide a contextual account of constitution-making and constitutional processes in Nepal and Bhutan respectively, where their focus is precisely on the contingent factors of politics, history and socio-economic realities that many contemporary scholars believe to be essential for a methodologically rigorous approach to their discipline. Responding to the call for bridging the gap between comparative politics and comparative constitutional law studies, Nelson's essay examining personal law reforms in India and Pakistan emphasizes the importance of focusing on political factors, such as authoritarian and dominant party regimes, beyond strictly legal categories. Similarly, the essay by Hoque seeks to keep the political contexts of Pakistan and Bangladesh in the foreground to drive home his analysis of aspects of constitutionalism in these orders. Methodologically speaking, the majority of essays in this volume employ the traditional methods of comparative law (defended robustly by Mark Tushnet against the charge laid by Ran Hirschl), pointing perhaps to some of the difficulties of conducting comparative constitutional scholarship in South Asia. Although none of the contributors in our volume makes use of large-scale empirical studies (and bearing in mind Upendra Baxi's caution about the new-found obsession with 'optimal constitutional design'), the volume as a whole does provide support for those interested in pursuing more quantitative research directions in relation to South Asian nations. It offers a much needed background and references to primary and secondary sources, especially in relation to jurisdictions, such as Bhutan and Nepal, on which little contemporary literature exists.

Many scholars writing in the field of comparative constitutional law have emphasized the continuing Eurocentric focus of much of the existing scholarship. Although there has been a discernible push towards including the perspectives of nations of the Global South in more recent publications, several challenges remain in making the enterprise of comparative constitutional law truly inclusive. An important contribution of this volume is to examine the impact of constitutional issues in a specific, under-studied region of the world, and provide new insights on the perennial problems of constitutionalism.

Taken together, the various essays in this book cover a large array of issues. Yet, given the many issues in South Asian constitutionalism that demand greater scrutiny, one volume can only scratch the surface of this terrain. Our hope is that others will be inspired, as we have been, to make contributions to South Asian constitutional law and help revive and redefine the field. It is, after all, a field that will be crucial to achieving South Asia's own future potential as a region that is more integrated and more at peace with itself.

CHAPTER ONE

Modelling 'Optimal' Constitutional Design for Government Structures

Some Debutant Remarks

Upendra Baxi

PREFATORY REMARKS

Constitution-makers everywhere remain concerned with the best constitutional design; however, that 'best' consists in 'shopping' around available models and adapting these to their needs and aspirations. The eventual mix, or more picturesquely put, the 'bricolage', is constrained by history interlaced with future-looking aspirations for transformation. South Asian constitutions (SAC) are no exceptions. This essay offers a cache of normative, and history-laden, concerns.

Here, the term 'South Asian constitutions' (hereinafter SAC) refers not just to the founding text and its subsequent re-writing (amendments/suspensions) but also to 'constitutionalisms' (the idea of a constitution, whether viewed in the frame of normative theory, as acts of utopic imagination, or as ideology-sets). In this way, the acronym may often mislead; the best I may do here is to let the appropriate contexts of my remarks unpack this usage.

This said, I summarize at the outset some perplexities of SAC. First, how viable is the notion of SAC, and indeed even 'South Asia'? Second, if SAC mark the early beginning of postcolonial forms, how best may we grasp elements of continuity with colonial constitutionalisms? Third, what aspects of discontinuity/change may we notice in choices of SAC as regards constitutional design? Fourth, how may we contrast the discourse of design alongside the experience of living under constitutions, which often manifests in the languages of constitutional nihilisms? Fifth, how far may a new discourse called 'constitutional economics'—preeminently concerned with the relationships between states and markets and with the extension of the methods of market analysis to non-market realms—assist any understanding of original (founding) constitutional choices and subsequent constitutional developments in the languages of economic rationality and rational choice theory? If, from this perspective, constitutional choices and developments are best grasped in the languages of 'optimizing governance', what may we be left with for conventional modes of understanding the histories of constitutional choices and development?

As it happens, even the most sophisticated constitutional minds in SAC remain blissfully unaware of this new discourse and perhaps wisely so in terms of a popular adage: when ignorance is bliss, it is folly to be wise!

I visit these and related concerns by way of a series of preliminary reflections. Doing more remains a task for another day and for framing a wider community, even a commune, of SAC minds.

'South Asia'

The appellation 'South Asia' constitutes variegated feats of colonial and imperial geographies, subsequently reinforced by the timeplaces of the Cold War and disciplines curiously named as 'area studies'.[1] All

---

[1] Allow me to say that the idea of South Asia remains both appealing and intriguing. Appealing because we all need to try to put together some available approaches to SAC in a common comparative frame not just with a view to learning what has been accomplished but also with a view to doing things differently in a future moment; intriguing because both the constitutional imagination and experience remain forbiddingly rich so far as to defy, among other things, the very idea of 'South Asia' and even 'constitutionalism'.

The very term 'South Asia' remains a colonial invention, further fostered by the Cold War regional/area studies. It entrenches the violent geographies of injustice, as do associated terms 'South East Asia', 'Indochina', the 'Middle East', and 'Africa'.

that I may say here is that a discursive object named as SAC may mislead at least for the following reasons. Were we to attend to what I may here name as constellations of the *conditions of early postcoloniality,* we would remain better equipped to recognize several elementary social facts, even truths. First, the intensity of colonial subjugation across and within the incipient postcolonial state-formation varied greatly. Second, so did the specific histories of movements of independence that framed and forged the era of *constitutionalism-to-come.* Third, the relation of the indigenous business and industrial classes with the new middle class fostered partly by the civil service and new professionals, and the nationalist leaders and movements, varies a good deal within 'South Asia'. Fourth, the balance of class forces as well as of the civilian and military relationships influence/condition the responsive capacity of the constitution-making elites to reshape inherited institutions. Understandably then, the processes of decision-making vary enormously across 'South Asia', and this further complicates the understanding of the revolution of rising public and popular expectations, especially of the prehistory of SAC. Fifth, given the 'genius' of colonial rule to produce 'severely divided societies suffused with "political" constructions of 'ethnicity',[2] questions concerning the enunciation of basic human rights of religious, cultural, and linguistic minorities haunt forms of 'South Asian' constitution-making and development. Sixth, mass impoverishment fostered by the colonial 'rule' or despotism and corresponding concerns about distributive justice dominate the varied landscapes of SAC. Last, the geopolitics of the constitutional orderings 'bloody' these in many a poignantly unjust mode.

APPROACHES TO SAC

The notion of 'constitutions' speaks to us about the *physics* of power and domination. Its 'other'—the imagery of constitutionalism— refers us to the *metaphysics* of power and domination. In this way,

---

They mask different penetrations of the global capital, the colonial as well as the contemporary. How I wish that our discussion would invent a new postcolonial nomenclature!

[2] To adapt here the phrase-regime of Donald Horowitz, *Ethnic Groups in Conflict* (University of California Press: Berkeley, 1985).

one may speak of the colonial constitutional form presented at one end of the spectrum by Ranajit Guha's withering phrase—regime of domination without hegemony[3]—and at the other end by what H.W.O. Okoth-Ogendo presciently names as 'constitutions without constitutionalism'.[4]

SAC present many a variation on this theme; I address here merely the forms of continuity and discontinuity. How may this binary relate to a second set—contingency/necessity in SAC—presents related but distinct concerns. These pairs do not carry any self-evident import. What may represent continuity may not always be a feature of necessity, and the contingent is not always an ally of discontinuity. The necessity of stable and effective governance does not by itself explain the originary constitutional choices: this much we surely learn from harvesting competing conceptions of such governance in the SAC constituent assembly debates as well as from debates over subsequent constitutional amendments. For example, the Indian constitution-making debates reveal alternate versions of constitutional ideas, yet different choices prevailed. If the figure of necessity obscures the elements of founding choice, the figure of contingency leaves nothing at all for the labours of understanding apt for the discipline that we may name either as doing constitutional history or perhaps its ethnography. A gifted narrative by Granville Austin finds a *modus vivendi*: Austin is thus moved to say that the Indian Constitution (IC) is at once a 'cornerstone' of the nation as much as it is a 'charter of social revolution'.[5] Let me start instead with an improvised category of 'tombstones'.

---

[3] Ranajit Guha, 'Dominance without Hegemony and Its Historiography', in Ranajit Guha (ed.), *Subaltern Studies*, No. 6 (Oxford University Press: New Delhi, 1989), pp. 210–309.

[4] See, H.W.O. Okoth-Ogendo, 'Constitutions without Constitutionalism: Reflections on an African Paradox', in C.M. Zoethout, M.E. Pietermaat-Kros, and P.W.C. Akkermans (eds), *Constitutionalism in Africa: A Quest for Autochthonous Principles* (Quint Deventer: Gouda, 1996), pp. 3–25.

[5] See, Granville Austin, *The Indian Constitution: Cornerstone of a Nation* (Clarendon Press: Berkeley, 1966) and Upendra Baxi, 'The Little Done, the Vast Undone: Reflections on Reading Granville Austin's *The Indian Constitution*', *Journal of the Indian Law Institute*, (1967), 9: 323–430.

WAYS IN WHICH SAC 'CORNERSTONES' INDEED BECOME SAC TOMBSTONES

The founding choices may often be calamitous. Violent social exclusion marked the first ever written SAC: the Afghanistan Constitution of 1923 denied the validity of existence of the impious or the heretic, a story that prefigures the subsequent Taliban 'constitutionalisms'. Put another way, 'sepulchral constitutionalisms' are indeed forms that do not merely deny recognition of the irreducible social fact of human social/cultural plurality but also further render this denial as the state-formative as well as a civic virtue. What such constitutions constitute is a code of terror, not just as a means to an end but as an end in itself. One ought to resist the temptation of denying the dignity of the idea of constitutionalism to such a state of affairs, if only because the underlying justifications of 'terrorist' constitutionality demand a fuller grasp.

Such justifications stand either inherited from the SAC colonial past or innovated in the writing of a new constitution. When the innovation lies primarily in imposing a comprehensive religious worldview as the basis of constitutional ordering, within-nation people of different faiths, and the explicitly named apostates and heretics remain subject to endless constitutionally sanctioned or state-tolerated violence, often bordering on terror. The Shari'a-based constitutionalisms in South Asia offer some poignant illustrations of cruelty and terror, most notably in Pakistan, in relation to the two million Ahmadiyya religious communities. Section 295(c) amending the Pakistan Penal Code (known as the anti-blasphemy law) continues to offer wide avenues for both the official prosecution of dissident faiths as well as 'civil society'–based persecution. Of course, constitutionalists and human rights folks continue to evoke, as is well known, a more 'authentic' Islamite understanding of the Shari'a. The narrative of Bangladesh, in my understanding at least, offers a different constitutional pluriverse.

Elsewhere in the 'South Asian' region, constitutional toleration of different religious worldviews remains the norm. The otherwise proclaimed 'Hindu' religious state (kingdom) in Nepal (now declared a constitutional secular state) offers a uniquely different narrative. So does the narrative of Indian constitutional secularism.

COLONIAL CONTINUITIES

Constitutions as Governance Machines

Far from being oxymoronic, colonial 'constitutionalism' signifies a complex domain of power and accountability. For most of South Asia, this means the internal constitution of power-governing—on the one hand, the relationship between the Board of Directors of the East India Company and its officials abroad, and on the other, between the Company itself and the Crown. Colonial constitutionalism is eminently a form of mercantilist despotism marking the flow of accountability obligations upwards/vertically among a predatory class of merchants and warriors standing at times in difficult relationship with the missionaries. Stage two of colonial constitutionalism marks the itineraries of a different type of domination when the Crown itself assumes powers of sovereign governance—students of Queen Victoria's 1858 Proclamation know fully well the significance of these passages of power.

If the Company Raj thus provides a paradigmatic instance of experiments with sepulchral constitutionalism in which the natives were no more than the vectors of raw imperial mercantilist prowess, the British Raj endows them with the dignity of being named as Her Majesty's loyal subjects. Important, of course, remains the idea of constitutionalism as a means of centralization of colonial/imperial power formations. I do not pursue here the complex, chaotic, and often cruel agendum of colonial governance of alien subjects by force and fraud.

In the confines of this conversation, I address only one element of the colonial constitutionalist lineages and inheritance—the imagery of the idea of constitutions as sheer *governance machines* placed at the service of dominance. The SAC conversion of 'cornerstones' into 'tombstones' thus occurs with routine poignancy. Most SAC forms continue to improvise this very colonial inheritance. This occurs variously. Most SAC continue the obnoxious colonial inheritance— such as the powers providing for preventive detention, proclamations of emergencies and martial law, and even the powers to 'suspend' the original constitutions; *this retention is made possible by the constitutional device of continuation of old colonial laws.* Pakistan, till today, continues with the perpetuation of 1901 Frontier Crimes Regulation (FCR), which authorize *carte blanche* arrests of tribal people without naming any crime and provides sanctions for collective crimes; it constitutes a perennial state of exception 'obnoxious to all recognized modern principles governing the dispensation of justice' (to quote the pungent remark of Chief Justice Cornelius).[6]

I desist from citing further examples such as the Indian constitutional penchant for retaining draconian colonial laws (for example, the Official Secrets Act or the offence of sedition). Even granting that the first task of the originary moment of many a SAC is to establish order and minimal collective security (especially in the Holocaustian moment of the Partition of the 'subcontinent'), such continuation of past colonial legality remains unconscionable for converting citizens into subjects of constitutional governance machines even in a *late colonial condition*, despite so many assurances of basic constitutional human rights and opportunities for sensible law reform.

Forms of Governance

To state the obvious, SAC founding choices remain ambivalent. Choosing forms of governance is never an endeavour at wiping the slate of history clean! More to the point, perhaps, are acts of re-writing that may render a little more legible some future histories of SAC. And there is 'more' to governance than entailed in formulation of constitutional texts, read merely as exercises in miming available EuroAmerican constitutional models!

Thus, we may not fully understand from an external standpoint the preference for hereditary kingship prevalent in the much understudied Bhutan and (until recently) in Nepal. Indian constitutionalism is, however, marked by 'integration' of about 600 odd princely states cancelling the British Indian Independence Act, which restored sovereignty to these entities with manifold constitutional and political impacts. The choice between 'monarchic' and 'republican' forms of governance was thus constitutively constrained; and so was the choice between the 'federal' and the 'unitary' forms.

Granville Austin's wry observation that the Government of India Act, 1935, had already accomplished the labour of history for the

---

[6] See, Abid Mehsud , 'Frontier Crimes Regulation: A Black Law', *The Frontier Times*, 23 June 2012.

IC-makers remains provocatively valid. However, a wider SAC context shows some distinctive points of departure. Until the birthing of Bangladesh, Pakistan offered an extraordinary instance of non-contiguous federalism. The IC did not exhaust, in any event, the situation of 'asymmetrical federalism',[7] even when it affirms the federal principle and design rather differently.[8] Military constitutionalisms—these occurred for a long while in Burma and equally intensely in Pakistan—offered some stunning variations in federal design and detail.

This essay does not allow room for exploring the choices concerned with founding governance design beset with much ambivalence. Erasure of precolonial and colonial times was simply not an available option; the concern here always was—and continues to be in some 'South Asian' contexts—to innovate the already heavily intermixed 'given'. And this 'intermix'/'intermeshing' may not ever be fully grasped by the new discourse of constitutional economics; its insistence on 'optimizing governance' remains, to say the least, unhelpful as an explanatory category.

Innovating Human Rights

Writing human rights in SAC has not been an easy task, given the already noted vast inheritance of the idea of constitutions as governing machines. Early SAC (especially those of India, Pakistan, and Sri Lanka) also did not have access to the development of international human rights enunciations beginning with the Universal Declaration of Human Rights. Yet, the very act of writing basic rights in SAC marks a radical discontinuity from colonial constitutionalism. I may indicate briefly the 'nature' of this discontinuity by a few summary remarks concerning the IC, which resonate over time elsewhere in South Asia.

First, the IC (much before the emergence of International Human Rights Covenants) fully anticipates and affirms social and economic

---

[7] See, M. Govinda Rao and Nirvikar Singh, 'Asymmetrical Federalism in India', (2004), http://eschola.rship.org/uc/item/4370m6p1 (last accessed on 2 October 2011). See also, Alfred Stephen, 'Multi-Nationalism, Democracy and "Asymmetrical Federalism"' (with some tentative comparative reflections on Burma), Technical Advisory Network on Burma, WP 02/02, at Online Burma/Myanmar Library.

[8] Granville Austin, *Working a Democratic Constitution: The Indian Experience* (Oxford University Press: New Delhi, 1999).

human rights as human rights. No doubt, the latter, clustered in Part IV as the directive principles of state policy, were not initially judicially enforceable as the here-and-now fundamental civil and political rights of Part III. However, this distinction between the promissory directives and the enforceable rights of Part III constitutes the future history of IC development, justifying the prophetic utterance of Austin that the IC is 'a charter of social revolution'. This division of rights soon spreads not just within SAC but also to some anglophonic African constitutionalisms—an aspect that requires mentioning, though without any further elaboration.

Second, the IC seeks to redress millennial past wrongs. The Right to Equality extends monumentally in Article 17 to abolish 'untouchability', forbidding its practice, and making discrimination on the ground of 'untouchability' a 'constitutional offence'. Article 35 suspends the principle and the detail of Indian federalism by casting on Parliament a series of constitutional obligations to enact laws crystallizing further this constitutionally named offence. Articles 15 and 16 variously mandate equality of opportunity in state-maintained educational institutions and state employment. Even Article 25—guaranteeing the right to freedom of conscience and religion—stands qualified by insistence on the rights of 'untouchables' to enter temples and other places of public worship. Further, the IC provides a system of political participation by 'untouchables' via the arrangement of legislative reservations in Parliament and state legislatures under which the principle of universal adult suffrage stands modified via reserved seats where only 'untouchables' (the Scheduled Castes) may contest electoral seats.

Third, much the same narrative extends to millennial injustices against the Indian indigenous people to whom also extend educational, employment, and legislative reservations. In this context remain crucial the Fifth and the Sixth Schedules of the IC.

Fourth, elevated forms of protection of minority rights remained a necessity for the making and development of the IC. In this way, Article 30's assurances of fundamental rights make near-absolute the basic human rights of religious and cultural minorities to establish and administer educational institutions.

Fifth, the IC contingencies of constitutional politics paradoxically strengthen the relative autonomy of the apex court and the legal profession thriving in its name. This means, summarily put, that each and every assertion of parliamentary supremacy meets its nemesis in an ever-increasing adjudicative constitutional scrutiny, paving the way for judicial governance of the nation.[9] Later in this essay I attend to aspects of rights-revolution that were un-anticipated by the makers of SAC.

In this summary I eschew large references to the ways in which all these constitutional arrangements have actually worked; for the present purpose, what remains significant is the radical IC symbolization of the principle of equality that is simply unparalleled in most postcolonial constitutional forms.

Imageries of Constitutions and Constitutionalism

With all this more or less acknowledged, one also needs to note the ways in which many a SAC development demands a more complex grasp of discontinuities. It is on this site that we may generalize Granville Austin's metaphor of 'charter of revolution' beyond the IC context. Even when most SAC makers imagined constitutions or constitutionalisms as no more than *governance machines*, they also innovated the very idea of constitutionalism as a site of *state formative practices*. Put another way, SAC constitutional imagination reconfigures the idea of constitution as complex and contradictory unfoldment of a quartet—namely, a *bricolage* of ideas about constitutions or constitutionalisms as praxes of governance with development on the one hand and justice and rights on the other. Decoding all this, however, poses many a narrative hazard.

All this remains a crazy quilt of IC, entirely un-amenable to modelling 'optimal constitutional design' (OCD) approaches! Surely, the IC remains far from OCD as signifying a paramount imagery of 'efficiency'—often to be thought of as an amoral virtue, signalling maintenance, repair, and overhauling. This virtue may however produce some lethal forms of Holocaustian 'governance'. Of

[9] See, for example, Granville Austin, *Working a Democratic Constitution: A History of the Indian Experience* (Oxford University Press: New Delhi, 2003); Upendra Baxi, *The Indian Supreme Court and Politics* (Eastern Book Company: Lucknow, 1980); Upendra Baxi, Alice Jacobs, and Tarlok Singh (eds), *Reconstructing the Republic* (Har-Anand Publications: New Delhi, 2000); S.P. Sathe, *Judicial Activism in India* (Oxford University Press: New Delhi, 2001); and Sudhir Krishnaswamy, 'Regional Emergencies under Article 356: The Extent of Judicial Review', *Indian Journal of Constitutional Law*, (2009), 3: 168.

course, most proponents of this virtue focus on governance 'efficiency' as a primary moral or social good serving other moral goods—such as societal 'wealth-maximization', 'development', 'welfare', 'human rights', and 'justice'. How 'efficiency' thus operates is a question, I believe, answered with tolerable certainty in the contemporary SAC grammars.

Colonial habits die hard in grasping some distinctive OCD issues, which remains a function of histories, both of the practices and structures of domination and of the movements and struggles of resistance. Even gifted historians are inclined to think that postcolonial SAC forms are merely a re-adaptation of the colonial. Sir Ivor Jennings was thus moved to say that the 'ghosts of Sidney and Beatrice Webb' stalk through Part IV of the Indian Constitution. Thus, narratives of inheritance of OCD often belittle, even as these do not altogether bypass, the variegated meanings of anti-colonial or imperial struggles. I do not gainsay (indeed, who may!) the political economy of foundational constitutional SAC choice-making; nor do I suggest that people make constitutions just as they please (to vulgarize 'Uncle' Marx's great saying about the making of history). I do suggest, however, a reading that coequally privileges the elements of mimesis with those of originality.

THE VARIETIES OF CONSTITUTIONAL NIHILISMS IN SAC

In the specific contexts of SAC, but assuredly not only on that site, 'con-theory' (the prefix indicating 'confidence') is often regarded by many as a kind of 'con-trick'. The prefix also invites considerations of calculation as when we talk about 'pros' and 'cons.' Further, in its Latin roots, the prefix further suggests ideas of working with or together. I think that the prefix is worth taking seriously in both its salutary and pejorative sense.

There are several ways of describing this—in terms of the 'alien' nature of con-theory, alienation of large masses of people from constitutional arrangements and the wielders of constitutional power, conflicted relationships between constitutional and societal cultures, and the crisis of legitimacy of the State. I may only speak here about the varieties of constitutional nihilisms, fraught of course with much narrative risk—in an eclectic adaptation here of Nietzsche's exposition of nihilism as entailing the 'devaluation of the uppermost values' ('passive nihilism') and their replacement by new ones ('active nihilism'). By values, put shortly, Nietzsche signifies 'constructs of domination' and, as Heidegger explains, this value is 'essentially the viewpoint of the increase or decrease of these centers of domination'.[10] I believe that the still-to-be-written histories of SAC may benefit from a close study of Nietzsche, even when he was not much concerned with constitutions and laws.

SAC constitutional nihilisms (CN) assume different historic visages; I describe briefly only CN from above and below. Both forms entail a loss of belief in the idea of a constitution as setting normative constraints on the power to rule and the capacity to resist and rebel. In CN from above, we have what Okoth-Ogendo presciently describes, in the context of imperial presidency in African constitutionalisms, as 'constitutions without constitutionalism'.[11] Burma exemplifies for the South Asian experience the most far-reaching CN manifesting an absolute will to power, rivalled only by the Taliban regime in Afghanistan. In contrast, military constitutionalisms in Pakistan for the most part, and Bangladesh for a while, furnish illustrations of militarized constitutionalism. Sri Lanka governs by forms of as-yet-interrupted Emergency rule. India undergoes national Emergency rule only for a brief period (1975–6). Nepal manifests different forms of CN within and against monarchical governance and now beyond.[12]

Despite these important differences, the CN-from-below critique suggests that the disadvantaged, dispossessed, and the depressed strata of South Asian people consider the actually existing constitutions as unworthy of their commitment or loyalty, even amidst some relatively 'successful' SAC plebiscitary forms of democratic governance. The critics point to the persistence of States of Emergency and constitutional authoritarianism cohabiting parliamentary regimes at the state and federal levels, and for a long while under the watch of a relatively independent adjudicature. No stark and simple narrative of CN from above may enable us to grasp the varieties of CN. All of this points to the difficult tasks ahead for SAC studies.

---

[10] M. Heidegger, *Nietzsche* (University of Chicago Press: Chicago, 1982), pp.55–6, 66 repectively.

[11] See, Okoth-Ogendo, pp. 3–25.

[12] See in this volume, Chapter 3 (Mara Malagodi, 'Constitutional Developments in a Himalayan Kingdom: The Experience of Nepal').

The SAC/CN spheres stand marked both by within-constitution movements and the variegated practices and insurgencies of the armed opposition groups which violently contest the postcolonial constitutional form (PCF). The latter contests a PCF version in which the right to people's self-determination stands normatively and historically *exhausted* with decolonization. The former pursue projects of devolution and decentralization and in the contexts of the federal SAC demand new political arrangements of power-sharing within the existing constitutional polity, prominently within-nation competitive politics of identity and difference. If the autonomists deploy violence as a contingent necessity, the secessionists pursue projects of ethical violence against the postcolony. This characterization remains infinitely complex in SAC. The experience of Sri Lanka especially shows ways in which autonomists have been regarded as secessionists (though it is true that the Tamil United Liberation Front [TULF] spoke both in the accents of a separate Elam and of a federal power-sharing[13]). No constitutional 'design' can be secession-proof[14] but the PCF remains particularly prone to armed insurgent movements seeking independence and a separate statehood.

If the armed opposition groups mark a twilight of the values of international human rights and humanitarian law, it also remains the case that so does the ethos of state managers and counter-insurgency elites who advance the justification of preserving the 'integrity' of a postcolonial state formation. This results in spiralling militarization of the constitutional state, in which the state itself is presented as a vulnerable entity or being. In this sense, constitutional nihilisms from above and below coalesce in constant and continual reproduction of the suffering and rightless SAC humanity.

PCF generally, and SAC specifically, cannot afford to ignore the timespaces of what Nietzsche also described as forms and practices

---

[13] See, Rohan Edrisinha, Mario Gomez, V. T. Thamilmaran, and Asanga Welikala (eds), *Power-sharing in Sri Lanka: Constitutional and Political Documents* (Colombo and Berghof Foundation for Peace Support: Berlin, 2008).

[14] The Burma Constitution of 1947 is, however, the only normative exception providing for the right to secession modelled on the Soviet Constitution; this now remains merely of historic interest. Perhaps not quite so: see, David C. Williams and Lian H. Sakhong, *Designing Federalism in Burma* (UNLD Press: Chiang Mai, Thailand, 2005).

of evaluative thought. Most historical, and specifically juridical, narratives of SAC ignore these 'revaluation' practices (installing new values in place of the old). I may here mention some SAC legendary figures: Mohandas Gandhi, Bhim Rao Ambedkar, Dalai Lama, Aung San Suu Kyi, Ariyaratne, and Jay Prakash Narayan. Fortunately, this list of names is not exhaustive. Even so, each one of these names evokes a different image of constitutionalism, which I term as a *caring* or *compassionate* PCF, not readily to be subsumed into the inherited categories of liberal/libertarian forms of constitutionalism. Their residual legatees in SAC are of course those whom I may summarily name as constitutional *optimists*. They believe in the languages, logics, paralogics, and movements of constitutional *restoration* and *reform*.

REVISITING CONSTITUTIONALISM(S)

The sophisticated literature concerning constitutional economics ignores, for the most part, the ways in which SAC forms complicate the idea of constitutionalism in terms of interestedness of four conflicted keywords: governance, development, justice, and human rights. We address some of these concerns later in this essay.

For the moment, we need to acknowledge at least the fact that SAC stands birthed in many a violent history of the holocaust of the Partition of India and Pakistan, and equally horrendous forms and practices of the Cold War that affect the making and unmaking of the Afghan, and the geopolitics of the Burmese constitutional experience. All these result in experiments with military SAC that foster the practices of neocolonialism, poignantly described by Kwame Nkrumah as 'power without responsibility' and 'exploitation beyond redress'.

Even so, and over time, judges and jurists in South Asia for the most part contribute to the re-democratization of SAC. The Pakistan Supreme Court offers a most resilient recent example.[15] So does the complex itinerary of the Supreme Court of India's doctrine of basic structure, which has travelled well to Bangladesh, Pakistan, and

---

[15] Upendra Baxi, 'Constitutional Interpretation and State Formative Practices in Pakistan: A Preliminary Exploration', Chapter 9, in M.P. Singh (ed.), *Comparative Constitutional Law: Essays in Honour of Professor P.K. Tripathi* (Eastern Book Company: Lucknow, 2011).

Nepal. This shows that apex justices may justifiably claim to share constituent power with the elected public officials, and sometimes even against their will to power; in this sense some recent CCS-type revival of understanding constituent power still remains Eurocentric.[16]

Crucially, the SAC experience suggests a typology of the fours 'Cs'. C1 designates the officially 'written' constitutional texts, almost always in the name of 'people'. These 'authorial' texts always contain 'unwritten' ones. The latter often remain at 'play' as well as at 'war' with the former. The 'play' is often represented and revealed by 'permissible' spheres of the wonders of adjudicatory leadership and interpretive feats, always held within the doctrine of the 'reason of the state'. The state of 'war' is signified by the triumph of the 'unwritten' over the 'written', explored poignantly with and since Carl Schmitt's drawing of contrasts between law as 'rule' and as 'decision'—or the 'state of exception'.

My second C—C2— speaks to the framing categories of juristic and judicial understanding that lawpersons know in terms of 'constitutional law'—a normative cache or chalice of grasping the idea of constitution as state-ordained 'meanings' of the written and unwritten C1. However, that peculiar something labelled as 'constitutional law' often seems to act against the legitimation of the executive–legislative combine. Surely, the labours of adjudicative leadership and performance remain severely contested, marking a profound ambivalence: How far the adjudicature—after all, an aspect of differentiation of the hegemonic state apparatus (a part, after all, of the 'governance machine')—may proceed to address and redress massive human/social suffering and rightlessness?

C3 marks histories of within-constitution meaning of citizen's interpretation of constitutionalism(s)—an aspect signifying patterns of political consensus and conflict, or more accurately put, the dialectic of sovereignty and resistance largely ignored in CSS. C3 is indeed of world-historic importance, as we learn variously from

---

[16] Today, there is much debate concerning forms of Islamic theocratic constitutionalisms which postulate a non-secular *grundnorm* articulating the will or reason of God as the criteria of all other legal norms. From the astigmatic perspectives of libertarian and even liberal constitutionalism this may be an egregious ethical error; yet Kelsen would guide us even today in taking these seriously. In this sense, one may yet read his gifted work, and even contrary to his manifest authorial intention, as providing a framework of constitutional plurality.

the shaking of the foundations of imperial legality by Mohandas Gandhi, of the questioning of the racist foundation of state power and authority in the struggles led and inspired by Martin Luther King Jr. and Nelson Mandela, and the enduring struggles of the workers', feminist, and ecological movements. Contrary to established C2 versions and visions, C3 pioneers the Herculean labours of transformative constitutionalism, often conscripting activist justices to their cause. C3 may indeed be read with Jacques Derrida in terms of 'the Enlightenment to come, rather than miming that Euro-American 'Enlightenment' said to have already come'! And to continue with his imagery, C3 may be read as 'two ways of going aground [*échouer*]: between running aground [*échouement*] and grounding [*échouage*]'.[17]

C4 offers a different register of insurgent reason in which CN from below finds its terminal manifestation. It seeks to combat both the foundational and reiterated violence of SAC, with a Utopian edge in pursuit of projects of 'ethical violence' in the name of emancipatory anti-constitutional 'people's' politics. Many a form of C1, C2, and even C3 constitutional retaliations thus occur within the full ambiguation constituted via the figurations of indiscriminate violence, named as 'state' and insurgent 'terror'. The SAC grammars respond differently to C4. The birthing of Bangladesh offers a complicated narrative; so does Sri Lanka in relation to the overcoming of the TLF and differently the narratives of constitutional state responses towards the 'Maoist' resurgences in Nepal and India. My naming of C4 at least directs attention beyond juridical SAC studies to what I would like to name as 'constitutional ethnography'.

MODELLING OCD

All this more or less fully said, I now turn briefly to the art and crafts of OCD neglected for too long by SAC scholarship. The theoretical foundations notably articulated by the work of James M. Buchanan, who, along with Gordon Tullock, spoke to us of a wider category— 'constitutional economics' that extended public choice theory and

---

[17] Jacques Derrida, 'The "World" of the Enlightenment to Come (Exception, Calculation, Sovereignty)', *Research in Phenomenology*, (2003), 33: 13.

rational choice models to understanding of basic constitutional choices and their further development.[18]

Many a crucial insight remains pertinent (and these have been further developed); for example, the distinctions between 'constitutional' decisions and the legislative ones, type of decision rules apposite to both the forms, choices about institutions under the constitution, and the electoral rules that constitute democratic representation.

This essay is scarcely a site for an overview of their main positions and subsequent critical extensions.[19] Yet at the outset, some extraordinary feats of adjudicatory leadership, such as the Indian doctrine of basic structure (a doctrine that has travelled to several SAC) and its essential features which may not be amended away without strict judicial scrutiny and even judicial veto, present some perplexities for this framework.

The overall Indian concerns and indeed some further ones of SAC were framed primarily in terms of parliamentary sovereignty confronted by a judicial will power. Important concerns thus raised by the proponents (including me) and opponents of the basic structure limitations focused on political ideology or theory, with a total disregard for the time costs and external costs[20] and the privileging by Buchanan and Tullock of the 'unanimity' rule of decision.

'Efficiency' is a keyword in constitutional economics; concerns of 'efficiency' predominate the understanding of constitutional arrangements for distribution of governance powers. Unlike the old

---

[18] See, J.M. Buchanan and Gordon M. Tullock, *The Calculus of Consent: Logical Foundations of Constitutional Democracy* (The University of Michigan Press: Ann Arbor, 1962); J.M. Buchanan, *Constitutional Economics* (Basil Blackwell: Oxford, 1991).

[19] See, for a recent re-visitation, Keith L. Dougherty and Julian Edward, *The Calculus of Consent and Constitutional Design* (Springer: New York, 2011).

[20] Dougherty and Edward phrase these costs in terms of a trade-off between decision costs and external costs: 'Decision costs are the time and effort needed to make a decision. External costs are the losses an individual expects to endure as the result of the coercive actions of others. Majority rule imposes moderate amounts of decision costs and external costs. Unanimity rule imposes no external costs but considerable decision costs. Whether one of these voting rules, or perhaps a supermajority rule, should be adopted depends on the context....' See, Dougherty and Edward, *The Calculus*, p. 9.

'(con)founding fathers' (since seldom do we encounter founding mothers!) the new ones are experts in constitutional design fostering new ways of OCD in which all constitutional arrangements, existing or proposed, must pass what stands named as an 'efficiency test'.[21] Constitutionalism now stands redefined in this genre not so much as ideology-sets but rather as myriad ways of processing 'information' for designing projects of 'efficient government'. Efficiency assessments entail some theory constructions which use formalized mathematical and statistical analyses, creating in the process a new breed of theoretically-challenged persons: I speak to you today as one such!

In this zodiac, efficiency in terms begins to get described as 'optimality'. This obligates us all to think with, and beyond, Pareto 'theorems'. That 'beyond' remains a veritable hornet's nest, unleashing the mighty furies of 'cost/benefit' analyses, 'externalities', theories concerning both endogenous and exogenous public goods, the 'economies of scale' as informing an understanding of centralized versus multi-level government structuring, the contrast between rent-seeking versus authority-reinforcing production of public policies (or even of politics for and by itself, to use here an 'antiquated' diction) and much else besides. Note that this remains the beginning of the story because some notable literature concerning the effects of constitutions requires a sustained grasp of micro-economic methods such as 'marching estimates', 'propensity score methods', 'instrumental variables estimates', and 'parametric selective corrections'.[22]

The 'efficiency' matrix is not concerned with the *aspirational* and cultural dimensions of constitutional design and developments but with its *instrumental* efficacy. In this way, 'efficiency', though not always a non-moral good, obscures from view political passion animating the birthing of constitutional normativity and the politics of passion that marks its subsequent development. Even so, this sovereign concern with 'efficiency' does remain imbued with a theory of government and regulation. Thus, Mancur Olson reminds us,[23]

---

[21] See, Robert D. Cooter, *The Strategic Constitution* (Princeton University Press: New Jersey, 2000).

[22] Mancur Olson, 'Toward a More General Theory of Governmental Structure', *The American Economic Review*, papers and proceedings of the ninety-eighth annual meeting of the American Economic Association, (1986), 76(2): 120–5.

[23] Ibid., p. 120.

a 'theory of government structure begins most naturally with [the question] why we need governments'. He suggests, in an act of rather rare transparent prose, that 'because governments are not needed to perform any functions that markets perform differently', a 'theory of government begins with market failures'. Even when, at the very outset, caveated by the recognition that most governments 'do not restrict themselves with market failures', Olson also significantly adds that the market failure approach helps to explain 'some crucial aspects of reality'.

For Richard Posner, efficiency relates to 'wealth-maximization'. Thus, laws and constitutions signify 'exploiting economic resources in a way that human satisfaction as measured by aggregate consumer willingness to pay for goods and services is maximized'.[24] While he only incidentally recognizes the 'function of the existing distribution of income and wealth in society', Posner still remains able to assert that 'a transfer of money from a rich man to a poor one' remains an unlikely candidate for improving the 'utility' of either.[25] For Posner then, at the end of the day, 'value' stands defined by 'willingness to pay'. However, this does not avoid the question of the initially unjust—that is, inefficient distribution of income and wealth in society.

Rational choice analysis as extended to regulation theory is not unfriendly to the wealth-maximization perspective. The groundbreaking contribution of Sam Peltzman remains premised on the recognition that 'what is basically at stake in regulatory processes is a transfer of wealth'.[26] In this way, constitutions become frameworks for the acquisition, management, distribution, and consumption/enjoyment of regulatory power. The elected and unelected constitutional agents or functionaries emerge as 'rent-seeking' self-interest maximizers (SIMS), pursuing two utility functions, namely, 'votes and money'—in sum, power.[27] The SIMS approach entails a distinctive theory of government which leads us

[24] Richard A. Posner, 'Utilitarianism, Economics and Legal Theory, *Journal of Legal Studies*, (1979), 8:103–40.

[25] Ibid.

[26] See, Sam Peltzman, 'Toward a More General Theory of Regulation', *Journal of Law and Economics*, (1976), 211–40.

[27] Ibid.

to the three core components of what has been labelled as 'Chicago Theory of Government', which direct attention to the fact that:

[1] Programmers of 'institutional change' remain a function of 'changes in the opportunities for using coercive power' to 'exact'/ 'capture rents'.

[2] 'Costs of effective political organization differ among economic interests and so affect who is likely to be the winning bidder in the competition to wield coercive power of the state to generate rents.'

[3] Thus arise forms of 'convergence of policy towards efficiency'.[28]

Finally (without being exhaustive), we ought to note that constitutional economics emerges in OCD discourse in terms of grand design and small bits–type questions. The latter typically concern the cost-benefit analysis of subsets of constitutional design, such as a choice between presidential or parliamentary method of government, for the methods of aggregating electoral choices. The empirically-based OCD discourse is indeed formidably based on mighty cross-country empirical studies that suggest different degrees of cost-effectiveness of such forms of governance, proportional versus first-past-the-post voting systems, bicameral versus unicameral forms of legislative structuring.[29]

A NON-CONCLUDING REMARK

There is no question that some OCD approaches need to be fully canvassed in relation to the extant SAC. Indeed, questions concerning the small bits–type design have occurred in SAC. India experiences these concerns in the brief history of debate during the internal emergency years (1975–6) concerning the presidential form of governance;[30] in Sri Lanka, more or less, the presidential form

[28] See, Sam Peltzman, Michael E. Levine, and Roger G. Noll, 'The Economic Theory of Regulation after a Decade of Deregulation', Brookings Papers on Economic Activity, *Microeconomics*, (1989), 1989: 1–59.

[29] See the impressive work of Torsten Persson and Guido Tabellini, *The Economic Effects of Constitutions: What Do the Data Say?* (MIT Press: Cambridge, 2003); Ibid., 'Separation of of Powers and Political Accountability', *Quarterly Journal of Economics*, (1997), 112: 1163–202. See also, Daron Acemoglu, 'Constitutions, Politics and Economics: A Review Essay on Persson and Tabellini's *The Economic Effect of Constitutions*, (2005), NBER working paper no. 11235.

[30] Granville Austin, *Working a Democratic Constitution.*

has withstood social criticism and designs for change; the recent adjudicative labours of the Supreme Court in Pakistan have limited the presidential powers.[31] Yet, the OCD literature played no part whatsoever, there being no epistemic communities able or disposed to take this seriously. It is not inconsistent, with some critical remarks thus far offered, for me to also say that the OCD studies may have contributed to the state of art and still carry future prospects for a more empirically-based and comparatively-informed public discussion.

All this fully said, it is not clear how far the available OCD studies may contribute to any superior understanding of the increasing and marked tendencies of adjudicative leadership[32] at least in India, Pakistan, Sri Lanka, and Bangladesh; how far coequal judicial governance practices developed by adjudicatory leadership may 'optimize' constitutional governance', or pass the 'efficiency test'.

To be sure, such approaches may help to relatively 'de-ideologize' some well-worn controversies concerning the role and function of judicial review and activist judicial dispositions in traumatically changeful SAC. Further we may be enabled to better understand the alternative choices of 'deregulation' of economic sphere (privatization of national economic resources) and forms of 're-regulation' (control over disinvestment, direct foreign investment, and capital flights). Concerning the growth of what I elsewhere name as systemic governance corruption, we surely need to understand relations between 'free markets' of corruption and 'costs' entailed in choice of regulatory models. And there is little doubt that patterns of legal education and research ought to move from obsessive compulsion for doctrinal/normative studies towards a nuanced understanding of

---

[31] See, Baxi, 'Constitutional Interpretation and State Formative Practices in Pakistan'. But see, as concerns the Indian SAL experience, Madhav Khosla, 'Addressing Judicial Activism in the Indian Supreme Court: Towards an Evolved Debate', *Hastings Int'l Law and & Comp. L. Rev,* (2009), 31(1): 55–100. Khosla creatively extends the analysis in Margit Cohn and Mordechai Kremnitzer, *Judicial Activism: A Multidimensional Model, Can J.L. & Juris,* (2005), 18: 333, 336.

[32] See, for this notion, Baxi, 'Public and Insurgent Reason: Adjudicatory Leadership in a Hyperglobalizing World: Apex Court as Exemplars of Public Reason', in Stephen Gill (ed.), *Global Crises and the Crisis of Global Leadership* (Cambridge University Press: Cambridge, 2011), pp. 161–78.

the place of human rights for all in some contexts of 'constitutional economics' and OCD studies.

Doing so, of course, opens up for SAC communities a whole new terrain of contestation of the hegemonic Global North OCD discourse. The SAC narratives, at any rate, challenge the notion of 'optimizing government structures' way beyond the idea of citizenship as being no more than atomized lustful gremlin-type SIMS, that make altogether insensible the idea of constitutional politics. And how may such new bodies of knowledge empower/dis-empower the militant subjects of social and human rights movements? This last remains a sovereign concern/question, at least for me.

What follows, then, for the forms of finite, even precious, lifetimes of SAC? Is a more prolonged sabbatical leave from the OCD discourse still called for? Or, do the future tasks lie in the direction of reconfiguring this discourse in some distinctive, even singular, SAC modes? And, in turn, how may these modes address the problematic of constitutional nihilisms from above and below?

CHAPTER TWO

How to Do Comparative Constitutional Law in India

Naz Foundation, Same Sex Rights, and Dialogical Interpretation

Sujit Choudhry*

INTRODUCTION

How should Indian courts do comparative constitutional law? What precise role should comparative materials— constitutional texts and comparative jurisprudence—play in the interpretation of the Indian Constitution? Is their use simply rhetorical, nothing more than legal window-dressing for a judgment that has already been reached on other grounds, and merely designed to demonstrate that Indian judges are cosmopolitan and to impress their foreign peers? Is the citation of comparative materials a judicial attempt to assert India's membership in the family of liberal democracies? Is legal globalization the counterpart to economic globalization, making open

* I presented an earlier draft of this essay at the Centre for Policy Research in Delhi; the Faculty of Law, University of Toronto; Georgetown University Law School; and the Columbia Law School. I thank Alan Brudner, Sidharth Chauhan, Markus Dubber, Jamal Greene, Meneka Guruswamy, Vicki Jackson, Sonia Katyal, Tarunabh Khaitan, Madhav Khosla, Karen Knop, Patrick Macklem, Audrey Macklin, Pratap Bhanu Mehta, Vikram Raghavan, Simon Stern, Arun K. Thiruvengadam, and Mariana Valverde. Rachel Park and Michael Sabet provided excellent research assistance.

trade in constitutional ideas the corollary to open access to markets? If the use of comparative constitutional materials does real work, does the practice of cosmopolitan citation carry with it the necessary implication that Indian constitutional adjudication is part of a transnational conversation on the relationship between rights, democracy, courts and the rule of law that knows no jurisdictional boundaries? Is the Indian Constitution merely a legal means to implement rights, that exist independently and apart from the Indian constitutional order, in universal principles of liberal political morality? Or is comparative analysis entirely inappropriate to the interpretation of a document that, as Rajeev Bhargava puts it, is the embodiment of India's 'first real exercise of political self-determination', and as Bhiku Parekh states, 'the clearest statement of the country's self-given identity'?[1]

In this chapter, I want to offer a provisional answer to these questions, by puzzling through the recent judgment of the Delhi High Court in *Naz Foundation* v. *Union of India*,[2] examining in particular the court's use of comparative constitutional law. Comparative law did real analytic work in *Naz Foundation*. Moreover, *Naz Foundation* neither used comparative materials in a way that was universalist, nor deemed them irrelevant because of a commitment to the particular and distinctive national character of the Indian Constitution. It rejected the choice between universalism and particularism as reflecting a false dichotomy. The court reasoned *dialogically* with comparative materials, and used them as interpretive foils to identify, reframe, and enforce the premises of the Indian Constitution that were articulated during its adoption. At the heart of *Naz Foundation* is the analogy between untouchability and sexual orientation. In a growing number of constitutional systems, courts have condemned discrimination on the basis of sexual orientation, and interpreted constitutional guarantees of liberty and/or privacy in a non-discriminatory manner to encompass sexual intimacy between same-sex partners. The question was whether the holdings

---

[1] R. Bhargava, 'Introduction', in R. Bhargava (ed.), *Politics and Ethics of the Indian Constitution* (Oxford University Press: New Delhi, 2008), pp. 1–42; B. Parekh, 'The Constitution as a Statement of Indian Identity', in Bhargava (ed.), *Politics and Ethics*, pp. 43–58. Neither Bhargava nor Parekh take any position on the use of comparative constitutional law in the interpretation of the Indian Constitution.

[2] (2009) 160 DLT 277 (hereinafter *Naz Foundation*).

and reasoning of those foreign courts resonated with pre-existing Indian constitutional premises. *Naz Foundation* held that they did. The court appeared to regard sexual orientation and untouchability as analogous, and accordingly seems to have reasoned that the Indian Constitution should condemn discrimination on the latter basis as much as on the former.

This chapter is an intervention in two debates. First, it contributes to the large and growing literature on Indian constitutional law, and in particular, the debate sparked by *Naz Foundation* over the role of comparative materials in that judgment. Second, it is part of a larger effort to change how we situate India in the field of comparative constitutional law. Although vibrant, the field narrowly focuses attention on a few central jurisdictions. The literature is organized around a relatively limited set of cases: Canada, Israel, Germany, New Zealand, South Africa, the United Kingdom, and the United States. India has suffered from comparative neglect. This is regrettable, because the Indian materials have much to contribute to a range of debates that are central preoccupations of the discipline.

One such debate is over the role of comparative materials in constitutional interpretation. Elsewhere, I have identified, elaborated, and defended the dialogical model of comparative constitutional interpretation through a detailed examination of its application in American, Canadian, and South African constitutional jurisprudence.[3] The dialogical model provides the best explanation for the use of comparative constitutional law in *Naz Foundation*. Moreover, a close reading of *Naz Foundation* provides an occasion for the refinement of the dialogical model. It illustrates the role of argument by analogy—in this case, the idea that a constitutional system may single out social groups who have experienced severe disadvantage for the highest degree of constitutional protection, and that comparative materials may serve to highlight that other social groups experience analogous forms and levels of disadvantage that warrant a comparable constitutional

---

[3] S. Choudhry, 'Globalization in Search of Justification: Toward a Theory of Comparative Constitutional Interpretation', *Indiana L.J.*, (1999), 74(3): 819–92; S. Choudhry, 'The *Lochner* Era and Comparative Constitutionalism', *International J. of Const. L.*, (2004), 2(1) 1–55; and S. Choudhry, 'Migration as a New Metaphor in Comparative Constitutional Law', in S. Choudhry (ed.), *The Migration of Constitutional Ideas* (Cambridge University Press: New York, 2006).

response. Additionally, *Naz Foundation* demonstrates that under the dialogical model, comparative materials can be used in a way that not only acknowledges, but also affirms, a distinct constitutional identity. Indeed, reasoning by analogy in *Naz Foundation* led the court to recover and reinterpret foundational constitutional premises that are core to the identity of the Indian constitutional order. The identity-affirming possibilities of comparative engagement have often been overlooked in the recent literature on comparative constitutional law, but are a common feature of constitutional argument across many jurisdictions.[4] What differs, of course, is the particular constitutional identity that is being affirmed through this shared interpretive method.

THE DOCTRINAL POLITICS OF *NAZ FOUNDATION*

Naz Foundation held the application of Section 377 of the Indian Penal Code to consensual sexual acts of adults in private to be unconstitutional, on the basis of Articles 14, 15, and 21 of the Indian Constitution. In addition to being substantively bold, the judgment is doctrinally innovative. As Vikram Raghavan has carefully explained, *Naz Foundation* breaks new ground on several fronts.[5] The judgment confidently asserts two propositions—that Article 21's 'right to life' encompasses the 'right to privacy' and that the right extends to persons and not places—as if those propositions were settled law, when in fact they are not.[6] It cites as precedents the Supreme Court's judgments in *Kharak Singh* v. *State of Uttar Pradesh*,[7] *Govind* v. *State of Madhya Pradesh*,[8] and *District Registrar and Collector* v. *Canara Bank*,[9] even though the support provided by those cases for the right to privacy set out by the court is weak. Without hesitation, *Naz*

---

[4] For a similar argument that focuses on the use of Indian constitutional doctrine in the interpretation of the Sri Lankan Constitution, see in this volume, Chapter 6 (Gary Jeffrey Jacobsohn and Shylashri Shankar, 'Constitutional Borrowing in South Asia: India, Sri Lanka, and Secular Constitutional Identity').

[5] V. Raghavan, 'Navigating the Noteworthy and Nebulous in *Naz Foundation*', *NUJS L. Rev.*, (2009), 2(3): 397–417.

[6] Article 21 provides in full: 'No person shall be deprived of his life or personal liberty except according to procedure established by law'.

[7] AIR 1963 SC 1295 (hereinafter *Kharak Singh*).

[8] (1975) 2 SCC 148 (hereinafter *Gobind*).

[9] (2005) 1 SCC 496 (hereinafter *Canara Bank*).

Foundation applied the doctrine of substantive due process under Article 21 to protect the right to privacy, even though that doctrine has been used sparingly since it was announced by the Supreme Court in *Maneka Gandhi* v. *Union of India*.[10] Prior to *Naz Foundation*, the principal target of the doctrine of substantive due process under Article 21 had been executive action. *Naz Foundation*—along with the Supreme Court's recent decision in *Selvi* v. *Karnataka*—may mark the beginning of the application of a substantive due process to legislation.[11] Moreover, *Naz Foundation* reformulated that doctrine, elevating the standard of review set out in *Maneka Gandhi*, that the violation of an Article 21 right not be 'arbitrary', to a requirement that the state demonstrate that it has a 'compelling state interest' for infringing the right, a much more stringent standard.[12]

Tarunabh Khaitan has noted the potentially dramatic implications of *Naz Foundation* for Indian equality doctrine.[13] The court held that Article 15 prohibits discrimination not only on enumerated grounds but also on grounds analogous thereto, including sexual orientation.[14] Moreover, it also ruled that Article 15 has horizontal

---

[10] AIR 1978 SC 598 (hereinafter *Maneka Gandhi*). For an overview of the Supreme Court's Article 21 jurisprudence, see, T.R. Andhyarujina, 'The Evolution of Due Process of Law by the Supreme Court', in R. Dhavan, B.N. Kirpal, R. Ramachandran, and G. Subramanium (eds), *Supreme But Not Infallible: Essays in Honour of the Supreme Court of India* (Oxford University Press: New Delhi, 2000), pp. 193–213; M. Mate, 'The Origins of Due Process in India: The Role of Borrowing in Personal Liberty and Preventive Detention Cases', *Berkeley J. Int'l L.*, (2010), 28(1): 216–60.

[11] (2010) INSC 340 (5 May 2010). For commentary, see, A. Chandrachud, 'Of Constitutional "Due Process"', *The Hindu* (24 May 2010).

[12] The doctrine of substantive due process is a product of reading Article 21 in light of the doctrine of non-arbitrariness developed under Article 14. For recent commentary, see, A. Chandrachud, 'How Legitimate is Non-Arbitrariness? Constitutional Invalidation in the Light of *Mardia Chemicals* v. *Union of India*', *Indian J. Constitutional L.*, (2008), 2: 179–91. See also, R. Gupta and D. Sharma, 'Doctrine of Arbitrariness and Legislative Action: A Misconceived Application', *Nalsar Student L. Rev.*, (2010), 6: 22–34.

[13] T. Khaitan, 'Reading Swaraj into Article 15: A New Deal for All Minorities', *NUJS L. Rev.*, (2009), 2(3): 419–32.

[14] Article 15 provides in full:
1. The State shall not discriminate against any citizen on grounds only of religion, race, caste, sex, place of birth or any of them.

effect and applies to private parties. *Naz Foundation* would subject distinctions on prohibited grounds to strict scrutiny, and thus intervenes in the larger jurisprudential debate over the strict scrutiny standard, whose applicability to violations of Article 15 has been the subject of controversy in *Anuj Garg* v. *Hotel Association of India*,[15] *Thakur* v. *Union of India*,[16] and *Subhash Chandra* v. *Delhi Subordinate Services Selection Board*.[17] Taken together, *Naz Foundation*'s holdings on the scope of Article 15 would revive a provision that has been overshadowed and rendered redundant by the general guarantee of equality in Article 14.[18] On Article 14, the court appeared to hold that the provision prohibits both direct and indirect (that is, disparate impact) discrimination, which in principle should also apply to Article 15.

These aspects of the judgment have generated considerable scholarly debate, both among its critics[19] and supporters.[20] The rich

---

2. No citizen shall, on ground only of religion, race, caste, sex, place of birth or any of them, be subject to any disability, liability, restriction or condition with regard to—

    a. access to shops, public restaurants, hotels and places of public entertainment; or

    b. the use of wells, tanks, bathing ghats, roads and places of public resort maintained whole or partly out of State funds or dedicated to the use of general public.

3. Nothing in this article shall prevent the State from making any special provision for women and children.

4. Nothing in this article or in Clause (2) or Article 29 shall prevent the State from making any special provision for the advancement of any socially and educationally backward classes of citizens or for the Scheduled Castes and the Scheduled Tribes.

[15] AIR 2008 SC 663.

[16] (2008) 6 SCC 1.

[17] For discussion of the strict scrutiny standard, see, T. Khaitan, 'Beyond Reasonableness: A Rigorous Standard of Review for Article 15 Infringement', *J. of Indian L. Institute*, (2008), 50(2): 177–208.

[18] Article 14 provides in full: 'The State shall not deny to any person equality before the law or the equal protection of the laws within the territory of India'.

[19] M.P. Singh, 'Decriminalization of Homosexuality and the Constitution', *NUJS L. Rev.*, (2009), 2(3): 361–80.

[20] Raghavan, 'Noteworthy and Nebulous'; S. Basheer, S. Mukherjee, and K. Nair, 'Section 377 and the 'Order of Nature': Nurturing 'Indeterminacy' in the Law', *NUJS L. Rev.*, (2009), 2(3): 433–43; P. Baruah, 'Logic and Coherence in *Naz*

tapestry of Indian constitutional jurisprudence defines the parameters of this discussion. What I want to explore, however, is the extensive reliance in *Naz Foundation* on comparative materials. Comparative constitutional law was a central feature of the judgment, and figured prominently at nearly every stage of the court's analysis. As Madhav Khosla has set out, comparative constitutional law was used in several different ways.[21] Four warrant special mention. First, the court cited comparative case law from the United States, the European Court of Human Rights, South Africa, Fiji, and Nepal, which interpreted the right to privacy as encompassing the right to intimate sexual relations, in support of its holding that Article 21 encompasses the right to engage in such conduct, and was, therefore, violated by the challenged provision.[22] This issue attracted the most serious and sustained engagement with comparative materials. Second, the court relied on comparative case law from Canada and South Africa to define the content of the right to dignity, also protected by Article 21, which the court held was violated as well.[23] Third, it turned to the decisions of the United States Supreme Court and the Constitutional Court of South Africa to hold that a facially neutral ban on 'unnatural sex' without reference to sexual orientation in fact deliberately targeted homosexuals as a class, because the prohibited sexual acts were closely associated with homosexuality.[24] Fourth, the court looked to decisions from the European Court of Human Rights and the United States Supreme Court to hold that popular disapproval of homosexuality on the grounds of morality, no matter how widespread, is not a legitimate reason to limit constitutionally protected rights.[25]

While the court relied on comparative materials extensively, it offered little in the way of explanation or justification for this interpretive move. On the scope of the right to privacy, the court

---

Foundation: The Arguments of Non-Discrimination, Privacy, and Dignity', *NUJS L. Rev.*, (2009), 2(3): 505–24; and S. Mandal, '"Right to Privacy" in *Naz Foundation*: A Counter-Heteronormative Critique', *NUJS L. Rev.*, (2009), 2(3): 525–40.

[21] M. Khosla, 'Inclusive Constitutional Comparison', *American J. Comp. L.*, (2011), 59(4): 909–34.

[22] *Naz Foundation*, at para 29.

[23] Ibid., at paras 26, 27, and 49.

[24] Ibid., at paras 94–6.

[25] Ibid., at paras 75–9.

justified its reference to the American jurisprudence by the fact that the Supreme Court had 'adverted' to these decisions in its own case law on privacy.[26] This is an argument from precedent. It is not a substantive justification for why that body of comparative jurisprudence is relevant, for the circumstances under which a court should have reference to it, for the issues with respect to which it is useful, and most fundamentally, for how precisely a court should rely on it. Even if the rote citation of precedent is adequate for the Delhi High Court, it will be insufficient for the Supreme Court. On the citation of comparative case law from other jurisdictions, in which courts found that criminal prohibitions on anal intercourse contravened a rights-protecting instrument, the court simply prefaced the recitation of these decisions under the heading 'global trends'. It failed to explain why these global trends were legally relevant to the interpretation of the Indian Constitution.[27]

The failure of *Naz Foundation* to justify its use of comparative materials is of legal consequence because of their importance to the constitutional challenge. To understand why this is so, compare the role of comparative materials in *Naz Foundation* and *Lawrence v. Texas*.[28] *Lawrence* was one of the three most important foreign precedents cited by *Naz Foundation*—the other two being the European Court of Human Rights' decision in *Dudgeon v. United Kingdoms*[29] and the judgment of the Constitutional Court of South Africa in *National Coalition for Gay and Lesbian Equality v. Minister of Justice*.[30] *Lawrence* provides a good analytical model for *Naz Foundation*, both because it involved the overruling of a criminal statute that prohibited anal intercourse and because it cited comparative jurisprudence with which the United States Supreme Court brought American constitutional doctrine into alignment. On one reading, *Lawrence* appears to have been a harder case than *Naz Foundation*, because of *Bowers v. Hardwick*,[31] which *Lawrence* had to overrule. According to this view, the comparative materials did important work, because they provided the

---

[26] *Naz Foundation*, at para 31.
[27] Ibid., heading preceding para 53.
[28] 539 U.S. 558 (2003) (hereinafter *Lawrence*).
[29] 45 Eur. Ct. H.R. (ser. A) (1981) (hereinafter *Dudgeon*).
[30] 1999 (1) SA 6 (hereinafter *National Coalition*).
[31] 478 U.S. 186 (1986) (hereinafter *Bowers*).

resources to overturn a relatively recent precedent. This is how Justice Scalia's dissent in *Lawrence* characterized the role of foreign law. And this work had to be done in a constitutional system that is famously resistant to comparative constitutional argument—albeit one where that is beginning to change.[32] By contrast, there is no equivalent to *Bowers* in India, since the constitutionality of the criminal prohibition on anal intercourse had never come before the Indian courts prior to *Naz Foundation*. So the comparative jurisprudence in that case was not counter-balanced by precedent. Rather, it was used to address a novel constitutional issue. Moreover, the foreign case law was cited in a system that has been open to comparative material from the outset. As Adam Smith has documented, the Supreme Court of India has cited comparative case law from its very inception and at a higher rate in its political and civil liberties cases than in its jurisprudence as a whole.[33]

Yet, upon closer examination, *Lawrence* is not as relatively difficult and *Naz* not as relatively easy, as this analysis would suggest. The reason for this is a long line of cases which originated before both *Lawrence* and *Bowers* on the right to privacy and intimate sexual relations: *Griswold* v. *Connecticut*,[34] *Eisenstadt* v. *Baird*,[35] *Roe* v. *Wade*,[36] and *Planned Parenthood* v. *Casey*.[37] Read against the jurisprudence as a whole, *Bowers* was a mistake, and *Lawrence* merely the application and slight extension of a long-standing line of precedents. Indeed, Justice Stevens' dissent in *Bowers*—which was endorsed by the majority in *Lawrence*—conforms to the narrative that the exceptional case that does not fit with the others was *Bowers*, not *Lawrence*. It was *Lawrence* that was demanded by precedent, not *Bowers*. Comparative constitutional law at best merely confirmed a result that flowed naturally from internal sources. *Naz Foundation* was very different. Even prior to *Naz Foundation*, the developing Indian jurisprudence on the right to

[32] V.C. Jackson, *Constitutional Engagement in a Transnational Era* (Oxford University Press: New York, 2009).

[33] A.M. Smith, 'Making Itself at Home: Understanding Foreign Law in Domestic Jurisprudence: The Indian Case', *Berkeley J. Int'l L.*, (2006), 24: 218–72.

[34] 381 US 479 (1965) (hereinafter *Griswold*).

[35] 405 US 438 (1972) (hereinafter *Eisenstadt*).

[36] 410 US 113 (1973) (hereinafter *Roe*).

[37] 505 US 833 (1992) (hereinafter *Casey*).

privacy, as commentators have noted, rested on unsure foundations.[38] Moreover, the issue of whether the right to privacy extends to sexual intimacy had not been decided by the Supreme Court of India, let alone raised in a single appeal. So the internal doctrinal resources available to *Naz Foundation* were meagre in comparison to those available to *Lawrence*. The external resources provided by comparative jurisprudence had to do a lot more work in *Naz Foundation* than in *Lawrence*. Comparative constitutional law mattered, and mattered centrally; indeed, it was the engine of doctrinal innovation in *Naz Foundation*. However, the court took the legal relevance of comparative constitutional law to be self-evident, when in actuality it was not.

Since the petitioner Naz Foundation and the respondent Voices Against 377 both cited these comparative materials, we might expect the justification for their relevance to the interpretation of the Indian Constitution to be found in these citations. This is not the case, however. Naz Foundation merely provides the arguments—or lack of argument—that the court later repeated in its judgment.[39] The submissions of Voices Against 377 shed considerable light on the global political-legal strategy of which *Naz Foundation* is a part. In a broad and increasing number of jurisdictions, spanning the developed and developing worlds, in both long-established and emerging liberal democracies, states have decriminalized anal intercourse between consenting adults in private. In some jurisdictions, these changes were brought about through legislation without the involvement of the courts. In other jurisdictions, judicial intervention—through domestic constitutional courts and international tribunals—has played an important role. Thus, Voices Against 377 refers to the cases of 'key jurisdictions' that have found unconstitutional criminal prohibitions on anal intercourse to be part of 'a contemporary international judicial trend' or 'global judicial trend'.[40] The implication is that the Indian courts should participate in this project of legal convergence by finding Section 377 unconstitutional. But again, this begs the question of why the fact of global judicial convergence should count as a reason in Indian constitutional argument.

---

[38] Raghavan, 'Noteworthy and Nebulous'.

[39] Submissions of Naz Foundation in *Naz Foundation*, at paras 42 and 173.

[40] Submissions of Voices Against 377 in *Naz Foundation*, at paras 1, 2, and 6.

Unfortunately, the legal literature offers insufficient assistance. Despite the fact that recourse to comparative materials is a widespread and long-standing feature of Indian constitutional interpretation, scholars have offered little by way of sustained explanation or justification. Sonia Katyal, Madhav Khosla, and Arun K. Thiruvengadam are notable exceptions.[41] Much of the torrent of legal commentary sparked by *Naz Foundation* mentions its comparative engagement largely in passing, and describes, but does not assess, the court's justifications for this interpretive practice.[42] Chief Justice Balakrishnan recently addressed the question extra-judicially.[43] However, his analysis raises more questions than it answers. Thus, while he acknowledges that Indian courts 'routinely cite' non-binding comparative case law because of its 'persuasive value', he does not set out the circumstances under which such citation is appropriate, or, more fundamentally, what about a foreign judgment would make it persuasive.[44]

Naz Foundation has a conceptual lacuna at its very heart, created by the court's failure to justify the centrality of comparative constitutional reasoning to its judgment. This space has been filled by critics who have politicized the court's use of comparative constitutional law. The parties who opposed the challenge engaged directly on the issue of comparative methodology. The Joint Action Council Kannur attempted to distinguish the foreign cases, on the basis that the

---

[41] S. Katyal, 'The Dissident Citizen', *UCLA L. Rev.*, (2010), 57(5): 1415–76; Khosla, 'Inclusive Constitutional Comparison'; A.K. Thiruvengadam, 'In Pursuit of 'the Common Illumination of our House': Trans-Judicial Influence and the Origins of PIL Jurisprudence in South Asia', *Indian J. Constitutional L.*, (2008), 2: 67–103; and A.K. Thiruvengadam, 'The Social Rights Jurisprudence of the Supreme Court of India from a Comparative Perspective', in C. Raj Kumar and K. Chockalingam (eds), *Human Rights, Criminal Justice and Constitutional Empowerment* (Oxford University Press: New Delhi, 2007), pp. 264–309. See also, S. Shankar, 'The Substance of the Constitution: Engaging with Foreign Judgments in India, Sri Lanka, and South Africa', *Drexel L. Rev.*, (2010), 2(2): 373–425.

[42] See, Singh, 'Decriminalization of Homosexuality', pp. 363, 371 (critical of use of comparative constitutional law); Raghavan, 'Noteworthy and Nebulous', pp. 401, 402, 409, and 413; T. Khaitan, 'Reading Swaraj', p. 424; and S. Narrain, 'Crystallising Queer Politics: The *Naz Foundation* Case and its Implications for India's Transgendered Communities', *NUJS L. Rev.*, (2009), 2(3): 455–68.

[43] K.G. Balakrishnan, 'The Role of Foreign Precedents in a Country's Legal System', *National Law School of India Rev.*, (2010), 22(1): 1–16.

[44] Ibid., pp. 7–8.

cases were brought by specific victims who adduced evidence of the breach of their rights and involved statutes that explicitly targeted homosexuals, which rendered those cases irrelevant to this appeal, which was brought by a public interest organization with respect to a facially neutral law.[45] But the stronger response came from the Union of India, which in its submissions before the Delhi High Court attacked the reliance on comparative constitutional law from the standpoint of cultural nationalism. Comparative jurisprudence was a mechanism to introduce foreign cultural norms into India that were at odds with norms deeply rooted in Indian tradition, religion and social practice. Thus, in defence of India's cultural distinctiveness, Indian courts should reject the use of comparative jurisprudence. The Union of India submitted that 'the Court should not interpret our Constitution in such a manner to thrust foreign culture in India where the [sic] morality standards are not as high as in India and where the society is governed by different laws and traditions'.[46]

These arguments have created a constitutional politics around *Naz Foundation*, which has driven defensive attempts to reinterpret it. For example, I think this context explains Justice Verma's narrow re-reading of the judgment.[47] Justice Verma starts from the premise that Section 377 impedes access to HIV/AIDS therapy by homosexuals, because they will not seek treatment for fear of criminal sanction. This effect renders Section 377 unconstitutional because of the interaction of Articles 47 and 21. Article 47 makes it a directive principle of state policy that the state improve public health; Article 21 protects the right to life. Justice Verma argues that reading Article 21 subject to Article 47 creates a right to medical treatment for persons infected with HIV. Section 377 is therefore unconstitutional because it is a barrier to accessing medical treatment. On this reading, *Naz Foundation* did not establish that Article 21 encompasses a right to privacy and that this right to privacy encompasses sexual intimacy, including between homosexuals. The point I want to highlight is that Justice Verma's reinterpretation of *Naz Foundation* relies largely

---

[45] Submissions of Joint Action Council Kannur in *Naz Foundation*, at para 9.

[46] Submissions of Union of India in *Naz Foundation*, at para 43.

[47] 'Justice J.S. Verma comments on the *Naz Foundation Judgment*', http://lawandotherthings.blogspot.com/2009/07/justice-jsvermas-comment-on-naz.html (last accessed on 31 August 2012).

on established internal legal sources, which in part reflects the fact that the court did not adequately defend the recourse to comparative constitutional law. To resist this impulse, advocates of *Naz Foundation* need to defend the use of comparative constitutional law more fully.

THREE MODES OF COMPARATIVE CONSTITUTIONAL INTERPRETATION

I approach this task by briefly placing *Naz Foundation* in context.[48] The centrality of comparative constitutional law in *Naz Foundation* is far from unique. Constitutional interpretation across the globe is taking on an increasingly cosmopolitan character, as comparative jurisprudence comes to assume a central place in constitutional adjudication. Extensive and detailed treatments of foreign materials have become familiar features of constitutional adjudication in many courts. As Alan Brudner writes: '[T]hose who interpret local constitutional traditions take a lively interest in how their counterparts in other jurisdictions interpret their own traditions.... This interest, moreover, is a professional one. Comparative constitutional studies are valued, not as a leisurely after-hours pastime, but for the aid they give to judicial...interpreters of a national constitution'.[49]

The growth in the use of comparative jurisprudence is part of a larger phenomenon: the migration of constitutional ideas across legal systems, which has emerged as one of the central features of contemporary constitutional practice. The migration of constitutional ideas occurs at various stages in the life-cycle of modern constitutions. The use of comparative law in constitutional interpretation is but one example. Another is the use of foreign constitutions in the process of constitution-making. Comparative materials are a source not only of models to be adopted and adapted, but also of lessons to be learned and dangers to be avoided.

Like any interpretive practice, the use of comparative constitutional law in constitutional interpretation requires justification. As Alexander Bickel explained over forty years ago, in liberal democracies that have opted for written constitutions enforced by unelected courts, the

---

[48] Choudhry, 'Globalization'; Choudhry, 'Lochner'; and Choudhry, 'Migration'.
[49] A. Brudner, *Constitutional Goods* (Oxford University Press: Oxford, 2004).

power of judicial review is a form of political power that cannot be legitimized through democratic accountability and control.[50] Courts must legitimize their power through both the processes whereby they determine whether issues come before the courts, and the reasons for their judgments, somehow distinguishing adjudication from other forms of political decision-making. The various features of legal reasoning—*stare decisis*, for example—are more than just the means through which courts arrive at decisions; they define and constitute the unique institutional identity of courts. The very legitimacy of judicial institutions hinges on interpretive methodology. So courts *must* explain why, how, and under what circumstances comparative law should count. And, if courts do not, judicial review is open to the charge of simply being politics by other means, cloaked in legal language and subject to attenuated democratic control.

Although Bickel wrote about constitutional interpretation in the United States, this is not a problem unique to that jurisdiction. In each and every country where the migration of constitutional ideas is on the rise, the demands of justification must be met. This is true even for countries such as South Africa, whose constitution provides that courts 'may consider foreign law' in interpreting its Bill of Rights and therefore licences comparative constitutional interpretation.[51] Left unanswered by this provision are the questions of how comparative law is to be considered, and why and in what context courts should engage with it at all.

Consider three different answers to these questions: the particularist, universalist, and dialogic models of comparative constitutional interpretation.

On the particularist conception, the migration of constitutional ideas, and the use of comparative jurisprudence in particular, stand at odds with one of the dominant understandings of constitutionalism: that the constitution of a nation emerges from, embodies, and aspires to sustain or respond to that nation's particular circumstances, most centrally its history and political culture. As Jürgen Habermas has explained, the citizens of a nation often use constitutional discourse

---

[50] A.M. Bickel, *The Least Dangerous Branch: The Supreme Court at the Bar of Politics,* 2nd Ed. (Yale University Press: New Haven, 1986).

[51] Constitution of the Republic of South Africa, Section 39(1).

as a means to 'clarify the way they want to understand themselves as citizens of a specific republic, as inhabitants of a specific region, as heirs to a specific culture, which traditions they want to perpetuate and which they want to discontinue, [and] how they want to deal with their history'.[52] Indeed, for some countries, particularly those with a diverse citizenry, lacking a prior or pre-political bond of ethnicity, religion, or race, constitutions are an integral component of national identity and reflect one way in which those nations view themselves as different from others. It is fair to say that constitutions continue to be widely understood in such a particular and local way.

The particularist conception of the nature and character of constitutions has implications for how those documents should be interpreted, and the use of comparative constitutional materials as interpretive aids. According to the particularlist view, constitutional interpretation should be situated or particular, and should rely on sources internal to specific political and legal systems. The use of local and particular sources in constitutional reasoning secures the legitimacy of judicial review. Comparative jurisprudence, by contrast, is of no assistance at all, precisely because it comes from outside a given legal system. At best, it represents a foreign curiosity of strictly academic interest and little practical relevance. At worst, its use is a foreign imposition or even a form of legal imperialism.

One possible challenge to this position is the increased convergence of constitutional texts, and, in particular, bills of rights. In particular, there is a core set of rights—for example, the right to life and the Right to Equality—that are found in most bills of rights. Moreover, the precise language of the provisions that entrench these rights is often very similar, reflecting the fact that the process of constitution-drafting is deeply comparative and draws on common models. In the face of this textual similarity, the particularist assertion of constitutional difference may be hard to sustain. However, committed particularlists emphasize differences where there appear to be none. On their account, the similarities between constitutions are rather superficial, and conceal profound differences not apparent

[52] J. Habermas, 'Struggles for Recognition in the Democratic Institutional State' in A. Guttman (ed.), *Multiculturalism: Examining the Politics of Recognition*, 2nd Ed. (Princeton University Press: Princeton, 1994), p.125.

at first glance. Particularists argue that in a post-realist world, it is beyond dispute that legal texts are inherently ambiguous and require reference to extra-textual sources for their interpretation and application in concrete cases. Moreover, although overarching principles of political morality provide some assistance, these arguments quickly run out, because the question then arises of which political morality to choose. For example, in choosing between the appropriate background principle against which to interpret a constitutional Right to Equality—found in many contemporary bills of rights—libertarian and egalitarian theories of justice would counsel divergent interpretations of the scope of the provision in the context, for example, of challenges to reservations or affirmative action. This disagreement on fundamental principle may explain the divergent approaches of the Indian and American supreme courts on precisely this issue.

Significantly, particularists claim that courts, as a matter of empirical fact, do not look outward to foreign experiences to facilitate the choice among these different theories; rather, they turn inward to sources that are internal to a particular country—variously described as the 'rhetoric and consciousness of those abroad…[that is,] what people believe that they are doing', the 'self-characterizations and self-perceptions' of actors within those legal systems (William Alford),[53] cultural and political history (Fred Schauer),[54] or 'the legal culture in which the [constitutional] dispute is embedded' (George Fletcher).[55] The reliance on a variety of internal sources leads particularists to be deeply sceptical of the viability of transplanting constitutional doctrine from one country to another. For example, Schauer argues that a German court may be able to distinguish between Nazi sympathizers and other peripheral political actors and uphold severe restrictions on the political activities of only the former, whereas an American court could not. This leads him to 'doubt the recent ease with which constitutional transplantation seems now to be embraced', because 'so long as cultural differences are reflected in categorical differences,…[there are

---

[53] W.P. Alford, 'On the Limits of "Grand Theory" in Comparative Law', *Wash. L. Rev.*, (1986), 61(3): 947.

[54] F. Schauer, 'Free Speech and the Cultural Contingency of Constitutional Categories', *Cardozo L. Rev.*, (1993), 14(3–4): 865–80.

[55] G.P. Fletcher, 'Constitutional Identity', *Cardozo L. Rev.*, (1993), 14(3–4): 737.

likely] to be pressures militating against the cross-cultural assimilation of cultural categories'.[56] But the differences that drive particularists need not be cultural, and may reflect instead deep disagreement over the fundamental values underlying the basic structure of political and economic rules and institutions. Thus, a constitution may reflect a commitment to a certain understanding of the relationship between politics and markets, which may in turn undergird the interpretation of constitutional rights to private property.

Next, consider universalists, who stand at the opposite end of the spectrum from particularists. They posit that constitutional guarantees are cut from a universal cloth, and that all constitutional courts are engaged in the identification, interpretation, and application of the same set of principles. Unlike particularists, who emphasize the differences among legal systems, universalists see unity in the midst of diversity. They exhort courts to pay no heed to national legal particularities when engaging in constitutional interpretation. Courts working in the universalist mode regard themselves as interpreting constitutional texts that protect rights that transcend national boundaries. The legitimacy of the reliance on comparative case law is buttressed by the empirical fact of convergence across constitutional systems. An emerging consensus among foreign legal systems—including foreign constitutional courts—is proof of a particular constitutional interpretation's truth or rightness. The law is something to be discovered or apprehended through a process of interpretive reflection; comparative jurisprudence offers a fund of similar reflections by courts and tribunals worldwide as an aid in that process.

In concrete legal terms, universalist interpretation may focus on both the interpretation of rights and their limitation. With respect to the former, universalists would hold that particular rights, such as freedom of expression, freedom of religion, or freedom of association, could each be based on political theories of what interests those rights are designed to protect. Universalists argue that these theories are the same for every constitution in which those rights are found. These theories flow from liberal political morality, which entails that respect for rights is a condition for the legitimate exercise of public power. Comparative jurisprudence becomes a repository of principles to be

[56] Schauer, 'Constitutional Categories', pp. 867, 879.

relied on as valuable articulations, explanations, and commentaries on the political theories underlying particular constitutional rights. Additionally, foreign judgments suggest how those rights are to be implemented through the crafting of constitutional doctrine, and then applied in concrete cases. A court no longer has to engage in the burdensome and time-consuming task of formulating the theories underlying particular rights, operationalizing those abstract guarantees through constitutional doctrine, or even applying those rights with respect to specific issues, since comparative case law offers a convenient shortcut to attaining these goals.

A parallel logic applies to the question of justifiable limitations. It is a common feature of contemporary constitutional adjudication that rights are not absolute. Constitutional rights may be limited, but those limitations must meet a test of justification. An emerging model for framing the judicial inquiry into justifiable limits on constitutional rights is provided by the doctrine of proportionality. According to this doctrine, rights can be justifiably limited if the limitation is undertaken for a sufficiently important reason, if the means chosen to vindicate this objective actually achieve the objective, if there are no other means available that are equally effective in pursuing the objective and impair the right less than the means chosen, and if the deleterious effects on the right are outweighed by the salutary effects of the rights-infringing measure. On the universalist account, this common template is integral to rights-based adjudication. How one court conceptualizes the notion of proportionality itself, frames the specific legal test that implements it, and applies it in specific cases should guide other courts because they are engaged in a common enterprise.[57]

In sum, following the universalist view, a court's reliance on comparative materials deliberately situates it as part of a transnational discussion among judicial tribunals about the interpretation and application of transcendent legal norms, which takes place through a universal legal language that shares a common grammar and underlying theoretical structure. The implicit image here is that of an international community of states and citizens that shares a basic commitment to a vision of constitutionalism based on the rule of law and the rights of individuals. The legal principles of universalist

---

[57] D. Beatty, *The Ultimate Rule of Law* (Oxford University Press: Oxford, 2004).

interpretation are the principles which animate constitutionalism in this community of nations.

Finally, consider the dialogical conception of constitutionalism. In its strongest form, legal particularism regards the mutual unintelligibility or incompatibility of legal systems as a fundamental barrier to the use of comparative jurisprudence. However, this position stands against the widely held—but often unarticulated—view that comparative constitutional law is an important tool for understanding one's *own* legal system, by serving as a stimulus to constitutional self-reflection. Dialogical interpretation proceeds by interrogating what a claim to constitutional difference actually means. Difference is an inherently relative concept; a constitution is only unique because it possesses some characteristic or feature which other constitutions do not. Moreover, since difference is defined in comparative terms, it follows that a keener awareness and a better understanding of difference can be achieved through a process of comparison. In this way, the use of comparative jurisprudence in the correct way, far from being in tension with a commitment to constitutional difference, may in fact both acknowledge it and even enhance an awareness of it.

Dialogical interpretation achieves this goal through three interpretive steps. The first step is to use comparative jurisprudence as a means to identify important assumptions, both factual and normative, that underlie the interpreting court's own constitutional order. There are a number of moves to this argument. The court begins by examining comparative jurisprudence, not primarily to gain an accurate picture of the state of the law in the other jurisdiction, but rather to identify the assumptions that lie underneath it. In the process of articulating the assumptions of comparative jurisprudence, a court will inevitably uncover its own. By asking why foreign courts have reasoned a certain way, a court will ask itself why it reasons the way it does; comparative jurisprudence serves as an interpretive foil.

At the second step, the court compares the assumptions underlying domestic and comparative jurisprudence, and engages in a process of justification. If the assumptions are different, the question becomes why they are different. It is now possible to ask this question because the court's own constitution and jurisprudence has been made 'strange' to it, by contrasting it with a different constitutional world.

Comparative constitutional law exposes the practices of one's own constitutional system as contingent, circumstantial, and mutable; not transcendent, timeless, and inevitable. If the assumptions are similar, one can still ask why—that is, whether those assumptions ought to be shared. A similarity in constitutional assumptions should not be considered fixed and immutable.

At the final stage, the court is faced with a set of interpretive choices. In cases of constitutional difference, if the court rejects foreign assumptions and affirms its own, the value of this exercise has been to heighten its awareness and understanding of constitutional difference, which in turn will shape and guide constitutional interpretation. A constitution can be interpreted not only by reference to what it is, but also in relation to what it is not. Negative anti-models can shape and drive constitutional interpretation, as illustrations of the path to be avoided. Conversely, in cases of constitutional similarity, if similarity once identified is embraced, dialogical interpretation grounds the legitimacy of importing comparative jurisprudence and applying it as law, on the basis of shared normative commitments. In either case, even if comparative constitutional reasoning does not lead to legal change, it nonetheless serves as a device to identify and affirm a constitutional identity. Dialogical interpretation, in other words, leads to a heightened sense of legal self-awareness through interpretive confrontation and clarification.

But the identification and attempted justification of constitutional assumptions through comparison may lead a court to challenge and reject those assumptions and search for new ones. From a starting point of constitutional similarity, a court may reject shared assumptions and stake out a new interpretive approach proceeding from radically different premises. Dialogical interpretation precipitates a shift from constitutional similarity to constitutional difference. Where the *status quo* is constitutional difference, a court may determine that difference to be unfounded. This new-found similarity, in turn, makes comparative jurisprudence a resource for constitutional interpretation. The process of dialogic interpretation can lead the court to fundamentally re-assess its previous judgments, and to use comparative jurisprudence as a means to initiate legal change. Comparison with a different constitutional perspective exposes one's assumptions as contingent, a first step to interpretive change. Comparative constitutional reasoning facilitates and enables constitutional choice.

Under dialogical interpretation, the constitutional premises that a court identifies, clarifies, and challenges fall into different categories.

Some premises set out the basic mission of the constitutional order as a whole. Consider an illustrative example from South Africa. Under the Interim Constitution, an important question was whether the Bill of Rights applied to the common law-governing relationships between private parties. In *Du Plessis* v. *De Klerk*,[58] a majority held that it did not, following the alleged trend among liberal democracies for bills of rights to apply only vertically against the State, not horizontally against private parties. Justice Johann Kriegler filed the leading dissent. He began by identifying the assumption underlying this supposed consensus. That consensus proceeded from the basis that the principal threat posed to individual rights comes from the repressive use of State power. Kriegler argued, however, that the assumption underlying the South African Bill of Rights was different, because the sources of oppression historically in South Africa were both public and private. He identified this assumption by reference, *inter alia*, to the Interim Constitution's Preamble, that gestured to a South African past which was not 'merely one of repressive use of State power[,]...[but] one of persistent, institutionalized subjugation and exploitation of a voiceless and largely defenceless majority by a determined and privileged minority'.[59] In the process of identifying that assumption, he justified it, both in terms of South Africa's racist past as well as the current 'stark reality of South Africa and the power relationships in its society'.[60] As a consequence, the interpretive choice was clear, and Kriegler held that the Bill of Rights applied both vertically and horizontally, expressly declining to follow the alleged consensus. But even though Kriegler reached this conclusion based on a recognition that the Interim Constitution was unique or different, he defined this difference in comparative terms. Although this premise shaped the interpretation of the provision governing the application of the Bill of Rights, because it was rooted in an

---

[58] 1996 (3) SALR 850 (CC).
[59] Interim Constitution, Preamble.
[60] *Du Plessis* v. *De Klerk*, 1996 (3) SALR 850 (CC) at 912.

underlying conception of the purpose of the entire constitutional order, it potentially had a bearing on other questions—for example, the degree of deference to be shown to political institutions that seek to redress power imbalances through measures targeted at private entities.

Other premises constitute part of the political theory underlying specific constitutional provisions, as opposed to the constitution as a whole. Justice Albie Sachs' judgment in another South African decision, *State* v. *Solberg*—which considered a constitutional challenge to the prohibition of liquor sales on Sundays—provides a useful example.[61] One ground of challenge, that the law amounted to an unconstitutional endorsement of Christianity, relied on American jurisprudence under the Establishment Clause. The argument was that this body of case law stood for the proposition that the very idea of freedom of religion encompassed the notion of State non-endorsement, and hence, that the specific South African provision guaranteeing freedom of religion should be interpreted accordingly. The majority judgment rejected this argument, and turned back the constitutional challenge. Although not fully theorized, the implicit argument in the majority judgment is that the combination of a specific constitutional permission for religious services in public facilities, and the discipline imposed by the equality guarantee on government activity, yields the principle of non-preferentialism rather than non-endorsement. Justice Sachs' dissent relied on American constitutional doctrine to challenge this unstated but central assumption. For Justice Sachs, the normative claim underlying the American Establishment Clause case law was the notion of political equality. However, he did not accept this principle in the manner of universalist interpretation. Rather, he used it as an invitation to peer into South African history and determine whether political equality was bound up with the freedom of religion in a way that justified its incorporation into the interpretation of the constitutional provision expressly guaranteeing the latter. This history betrayed a deliberate and express state preference for Christianity in public policy, based on the view that other faiths were not only different, but also deviant and inferior. Against this backdrop, the social meaning of any

[61] 1994 (4) SALR 1176 (CC).

contemporary preference for Christianity is to serve as a reminder of the historically subordinate position of other faiths. As a consequence, Justice Sachs concluded that prohibiting State endorsement as a means to political equality through an idea drawn from American jurisprudence had 'special resonance in South Africa' and therefore was a South African constitutional assumption too.[62] Doctrinally, the notion of political equality translated into a bar on the enactment of laws for religious reasons under the constitutional guarantee of freedom of religion.

Finally, the premises may concern the application of constitutional guarantees in specific cases. Consider Mayo Moran's contrast of the American and Canadian constitutional jurisprudence on hate speech targeted at racial and religious minorities.[63] American constitutional doctrine bars the criminal prohibition of hate speech, while Canadian constitutional doctrine permits it. Moran argues that the diametrically opposed conclusions of the American and Canadian courts—both adjudicating rights-protecting constitutional instruments in countries that are widely acknowledged to be liberal democracies and enjoy a high degree of political freedom—cannot be explained by differences between the relevant constitutional texts. Rather, this difference turns on divergent background assumptions about the nature of hate speech, the interests at stake in its regulation, and the nature of the State, which are exposed through constitutional comparison. In the American constitutional tradition, hate speech is regarded as a form of extreme political expression, whereas in Canada it is the verbal manifestation of racial and religious discrimination. This difference in turn leads to differing accounts of the interests at stake. In the United States, the criminal regulation of hate speech pits the individual against the coercive State, which is the only source of threat to individual freedom. In Canada, the targets of hate speech are conceptualized as victims, meaning that the criminal regulation of hate speech is a contest between differing private interests, which the State must balance. Through criminalizing hate speech, the State acts to protect the freedom of its victims. Moreover,

[62] Ibid., at 1229.

[63] M. Moran, 'Talking About Hate Speech: A Rhetorical Analysis of American and Canadian Approaches to the Regulation of Hate Speech', *Wisconsin Law Review*, (1994), 6: 1425–514.

in the Canadian view, there are important public interests at stake, because hate speech impedes equal participation in political debate and democratic decision-making by its victims. Finally, the State is viewed with relatively greater suspicion as a potential source of political repression in American constitutional doctrine than under Canadian jurisprudence, where the state is more likely to be regarded as a trustworthy custodian of public interest.

Dialogical interpretation can reinforce moments of constitutional difference, but can also fuel convergence across different constitutional systems. Since convergence is also the outcome of universalist interpretation, this raises the question of how the dialogical and universalist interpretive modes are related—indeed, whether they are different modes at all. Consider two different accounts of dialogical interpretation. One view would hold that universalist interpretation is nested *within* the dialogical model. Under this view, arguments for convergence necessarily rely on universalist premises. Thus, a blanket prohibition on torture, which one court has interpreted as entailing a corresponding prohibition on deportation to torture, should lead another court to reach the same result, on the basis of a shared commitment of the two constitutional systems to a universal principle of liberal political morality. Conversely, the absence of universal norms would open the space for—but not require—constitutional difference. The identity-affirming aspects of dialogical interpretation, on this account, could only operate within the space left over by a universal principle. The notion of the 'margin of appreciation', central to European human rights law, captures this idea. Now, to be sure, the space for national constitutional difference in fact is fairly large. The rights with respect to which universalist interpretation can be invoked are relatively limited in scope. The central case may be those rights that affect the physical security of the individual. By contrast, even the traditional liberal freedoms (such as expression, religion and conscience, association, and assembly), although enshrined by many constitutions, are more normatively contentious. Though courts of various jurisdictions agree on the importance of these rights, they have differed sharply on their interpretation. These differences in interpretation manifest themselves in different ways. In some cases (for example, the interpretation of rights to equality), courts might diverge on the scope of the right. But in many others, courts may diverge in proportionality analyses, with respect to the range of legitimate reasons for which rights can be violated, the degree of deference to be shown to the state, and so on.

But there is a second view of dialogical interpretation that sharply distinguishes it from the universalist interpretation. This view takes distinct national constitutional identities seriously, but nonetheless charts a path to constitutional convergence in the teeth of such difference. It proceeds from the starting point that constitutional interpretation is a form of reasoning within a distinct national constitutional tradition that must occur on its own terms. National constitutional traditions are distinctive in three ways. First, a constitutional tradition consists of the total set of outcomes of constitutional interpretation. This set of outcomes will differ across systems, because of the contingency of the range of constitutional issues that arise under each system, and the inevitability of divergent interpretations on some common issues. Second, national constitutional traditions will be necessarily distinct if a court habitually relies on interpretive methods that incorporate by reference particular features of a nation's constitutional practice—its constitutional text, the particular historical circumstances that surrounded the adoption of the document, and the views of its framers on the meaning and applications of the constitutional text.

The third dimension of the distinctiveness of national constitutional traditions is methodological distinctiveness. To be sure, methodological diversity does not mean that the kinds of arguments that are acceptable in constitutional systems are radically different. On the contrary, as Jeff Goldsworthy has recently argued, courts in Australia, Canada, Germany, India, South Africa, and the United States rely on a shared set of interpretive methods. These include textual (including intra-textual methods), originalist (both original intent and original meaning), teleological or purposive, doctrinal or precedent-based, structuralist (drawing inferences from a single provision or sets of related provisions), prudential, and ethical or moral approaches to constitutional interpretation.[64] But each national constitutional tradition differs in the relative emphasis and interrelationship they

---

[64] J. Goldsworthy, 'Conclusions', in J. Goldsworthy (ed.), *Interpreting Constitutions* (Oxford University Press: Oxford, 2006), pp. 325–45.

accord to those methods. The methodological matrix of a national constitutional tradition defines an argumentative space within which acceptable forms of constitutional argument occur. For example, in the United States, Mark Tushnet argues that precedent and considerations of administrability are the most important components of constitutional interpretation, followed in descending order of importance by constitutional text and original intent and meaning, structure, and ethical or moral considerations.[65] By contrast, Donald Kommers suggests that structural, purposive, and ethical reasoning are of much greater relative importance in Germany.[66]

So where does this leave dialogical interpretation? Within a given constitutional tradition, a particular constitutional outcome may be demanded by the combination of local sources and by the methodological distinctiveness of that tradition. But in most cases, those contingent features of a constitutional tradition merely rule out, and do not require, specific constitutional decisions. Rather, they create an argumentative space within which a tradition is open to elaboration, reinterpretation, contestation, and change. Comparative constitutional materials can figure into this process and lead to constitutional convergence. They do so by dispelling the illusion of false necessity, and by illustrating concretely other constitutional possibilities. The possibility of convergence is greatest in those constitutional spaces where ethical or moral arguments hold sway. But under the dialogical model, historical, teleological/ purposive, structural, and prudential arguments also benefit from comparative materials.

Consider again the distinction between specific prohibitions on Nazi speech and the right to engage in other forms of advocacy of extreme political opinions. This distinction is permissible under German constitutional law but prohibited under American constitutional law. To Schauer, the sustainability of this distinction in Germany is dependent on the experience of Germany with Nazi rule, which subverted democracy from within.[67] The absence of

[65] Mark Tushnet, 'US: Eclecticism in the Service of Pragmatism', in Goldsworthy, *Interpreting Constitutions*, pp. 7–54.

[66] D. Kommers, 'Germany: Balancing Rights and Duties', in Goldsworthy, *Interpreting Constitutions*, pp. 161–211.

[67] Schauer, 'Constitutional Categories'.

such an experience in the United States explains the unsustainability of this distinction in American constitutional doctrine. However, a third jurisdiction may have experience with a past totalitarian regime similar to Germany's that seized power from within, which may serve to support the constitutionality of a parallel distinction. Constitutional convergence would proceed not from universal principles but from a combination of teleological and historical analogy. The interpretive power of the analogy is contingent on a comparable historical experience.

Under the dialogical model of comparative constitutional interpretation, reasoning by analogy can play an important role. Legal argument—especially in the common law world—often proceeds by analogy.[68] The use of analogy captures the basic intuition that like cases should be treated alike. To state that two cases are analogous accordingly requires the identification of the underlying rationale that explains and justifies the treatment of the first case and argues that the second case should be treated in the same way. The response to an argument from analogy is to counter that the cases are in fact unlike, again by reference to this underlying rationale. Arguments from analogy figure prominently in the incremental development of legal doctrine under common law systems. In the adjudication of rights-protecting instruments, arguments by analogy can figure into each stage of analysis. An argument from analogy can figure into the interpretation of the scope of a right (for example, what activities fall within the scope of the Right to Liberty or privacy or what kind of treatment is prohibited by the Right to Equality), and under proportionality analysis (for example, what kinds of speech are sufficiently harmful to justify their criminal prohibition).

Arguments from analogy can draw on comparators that are internal or external to a legal system. Internal analogies emerge from within a legal order. They accordingly combine arguments from principle with arguments from authority, since the first case exerts some binding force on the adjudication of the second case, captured by Ronald Dworkin's notion of 'articulate consistency'.[69] However, an

---

[68] C. Sunstein, *Legal Reasoning and Political Conflict* (Oxford University Press: New York, 1996), Chapter 3.

[69] R. Dworkin, *Taking Rights Seriously* (Duckworth: London, 1977).

argument from analogy can proceed without a claim to authority—that is, by an appeal to principle alone. This is how an analogy that is external to a legal system functions in legal argument. On this model, the first case compels a court to explain and justify why the second case should be treated any differently, without any legal obligation to treat the two cases identically. Thus described, arguments from analogy are an important tool in dialogical interpretation, since they facilitate the process of interpretive confrontation and clarification by forcing courts to explicitly identify the premise to a doctrinal position. Moreover, analogies are not restricted to historical ones, as I will argue below by reference to *Naz Foundation*.

NAZ FOUNDATION AND DIALOGICAL INTERPRETATION

Do these analytical models for the use of comparative constitutional law in constitutional interpretation shed light on *Naz Foundation* and the debates it has spawned? I think that they do. The argument against the role of comparative constitutional law offered by the Union of India before the Delhi High Court (it has since dropped its opposition to the challenge to Section 377) is clearly a particularist argument, which I term as *cultural nationalism* for the sake of convenience. Albeit highly compressed and devoid of any extended defence, it entails the following claims: (a) the Constitution should be interpreted to be consistent with Indian cultural norms; (b) when interpreting the fundamental rights provisions of the Constitution, courts should prefer interpretations that are consistent with Indian cultural norms and reject interpretations that are inconsistent with them; (c) when determining whether violations of rights are justifiable, courts should defer when legislation reflects Indian cultural norms; and (d) comparative materials are an irrelevant and illegitimate aid to constitutional interpretation, since by definition they come from outside the Indian cultural context.

In *Naz Foundation* itself, the asserted cultural norm was the disapproval of homosexuality. Within the particularist framework, the rejection of comparative constitutional law therefore meant that: (a) the Constitution should be interpreted in a manner that is consistent with the rejection of homosexuality; (b) the right to privacy should not be interpreted as protecting the right to sexual intimacy among homosexuals, and the Right to Equality should not be interpreted as prohibiting distinctions drawn on the basis of sexual orientation because that would be inconsistent with Indian cultural norms that disapprove of homosexuality; (c) if those rights have been violated, the court should defer because Section 377 reflects an Indian cultural norm that disapproves of homosexuality; and (d) comparative jurisprudence which holds to the contrary on one or more of these points is irrelevant.

Naz Foundation placed comparative constitutional law at the heart of its reasons. So it must have rejected the argument from cultural nationalism. But how did it do so? There are in fact two ways to read the judgment: one that applies the universalist model, another that applies the dialogical model. I will consider each in turn.

The most straight-forward reading of *Naz Foundation* is that it endorses and applies a universalist understanding of the place of comparative jurisprudence in the adjudication of rights-protecting instruments. The universalist response to cultural nationalism in *Naz Foundation* would consist of the following propositions: (a) the Constitution should be interpreted to be consistent with the principles of liberal political morality; (b) Article 21 should be interpreted as protecting the right to privacy, which in turn entails the right to sexual intimacy, including for homosexuals, and Articles 14 and 15 should be interpreted as prohibiting discrimination on the basis of sexual orientation; (c) even if Section 377 reflects an Indian cultural norm that disapproves of homosexuality, courts should not defer to Section 377 simply because it reflects Indian cultural norms; and (d) the court should cite and apply comparative materials that stand for one or more of these propositions as if they were law.

Much of *Naz Foundation* fits this account. Consider the following examples. In its analysis of the scope of the right to privacy under Article 21, the court shuttles back and forth between Indian and American jurisprudence and in effect treats the two as if they were one integrated body of case law. To reiterate, it was the American decisions, not the Indian decisions, which historically located sexual intimacy in the right to privacy (although its current constitutional foundation is the Right to Liberty). The American cases are cited as establishing propositions for what privacy means, and those propositions are applied to the interpretation of Article 21, without any apparent regard for the fact that those decisions emerged from a foreign constitutional system and involved the interpretation of a different constitutional rights-protecting instrument. Thus, the court begins its analysis of the right to privacy with American cases, including those on sexual intimacy (*Griswold*, *Eisenstadt*, *Roe*, and *Casey*), which are taken to set out the parameters of American privacy constitutional doctrine; the court then turns to the Indian case law on privacy (*Kharak Singh*, *Govind*, *Rajagopal*, and *Canara Bank*), and then sums up that the right to privacy encompasses

> ...a sphere of private intimacy...which allows it to establish and nurture human relationships without interference from the outside community. The way in which one gives expression to one's sexuality is at the core of this area of private intimacy. If, in expressing one's sexuality, one acts consensually without harming the other, invasion of that precinct will be a breach of privacy.[70]

The conclusion implicitly assumes that this proposition holds true for any constitutional bill of rights that guarantees the right to privacy. The right to privacy is wrenched out of its jurisdictional context and appears to be a transcendent constitutional norm that is implemented in specific national bills of rights.

Another example of universalist interpretation at work in *Naz Foundation* appears in its response to the question of reasonable limits on rights. Recall that the Court held that moral disapproval was an inadmissible reason to justifiably limit constitutional rights. How did the Court derive this doctrine? It began with *Govind*, which, it stated, held that only a compelling state interest could justify the limitation of a fundamental right. It then stated that the mere enforcement of public morality was insufficiently important to rise to the level of a compelling state interest. As support for this development of the compelling state interest doctrine, it cited *Lawrence*, *Dudgeon*, and *Norris* v. *Ireland*[71] (another decision of the European Court of Human Rights), which all took this view in challenges to criminal prohibitions on anal intercourse, but within the context of interpreting and applying the American Constitution

---

[70] *Naz Foundation*, at para 40.
[71] 142 Eur. Ct. H.R. (ser. A) (1988).

and the European Convention on Human Rights. It then concluded: 'Thus popular morality or public disapproval of certain Acts is not a valid justification for restriction of the fundamental rights under Article 21'.[72] Unlike the right to privacy, where there was at least some Indian case law, the precedents cited and applied here were entirely comparative. Once again, this principle appears to float above the Indian constitutional system, as part of a trans-jurisdictional body of constitutional doctrine.

I suspect that this is how both *Naz Foundation*'s proponents and opponents would characterize it. However, this reading of *Naz Foundation* cannot explain one of the most striking features of the judgment—its invocation of the ideals animating the adoption of the Indian Constitution, as described by scholars and reflected in the writings and speeches of its most important framers. For example, at the end of its treatment of Article 21, the court noted that the 'fundamental rights had their roots deep in the struggle for independence' and referred to Granville Austin's explanation that 'they were included in the Constitution in the hope and expectation that one day the tree of true liberty would bloom in India'.[73] In a parallel fashion, after the court concluded that public morality could not justify the limitation of rights, it referred to Austin's argument that one of the basic purposes of the Indian Constitution was to achieve or foster a 'social revolution', which the court defined as the creation 'of a society egalitarian to the extent that all citizens were to be equally free from coercion or restriction by the state, or by society privately'.[74] Finally, at the end of its reasons, after it had addressed all the constitutional issues—including the appropriate remedy—the court invoked Jawaharlal Nehru and his speech on the Objective Resolution in the Constituent Assembly to argue that one of the underlying themes in the Indian Constitution is 'inclusiveness'. It continued:

This Court believes that [sic] Indian Constitution reflects this value deeply ingrained in Indian society, nurtured over several generations. The

---

[72] *Naz Foundation*, at para 79, citing Granville Austin, *The Indian Constitution: Cornerstone of a Nation* (Oxford University Press: New Delhi, 1966).

[73] *Naz Foundation*, at para 52.

[74] *Naz Foundation*, at para 80.

inclusiveness that Indian society traditionally displayed, literally in every aspect of life, is manifest in recognising a role in society for everyone. Those perceived by the majority as 'deviants' or 'different' are not on that score excluded or ostracised.

Where society can display inclusiveness and understanding, such persons can be assured of a life of dignity and non-discrimination. This was the 'spirit behind the Resolution' of which Nehru spoke so passionately.[75]

This material on the point and purpose of the Indian Constitution is a world away from the constitutional cosmopolitanism that sets the character and tone of the rest of the judgment. It is a direct and decisive response to the argument from cultural nationalism, as I will explain below. However, two aspects of how the court situated this material in its judgment undermine its power. First, the passages that raise these arguments occur *after* the court reaches the legal conclusion to which they relate. Their location suggests that their absence would have made no legal difference to the judgments; they did not do any work, but were afterthoughts. Moreover, the sections that did do the work were framed around comparative constitutional law. This leads to a second and more fundamental point. The judgment, in a very basic sense, speaks in two voices: a global voice that draws heavily on constitutional jurisprudence from abroad, and an Indian nationalist voice that gives pride of place to the political project underlying the adoption of the Indian Constitution. In addition to failing to justify its use of comparative constitutional law, the court also fails to provide any explanation for how the externally and internally driven parts of its reasons are connected. Given the location of its treatment of Indian constitutional history, it seems that the external sources mattered more than the internal ones.

However, there is a more complex reading of the judgment that shows how the apparently divergent parts of the reasons are in fact closely linked. Here is the key passage:

> The criminalisation of homosexuality condemns in perpetuity a sizable section of society and forces them to live their lives in the shadow of harassment, exploitation, humiliation, cruel and degrading treatment at the hands of the law enforcement machinery. The Government of India

[75] *Naz Foundation*, at paras 130–1.

estimates the MSM number at around 25 lacs. The number of lesbians and transgenders is said to be several lacs as well. This vast majority (borrowing the language of the South African Constitutional Court) is denied 'moral full citizenship'. Section 377 IPC grossly violates their right to privacy and liberty embodied in Article 21 insofar as it criminalises consensual sexual acts between adults in private. These fundamental rights had their roots deep in the struggle for independence and, as pointed out by Granville Austin in *The Indian Constitution: Cornerstone of a Nation*, 'they were included in the Constitution in the hope and expectation that one day the tree of true liberty would bloom in India'.[76]

The passage combines a reference to South African constitutional jurisprudence with one to the purposes animating the adoption of the Indian Constitution. The link between the two, however, is not set out. Moreover, the quote is unattributed. As it turns out, it is a slight misquote. The original reads 'full moral citizenship', and comes from the separate concurring judgment of Justice Albie Sachs in *National Coalition*, the South African analogue to *Naz Foundation*.[77] One of the issues raised in *National Coalition* was the relationship between the Right to Equality and the right to dignity, which are two textually distinct rights under the South African Constitution. It had been argued that the textual distinction between the two meant that the two rights should be doctrinally distinct—in particular, that equality be interpreted without reference to dignity. Justice Sachs rejected this position, and held instead that to treat someone in a way that is dignity-demeaning is the very essence of unequal treatment. He wrote:

In the case of gays, history and experience teach us that the scarring comes not from poverty or powerlessness, but from invisibility. It is the tainting of desire, it is the attribution of perversity and shame to spontaneous bodily affection, it is the prohibition of the expression of love, it is the denial of full moral citizenship in society because you are what you are, that impinges on the dignity and self-worth of a group. … Gays constitute a distinct though invisible section of the community that has been treated not only with disrespect or condescension but with disapproval and revulsion; they are not generally obvious as a group, pressurized by society and the law to remain invisible; their identifying

[76] *Naz Foundation*, at para 52.
[77] *National Coalition*, note 31 at para 127.

characteristic combines all the anxieties produced by sexuality with all the alienating effects resulting from difference; and they are seen as especially contagious or prone to corrupting others. ... At the heart of equality jurisprudence is the rescuing of people from a *caste-like status* and putting an end to their being treated as lesser human beings because they belong to a particular group.[78]

The analogy drawn by Justice Sachs in *National Coalition* between sexual orientation and caste is highly suggestive of the possible influence of his reasons on *Naz Foundation*. An illuminating source of insight is an edited transcript of the hearing.[79] Although the transcript is not verbatim, this limitation is counter-balanced by the fact that the transcript is actually a narrative description of the oral argument that describes the interplay between the bench and counsel. Here is the account of the portion of the proceedings during which *National Coalition* was raised in argument:

> As Mr. Grover [counsel for *Naz Foundation*] was reading from the South African decision, the visibly moved judges began conferring amongst themselves.... Chief Justice Shah, noticing that the Additional Solicitor General was not present in court, remarked, 'I don't know what assistance we are going to get from the government. The ASG is not here. He should have been here to listen to this'. He [Grover] then compared discrimination based on sexual orientation to discrimination based on caste. 'If you belong to the "untouchable" category, you suffer a disadvantage in every aspect of life. The effect of criminalisation (of homosexuality) is like treating you as a member of a scheduled caste', he said. ... The judges asked Mr. Divan [counsel for Voices Against 377] if it was possible to link the petitioners' arguments to the constitutional provisions in Article 17 and 23 that deal with untouchability.[80]

Thus, the missing link between the comparative jurisprudence on same-sex rights and the basic premises of the Indian Constitution is the analogy between sexual orientation and untouchability. The

---

[78] *National Coalition*, at paras 127–9 (emphasis added).

[79] 'Edited Transcripts of Day-to-Day Proceedings before the Delhi High Court in the Matter of *Naz Foundation* v. *Union of India*', in A. Narrain and M. Eldridge (eds), *The Right that Dares to Speak Its Name—Naz Foundation v. Union of India and Others: Decriminalising Sexual Orientation and Gender Identity in India* (Alternative Law Forum: Bangalore, 2009), p. 48.

[80] Ibid., p. 54.

Indian Constitution singles out untouchability for special and selective condemnation. Article 17—mentioned by the Bench in *Naz Foundation* in oral argument—lies at the heart of this constitutional project. Article 17 provides in full: '"Untouchability" is abolished and its practice in any form is forbidden. The enforcement of any disability arising out of "Untouchability" shall be an offence punishable in accordance with law'. This is a unique constitutional provision. The other provisions of Part III ('Fundamental Rights') apply to government, and direct it to act or refrain from acting in certain ways. Article 17, by contrast, purports to abolish a social status, and the social practices that revolve around that status, which exist apart and independent from State action. In other words, Article 17 applies horizontally. Moreover, it goes much further, and mandates that the private breach of this constitutional duty must be punishable by criminal sanction. Article 17 is accordingly the constitutional underpinning of the Anti-Untouchability Act, 1955 and the Scheduled Castes and Scheduled Tribes Act, 1989, which criminalize the preaching and practice of untouchability.

Article 17 reflects the view, as Gopal Guru puts it, that 'dignity may not easily come forth from the upper castes; it will have to be forcibly extracted from the recalcitrant members of twice-born civil society'.[81] The whole constitutional architecture of reservations for Scheduled Castes—found in Articles 15(4), 16(4), 29(2), 330, and 332—which aim to fundamentally redistribute economic, political, and social power towards the Scheduled Castes, is designed to compensate for millennia of neglect and exploitation. As Guru explains, the nationalist movement was not just about the advocacy of self-government to oppose 'the colonial configuration of power', but also about the promotion of social justice to challenge 'local configurations of power'.[82] Indeed, it was 'one of the central organizing and mobilizing principles of the nationalist movement'.[83]

What analogy did the court see between untouchability and sexual orientation? Unfortunately, the court does not say. Indeed, it does

---

[81] G. Guru, 'Constitutional Justice: Positional and Cultural', in R. Bhargava (ed.), *Politics and Ethics of the Indian Constitution* (Oxford University Press: New Delhi, 2008), pp. 230–48.

[82] Ibid., p. 232.

[83] Ibid.

not refer to Article 17 at all in its judgment, notwithstanding its significance during the hearing. But perhaps the argument is this. *Naz Foundation* held that the effect of Section 377 was to create a status offence—to 'be classified as criminal as such'.[84] Since Section 377 criminalizes 'these sexual acts which…are associated more closely with one class of persons, namely the homosexuals…Section 377…has the effect of viewing all gay men as criminals'.[85] Section 377 effectively brands homosexuals as outlaws who do not enjoy the law's protection. The court described the effects of this status offence:

> Even when the penal provisions are not enforced, they reduce gay men or women to what one author has referred to as 'unapprehended felons', thus entrenching stigma and encouraging discrimination in different spheres of life. Apart from misery and fear, a few of the more obvious consequences are harassment, blackmail, extortion and discrimination. There is extensive material placed on the record in the form of affidavits, authoritative reports by well known agencies and judgments that testify to a widespread use of Section 377 IPC to brutalise [the] MSM and gay community.[86]

But what is the link between sexual orientation and untouchability? The treatment which homosexuals experience today is similar in kind to that which 'untouchables' experience and which prompted the adoption of Article 17, and likewise flows from their social status. As was noted during the Constituent Assembly Debates, the purpose of Article 17 was 'to save one-sixth of the Indian population from perpetual subjugation and despair, from perpetual humiliation and disgrace'.[87] This manifest injustice was delivered not by the hands of the State, but 'by a vast mass of Hindu population which is hostile to them and which is not ashamed of committing any inequity or atrocity against them'.[88]

Where does this leave us? The comparative jurisprudence on the criminal prohibition of anal intercourse was not simply applied as

---

[84] D. D'Souza, *Branded by Law: Looking at India's Denotified Tribes* (Penguin: New Delhi, 2001), p. 57.

[85] *Naz Foundation*, at para 94.

[86] *Naz Foundation*, at para 50.

[87] Voices Against 377, 'Note on the Constituent Assembly Debates and Equality', supplemental submission in *Naz Foundation*, at p. 2 (quoting speech of Monomohan Das).

[88] Ibid., at p. 3.

the universalist model of comparative constitutional interpretation would suggest. The picture is more complex. Comparative materials led the court to revisit and update the premises of the Indian Constitution. The engine of this change is the analogy between untouchability and sexual orientation. The court may have reasoned that the two were indeed analogous, and accordingly that the Indian Constitution should condemn discrimination on the latter basis as much as on the former. This mode of comparative constitutional reasoning is dialogical. External legal sources were used as a foil to constitutional self-reflection, and to nourish and reframe the judges' reading of internal constitutional sources. The question was whether comparative constitutional law resonated with pre-existing Indian constitutional premises. *Naz Foundation* held that it did.

The doctrinal implications of this reading of *Naz Foundation* are unclear, and remain to be worked out, perhaps by the Supreme Court of India, when it renders its judgment on appeal. It may be that Article 17 has a constitutional significance beyond its express prohibition on untouchability. *Naz Foundation* could stand for the proposition that there is a constitutional doctrine that grows out of Article 17, whereby groups that experience disadvantage analogous to that experienced by 'untouchables' are entitled to the highest degree of constitutional protection. This disadvantage occurs along multiple dimensions—social, economic, and political—which are mutually reinforcing. This doctrine may be analogous to the suspect class doctrine under American constitutional law, which on one interpretation enables those groups that experience disadvantage analogous to that experienced by African-Americans to deploy the full force of the Equal Protection Clause. With respect to such groups, for example, this doctrine might counsel a particularly stringent approach to equality claims brought under Articles 14 and/or 15 that does not shy away from the prohibition of indirect discrimination, which is often proof of legislative animus towards the most disadvantaged. It could render inadmissible public morality as the justification for the infringement of constitutional rights of such groups, because public morality is particularly likely to reflect a bare naked preference to harm those groups. Finally, it may mean that the interpretation of other fundamental rights is infused with equality, so that a court is particularly alert to the importance of the interests protected by those rights to the group in question, and ensures that the scope of the right is defined accordingly. For example, against the backdrop of pervasive cultural disapproval of homosexuality in terms of sexual perversity, this doctrine provides an additional reason for including sexual intimacy within the right to privacy under Article 21, which, of course, is the main holding in *Naz Foundation*.

Naz Foundation refers to the Indian Constitution as an instrument of 'social revolution'.[89] The idea of a constitution as a dynamic, evolving instrument of social change is arguably the principal influence of the Indian constitutional experience on the way that South Africans understand the purpose of a constitution, and the task of its constitutional court. This understanding of the mission of a constitutional system is captured by the notion of 'transformative constitutionalism'.[90] The Constitutional Court of South Africa recently stated that the legal implication of this theory of constitutionalism is that 'the founding values' of the new constitutional order should inform 'the assessment of the prevailing boni mores of our society'.[91] This is precisely what *Naz Foundation* did. It is therefore fitting that South African constitutional jurisprudence should now inspire the Indian courts to revisit and reinforce this dimension of the Indian constitutional experience.

CONCLUSION: THE POLITICS OF COMPARATIVE CONSTITUTIONAL LAW

So here is the argument in brief. The use of comparative constitutional law was central to *Naz Foundation*. On the particularist model, this reliance on comparative legal materials was irrelevant and illegitimate. There are two ways to respond to the particularlist challenge. The universalist model holds that the citation and application of comparative constitutional law was necessary and appropriate. The dialogical model holds that comparative materials were a means to revisit and extend the premises of the Indian Constitution. Both

---

[89] *Naz Foundation*, at para 80.

[90] K. Klare, 'Legal Culture and Transformative Constitutionalism', *S. Afr. J. Hum. Rts.*, (1998), 14: 146–88.

[91] *Hassam v. Jacobs*, (2009) ZACC, at para 28.

the universalist and dialogical accounts of *Naz Foundation* fit the judgment imperfectly. But which is the better approach?

Universalists hold that constitutional guarantees are cut from a universal cloth, and that all constitutional courts are engaged in the identification, interpretation, and application of the same set of principles. Comparative jurisprudence serves an evidentiary function, providing valuable articulations of the political theories underlying particular rights and how those rights are to be applied in concrete cases. This may be particularly attractive to a newly established constitutional court, in jurisdictions with little or no prior experience of constitutional judicial review. The use of comparative constitutional law anchors the legitimacy of the court's decisions, and counters the impression that by looking to foreign sources, the court is looking outside the law. In countries beginning their experience with constitutional judicial review, the use of comparative law makes normal and routine what would otherwise appear revolutionary and dramatically new. Moreover, universalist interpretation will internationalize a nation's constitutional culture, by working the assumption that a nation's particular constitutional guarantees are shared with other countries and transcend borders into the culture of constitutional argument. Tying these points together, universalist interpretation posits that within the family of liberal democracies committed to the rule of law and human rights, comparative jurisprudence offers guidance and wisdom to newer constitutional democracies that are beginning their journey on how best to proceed down the road ahead.

But universalist interpretation is vulnerable to serious criticism. Recall that universalist interpretation relies on the empirical fact of convergence—on the theories underlying constitutional provisions, on the doctrinal tests which implement those theories, and on particular outcomes on specific issues—as proof of the correctness of those legal propositions. Empirical convergence is proof of moral truth, which is a reason for a court to follow foreign jurisprudence. Universalist interpretation is therefore open to criticism on the ground of cultural relativism, which holds that moral and political values are not universal but are tightly connected to particular cultural contexts. Whatever the merits of this criticism, it means that universalist interpretation is fraught with controversy.

As a consequence, universalist modes of comparative constitutional reasoning will constantly be put into question. This poses the additional danger that the universalist methodology may in fact corrode the legitimacy of constitutional interpretation itself.

Moreover, the strong normative claims underlying universalist interpretation limit its scope of application to those rights which are truly universal. The most universal of human rights are those that affect the physical security of the individual, such as the right to life and physical liberty. By contrast, even the traditional liberal freedoms—such as expression, religion and conscience, association and assembly—although enshrined in many constitutions, are more normatively contentious. Though courts of various jurisdictions agree on the importance of these rights, they have differed sharply on their interpretation. In the face of such normative diversity, universalist arguments become difficult to make.

Dialogical interpretation, by contrast, does not require the kind of consensus across jurisdictions that universalist interpretation does. Indeed, far from being an obstacle to the use of comparative jurisprudence, normative disagreement drives dialogical interpretation, because it forces courts to identify and justify the sources of that disagreement as a means to developing a sharper awareness of constitutional difference. Moreover, for dialogical interpretation to be possible, there need only exist corresponding provisions and jurisprudence in two or more jurisdictions. More fundamentally, dialogical interpretation makes no normative claims regarding comparative jurisprudence. It uses comparative case law instrumentally, as a means to stimulate constitutional self-reflection. Dialogical interpretation is more a legal technique than a theory of constitutional interpretation. Comparative materials are not asserted to be true or right; rather, they reflect a particular way of articulating underlying values and assumptions. The reliance on comparative constitutional materials does not necessarily assimilate constitutional actors into a larger transnational conversation about rights, courts, and democracy. A sophisticated and literate comparativism need not be tantamount to universalist conceptions of constitutionalism. It does not raise the spectre of illegitimacy in the manner that the universalist interpretation does. Rather, it facilitates and enables the development of, and reasoning within, an established constitutional tradition.

At a moment of high political controversy over the merits of a constitutional dispute—such as the one presented by *Naz Foundation*—dialogical interpretation offers significant political advantages to a court. But the very source of its strength also limits its reach, because it is subject to the vagaries of the contingent nature of the space of acceptable constitutional argument, which creates the possibility for dialogical interpretation. My interpretation of *Naz Foundation* suggests that the court drew an analogy between untouchability and sexual orientation. The drawing of this analogy turned on a contingent feature of the Indian Constitution— Article 17. Were Article 17 absent, the judgment would have to be defended on a different basis.

Let me conclude with this thought. In *Gopalan* v. *Madras*,[92] the Supreme Court of India declined to interpret the phrase 'procedure according to law' in Article 21 as encompassing substantive limits on the deprivation of the interests—life and personal liberty— protected by the provision. It did so through dialogical reasoning, in this case arguing that the deliberate rejection by the Constituent Assembly of the phrase 'due process of law' was specifically designed to avoid the American doctrine of substantive due process.[93] *Maneka Gandhi* overruled this aspect of *Gopalan*. But is it possible to accept that *Gopalan* is no longer good law while valuing its interpretative methodology, in which comparative constitutional experience can serve as a negative model and provide the impetus for, and resources to strengthen, moments of constitutional difference? This too is an instance of dialogical interpretation. Indeed, it may help to explain the role of American constitutional doctrine on affirmative action in the Indian jurisprudence on reservations—for example, in *Indra Sawhney* v. *Union of India*—as an anti-model of comparative constitutional experience.[94] How this could play out in the Indian context—while preserving the correctness of *Naz Foundation*—is a topic for another occasion.

[92] 1950 SCR. 88 (hereinafter *Gopalan*).
[93] In particular, see the judgment of Chief Justice Kania, *Gopalan*, at 108.
[94] AIR 1993 SC 447.

CHAPTER THREE

Constitutional Developments in a Himalayan Kingdom
The Experience of Nepal

*Mara Malagodi**

This essay provides an account of Nepal's constitutional developments over the years in light of the 'interaction between indigenous law and transplanted law'.[1] It seeks to maintain a comparative perspective, especially within the South Asian context, and reflects upon the modalities of the political transformations that have occurred in Nepal over the past 250 years, with particular reference to the influence of external legal and political concepts. Imported models have been progressively implanted into autochthonous juridical and political structures, and the interplay of different systems has generated a situation of legal pluralism in Nepal.

The aim of this essay, in the first place, is to investigate the process of reception of Nepal's autochthonous legal elements in its various constitutions, and to demonstrate that this process has produced a specifically Nepali synthesis. Second, in a historical analysis of Nepal's

* I am grateful to Michael J. Hutt for his thoughtful and insightful comments on this essay. My research in Nepal in 2006 and 2007 was supported by the generous grant received from the University of London Central Research Fund in 2006.

[1] Masaji Chiba, *Legal Pluralism: Towards a General Theory through Japanese Legal Culture* (Tokai University Press: Tokai, 1989), p. 8.

constitutional developments, it endeavours to explain why the 1990 democratic Constitution came to occupy such a central place in Nepal's post-1990 political discourse. The analysis intends to evaluate the reasons, modalities, and implications of the abrogation of the 1990 Constitution, and the adoption on 15 January 2007 of the new Interim Constitution—the sixth in Nepal's history. The Interim Constitution led Nepal to the elections, on 10 April 2008, of the Constituent Assembly (CA) whose term to draft a new constitution has been extended several times, the latest until May 2012. The CA in its first session on 28 May 2008 abolished the monarchy and declared Nepal a federal republic through the Interim Constitution's Fourth Amendment. The essay ultimately seeks an answer to the following question: what kind of story does the demise of the 1990 Constitution tell us, both about political processes in Nepal between 1990 and early 2007, and about democratic politics in the country more generally?

PRE-1990 LEGAL DEVELOPMENTS IN NEPAL

The military campaigns launched in 1744 by King Prithvi Narayan Shah of Gorkha—a small kingdom in the hills, west of the Kathmandu Valley—progressively brought modern Nepal into existence. Conventionally, the Gorkhali conquest of the last of the three kingdoms of the Kathmandu Valley in 1769 is taken to represent the beginning of the history of Nepal as the political entity we know today. The Gorkhali expansion led to the annexation of many small principalities in the central Himalayan range and in the early nineteenth century, the sovereignty of the Gorkhali kingdom extended from the Kangra Valley in the west to Sikkim in the east. The Gorkhali kingdom's territorial extension was considerably reduced with their defeat in the Anglo-Nepali War (1814–16). The Treaty of Sagauli in 1816 fixed the Gorkhali southern border with the territories of the East India Company approximately as it is nowadays, and interestingly referred to the Gorkhali kingdom—for the first time—as 'Nipaul', a term which traditionally designated only the Kathmandu Valley.[2] The Shah period established the narratives

---

[2] Ludwig Stiller, *The Silent Cry: The People of Nepal: 1816–1839* (Sahayogi Press: Kathmandu, 1976), p. 22.

informing an eminently Nepali legitimation of state power. Prithvi Narayan Shah described his country as a 'true Hindu kingdom, a garden of the four *varna* and thirty-six *jāt*'.[3] This now rather notorious statement established the centrality of Hinduism in the creation of a distinct Nepali identity especially vis-à-vis neighbouring India, similar to the scope of Buddhism in Bhutan as elucidated by Whitecross' essay in the present volume.[4] In Prithvi Narayan's vision, the subdued communities—diverse in terms of their culture, religion, and language from those of the Gorkhali rulers—were subordinate to the hegemony of the conquerors. Such hegemony was rooted in the culture of the dominant social group which—in Gorkha like in the other hill kingdoms of central and west Nepal—was the Parbatiya or Indo-Nepali Hindus. The Parbatiya caste structure entrenched the dominance of the Bahun (Brahmins) and the Chetri (Kshatriya).

The Rana Regime (1846–1951)

In 1846 a young aristocrat, Jang Bahadur Kunwar, succeeded in ending the period of political instability inaugurated by the death of Prithvi Narayan Shah in 1775. He staged a coup, neutralized the power of the Shah King and the aristocratic elites, and progressively assumed absolute powers by making the office of the Prime Minister (PM) hereditary within his family. However, he chose to retain the monarchy—although divested of effective power—as the living symbol of the unity of the kingdom vis-à-vis the internal diversity of its subjects. This was an arrangement that lasted for over a century. Jang Bahadur Rana, as he came to be known, also realized that an alliance with the British East India Company was crucial—both internally for his survival as the supreme political leader, and externally for the preservation of the country's independence. Thus, in 1850, he undertook a journey to England and France as the ambassador of the King; the power and wealth of the European countries made a lasting impression on him.[5]

---

[3] Ludwig Stiller, *Prithvi Narayan Shah in the Light of Divya Upadesh* (Ludwig Stiller: Kathmandu, 1968), p. 44.

[4] Richard Burghart, *The Conditions of Listening: Essays on Religion, History and Politics in South Asia* (Oxford University Press: New Delhi, 1996), p. 268.

[5] John Whelpton, *Jang Bahadur in Europe* (Sahayogi Press: Kathmandu, 1983).

In particular, Jang Bahadur seems to have regarded Napoleon as his political exemplar and taken the *Code Napoléon* as a model for legal reform in Nepal through which he envisioned as a further consolidation of his power.[6] In fact, after his return from Europe, the Prime Minister promulgated the *Muluki Ain* (Law or Code of the Country).[7] The 1854 Code aimed at codifying traditional social conditions, subsumed the various ethno-linguistic groups within the Parbatiya Hindu caste hierarchy and imposed its rules on them as part of the state-driven process of Sanskritization. The Code contained both civil and criminal law provisions and its sources were the *Dharmashāstra*, the *Arthashāstra*, Mughal legislation, and possibly Anglo-Indian law.[8] The *Muluki Ain* was technically not a constitution and its provisions were more or less limited to the fields of personal and administrative law.[9] However, by claiming to be a body of legislation applicable to the entire population of the kingdom, it represented the Nepali State's first attempt to impose legal uniformity. In this regard, the Nepali historian Mahesh C. Regmi maintains that the Code had a constitutional value.[10] The *Muluki Ain* had also a clearly political rationale: it was an endeavour to legitimize the identity of the Nepali polity by depicting it as culturally distinct, and to sway the solidarity of its population towards the state.[11]

The political, institutional, and ideological structures established under Jang Bahadur's reign (1846–77) led to the consolidation of the Rana regime, and until its displacement in 1951, few changes within the Nepali political system occurred. The British departure from the subcontinent in 1947 and the emergence of India as an independent democracy marked a watershed in Nepal's political history. The rhetoric employed by the Nepali State also changed

---

[6] John Whelpton, *Kings, Soldiers and Priests: Nepalese Politics 1830–1857* (Manohar: New Delhi, 1991), p. 218.

[7] *Shrī Surendra Vikram Shāhdevkā Shāsankālmā Baneko Mulukī Ain*, 1910 BS (Jang Bahadur Rana's *Muluki Ain*, 1854).

[8] Andras Höfer, *The Caste Hierarchy and the State in Nepal* (Universitatsverlag Wagner: Innsbruck, 1979), p. 41.

[9] Ibid., p. 40.

[10] Mahesh C. Regmi, 'Preliminary Notes on the Nature of Rana Law and Government', *Contributions to Nepalese Studies*, (1975), 2(2): 103–15.

[11] Höfer, *Caste Hierarchy,* p. 40.

significantly: the ideas of equality and democracy made persuasive by the Indian anti-colonial struggle could no longer be ignored in Nepal if the Rana elites were to retain political power in the country. Prime Minister Padma Shamsher Rana understood this and on 1 April 1948 he promulgated the first ever written constitution of Nepal.[12] The document contained a mix of innovative and conservative provisions which endeavoured to 'mould the electoral system of the West to the Panchayat system, which is an essential part of our heritage and culture', as stated Prime Minister Padma Shamsher Rana in his address upon the inauguration of the Government of Nepal Act, 1948.[13]

The new constitution was drafted with the aid of three Indian constitutional experts who visited Nepal in June 1947 and worked with a Reform Committee appointed by the Prime Minister.[14] The outcome was a hybrid document that drew heavily on the institutional framework of British India and attempted to adapt it to a unique Nepali system. In his address marking the inauguration of the constitution, the prime minister stated that 'the powers and functions of the legislature are generally of the nature conferred by the Government of India Act, 1935'. Although the Preamble described Nepal as 'this sacred country of Lord Pashupatinath', the constitutional text did not make use of Hindu symbols to legitimize state authority and the fundamental rights provided in Article 4 included freedom of worship and equality of Nepali citizens in the eyes of the law. The inclusion of Fundamental Rights was based on discussions occurring in India at the time, but with some restrictions to guarantee 'public order and morality', as expounded by the Prime Minister in his address.

The Act introduced a bicameral central legislature with limited jurisdiction, and a party-less legislative structure called the Panchayat.[15] The Rana Prime Minister remained at the apex of the new political

---

[12] *Nepāl Sarkār, Vaidhānik Kānūn,* 2004 BS (Rana Constitution, 1948).

[13] Shastra Dutta Pant, *Comparative Constitutions of Nepal* (SIRUD: Kathmandu, 2001), p. 321.

[14] Narayan Agrawal, *Nepal: A Study in Constitutional Change* (Oxford and IBM Publishing Co: New Delhi, 1980), p. 9.

[15] The central legislature could not discuss: (a) any matter concerning the Shah King and the Rana Prime Minister; (b) the list of expenditures charged upon the

structure and directly controlled the Council of Ministers which held all the executive powers. The 1948 text did not represent a real break with the past—nor was it ever implemented, due to the fact that Padma Shamsher resigned from the office of prime minister shortly after the Constitution was prepared. However, the 1948 document marked the entry of debates about modern constitutionalism and democracy into Nepal's official political discourse.

The Democratic Interlude (1951–60)

On 6 November 1950, King Tribhuvan fled to the Indian Embassy in Kathmandu and asked for political asylum. Meanwhile, the newly created Nepali political parties, based in India,[16] had become more active in their opposition to the Rana regime. They launched an armed insurgency and received assistance from independent India which was increasingly unwilling to support the autocratic Rana oligarchy. Following the 1950 uprising in Nepal, India was deeply involved in the negotiations that took place between the Ranas, King Tribhuvan, and the parties. An agreement known as the 'Delhi Compromise' led to the establishment of a Rana–Congress government to guide the country towards a democratic establishment.

In his Royal Proclamation of 18 February 1951, King Tribhuvan declared: '...hereafter our subjects shall be governed in accordance with a democratic constitution to be framed by the Constituent Assembly elected by the people'.[17] On 11 April 1951, he promulgated the Interim Government of Nepal Act, 1951, the first democratic constitution ever enforced in the Himalayan kingdom.[18] The new constitution was a provisional document under which the country was to be governed for two years until a definitive document could be drafted. It was prepared under the guidance of Ram Ugra Singh of Lucknow University and relied heavily on the

revenues of the State; and (c) a demand for a grant without the permission of the prime minister (Agrawal, *Nepal*, p. 14).

[16] The Nepali National Congress was founded in 1947 and the Communist Party of Nepal in 1949, both in India; see, Krishna Hachhethu, *Party Building in Nepal: Organization, Leadership and People* (Mandala Book Point: Kathmandu, 2002).

[17] Hari Bansh Tripathi, *Fundamental Rights and Judicial Review in Nepal* (Pairavi Prakashan: Kathmandu, 2002).

[18] *Nepālko Antarim Shāsana Vidhān*, 2007 BS (Interim Constitution, 1951).

Interim Government of India Act.[19] Joshi and Rose defined it as 'a hastily prepared adaptation of the 1950 Indian Constitution which was promulgated in Nepal with no evident concern for the lack of prerequisites and concomitants which gave meaning to the Indian document'.[20] The Interim Constitution introduced a democratic form of government with the Shah King as the head of state. Political parties operating on a mass scale were to be legitimate vehicles for political action. The text made no explicit reference to Hinduism and left the issue of whether or not Nepal was a Hindu state to the permanent constitution. Executive powers were vested in the King and the Council of Ministers, an Advisory Assembly General enjoyed limited legislative functions, and an independent judiciary was established. Article 17 defined the Fundamental Principles of Law guaranteeing basic fundamental rights to all Nepali citizens, with the notable exception of freedom of worship. The fundamental rights were not given a separate section, but were incorporated into the section of directive principles of state policy, making them non-justiciable.[21] Interestingly, this section also included Article 10 about the need to 'secure a Uniform Civil Code throughout Nepal' on the basis of Article 44 of the Indian Constitution. Nepal's first democratic constitution opened the way for wider political participation in the country and laid down the founding principles of democracy.

The first years of the new dispensation were characterized by transitional politics and great instability, exacerbated by bitter inter-party disputes. The death of King Tribhuvan in 1955 and the ensuing coronation of his son Mahendra led to a more central role of the Shah monarchy in the conduct of Nepal's political affairs. King Mahendra advocated a more assertive and proactive role for the monarchy in Nepal's political arena. According to one analysis, '[King Mahendra] aspired to exercise an active leadership in accordance with Hindu traditions and these aspirations were manifested by his refusal to

---

[19] Bishal Khanal, *Regeneration of Nepalese Law* (Bhrikuti Academic Publications: Kathmandu, 2001), p. 34.

[20] Bhuvan Joshi and Leo Rose, *Democratic Innovations in Nepal* (University of California Press: Berkeley, 1966), p. 488.

[21] Hari Bansh Tripathi, *Fundamental Rights and Judicial Review in Nepal (Evolution and Experiments)* (Pairavi Prakashan: Kathmandu, 2003), p. 28.

hold elections for a Constituent Assembly, and the desire to write the constitution himself with no sovereignty being vested in the people'.[22]

In March 1958—ignoring continued demands for the election of a Constituent Assembly—King Mahendra invited British constitutional expert Sir Ivor Jennings to guide the impending constitution-making process and independently appointed a Commission to draft the new constitution. Jennings was convinced that a modified Westminster model would be easy to transplant in Nepal assuming that the Nepali constitutional edifice would revolve around the principles of constitutional monarchy as expounded in the UK.[23] The King promulgated the new constitution on 12 February 1959.[24] The document established a democratically elected parliamentary system under a constitutional monarchy, even if the King retained ultimate sovereignty, as stated in the Preamble: 'I, King Mahendra Bir Bikram Shah Dev in the exercise of the sovereign powers of the Kingdom of Nepal....' The monarch enjoyed wide discretionary powers and was granted residuary and emergency powers. Executive powers were vested in the King as well, although the Constitution created a cabinet of ministers responsible to Parliament to aid His Majesty in performing the executive functions. The legislative body was constituted by a bicameral Parliament comprising the Senate and the House of Representatives. The section on Fundamental Rights featured the Right to Equality before the law without discrimination on the grounds of religion, sex, race, caste or tribe in Article 4, and the Right to Religion in Article 5. However, the Right to Religion—for the first time in Nepali constitutional history—was limited and defined religion 'as handed down from ancient times'. It also 'provided that no person shall be entitled to convert another person to his religion'.

Nepali history and traditions acquired a paramount position in the 1959 Constitution. The Preamble defined His Majesty, for the first time in a Nepali constitution, as 'a descendant of the illustrious King Prithvi Narayan Shah, adherent of the Aryan Culture and Hindu religion', and stated that the sovereign powers of the Kingdom of Nepal were vested in the King 'in accordance

[22] Surya Dhungel, Bipin Adhikari, B.P. Bhandari, and Chris Murgatroyd, *Commentary on the Nepalese Constitution* (DeLF: Kathmandu, 1998), p. 24.

[23] Khanal, *Regeneration*, p. 25.

[24] *Nepāl Adhirājyako Samvidhān*, 2015 BS (Constitution of Nepal, 1959).

with the traditions and customs of our country and which devolved on "Us from Our August and Respected Forefathers"'. For the first time in Nepal's constitutional history the notion of Hindu kingship was institutionalized in positivist legal form. In fact, the 1959 Constitution granted the Shah Hindu monarchy higher standing, both institutionally and ideologically. King Mahendra ultimately aimed to create a full-fledged Nepali nationalist discourse centred on the permanence of the Shah monarchy in the country.

In 1959, the Nepali Congress achieved a victory in the first general elections and its leader, Bishweshwar Prasad Koirala, became Prime Minister. In December 1960, however, the Nepali Congress government was dismissed by King Mahendra and its leaders were either detained or driven into exile in India. Mahendra claimed that the country's fragile democratic process was endangering national sovereignty and failing to maintain internal order.

The Panchayat Period (1960–90)

In 1960 King Mahendra staged a 'royal coup': he assumed emergency powers, banned all political parties and suspended the short-lived 1959 Constitution. He claimed that Nepal was unprepared to function according to the rules of a Western-style parliamentary democracy. Instead, he sought to engineer an essentially brand new political system called the 'Panchayat system', nominally based on Nepal's traditions, as the country's alternative route to modernization and development as highlighted by Burghart.[25] The notion of the 'Panchayat system' was created to legitimize the central and preponderant role of the Shah monarchy in Nepal's constitutional edifice.

King Mahendra held absolute power for two years and on 16 December 1962 promulgated the so-called Panchayat Constitution.[26] The new document was the result of the research conducted by a four-member committee under the chairmanship of Minister Rishikesh Shaha. The committee had been appointed by the king to study the constitutional frameworks of Yugoslavia,

---

[25] Richard Burghart, 'The Political Culture of Panchayat Democracy', in Michael Hutt (ed.), *Nepal in the Nineties: Versions of the Past, Visions of the Future* (OUP: New Delhi, 1993), p. 1.

[26] *Nepālko Samvidhān,* 2019 BS (Panchayat Constitution, 1962).

Egypt, Pakistan, and Indonesia. The final outcome was an ingenious combination of various features of these countries' constitutions, adapted to devise a specifically Nepali one.[27] The 1962 Constitution established the involvement of the king in every branch of government, making the principle of separation of powers enshrined in the 1959 Constitution entirely meaningless.[28] The active leadership of the king in the Panchayat system entailed a complete absence of political opposition, ensured by the outlawing of political parties. The plan was to re-establish the relationship between the King and his people, unmediated by any political actor. The Constitution created a central legislative body, the National Panchayat, which enjoyed only advisory powers. The membership of the National Panchayat was partly nominated directly by the king and partly elected indirectly. The Panchayat system was constituted by four tiers of representative institutions elected at different levels. Direct popular elections with universal adult suffrage took place only at village (*gaum*) and town (*nagar*) levels. The elected representatives of these assemblies voted for the members of the seventy-five assemblies at district (*jilla*) level, who then elected the members of the fourteen assemblies at zone (*anchal*) level, who finally voted for the elected representatives in the National Panchayat.[29] The system was a pyramidal structure in which only the lowest level was directly elected by the people, while the members of the higher assemblies were selected by and from amongst the representatives on the level immediately below.

The Panchayat Constitution was the first constitutional document to precisely define and institutionalize the connotations of Nepal's national identity. In the preliminary section, Article 2 stated that 'the Nepalese People, irrespective of religion, race, caste or tribe, collectively constitute the Nation', while Article 3 declared Nepal as 'an independent, indivisible and sovereign monarchical Hindu state'. The Preamble vested in the king state sovereignty and powers, as a sort of royal prerogative defined 'in accordance to the constitutional law, custom and usage of Our country as handed down to Us by Our August and Revered Forefathers'. For the first time the 1962

[27] Joshi and Rose, *Democratic Innovations*, p. 396.

[28] Dhungel et al., *Nepalese Constitution*, p. 30.

[29] Leo Rose and Margaret Fisher, *The Politics of Nepal: Persistence and Change in an Asian Monarchy* (Cornell University Press: Ithaca and London, 1970), p. 53.

Constitution legally made Nepal a Hindu kingdom. However, the constitution contained an extensive section on fundamental rights and duties. Article 10 guaranteed equality before the law without discrimination on the grounds of religion, sex, race, caste or tribe, and Article 14 the Right to Religion, although this was limited—as in the previous 1959 Constitution—to 'religion as handed down from ancient times' and to its practice 'with regard to the traditions'. Moreover, Article 14 reiterated the ban on conversion. The emphasis on 'Nepali traditions' became part of the propagandistic rhetoric of the Panchayat system. The 1962 Constitution was imbibed with the spirit of modern nation-building which was, Mahendra believed, the ideal strategy to tighten his hold on power and create favourable circumstances for Nepal's socio-economic development and modernization. Moreover, the new constitution fixed the coordinates for the construction of a Nepali nationalistic discourse: Hinduism, the Shah monarchy, and the Nepali language became the 'triumvirate of official Nepali national culture'.[30]

In 1963, King Mahendra—as part of his modernizing efforts—promulgated a new *Muluki Ain*,[31] with significant departures from the 1854 legal document. This seems in line with Nelson's argument that changes in religious laws in India and Pakistan occurred when political elites were 'unrivalled'.[32] In fact, to the present day, the new Code constitutes the central pillar of Nepal's civil and criminal law systems. It recognizes the different customs of the various groups within Nepali society, and deviations from the norm are considered legal if they can be regarded as part of the traditions of a specific group.[33] It is also important to emphasize that in Nepal there is no personal law system like that which exists in India, and that the provisions of the *Muluki Ain* are meant to apply to all the citizens of Nepal, irrespective of their religious affiliations. The new Code remains implicitly anchored in Hindu values and sources, although discrimination on the basis of caste or ethnicity has been formally

---

[30] Pratyoush Onta, 'Ambivalence Denied: The Making of Rastriya Itihas in Panchayat Era Textbooks', *Contributions to Nepalese Studies*, (1996), 23(1): 214.

[31] *Mulukī Ain,* 2020 BS (*Muluki Ain*, 1963).

[32] See in this volume, Chapter 7 (Mathew J. Nelson, 'Inheritance Unbound: The Politics of Personal Law Reform in Pakistan and India', "Introduction").

[33] Rose and Fisher, *The Politics of Nepal*, p. 89.

abolished. Höfer further explains: 'Contrary to the wide-spread view, modern legislation has not explicitly abolished the caste hierarchy. Although there is no longer an inequality before the law, based on caste affiliation, the system of relations constituting the caste hierarchy remains unchanged and is tacitly sanctioned'.[34]

In the 1970s and 1980s the Panchayat system became progressively delegitimized. Its proponents were implicated in one scandal after another, the country's economy failed to grow, the regime's mantra of development remained unfulfilled, and the system came under attack from the underground parties and civil society. The death of King Mahendra in 1973 and the succession to the throne of his son Birendra marked a shift in the trajectory of political affairs in Nepal. The new king attempted to re-legitimate and preserve the Panchayat system against mounting opposition and public dissent by introducing partial reforms. He even held a referendum in 1980. However, the contradictions of the system were becoming increasingly evident and the opposition was growing in strength. The economic crisis of 1989 ignited by the Indian trade embargo and refusal to renew its economic agreements with Nepal significantly contributed to uprooting the legitimacy of the Panchayat regime.

THE POST-1990 ESTABLISHMENT

On 15 January 1990, seven communist parties united under the United Left Front (ULF) and formed a tactical alliance with the Nepali Congress against the Panchayat regime. Most of the banned political parties took part in the pro-democracy alliance and launched a *Jan Āndolan* (People's Movement) to seek the restoration of multi-party democracy. On 16 April 1990, after two months of protests, mass demonstrations and strikes, the king dissolved the government and the national Parliament, and a few days later allowed for the creation of an interim government under the Premiership of Krishna P. Bhattarai, the General Secretary of the Nepali Congress. The Cabinet included other Congress members, delegates of the United Left Front (ULF), independents, and royal nominees.[35] The political

---

[34] Höfer, *Caste Hierarchy*, p. 204.
[35] Rishikesh Shaha, *Politics in Nepal 1980–1991* (Manohar: New Delhi, 1993), pp. 217–18.

overture and the climate of dialogue allowed for a meaningful debate about the drafting of a new constitution to establish a functioning democracy in the country.

DRAFTING THE 1990 CONSTITUTION

The process of drafting a new democratic constitution in 1990 reflects the political dynamics of the historical moment following the *Jan Āndolan* and is instrumental to the understanding of the dissatisfaction with the 1990 document. Criticism of the 1990 Constitution arose even during the drafting of the document because of the body which prepared it. The new constitution was, once again, not drafted by an elected Constituent Assembly, but by a small nine-member commission nominated by the political elites of the country, and finalized by a government committee composed of three ministers. Some of the more radical communist parties, like the CPN (Masal) and the CPN (Mashal),[36] had demanded the immediate promulgation of an interim constitution to pave the way for the election of a Constituent Assembly, but their proposal was rejected as they were small groups outside the ULF without much political leverage.

In fact, on 31 May 1990, King Birendra—following his unsuccessful attempt on 11 May to single-handedly nominate a Commission without consulting the Council of Ministers—formed a new Constitution Recommendation Commission (CRC) again under the chairmanship of Chief Justice Bishwa Nath Upadhyaya. The Commission was entrusted with drafting a new constitution in three months, explicitly within the mandate of constitutional monarchy and parliamentary democracy.[37] Although the Royal Communiqué

---

[36] The CPN (Masal) seceded in 1983 from the CPN (4th Convention) and the CPN (Mashal) separated in 1985 from CPN (Masal) itself. The leader of Mashal Party was 'Prachanda' ('the fierce one', a.k.a. Pushpa Kamal Dahal), the supreme leader of the Maoists.

[37] The Royal Palace Communiqué issued by the Palace Chief Secretariat on 31 May 1990 (16 *Jest* 2046) formed the Constitution Recommendation Commission (CRC) under the chairmanship of Supreme Court Chief Justice Bishwa Nath Upadhyaya. The other eight members were: Pradyumna Lal Raj Bhandari, Ram Nanda Singh, Laxman Prasad Aryal, Mukunda Regmi, Daman Nath Dhungana, Nirmal Lama,

did not specify the political affiliation of the Commission members, it was clear that the Palace, the Nepali Congress, and the ULF had three delegates each in the Commission. The CRC composition was criticized from the outset as exclusionary; in fact, many smaller political parties were not included in the Commission, while women, ethno-linguistic and religious minorities found no direct representation in it. As a result, it has been argued that the composition of the Commission negatively affected the treatment of minorities and women due to the predominant involvement and hegemony of high-caste male Hindus in the constitution-drafting process, and generally in the political sphere.[38]

The fact that the mandate of the Commission was conditional to devising a frame of government within the parameters of constitutional monarchy and parliamentary democracy played an important role in the selection of the various institutional models. CRC Secretary Surya Nath Upadhyaya set up a secretariat to assist the Commission in its work and collected more than 150 constitutions from all over the world to provide inspiration to the constitution-makers.[39] However, the structure of the Commission's draft relied on Nepal's previous constitutional documents, especially the 1962 Panchayat Constitution.[40] In terms of content, the CRC members intended to improve on the short-lived 1959 Constitution of Nepal, which was perceived as the institutionalization of the achievements of the 1950–1 revolution against autocracy. The Westminster model represented, once again, the institutional framework and point of reference for the drafting process, especially because the UK was considered the archetypical and most stable constitutional monarchy worldwide.[41] Moreover, many Nepali political leaders and members of the elite had received their education and formed their political

---

Bharat Mohan Adhikari, and Madav Kumar Nepal. Surya Nath Upadhyaya was the Secretary of the Commission, but he did not enjoy voting powers.

[38] Mahendra Lawoti, *Towards a Democratic Nepal: Inclusive Political Institutions for a Multicultural Society* (Sage Publications: New Delhi, 2005).

[39] Interview with Surya Nath Upadhyaya, Kathmandu, 22 March 2007.

[40] Mukunda Regmi, *Samvaidhānik Vikās ra Nepāl Adhirādyako Samvidhān 2047* (Constitutional Development and the Constitution of the Kingdom of Nepal, 1990) (Millennium Press: Lalitpur, 2004), pp. 1771–846.

[41] Interview with Daman Nath Dhungana, Kathmandu, 9 April 2007.

views in the milieu of the institutional and political arrangements of British India and the newly-independent Indian Republic; hence the Constitution of India was also a very important point of reference.[42] The Commission adopted a centralized unitary state structure, a British-style first-past-the-post majoritarian electoral system, and the principle of 'King in Parliament'. The document set up a bicameral legislature with a cabinet of ministers responsible to Parliament under the premiership of the leader of the party holding the majority in the Lower House.

Article 3 vested state sovereignty exclusively in the people of Nepal and not in the king for the first time in Nepali history; this shows the Commission's desire to also act in line with the democratic spirit of the People's Movement. Executive power was vested in the king and the Council of Ministers in Article 35(1), no issue concerning any action of the monarch could be raised in any court nor discussed in Parliament under Article 31, the king's name was included in the name of most constitutional bodies, and he was made the Supreme Commander of the Army in Article 119. The position and powers of the king represented the most contentious issue debated by the Commission. While the communist members tried to curtail the role of the monarchy considerably, the Nepali Congress and the Palace delegates managed to impose a 'constitutional monarchy with higher status and privileges' through a majority vote.[43]

The Commission established an independent judiciary and the Supreme Court was granted extraordinary jurisdiction to enforce the fundamental rights enshrined in the Constitution. Article 88 granted the apex court the power of judicial review, to settle any legal question in matters of public concern (Public Interest Litigation or PIL), and issue orders to enforce such rights. The document also included an extensive section on fundamental rights centred on the Right to Equality and the principle of 'non-discrimination on grounds of religion, race, sex, caste, tribe or ideological conviction' enshrined in Article 11. The Commission's awareness of the disadvantaged

[42] Mara Malagodi, 'Minority Rights and Constitutional Borrowings in the Drafting of Nepal's 1990 Constitution', *European Bulletin of Himalayan Research*, (2010), 37: 56–81.

[43] Krishna Hachhethu, 'Transition to Democracy: Negotiations behind Constitution Making, 1990', *Contributions to Nepalese Studies*, (2004), 21(1): 103.

socio-economic position of many ethno-linguistic minorities, lower castes, and women resulted in the insertion of Article 11(3) on non-discrimination on the part of the State: 'Provided that special provisions may be made by law for the protection and advancement of women, children, the aged or those who are physically or mentally incapacitated or those who belong to a class which is economically, socially or educationally backward'.

This sub-clause was devised to allow for future enactments of special legislation for the advancement of unprivileged segments of Nepali society. It is similar to Article 15(4) of the Indian Constitution introduced by the First Amendment, even though in Nepal no groups were identified as Scheduled Castes and Scheduled Tribes. The provision opened the door for some form of future positive discrimination as defined by the legislator. The CRC members rejected an outright 'minority approach' and refused to include any provision for an Indian-style reservation system. Nirmal Lama, himself a member of an ethnic minority although originally from the Indian district of Darjeeling, forcefully condemned the minority approach as a path leading to communal tension.[44] The Indian experience of communal violence and the findings of the Mandal Commission Report, together with the Janata Dal–led government's decision to implement it at the time of the CRC work, negatively influenced the Nepali Constitution–making process with regard to the question of introducing affirmative measures in the draft.[45]

Nepal's great degree of socio-cultural diversity was, in fact, taken into account by the constitution-makers only to a limited extent in 1990. The Commission recognized Nepal's diversity in Article 4(1) by declaring the State—for the first time in the country's history—as 'multiethnic and multilingual', but omitted the term 'multi-religious'. The preservation of the Shah monarchy in the 1990 constitutional arrangements entailed the perpetuation of 'traditional' nationalist identity-markers centred on Hinduism, the Hindu monarchy, and the Nepali language to legitimize political power in Nepal. In fact, the Commission qualified the monarchy as Hindu in Article 4(1)

---

[44] Dhungel et al., *Nepalese Constitution,* p. 39.
[45] Interview with Laxman Prasad Aryal, Kathmandu, 9 April 2007.

while it could not agree whether to define the state itself as Hindu. The national anthem, the national animal, the national colour, and the national flag, however, all reflected Hindu symbolism.[46] The Right to Religion in Article 19 was guaranteed but again limited to 'religion as handed down from ancient times and having due regards to traditional practices', and the ban on conversion was also reiterated without much debate.[47] Article 6 again declared Nepali as both the language of the nation (*rāshtrabhāsā*) and the official language, while the other languages were recognized as mother tongues, but defined as national languages (*rāshtriya bhāsā*). Article 18 was included in the fundamental rights to guarantee cultural and educational rights, allowing the various communities of Nepal to promote their languages and cultures and to run schools up to primary level in their own language.

Public participation in the 1990 Constitution–making process was limited. Written submissions were sent to the Commission in Kathmandu and eight of the CRC members travelled around Nepal to collect suggestions from the general public, while two travelled to the UK and the USA. Interestingly, most of the suggestions from Nepal concerned religious, ethnic, and regional issues.[48] In fact, with the democratic opening of 1990, ethno-linguistic and religious minorities had become increasingly vocal and active in the public sphere, and various groups had united under the umbrella organization of the Nepal Janajati Mahasangh (Nepal Federation of Indigenous Nationalities). The minorities were pressing for a constitutionally-established secular state and for the full recognition of their cultural and religious rights. However, the formal recognition in the constitution of Nepal's socio-cultural diversity did not lead to discussions about federalism or social inclusion.[49] The Commission's preoccupation with strengthening national unity prevailed in view of preserving Nepal's security and independence, especially vis-à-vis India. The recognition of diversity in the constitutional structure was

---

[46] International Crisis Group, *Towards a Lasting Peace in Nepal: The Constitutional Issues*, International Crisis Group: Asia Report No. 59, (2005), pp. 13–14.

[47] Interview with Madhav Kumar Nepal, Kathmandu, 10 April 2007.

[48] Michael Hutt, 'Drafting the 1990 Constitution', in Hutt (ed.), *Nepal in the Nineties*, pp. 35–6.

[49] Interview with Daman Nath Dhungana, Kathmandu, 9 April 2007.

perceived by the Commission members as a divisive and weakening factor for the Nepali State.

On 10 September 1990, Chairman Bishwa Nath Upadhyaya submitted the CRC draft to the king who, in turn, handed it over to PM Bhattarai for finalization. The PM set up a three-minister Cabinet Committee coordinated by ULF Minister Nilamber Acharya and composed of the Congress Home Minister Yog Prasad Upadhyaya and the royal nominee Keshar Jung Rayamajhi, the Minister of Education. The three ministers worked for eight days to finalize the document.[50] Three significant changes were made to the CRC draft. First, Nepal became constitutionally a Hindu kingdom. The Cabinet Committee inserted a comma in Article 4, specifically defining the state as Hindu and not just the Shah monarchy. Second, in the draft, every provision was amendable by Parliament with a two-thirds majority. The ministers introduced a limitation allowing only for amendments which 'do not prejudice the spirit of the Preamble' in Article 116 on the basis of the Indian-derived 'basic structure doctrine'. Lastly, the Committee specified that treaties of an ordinary nature concerning peace and friendship and natural resources could be ratified by a simple majority in Article 126. The Committee also received from the Palace Chief Secretary, Reabatti Raman Khanal, a list of approximately eighteen points to be revised, mostly concerning the position of the monarchy.[51]

On 11 October, the Prime Minister handed over the finalized version of the constitution to King Birendra for promulgation. However, the King kept postponing the promulgation of the document. His dissatisfaction with the draft manifested itself openly on 22 October 1990 when the *Gorkhāpatra*, the government-owned daily newspaper, published an article stating that the Palace had prepared a separate draft following a leak from one of the CRC members.[52] There was a public outcry and the king came in for heavy criticism. Then King Birendra finally promulgated the new constitution as revised by the Cabinet on 9 November 1990.

[50] Interview with Keshar Jung Rayamajhi, Kathmandu, 15 April 2007.
[51] Interview with Nilamber Acharya, Kathmandu, 12 April 2007.
[52] Interview with Bharat Mohan Adhikari, Kathmandu, 18 May 2007.

The Interpretation and Implementation of the 1990 Constitution

The debates concerning the 1990 Constitution of Nepal need to be understood in the context of the historical and political developments in the country. The initial dissatisfaction with the 1990 document was progressively exacerbated by political instability, restrictive interpretations of the Constitution in many post-1990 Supreme Court cases, and by the deepening political predicament of the country, caught up between the Maoist armed insurgency and the progressive militarization of the state under the king's direct rule.

The 1991 elections, the first under the 1990 Constitution, produced a Congress majority government and four years of relative stability for the country. However, since the dissolution of the House of Representatives by Prime Minister Girjia P. Koirala and the resulting mid-term elections in 1994, Nepali politics has been extremely unstable. The 1994 elections produced a hung Parliament and eight governments in five years.[53] For ten years, beginning in 1996, Nepal also endured an armed insurgency launched by the Communist Party of Nepal (Maoist) and suffered two bouts of autocratic monarchical rule, in 2002–3 and 2005–6. In February 1996, the Maoists submitted a list of forty demands to the government that included a demand that 'a new constitution should be drafted by the People's representatives'. After five years of conflict and the (apparently unrelated) massacre of King Birendra and his family, the Maoists and the government sat down to negotiate in the autumn of 2001. These talks broke down when it became clear that the Maoists' demand for a new constitution framed by a constituent assembly was non-negotiable. The 1990 Constitution became the focus of the negotiations: its abrogation became the *conditio sine qua non* for the Maoists to come to a negotiated agreement. In the meantime, the fact that King Gyanendra legitimized his second takeover on 1 February 2005 by making use of the 1990 Constitution made the document increasingly embattled. The king claimed to be acting within the Constitution's boundaries through Article 127, granting him the 'power to remove difficulties' and to be upholding its democratic spirit. Thus, if the Maoists had

[53] See, Table 3A.1 in the Annexes of this essay for a complete list of post-1990 governments.

gravely compromised the position of the 1990 Constitution, it was King Gyanendra who dealt the final blow to its legitimacy. In the Twelve-Point Agreement concluded in November 2005 in India, the Maoists and the seven main parliamentary political parties united against King Gyanendra's autocratic rule and committed to 'establish permanent peace in the country through Constituent Assembly elections and forward-looking political outlet'. This was the death sentence for the 1990 Constitution. In April 2006, the second *Jan Āndolan* (People's Movement) launched jointly by the Maoists and the seven-party alliance succeeded in putting an end to monarchical autocracy. Parliament was restored and in November 2006 the Maoists and the political parties signed the Comprehensive Peace Agreement. Following the promulgation of the Interim Constitution on 15 January 2007, the Maoists entered the Interim Parliament and joined the government committing Nepal to the process of constitutional change and state-restructuring they had envisioned.

Much of the dissatisfaction with the 1990 Constitution from the time of its promulgation was due to the kind of Nepali identity it promoted and its exclusionary nature. It seems that the way in which the 1990 Constitution constructed and institutionalized a Nepali identity based on the Shah monarchy, Hinduism and the Nepali language represented for many a legacy of the Panchayat ideology, which regarded these as the three pillars of official Nepali national cultural identity. In fact, the wording of the articles of the 1990 Constitution defining His Majesty (Article 27), the State (Article 4), and the Language of the Nation (Article 6) is essentially the same as that of the corresponding articles of the 1962 Panchayat Constitution.[54] Notwithstanding a timid gesture towards a more inclusive system recognizing the great extent of socio-cultural diversity within Nepal, the 1990 Constitution was still informed by the traditional legitimization of political power derived from Nepal's specific patterns of state-building and nation-building anchored in the notion of Hindu kingship. Thus, it is not surprising that the 1990 document has been heavily criticized, for promoting male Parbatiya

---

[54] In the 1962 Panchayat Constitution, Article 20 referred to His Majesty, Article 3 to the State, and Article 4 to the National Language.

high-caste Hindu values, by religious and ethnic minorities, women and dalit activists and concerned intellectuals.[55] This criticism raises a very important question: in the post-1990 democratic era, to what extent could the various groups of Nepali society identify with the idea of 'Nepaliness' promoted by the 1990 Constitution? To answer this question it is essential to analyse some concrete examples of the application of its provisions.

The outright rejection of the 1990 Constitution by the Maoist insurgent groups was accompanied by a growing dissatisfaction of Nepali society with the implementation and judicial interpretation of the 1990 document. In the political sphere, the first case to test the constitutional limits to the power of the monarchy was the *Ambassador Appointment* case.[56] Minister Nilamber Acharya leaked to the press that the appointment of K.L. Adhikari, already the Royal Ambassador to France, as Ambassador to Spain and Israel as well had been conducted by the king without consulting the Council of Ministers. Advocate R. Adhikari then filed a petition in the form of Public Interest Litigation to the Supreme Court challenging the validity of the appointment. The Court dismissed the petition refusing to interfere in any communication between the king and the prime minister. Another instance of the king acting independently without following the constitution was his unilateral appointment of the ten members of the Upper House, whom the king was supposed to nominate on the advice and consent of the Council of Ministers according to Article 46(1). However, in practice this became a prerogative of the king, and this too went largely unchallenged.

It is interesting to analyse the instability of post-1994 governments, in connection with the judicial interpretations provided by the Supreme Court, in two landmark decisions. The Supreme Court judgment in the first House Dissolution case sanctioned the decision of Prime Minister Girjia Prasad Koirala to dissolve the House of Representatives and hold mid-term elections.[57] However, as Sangraula points out, the Prime Minister decided to dissolve the House because

---

[55] Lawoti, *Towards a Democratic Nepal,* pp. 113–53.
[56] *Radheshyam v. Council of Ministers,* NKP, 2048, Vol. 33, No. 12, p. 810.
[57] *Hari Prasad Nepal v. Prime Minister,* NKP, 2052, Vol. 37, No. 1, p. 88.

of a dispute within his own party, the Nepali Congress: it was a party crisis, not a national crisis.[58] Interestingly, the Court took the opposite view a year later in a similar case in which the UML Prime Minister Man Mohan Adhikari sought the dissolution of the Lower House.[59] The Special Bench of the Supreme Court held the recommendation of the prime minister unconstitutional on the ground that it violated both the spirit and the letter of the constitutional text. The apex court withdrew from a debate which was essentially political, and ordered the House of Representatives to be reinstated.

Three years later, the Supreme Court adjudicated a case presented to it by the king regarding the recommendation made by Prime Minister Surya Bahadur Thapa to dissolve the Lower House.[60] The king—before dissolving the House—sought an opinion from the Supreme Court. The Court relied on the precedent established by the second House Dissolution case and gave priority to a special session of Parliament which would consider a no-confidence motion before the king could dissolve the House. It was the dissolution of the House of Representatives carried out by the Nepali Congress Prime Minister Sher Bahadur Deuba on 22 May 2002, together with his recommendation to postpone mid-term polls to October, and the fact that the Supreme Court upheld the validity of the Prime Minister's action in its decision on 6 August 2002, which provided King Gyanendra with the opportunity to make a direct intervention in the political affairs of the country.[61]

In relation to the Nepali language and Hinduism, the formulation of the corresponding articles in the constitutional text was sufficiently ambiguous to allow ample room for very different kinds of judicial interpretation. The Supreme Court's decisions in the matter of linguistic rights, however, have been conservative. There have been two notable rulings on this issue by Nepal's apex court. The first, in 1997, made Nepali the only language in which candidates were

[58] Yubaraj Sangroula, *Nepalese Legal System: Human Rights Perspective* (KLS: Kathmandu, 2005).

[59] *Ravi Raj Bhandari* v. *Prime Minister,* Sarvocca Adalat Bulletin, 4, *Bhadra* 16–31, 2052.

[60] *House Dissolution (N. 3) case,* 6 Sarvocca Adalat, 1, *Magh* 16–30, 2054.

[61] See Table 3A.2 in the Annexes of this chapter for a complete list of post-2002 governments.

allowed to take the examination for the Public Service Commission.[62] The second, in 1999, forbade the use of any language other than Nepali in local government bodies.[63] Moreover, if we look at the implementation of Article 18 on Cultural and Educational Rights the government has not invested many resources in the promotion of languages other than Nepali and Sanskrit.

The issue of Nepal being constitutionally a Hindu kingdom has emerged in a few cases, mostly pertaining to interpretations of the *Muluki Ain*. A leading case on religious conversion, referred by the Supreme Court in 1989, provided the interpretation of the limited Right to Religion vis-à-vis the connotation of the Nepali State as Hindu.[64] The defendants, who were originally Christian, were charged with the offence of religious proselytism and conversions of Hindus to Christianity, while the defendants, who were originally Hindu, were charged with having converted from one religion to another. The appellate court acquitted the Christian defendants, but convicted the converts and ordered their conversion back to Hinduism. The Supreme Court overturned the earlier judgment and convicted the Christian defendants to six years' imprisonment. It ruled that the Right to Religion 'seems to have guaranteed to practice one's religion as handed down from ancient times and to perform religious rites under that religion. However, a religion which has not been handed down from ancient times does not seem to have got protection under the Constitution'. Ironically, since the formulation of the Article pertaining to the Right to Religion in the 1990 Constitution was almost identical to that of the Panchayat Constitution and the Nepali State was still defined as Hindu, the Supreme Court's decision in the *Charles Mendez* case remained valid even after 1990.

Another landmark decision of the Supreme Court in relation to the Right to Religion is the case of Man Bahadur Vishwakarma which disputed discriminatory practices related to untouchability.[65]

---

[62] *Chudanath* v. *Public Service Commission*, NKP, 2054, Vol. 39, No. 7, p. 360.

[63] *Adv. Lal Bahadur Thapa and Others* v. *Kathmandu Metropolitan City and Others*, unpublished decision, Supreme Court, 2056.

[64] *HMG/N* v. *Charles Mendez and Others*, NKP, 2046, Vol. 31, No. 6, p. 648.

[65] *Man Bahadur Vishwakarma* v. *Ministry of Law and Justice*, NKP, 2049, Vol. 34, No. 12, p. 1010.

The petitioner challenged the constitutional validity of the clause of the *Muluki Ain* that provides that customary practices of any temple or religious denomination in place since time immemorial shall not be deemed discriminatory. The Supreme Court's judges interpreted the clause as ambiguous and struck it down to reaffirm the supremacy of the Constitution which clearly makes caste-based discrimination punishable by law in Article 11(4). The reasoning of the judges, however, focused on the legalistic formal aspect of the case they were referring to, rather than the substantial provisions against untouchability.

In 1996, the Supreme Court entertained the petition filed in the *Chanda Bajracarya* case challenging the constitutionality of various provisions of the *Muluki Ain* relating to women's rights, on the grounds that Nepal is a Hindu and patriarchal society, and ultimately that sudden societal changes are undesirable.[66] The Court relied on the precedent established in the famous *Mira Dhungana* case on women's inheritance rights, which had been decided the previous year.[67] The judges relied on both the reasoning and the solution adopted in this earlier case, and issued an order to the government to introduce an appropriate Bill in Parliament to address the issue of women's rights instead of exercising its extensive powers of review. Other cases between 1996 and 2001 challenged the constitutionality of certain provisions of the *Muluki Ain* with regard to women's inheritance rights,[68] marital rape,[69] rape of a prostitute,[70] and incest.[71] The Supreme Court adopted a similar approach in all of the aforementioned cases claiming to preserve Nepal's social stability and its traditions as influenced by Hinduism. Similarly, cases on cow

[66] *Chanda Bajracharya* v. *Secretariat of Parliament*, NKP, 2053, Vol. 38, No. 7, p. 537.

[67] *Meera Dhungana* v. *Ministry of Law and Justice*, NKP, 2052, Vol. 37, No. 6, p. 462.

[68] *Sapana Pradhan-Malla for FWLD* v. *Ministry of Law and Justice*, 5 Sarvocca Adalat Bulletin, 1, *Asoj* 16–30, 2053.

[69] *Meera Dhungana* v. *Ministry of Law and Justice*, Publication of Decisions relating to Human Rights, 2059, Special Issue, Supreme Court, p. 129.

[70] Writ petition filed by Advocate Sapana Pradhan-Malla for *FWLD* v. *HGM/N*, Publication of Decisions relating to Human Rights, 2059, Special Issue, Supreme Court, p. 144.

[71] *Tara Devi Poudel* v. *Cabinet Secretariat*, NKP, 2058, Vol. 43, No. 7/8, p. 375.

slaughter have been criminalizing Nepali citizens who are not Hindu and do not worship the cow.[72]

It seems that in most of the post-1990 cases which question the societal order and stability of Nepali society as defined by a certain type of Hinduism, the *Muluki Ain*—with its undeniable Hindu bias—has prevailed over the 1990 Constitution and the fundamental rights it enshrines. It seems useful to compare the liberal judgment of the apex court in the *Reena Bajracharya* case on equal remuneration for equal work by different genders[73] with its irresolute decisions in the many cases on women's property rights, inheritance rights, and so on which impinged on more 'traditional' aspects of Nepali society. While we witness a positive example of judicial activism in the *Reena Bajracharya* case, in other cases we observe the Court admitting that there is a gender bias within Nepali society, then telling the government to do something about it, and ultimately washing its hands clean of the possible legal disarray that a more direct intervention might have caused. The response of the Court to the petition filed by Advocate Achyut Prasat Kharel to the Supreme Court in 2004 to ban the Blue Diamond Society (BDS) is another example of the Court's cautious approach to reform at that time.[74] The petitioner accused the BDS of attempting to make 'homosexual activities legal' and demanded that such activities be banned by the government because they were a criminal offence in Nepal. The petitioner claimed that Clause 4 of the Chapter on Marriage of the *Muluki Ain* criminalizes 'unnatural sex' and that homosexuality is against Hinduism. The Code, however, does not define 'unnatural sex' in any of its parts and never mentions homosexuality. The Supreme Court nonetheless did not get entangled in the potential frenzy that such a case might have caused and issued a show-cause notice to the Home Ministry seeking a written reply on 'why open homosexual activities should not be banned in Nepal'. It was left to the Ministry to respond that there is no legal provision to ban or punish homosexual activities in the country, even if the Supreme Court is the body deputed to provide the final and binding interpretation of the country's constitution and laws.

---

[72] *Unequal Citizens* (The World Bank: Kathmandu, 2006), p. 43.

[73] *Reena Bajracarya* v. *HMG Secretariat of the Council of Ministers*, Writ N. 2812 of 2054 (1997), unpublished decision, Supreme Court decision, 2057.

[74] Petition filed by Advocate Achyut Prasat Kharel, 4 *Asadh* 2061.

CONCLUSION

Nepal's political instability since the mid-1990s and the increasing recorded patterns of legally-sanctioned social exclusion led to a growing disaffection towards the 1990 Constitution amongst Nepalis.[75] The various governments could not respond adequately to the demands for constitutional change arising from different segments of society, and not a single amendment bill was ever tabled in Parliament. Moreover, the permanence of the 1990 document was increasingly viewed as the main obstacle to peace talks with the Maoists, and, ultimately, as an ineffective limitation on the powers of the king. The increasing militarization of the state under the king's direct rule since late 2002 was justified in response to the Maoist insurgency and legitimized by a neo-traditionalist ideology based on the Panchayat narratives. Furthermore, King Gyanendra's claim to be upholding the 1990 Constitution to justify his autocratic rule led to the alliance of the main seven political parties with the Maoists. The anti-monarchical forces launched a pro-democracy movement in April 2006 which succeeded in putting an end to the king's rule. The first act of the restored Parliament on 30 April 2006 was to pass a resolution to hold elections for a Constituent Assembly, accommodating the main demand of the Maoists. The Interim Constitution was then promulgated on 15 January 2007 to pave the way for the elections of the Constituent Assembly, held in April 2008, whose first meeting declared Nepal a Republic, putting an end to the Shah monarchy.

The 1990 Constitution was hailed as the best constitution in the world at the time of its promulgation by Nepali politicians, but by 2006 it had become the worst. But this is political rhetoric and propaganda which bears little significance for a persuasive analysis of the 1990 constitutional experience. This brings us back to the initial question about what kind of story 'the rise and fall of the 1990 Constitution' tells about post-1990 Nepali politics. The 1990 constitutional experience tells a story of exclusion, of high hopes which were not fulfilled, of aspirations for a more equitable environment which were not met.

---

[75] World Bank/DFID, *Unequal Citizens: Gender, Caste and Ethnic Exclusion in Nepal: Executive Summary* (World Bank Nepal Office: Kathmandu, 2006).

However, the blame should not be put exclusively on the document itself. The 1990 Constitution was the result of a political compromise; hence it was formulated in such an ambiguous manner that it could have supported many different interpretations. The 1990 document did introduce parliamentary democracy and extensive fundamental rights; and its spirit was undoubtedly a democratic one. Nonetheless, its values were often not respected and its provisions manipulated. For a constitution to be implemented properly a strong commitment to its values is required from the political establishment and the judiciary, otherwise the constitution remains a dead letter. The 1990 document could have also been amended, especially the Articles defining the coordinates of Nepali identity. This raises another important question: does the abrogation of the 1990 Constitution now require a redefinition of 'Nepaliness'? The promulgation of the 2007 Interim Constitution has endeavoured to ignite a process of state restructuring and the creation of a 'New Nepal'. In this changing context, what does being Nepali mean? We are witnessing the rise of ethnic politics and the abandonment of the old nationalistic narratives—or an attempt to achieve their abandonment—so what kind of collective identity, informing the forthcoming constitution, could be truly inclusive? It seems that a new document recognizing Nepal's inner plurality, rooted in social hybridity as highlighted by Gellner,[76] and fostering a civic sense of belonging with an emphasis on citizenship and rights might be a valid instrument for institutional change, rather than constitutional arrangements based on polarized essentializing identity lines. It is, however, important to bear in mind that although change might begin with a new document, it is certainly not guaranteed by it. Positive institutional transformation is a long process which requires great political responsibility. This seems to be the main lesson that should be learnt from Nepal's 1990 constitutional experience. The long-term success of the political process currently underway to establish lasting peace in Nepal will depend ultimately upon whether the present constitution-making endeavours achieve consensus and stability.

[76] David Gellner, 'From Group Rights to Individual Rights and Back: Nepalese Struggles over Culture and Equality', in Jane Cowan, Marie-Bénédicte Dembour, and Richard E. Wilson (eds), *Culture and Rights: Anthropological Perspectives* (Cambridge University Press: Cambridge, 2001), p. 192.

ANNEXES

Table 3A.1 Elections for the House of Representatives

Date of Election	Type of Election	Govt No.	Type of Government
12 May 1991 (29 *Baishak* 2048)	General Elections NC Majority	1	27 May 1991 (13 *Jesht* 2048); PM G.P. Koirala (NC); (NC-majority govt)
			December 1991, Cabinet reshuffle in NC; PM G.P. Koirala (NC)
15 November 1994 (29 *Kartik* 2051)	Mid-term Elections Hung Parliament	2	29 November 1994–September 1995 (13 *Mangsir* 2051); PM Man M. Adhikari (UML); (UML-minority govt)
		3	11 September 1995–March 1997 (26 *Bhadra* 2051); PM Sher B. Deuba (NC); Centre–Right coalition (NC, RPP, NSP)
		4	10 March–October 1997 (27 *Phalgun* 2053); PM Lokendra B. Chand (RPP-C); Right–Left coalition (UML, RPP)
		5	6 October 1997–March 1998 (20 *Asoj* 2054); PM Surya B. Thapa (RPP-T); Right–Centre coalition (NC, RPP, NSP)
		6	26 March–August 1998 (30 *Chaitra* 2054); PM G.P. Koirala (NC); Centre–Right coalition (NC, RPP, NSP)
		7	26 August–December 1998 (10 *Bhadra* 2055); PM G.P. Koirala (NC); Centre–Left coalition (NC, CPN (ML))

(Cont'd)

Table 3A.1 (*Cont'd*)

Date of Election	Type of Election	Govt No.	Type of Government
		8	10 December 1998 (24 *Marg* 2055); PM G.P. Koirala (NC); (NC-minority govt)
		9	23 December 1998–May 1999 (8 *Poush* 2055); PM G.P. Koirala (NC); Centre–Left coalition (NC, UML, NSP)
3–17 May 1999 (20 *Baishak* – 3 *Jest* 2056)	General Elections NC majority	10	27 May 1999–March 2000; (13 *Jest* 2056); PM K.P. Bhattarai (NC); (NC (Bhattarai faction)-majority govt)
		11	20 March 2000–July 2001 (7 *Chaitra* 2056); PM G.P. Koirala (NC); (NC (Koirala faction)-majority govt)
		12	23 July 2001–May 2002 (8 *Shavan* 2057); PM Sher B. Deuba (NC)
22 May 2002	Deuba dissolves Parliament and calls fresh elections due to political confrontation over extending the State of Emergency		

Table 3A.2 Post-2002 Series of Unelected Governments

Date of Formation	Date of Dissolution	Govt No.	Prime Minister
4 October 2002 (18 *Asoj* 2059 BS)			***First royal takeover;*** **King Gyanendra sacks Deuba government**
12 October 2002 (Royal nomin.)	30 May 2003 (resignation)	1	Lokendra Bahadur Chand (RPP)
4 June 2003 (Royal nomin.)	7 May 2004 (resignation)	2	Surya Bahadur Thapa (RPP)

2 June 2004 (Royal nomin.)	1 February 2005 (sacked)	3	Sher Bahadur Deuba (NC-D)
1 February 2005 (**9** *Magh* **2061** BS)			***Second royal takeover;*** **King Gyanendra sacks Deuba government**
1 February 2005 (Royal nomin.)	26 April 2006	4	King Gyanendra Shah
26 April 2006 (**13** *Baishak* **2063** BS)			***Jan Andolan II;*** **Second popular movement**
27 April 2006	25 March 2007	1	Girjia Prasad Koirala (NC)
15 January 2007 (**1** *Magh* **2063** BS)			***Formation of Interim* Parliament including the Maoists**
26 March 2007	–	2	

CHAPTER FOUR

Separating Religion and Politics?
Buddhism and the Bhutanese Constitution

༄༅

*Richard W. Whitecross**

On 18 July 2008, the first written Constitution of Bhutan was formally enacted by the fifth king, His Majesty Jigme Khesar Namgyal Wangchuck.[1] Bhutan is a landlocked country to the northeast of India with an approximate population of 560,000. Unlike Pakistan, India, or Sri Lanka, Bhutan was not colonized by the British, and its legal and constitutional development has followed a different historical trajectory. Looking north to Tibet, the character of the Bhutanese State that emerged in the seventeenth century drew upon Tibetan religious and political structures that lasted into the twentieth century and, arguably, into the twenty-first. This essay addresses the recent changes in Bhutan, the last surviving Himalayan kingdom. In particular, it sets out and reflects on the relationship

* The research for this essay was made possible by awards from the Economic and Social Research Council (ESRC), Carnegie Trust for the Universities of Scotland (2002), ESRC Postdoctoral Fellowship (2003), Society for South Asian Studies, UK (2003), Frederick Williamson Memorial Trust, Cambridge (2003), and the University of Edinburgh Research Award (2004). Fieldwork was conducted between 1999 and 2001, 2003, and 2004. Supplementary interviews were conducted in 2005 and 2006. I would like to thank the editors for their invaluable comments and suggestions. All errors are, of course, my own.
[1] http://www.constitution.bt (last accessed on 5 May 2012).

between Buddhism, the new Constitution and the avowed secular nature of the contemporary Bhutanese State.

In order to explore the implications of the Constitution and the changing role of Buddhism in Bhutan, I first need to set out the context and introduce the reader to Bhutan. Accordingly, the first section of the essay outlines the emergence of Bhutan as a 'religious estate' during the seventeenth century, and the transformation from theocracy to monarchy in the early twentieth century. In this section, I focus on the difficulty of separating Buddhism from the state due to its embedded role in the creation and expansion of the Bhutanese State in the seventeenth century. The section ends by illustrating how even during a period of major political reforms in the 1950s and 1960s, the links between the State, the state-sponsored official Monk Body and Buddhism remained unbroken. The second section focuses on the drafting of the Constitution and specifically, the role of Buddhism and Buddhist religious institutions within the new political framework as re-imagined by the Constitution-drafting committee. The third section reflects on the implications and impact of the Constitution and considers what 'secularism' in a Bhutanese context may mean. Unlike other essays in this volume which draw on case law or ongoing legal debate in Sri Lanka, Pakistan, Nepal, or India, at present there has been no case law on the interpretation of the Constitution. Therefore, the conclusion set out is tentative and seeks to contextualize the intentions of the constitutional drafters within the broader understanding of contemporary Bhutanese.

While the 1990 Constitution of Nepal affirmed that Nepal was a 'Hindu' constitutional monarchy, the Bhutanese Constitution acknowledges that 'Buddhism is the spiritual heritage of Bhutan' (Article 3(1) of the Bhutanese Constitution) while specifically refraining from declaring Buddhism to be the official state religion. Although some do read this Article as declaring Buddhism to be the State religion, that was not the intention of the Drafting Committee. Furthermore, Article 1 sets out the key features and emblems of the Kingdom—a democratic constitutional monarchy, national flag, and anthem—but specifically does not declare Buddhism as a key symbol of Bhutan. The Constitution sets out the separation of church and state, yet repeatedly re-emphasizes the linkages between politics and religion, the Dual System (*Chhoe-sid-nyi*) established by the unifier of Bhutan, the Tibetan religious hierarch, Zhabdrung Ngawang Namgyal, in the seventeenth century.[2] Finally, the Constitution introduces a hitherto unfamiliar concept to the Bhutanese people: secularism and the separation of church and state.

There is a particular challenge in seeking to examine and discuss secularism in the context of Bhutan. Unlike India, where the interrelationship between the Constitution, law, and religion can be examined through Acts and case law, my approach to constitutionalism, religion, and secularism within the Bhutanese context focuses on the impact of the first written constitution on the landscape of the Bhutanese state and its relationship with Buddhism. The discussions in the other essays of this volume draw heavily on case law, judicial decisions, and debates about religion, religious laws, and their relationship with their respective political constitutions. Indeed, when we consider secularism in India, we are confronted by an extensive legal and academic literature that continues to develop. During the preparation of the Bhutanese Constitution, K.K. Venugopal, a prominent senior advocate at the Supreme Court of India and constitutional law expert, provided advice on the first draft of the Constitution. Therefore, it remains to be seen to what extent, if any, the Supreme Court of Bhutan will look to Indian constitutional law as Gary J. Jacobsohn and Shylashri Shankar discuss in the Sri Lankan context in this volume. Like Thailand, the Bhutanese Drafting Committee opted for the principle of constitutional secularism. Why not like India? Whereas the Indian Constitution has the entrenched principle of non-establishment, we cannot describe the Bhutanese Constitution in the same terms. While the Bhutanese Constitution sets out official indifference to religion and recognizes religious freedom and equality on the grounds that to recognize Buddhism could create social division within the country, the apparently secular nature of the new Bhutanese State is modified by the following considerations (mirroring the 1997 Thai Constitution):[3]

---

[2] I outline the Dual System in more detail in the first part of this essay. It refers to the combination of religious and secular authority. The Dzongkha term *Chhoe sid nyi* (*Dz: chos srid gnyis*) means 'dharma (religion) and secular together/combined'. In Tibet, it is generally referred to as *Chos srid zungdrel* or *chos srid gdan*.

[3] I draw here on Andrew Harding, 'Buddhism, Human Rights and Constitutional Reform in Thailand', *Asian Journal of Comparative Law*, (2007), 2(1): 1–25.

(a) The King (monarch) must be Buddhist (Article 2(1)). However, the monarch will also act as protector of all religions (Article 3(2)).

(b) Buddhist monks and nuns are prohibited from voting or standing as candidates for election (Article 3(3)).

(c) The State will continue to provide adequate funds and facilities to support the Zhung Dratshang (Monk Body) (Article 3(7)).

Rather, on reading the Bhutanese Constitution and comparing it with the Sri Lankan and Cambodian Constitution (1993), of which each proclaimed Buddhism to be the state religion, we see a subtle yet meaningful transformation of the political and social landscape of Bhutan. I discuss these further later. However, I would argue that the decision to break with tradition and to not declare Buddhism to be the state religion reflects two key considerations. The first, discussed at more length in this essay, is the focus on the monarchy. The second, and which is not explicitly addressed in the Constitution or elsewhere, is a response to earlier, potentially de-stabilizing inter-community tensions between the majority Buddhists and the minority Hindu Lhotshampas (ethnically Nepalese Bhutanese) in the late 1980s and the early 1990s. Tensions between adherents to different traditions within Buddhism—Druk Kagyu in the west and Nyingma tradition in central and eastern Bhutan—led to short-lived conflict in the mid-1990s. If Buddhism had been proclaimed as the state religion, or the Druk Kagyu tradition specifically, it is possible that these tensions, which have eased considerably over the last decade, could lead to 'mistrust between the majority and the minorities, and afford in some indirect way an acceptable basis for those who would seek to oppress and abuse religious minorities'.[4]

FROM THEOCRACY TO MONARCHY

The Zhabdrung's Arrival: Creating The Dual System

The arrival of the Druk Kagyu religious hierarch, the Zhabdrung Ngawang Namgyal, in 1616 from Ralung monastery in southern central Tibet, marked the beginning of the process of state construction

[4] Ibid, p. 5.

and unification in Bhutan.[5] The Zhabdrung's new religious state based upon the teachings and practices of the Druk Kagyu order was to be ruled according to the Dual System. Although this system was widely invoked as a theory of governance in Tibet, its implementation varied across the Himalayas and Tibetan cultural areas significantly.[6] The Zhabdrung, in seeking to consolidate his authority, constructed a series of *dzong* (fortress/monastery) throughout Bhutan. Unlike the administrative fortresses of Tibet, the *dzong* of Bhutan were simultaneously administrative centres and monasteries and, for a long period of time, it was the Druk Kagyu monks who were the administrators of the newly created 'Drukpa' state.[7]

Unlike the Dalai Lamas of Tibet, the Zhabdrung did not separate religious and secular authority. The Dual System, as it operated in Tibet, separated the ecclesiastical and secular authorities with civil officials typically having their monastic counterparts. However, the nature of the 'State' as developed in Bhutan did not allow for a clear distinction between religious and secular authority. In Bhutan, under the theocracy created by the first Zhabdrung, the Zhabdrung—and his subsequent incarnations—was the pinnacle of the government. A subordinate position, the 'Desi', was created, and it was responsible for civil administration with the assistance of the three regional governors of Paro, Daganna, and Jakar, as well as the district administrators of Thimphu, Wangduephodrang, and Punakha. All lay officials assumed a semi-monastic character; if a lay official rather than a full monastic was appointed as Desi, he was required to take *getshul* (partial ordination) vows and received a new, monastic name.

In 1729, Tenzin Chogyel prepared a law code on the order of the ninth Desi, Mipham Wangpo. The code written by Tenzin Chogyel organized 'along Buddhist lines the relationship between

---

[5] Druk Kagyu refers to an offshoot of the Kagyu tradition of Tibetan Buddhism. Zhabdrung is the formal title of the unifier of Bhutan, Ngawang Namgyal.

[6] For an excellent discussion of the Dual System in Bhutan, see, John Ardussi, 'Formation of the State of Bhutan (Brug gzhung) in the 17th Century and its Tibetan Antecedents', *Journal of Bhutan Studies*, (2004), Issue 11: 10–32. See also, Michael Aris, *Sources for the History of Bhutan* (Arbeitkreis fur Tibetische und Buddhistische Studien Universitat Wien: Vienna, 1986) and Michael Aris, *Bhutan: The Early History of a Himalayan Kingdom* (Aris and Philips: Warminster, 1979).

[7] Drukpa is a contraction of Druk Kagyu.

the Drukpa Kagyu monastic community, representing the State and lay patrons (*jinda*) and subjects in the judicial and economic fields'.[8] The centrality of Buddhism, or rather the monastic community to the Dual System cannot be overestimated. In a recent history of the Druk Kagyu in Bhutan, Dargye notes that 'under the dual system of government, the monk communities rose to occupy a powerful position in Bhutanese society...and exerted immense influence in every facet of life. Almost all senior monks participated in political matters'.[9] The norms of church and state were 'deeply fused and intermingled...in the consciousness of the Bhutanese' and as a consequence, it was impossible to distinguish secular and religious spheres.[10] This framework remained in place until the early twentieth century when the post of Desi was abolished and a hereditary monarch appointed.

Modernizing Bhutan: The Supreme Laws and Political Reform

The abolition of the position of Desi made way for the establishment of the monarchy. In 1907, Ugyen Wangchuck (reign: 1907–26) was elected king and Bhutan moved from theocracy to monarchy. The first two kings consolidated royal power without disturbing the pre-existing institutional framework. The second king, Jigme Wangchuck (reign: 1926–52) focused on reforming a complicated tax system and strengthened the financial basis of the monarchical government. In 1952, Jigme Dorji Wangchuck (reign: 1952–72) came to the throne and embarked on a major programme of political and social reforms. The main social reforms began with the abolition in 1953 of various categories of serfs and slaves that existed in Bhutan. The introduction of Five-Year Plans from 1961 saw the gradual development of secular education, health care provision, and increased government control of the economy. The political and social developments initiated by the third king relied on the creation of new political and legal

[8] See, Francoise Pommaret, 'The Birth of a Nation', in F. Pommaret and C. Schicklgruber (eds), *Bhutan: Mountain Fortress of the Gods* (Serindia: London, 1997), p. 199.

[9] Yonten Dargye, *History of the Drukpa Kagyud School in Bhutan: Twelfth to Seventeenth Centuries* (Omega Traders (India): New Delhi, 2001), p. 216.

[10] Harding, 'Buddhism', p. 24.

institutions and a series of laws as part of the overall modernization and development of Bhutan.

As with Thailand and the legal reforms instigated in the late nineteenth century under Chulalongkorn, Bhutan sought to effect legal and cautious political reforms to protect its independence and to tackle political pressures both from within—notably the appearance in 1952 of the Bhutan State Congress Party, an association of Lhotshampa—and externally with the Chinese occupation in the north.[11] The third king began by creating a new administrative system partly based on Western models and adapted to the pre-existing structures and traditions of the Dual System that had remained in place into the twentieth century.

Central to the reforms instigated by the third king was the first consolidation of laws in a recognizable legal code. The Supreme Laws are often presented as a codification of the traditional laws of Bhutan, and the foreword to the original law code describes a process of canvassing the elders for 'what was good and rejecting that which was not good'.[12] In reality, the drafters of the Supreme Laws drew widely on a range of non-indigenous sources, notably from India.[13] However, this apparent continuity with the past was significant for the legitimacy it provided the new national law code and its acceptance by the Bhutanese.

The language of the Supreme Laws draws on classical Tibetan, the language of religious texts, and this link with pre-existing literary forms is important. Rather than creating a rupture with the past and earlier, extant law texts, the Supreme Laws maintains through its language, rather than through the actual laws, the connection with the past, notably with the earlier laws introduced by the Zhabdrung who founded Bhutan as a unified country in the

---

[11] For a discussion on the development of Thailand, see, David Engel, *Code and Custom in a Thai Provincial Court: The Interactions of Formal and Informal Systems of Justice* (University of Arizona Press: Tucson, 1978) and David K. Wyatt, *Thailand: A Short History* (Yale University Press: New Haven and London, 1982).

[12] My translation is based on a copy of the original text of the Supreme Laws given to me by Michael Aris in March 1998. Royal Government of Bhutan, *Thrimszhung Chenmo*, Thimphu.

[13] This is, in my opinion, apparent in the sections dealing with land and restricting landholdings to twenty-five acres.

early seventeenth century.[14] As the national language, Dzongkha, developed over the past fifty years, subsequent legislation has been drafted and promulgated in the national language promoted from the 1960s. The role of Dzongkha as the official language, drawing as it does on its roots in classical, and therefore religious, language illustrates the intricate intertwining of the promotion of Dzongkha as the official national language since 1961 and the development of a homogenized political and legal vision of Bhutanese national identity since the 1950s.[15] Furthermore, for one of the most important authoritative texts issued from the political centre, the choice of language emphasized how the Bhutanese government imagined the Bhutanese State, which, despite the egalitarian vision expressed in the opening section of the law code, emphasized continuity with the past.[16] In both the foreword and the epilogue to the Supreme Laws, the language employs religious metaphors and imagery—a swirling sea of *dharma* protectors subduing the enemies of the 'Glorious Drukpa', praise to various religious figures and the noble lineage of 'bodhisattva' monarchs culminating in the third king and his enlightened reforms.[17] The image of the Bhutanese polity, founded by the Zhabdrung, blessed by the buddhas, draws on the language

---

[14] See, Aris, *Sources for the History of Bhutan*.

[15] For an excellent overview, see, Pommaret, 'The Birth of a Nation'. See also, two articles by Karma Ura: 'Decentralisation and Development in Medieval and Modern Bhutan', in M. Aris and M. Hutt (eds), *Bhutan: Aspects of Culture and Development* (Kiscadale Asia Research Series No.5: Gartmore, 1994); and, 'Tradition and Development', in F. Pommaret and C. Schicklgruber (eds), *Bhutan: Mountain Fortress of the Gods* (Serindia: London, 1997).

[16] Section OM AH HUM at the beginning of the Supreme Laws states that all Bhutanese, with the exception of the king, will be treated equally under the law. This is discussed further in Richard W. Whitecross, '"Keeping the Stream of Justice Pure": The Buddhicisation of Bhutanese Law?', in F. Benda Beckman, K. Benda Beckman, and A. Griffiths (eds), *Law and Anthropology in a Trans-national World*, (Berghahn Press: Oxford, 2009). Also, Richard W. Whitecross, 'The *Thrimzhung Chenmo* and the Emergence of the Contemporary Bhutanese Legal System', in K. Ura and S. Kinga (eds), *The Spider and the Piglet: Collected Papers on Bhutanese Society* (Centre for Bhutanese Studies: Thimphu, 2004).

[17] The term 'Glorious Drukpa' (Pelden Drukpa) continues to be used and can be found in the 2008 Constitution. A 'bodhisattva' is an enlightened being (a buddha) who chooses not to enter nirvana but remains to liberate all sentient beings from *samsara*.

and imagery of earlier texts and served to metaphorically link the new political and legal institutions with the Dual System, underscoring the continuing relevance to the Bhutanese authorities of the Dual System, and its place in the minds of ordinary Bhutanese.

The Monk Body: Religious Representation in the New Order

As part of the political reforms, the third king created a series of new institutions between 1953 and 1968. The first was the National Assembly. Established in 1953, the National Assembly (*Tshogdue Chenmo*) prior to its dissolution in 2007 had 150 members; 106 were elected representatives of the people, including six Royal Advisory Councillors, ten representatives of the Central Monk Body, ten elected Council of Ministers, and twenty-four nominated representatives of the government. The people's representatives were directly elected by the people of their respective constituencies through secret ballot.[18] The representatives of the government were nominated by the king from among senior civil servants. All the members, including those from the Central Monk Body, served for a term of three years. The speaker and the deputy speaker were elected by the National Assembly from among its members.

The Monk Body comprises the Central Monastic Body and the District Monastic Bodies. The representatives of the clergy were elected by the Central Monk Body and the concerned District Monk Bodies. The current strength of the Monastic Body is about 9,287 registered monks, and it is financed by an annual grant from the royal government.[19] The Central Monk Body is the sole arbiter on religious matters. His Holiness, the Je Khenpo, who shares the same rank as the king, is chosen from amongst high-ranking monks and acts as the head of the Central Monk Body. The Je Khenpo is assisted by five high-ranking monks (recently increased from four due to the Je Khenpo's increased public commitments).

The Royal Advisory Council (*Lodey Tshogdey*) was formally established in 1965 to advise the king and government ministers,

---

[18] Information drawn from the website of the National Assembly. http://www. nab.gov.bt (last accessed on 29 June 2010).

[19] According to the *Bhutan Observer*, 2 February 2007, this comprises 7,437 monks, 169 lams, 1,593 lay monks, and 88 nuns.

and to supervise the implementation of programmes and policies laid down by the National Assembly. Although formally established in 1965, the origins of the Royal Advisory Council can be traced back to the State Council that was created by the Zhabdrung in the seventeenth century. The Royal Advisory Council served as a consultative and advisory body. There were nine members of the Royal Advisory Council including the chairman. Six members are elected representatives of the public, two elected representatives of the clergy, and one nominated by the government who functions as a chairman of the Council. Thierry Mathou notes that 'having in the same body high ranking civil servants...former *chimis* (elected members of the National Assembly), businessmen and monks, is a good way to give the opportunity to various channels of influence... to participate in the decision making process'.[20]

By way of illustrating the role of the Monk Body in Bhutan before the reforms introduced by the 2008 Constitution, it is worth considering how young Bhutanese people were taught about its function and role within the Bhutanese political framework. In a school textbook published in 1999, it stated that the 'monastic establishment does not form part of the political structure of Bhutan'[21] yet in the same textbook, when describing the executive and the legislature, it unquestioningly noted monastic representation on the Royal Advisory Council and in the National Assembly. Furthermore, the text specifically states that 'the importance of the Buddhist tradition is...recognized in the provision for the guaranteed representation of the monastic establishment in the National Assembly, in the Royal Advisory Council and the Cabinet'.[22] This rather confused text suggests a sense of tension—a desire to keep the Monk Body removed from secular affairs yet unable to deny its presence in two major political forums and the centrality of Buddhism to Bhutanese political as well as religious identity.

I have focused on illustrating both the presence and the role of the Monk Body in the new political institutions, notably the National Assembly and the Royal Advisory Council. The inclusion of the

[20] See, Thierry Mathou, 'Bhutan: Political Reform in a Buddhist Monarchy', *Journal of Bhutan Studies*, (1999), 1(1): 123.

[21] Ibid., p. 75.

[22] Ibid., p. 76.

Monk Body in these new institutions was undoubtedly intentional, as was the resurrection of a long defunct advisory council originally instituted by the Zhabdrung. Just as secular and temporal affairs were intermingled between the seventeenth and the nineteenth centuries, the political reforms of the twentieth century did not seek to separate church and state. The Je Khenpos continued to exert authority over religious matters and did not participate directly in the political process; however, their views have undoubtedly been expressed in the National Assembly and in the Royal Advisory Council through the Central Monk Body representatives.

Although some Bhutanese officials claim that monastic representatives only spoke on religious matters, such claims must be very carefully scrutinized. Even a casual reading of the National Assembly debates reveals that the monastic representatives were far from silent. In a series of debates in the late 1990s, when other representatives called on the High Court to apply the death penalty, the monastic representatives declared that the use of death penalty in a Buddhist country was unthinkable.[23] Based on a close reading of the National Assembly debates, the contributions of the monastic representatives have, on occasion, acted as a guiding moral conscience, restraining more extreme reactions to problems. At other times they have displayed a deeply conservative response to new social conditions and to the effects of modernization on Bhutanese society and culture. However, it is necessary at this point to note that despite the intertwining of religious and temporal authority, it would be difficult to say that the laws promulgated, either under the Zhabdrung and his incarnations or under the monarchy, were 'Buddhist'. Here, an important distinction needs to be marked between Bhutan's Buddhist tradition and other religious communities in South Asia that have distinct religious laws, notably the Muslims and the Hindus. There are no specifically Buddhist religious laws—rather as French notes in respect of Tibetan laws, Bhutanese laws were and remain, 'based in Buddhism but secular in

---

[23] The debate is discussed in more depth in Richard W. Whitecross, *The Zhabdrung's Legacy: State Transformation, Law and Social Values in Contemporary Bhutan*, unpublished thesis, University of Edinburgh, 2002; and in Richard W. Whitecross, 'Signs of a Degenerate Age: *Chorten* and *Lhakhang* Robberies', *Journal of Bhutan Studies*, (2000), 2(2).

nature'.[24] Indeed, there are ongoing debates among comparative law scholars and other academics about to what extent it is possible to discuss 'Buddhist law'.[25]

Before turning to consider the Constitution, it is necessary to contextualize the political background to the shift, between 1998 and 2008, from absolute to constitutional monarchy. In addition to the political crises of the early 1990s between the Lhotshampa and the government, the Druk National Congress Party (DNC) was established by Rongtong Kuenlay, a Kheng from central Bhutan.[26] The DNC sought to promote unrest and disaffection among the other main ethnic group, the Sharchop, who are primarily located in the eastern districts of Bhutan. The DNC argued that the government did not share resources equally, either based on ethnicity or geographic location, and that the western districts received a disproportionately high amount of investment compared to the eastern ones. The DNC was crushed in the east during a campaign by the Royal Bhutan Army in 1997.[27] Following the campaign, a number of disaffected young men left Bhutan to avoid potential charges of treason being raised against them.

In June 1998, the fourth king, Jigme Sangye Wangchuck (reign: 1972–2006), surprised the Bhutanese people and external observers by transferring royal authority to an elected cabinet, effectively ending, at least on paper, direct royal government. In addition to these internal challenges, was the threat presented by the presence of guerrilla bases in remote areas of southeastern and southern Bhutan. From the early 1990s onwards, possibly slightly earlier, guerrillas from a variety of armed insurgent groups from the northeast region of India—ULFA–Bodo, KLO, and others—established camps

[24] Rebecca Redwood French, *The Golden Yoke: The Legal Cosmology of Buddhist Tibet* (Cornell University Press: Ithaca, NY, 1996).

[25] See, Andrew Huxley (ed.), *Thai Law, Buddhist Law: Essays on the Legal History of Thailand, Laos and Burma* (White Orchid Press: Bangkok, 1996).

[26] For a presentation of the problems that arose in the 1980s and 1990s, the main work is Michael Hutt, *Unbecoming Citizens: Culture, Nationhood, and the Flight of Refugees from Bhutan* (Oxford University Press: Oxford, 2003). Kheng is one of the twenty ethnic/linguistic minorities in Bhutan.

[27] AI Index: ASA 14/02/98 21 January 1998 Bhutan: 'Crack-down on 'anti-nationals' in the east'.

in southeast and southern Bhutan.[28] After years of negotiation between the government—notably the king—and the guerrillas, the Royal Bhutan Army and a militia force raised in 2003 launched an apparently brief campaign to drive the guerrillas out of their camps.

Political reform became imperative. Internal and external threats were recognized. At the same time, other changes were making their impact on Bhutanese society—notably, the creation of an educated youth and the intangible, yet real, effects of globalization. In the following section, I turn to look at the preparation and enactment of the first written constitution and the transformation of the role of the Central Monk Body. Implicit within this discussion is the role of Buddhism.

THE DRAFT CONSTITUTION AND BUDDHISM

In October 2001, the fourth king instructed the cabinet of ministers that Bhutan should have a written constitution. During three years following the king's *kasho* (royal decree) in 2001 and the creation of the Drafting Committee, the form and content of the Draft Constitution was a major source of speculation and deep concern among many Bhutanese. In this section, I discuss the main Articles from the written constitution published on 25 March 2005 and contrast the official version with an alternative version launched by the National Front for Democracy in Bhutan at the Mechi Bridge, on the border between Nepal and Bihar, on 17 July 2006.

The King's Kasho: Drafting The Constitution

Following the king's announcement that Bhutan should have a written constitution, a Drafting Committee of thirty-nine members was established under the chairmanship of the Chief Justice, Lyonpo Sonam Tobgye. The Drafting Committee was drawn from a broad cross-section of Bhutanese society and included two representatives

---

[28] ULFA is the acronym for the United Liberation Front of Assam. KLO is the acronym for the Kamtapur Liberation Organisation. Bodo/NDFB (National Democratic Front for Bodoland) refers to the tribal people in the North East region of India who are seeking to create an independent state. NDFB is one of a number of political organizations seeking independence.

of the Central Monk Body (there were an additional two monastic representatives representing other institutions) as well as one Lhotshampa representative. The Drafting Committee met on at least six occasions in various locations throughout Bhutan. At present, its deliberations and discussions are not available for us to follow the debates of the Drafting Committee, though they were recorded and transcribed. However, it was widely rumoured in Thimphu (rumour being one of the most important sources of information in the capital), that the Drafting Committee were split over two key issues. The first was the future role of the Central Monk Body and the other, whether or not Buddhism should be declared the State religion of Bhutan. In the absence of transcripts of the discussions, it is difficult to say how accurate these rumours were. However, it is probable, given that two of the four *lopons* (*lopon* means teacher) of the Monastic Body were on the Drafting Committee and the generally conservative nature of the National Assembly representatives, that the roles of Buddhism and the Central Monk Body in the new constitutional arrangements for Bhutan were highly contested.

After undergoing several rounds of revisions, including a review by K.K. Venugopal, an Indian constitutional expert, between October 2003 and June 2004, the Constitution was published on 26 March 2005. The Draft Constitution began with a Preamble, easily overlooked yet worth commenting briefly on. The Preamble was set within a *mandala*—an outer circle of fire, a *vajra* fence, a mantra in the stylized Sanskrit script known as Lentsa with dharma wheels punctuating the mantras. The Preamble states:

We, the people of Bhutan
    Blessed with the luminous benedictions of the Triple Gem, the protection of our guardian deities, the wisdom of our leaders, the everlasting fortunes of the Pelden Drukpa, and the command of His Majesty the Druk Gyalpo, Jigme Singye Wangchuck;
    Solemnly pledging ourselves to strengthen the sovereignty of Bhutan, to secure the blessing of liberty, to ensure justice and tranquillity and to enhance the unity, happiness and well being of the people for all time;
    Do hereby ordain and adopt this Constitution for the Kingdom of Bhutan on this...Day of the...Month of the Year...[29]

---

[29] Royal Government of Bhutan, *Draft Constitution*, Thimphu, Bhutan, 2005.

The opening statement, 'We, the people of Bhutan' is reminiscent of other constitutions and importantly suggests a shift in the location of sovereignty. The following paragraph contains a standard and familiar invocation of the three jewels of Buddhist refuge—the Buddha, the Dharma, and the Sangha. The protective deities referred to are a major focus in the daily and annual rituals of the Monk Body, who invoke and propitiate these deities on behalf of the Bhutanese State. It is important to recognize that this opening paragraph firmly orientates public understanding of the Constitution by explicit reference to Bhutan's Buddhist heritage and the Druk Kagyu tradition. These opening words are even more significant for the Constitution refrains from declaring Buddhism the official State religion, and the Monk Body ceases to be officially guaranteed representation in the new National Assembly.

Throughout the text there are prominent statements emphasizing the maintenance of the Dual System. However, the Dual System is redefined and its embodiment reconceived. The king, under Articles 2(2) and 3(2), is the head of the Dual System. The details of the new National Assembly, as the Lower House of a new bicameral structure, did provide for reserved seats for the Monk Body. The former Royal Advisory Council was transformed into a National Council, creating a new Upper House.[30] Following the election of twenty members of the National Council between December 2007 and January 2008, the remaining five members were appointed by the fifth king, Jigme Khesar Namgyal Wangchuk, in March 2008. No monastic representatives were appointed to the National Council, emphasizing the king's role in supporting the constitutional separation of religion and politics.

Article 3 of the Constitution, at least initially, provoked calls during public meetings for Buddhism to be declared the official religion of Bhutan. Indeed, one can perhaps see in the public debates some of the issues the Drafting Committee almost certainly had to address.

---

[30] Before the elections in 2007, the Bhutanese with whom I discussed the Constitution between 2001 and 2007 generally thought that the king would perhaps appoint under Article 10, Section 1(b), at least one, possibly two, prominent monastic figures nominated by the Central Monk Body. In fact, this has not been the case suggesting that the king is keen to ensure that the Monk Body is not involved in politics.

In *Kuensel*, at the time the only national newspaper, report of a public discussion between residents of the capital, Thimphu, and attended by the king and other members of the royal family in October 2005, speakers suggested that the spiritual heritage of Bhutan should be specifically described as 'Drukpa Kagyu and Nyingma' rather than as the more general 'Buddhism'.[31] Such statements reflect the more local understanding and approach to Buddhism in which the two main sects dominant in Bhutan provide the main points of reference for the majority of Bhutanese. Often referred to by the contraction 'Ka-Nying', it is precisely this phrase that was specifically used by the opposition groups in their alternative constitution.[32] The National Front for Democracy in Bhutan inserts in Article 3(2) the following sentence: 'Bhutan shall continue to be a Buddhist nation with the Kanying-Zungdrel existing in complete peace and harmony'. This alternative clause was possibly more in accord with popular sentiments than the official draft, referring as it does to both the Kagyu and the Nyingma traditions.

Other speakers during public debates on the Constitution argued that there should be no separation of religion and politics 'since Bhutan had prospered throughout history because of the harmony between religion and politics'. In response, the Chief Justice addressing the assembled people advised that the Drafting Committee had sought to look to the long-term future of the Constitution and decided that it was not appropriate to mention different sects. Indeed the Chief Justice stated that, on reflection, the Drafting Committee considered it essential to separate church from state to ensure religion and politics 'flourish *without interference* from each other'.[33] The remarks by the Chief Justice emphasized the importance placed on ensuring the effective separation of State and religion.

When the draft was released, the initial reaction from the populace, as presented by *Kuensel*, was one of deep concern that Buddhism was

[31] *Kuensel*, 29 October 2005, 'A constitution for the Future of Bhutan', http://www.kuenselonline.com/2011/?p=673 (last accessed on 13 May 2012).

[32] See Table 4A.2 for excerpts from the alternative version of the Constitution launched by the National Front for Democracy in Bhutan.

[33] *Kuensel*, 29 October 2005, 'A constitution for the Future of Bhutan', http://www.kuenselonline.com/2011/?p=673 (last accessed on 13 May 2012). (Emphasis added.)

not to be the declared official religion of Bhutan. There was less publicly voiced surprise over the absence of any stated political role for the Central Monk Body. On one level, the overwhelming majority of people respect the current Je Khenpo and his popularity is highlighted by the long queues of people who line the road from Punakha to Thimphu each year to receive his blessing, turning what would otherwise have been just a two- to three-hour car journey into a two-day event. Yet at the same time, many Bhutanese are critical of the Monk Body which continues to receive State support when there are other private religious institutions and religious figures that are revered but neither receive state assistance nor participate in national politics. Others, especially those from eastern Bhutan, argued that the attitude of the Druk Kagyu Monk Body towards Nyingma lamas and practitioners was divisive and that a total withdrawal of State support would be widely supported. It is hard to gauge the depth of such feelings; however, it is important to point out that tensions based on rivalries between the two Buddhist traditions in Bhutan were probably the basis for the rejection of State-funding for the Monk Body in the alternative Constitution proposed by the opposition. These tensions were rarely discussed outside the privacy of the household, and seldom touched upon by Western writers more attuned to the official views from Thimphu. During a recent brief visit to Bhutan, I discussed the changes introduced by the Constitution with a highly educated Nyingma abbot. From his perspective, relations have significantly improved between the Monk Body and the non–State supported institutions. The easing of relations between the two traditions, with neither given prominence, may well reflect the desire by the constitutional drafters to avoid perpetuating subtle divisions within Bhutanese society.

Separation of Church and State: The Dual System Re-Imagined

Prior to the 2008 Constitution, the Dual System was treated as either having fallen into desuetude or as a continuing legacy from the Zhabdrung. According to the school text cited earlier, 'with the creation of the hereditary monarchy, there was no longer a dual authority in the administration of the state'.[34] Therefore, the Constitution,

---

[34] Royal Government of Bhutan, *Bhutan Civics* (Ministry of Education: Thimphu, 1999), p. 75.

notably in its revised form, emphasizes a major transformation in the relationship between the monastic body and the State. There are no special reservations or specific provision for monastic representation in either the National Council or the National Assembly. There was some debate over whether or not the king, exercising his power under Article 10(1)(b), would choose to appoint a representative from the monastic body to the National Council. However, the king did not appoint any monastic representatives. A similar appointment could, in theory, have been made to the Privy Council. Instead, the king has adhered to Article 3(3) that stresses that 'religion remains separate from politics in Bhutan'. It is also important to note the references in both the official and alternative Constitutions to the use of ceremonies introduced by the Zhabdrung to mark the opening and closing of Parliament. Article 10(6) states: 'At the commencement of each session of Parliament, the Druk Gyalpo shall be received in a joint sitting of Parliament with Chibdrel Ceremony and the session shall be opened with a Zhug-drel-phunsum tshog pai ten drel, and each session shall conclude with the Tashi mon-lam'.

These ceremonies, part of the *driglam namzha* or code of etiquette introduced in the seventeenth century and actively promoted since the late 1980s as a key part of Bhutanese identity and customs, are essentially Buddhist in their ethos.[35] Accordingly, although not declared the official religion of the country, Buddhism as the State religion is embedded in other ways in the Constitution.

Under Article 3(5), the Je Khenpo's authority is specifically restricted to religious affairs and the organization of the Monk Body. Rather, echoing the tenor of the *Thrimzhung Chenmo*, it is the monarch who embodies the Dual System. Article 2(2) specifically states that 'the Chhoe-sid-nyi of Bhutan shall be unified in the person of the Druk Gyalpo who, as a Buddhist, shall be the upholder of the Chhoe-sid'. The alternative Constitution proposes something similar and yet different—that the monarch be viewed as 'unifying' not the Dual System; rather the 'Kanying-Zungrel' or 'Co-existence of Kagyupa and Nyingmapa of the Mahayana Buddhism shall be

---

[35] The *chibdrel* is a procession to receive and honour an important person. The *zhug-drel phunsum* seeks to attract the three blessings of 'grace, glory and wealth' during formal occasions and the final are prayers for the fulfilment of 'good wishes and aspirations'.

unified in the person of the monarch'. Mention of the Dual System is conspicuously absent. Instead the emphasis is on the two main Buddhist sects in Bhutan and appears to reflect a different approach to the Dual System that seeks to balance the spiritual role of the Druk Kagyu with that of the Nyingma.

What of secularism? As a concept, it is a relatively new one for educated Bhutanese, many of whom have studied in India and may be aware of debates around secularism in India. For the majority of Bhutanese mainly living in rural communities, secularism and the doctrine of separation of church and state are unfamiliar concepts. How meaningful secularism or its application will be depends on two factors: (a) the role of the Supreme Court and (b) the acceptance and equality of minority religions in Bhutan. As the guardian of the Constitution, the recently created Supreme Court will function as the constitutional court. As such, it will be responsible for interpreting Article 3. The Drafting Committee, and, in particular, the Chief Justice who was its chairman, would have been conscious of the critical role of the Supreme Court in establishing and upholding the freedoms and democratic values that the Constitution espouses. The decision to specifically not declare Buddhism as the official religion and to remove the political representation of the Monk Body probably indicates a desire to separate church and state in a new, democratic Bhutan. Yet, it remains to be seen how far the Supreme Court will support secularism, as it develops, in Bhutan. Or will the Supreme Court in its future considerations take into account, or be swayed by, public sentiments? The judiciary has been active not only in modernizing its procedures and formalizing the training of its personnel based on Western models, but also, as already noted, in attempting to ground Bhutanese law in its Buddhist heritage. However, the appointment of the former Chief Justice, Lyonpo Sonam Tobgye, as Supreme Justice of the Supreme Court in November 2009 suggests that the Supreme Court will not be swayed by public sentiment. Rather, although in private life a devout Buddhist, the new Supreme Justice will, based on his comments during the public consultation on the Draft Constitution, uphold, if required, the separation of religion and politics.

On the second issue of equal status for all religions, it should be noted that while the king is to be regarded as the protector of all religions (Article 3(2)) and there is freedom of belief (Article 7(3)), there is a prohibition on proselytizing. The Bhutanese do not view Hindus as different—there is a tendency to describe Buddhism and Hinduism as being closely linked, and therefore Hinduism as a religion is unproblematic. It is not uncommon to see sadhus wandering through villages and being offered food or money by non-Hindu villagers. There are no published figures that accurately provide the division of the Bhutanese population between Buddhists and Hindus. It is possible that the Buddhist majority form about 70 to 75 per cent and the Lhotshampa (mainly, though not exclusively Hindu) about 25 to 30 per cent of the population. During discussions with several Lhotshampa descended from migrants from eastern Nepal, although nominal Hindu, they noted that 'we are born Hindu, but die Buddhist'. This reflected not a need to become Buddhist but rather a syncretic approach to religious belief and practice. This approach is also found in the ritual practices of ordinary Bhutanese which reflect Bon or non-Buddhist origins. Of course, it has to be noted that according to Hutt, in the early 1990s, Sanskrit schools were closed and Hindu temples damaged during the conflict between the Lhotshampa and the royal government.[36] However, while religious identity can be the cause of communal strife elsewhere in South Asia, religious difference has not been the primary cause of conflict. Indeed, there was historically probably more tension between eastern Bhutanese—who follow the Nyingma tradition of Himalayan Buddhism—and the Druk Kagyu tradition than between Buddhists and the Hindus. This tension between the two Himalayan Buddhist traditions has dissipated over the last ten years. Rather, mirroring concerns in Sri Lanka discussed by Deepika Udagama in this volume (Chapter 5), the problem lies rather with perceptions of Christianity and with proselytization.

Bhutan, as with other parts of South Asia, has been targeted by various Christian missionary organizations. To date, the majority of converts are from the Lhotshampa community, notably after the tensions in the late 1980s and early 1990s. As a result, the act of conversion carries with it political undertones. A common misapprehension is that active proselytization would, if permitted,

[36] See, Huxley (ed.), *Thai Law, Buddhist Law*.

seriously undermine belief in Buddhism thereby undermining Bhutanese cultural values. I suggest that this may be extended to include a concern that conversion to Christianity may be perceived as potentially introducing an alternative political outlook that would challenge or question the existing order. This is perhaps the rationale in the Constitution that political parties based on ethnicity, language, or religion will not be permitted in Bhutan. The implications of these caveats on the formation of political parties hint at a deep concern over potential sources of internal conflict—ethnicity, regionalism, and religion.

Bhutan is an ethnic mosaic of twenty minority languages and ethnic groups. The only non-Buddhist group are the Lhotshampa. The other two largest minorities are the Sharchop in eastern Bhutan and the Ngalong in western Bhutan. Below these three main ethnic/linguistic groups are seventeen ethnic/linguistic groups that are Buddhist and range in size from a few hundred to several thousands. These groups share a cultural and religious identity with the Ngalong and Sharchop. Following the conflicts in the 1990s between the royal government and members of both the Lhotshampa and Sharchop communities, the Bhutanese State has emphasized a shared, national identity respectful of minority cultural and linguistic traditions. Equally, the Bhutanese authorities are aware of the problems experienced elsewhere in South Asia as a result of ethnic, regional, and religious differences.[37] Indeed, the presence of guerrillas fighting for an independent state in the northeastern territories of India had a direct impact on the eastern districts of Bhutan. Based on its own experience of internal conflicts as well as communal violence and civil war elsewhere in South Asia, and due to increasingly encountering and engaging with international legal and political norms, the Bhutanese State has sought to transform the political landscape without creating division within its heterogeneous population.[38]

---

[37] A 'One Nation, One People' policy was introduced in the mid-1980s and is often referred to as a cause of the conflict between the royal government and the Lhotshampa in the early 1990s.

[38] I think it is important to recognize the complexity of Bhutanese society. The emergence of a shared Bhutanese identity is ongoing and my sense is that this was recognized by the fourth and fifth kings and the Drafting Committee.

From Elected to Sacral Monarchy

The establishment of the monarchy in 1907, based on a contract signed by the leading figures of the period, drew on and developed notions of authority and legitimacy recognized within the Bhutanese system. Although it is usually described as an election, there is little documentary evidence to support this claim.[39] During the National Assembly in 1999, representatives speaking about the king's transfer of powers and the right of the National Assembly to remove the monarch called for the country to reaffirm the contract of monarchy.[40] Yet, the Bhutanese State has been transformed, the power of the monarch passed (in theory, if not entirely in practice) first to a cabinet of ministers and, since March 2008, to an elected government. However, in the redistribution of power, authority, and especially the moral authority of the monarch, rather than of the Royal House, has been arguably re-emphasized. As provided for in the Supreme Law, *kasho* and *kaydon* issued by the crown cannot be scrutinized and are effectively law. Royal *kasho* continue to shape and direct government policy and it remains unclear from the Constitution how future royal *kasho* will be treated now that the Constitution is in force.

Even the most cursory reading of the 2008 Constitution will provide the reader with a strong sense of the centrality of the monarchy, or the Druk Gyalpo, to the reformed political framework. The term 'Druk Gyalpo', King of Bhutan, is the most common term found in the entire Constitution. By contrast, the term 'Buddhism' appears only twice. There are signs that the nature of monarchy has been transformed from the mid-1990s onwards. The fourth king became associated not only with the exercise of temporal authority but as possessing spiritual authority as well.[41] Although this sacral

---

[39] For discussion on the establishment of the monarchy and the Wangchcuck dynasty, see, Michael Aris, *The Raven Crown: The Origins of Buddhist Monarchy in Bhutan* (Serindia Press: London, 1998).

[40] 77th National Assembly Supplement, *Kuensel*, 17 September 1999. This is the theme of much of the reporting.

[41] Thierry Mathou notes: '…the current evolution will enhance the King's sacred dimension' in Thierry Mathou, 'Bhutan: Political Reform in a Buddhist Monarchy', *Journal of Bhutan Studies*, (1999), 1(1): 130.

dimension of the monarch was denied by Bhutanese officials, for many Bhutanese this description of the fourth king as a '*bodhisattva*', as well as his late father, is accurate.[42] Once, following a brief speech by the fourth king encouraging Bhutanese to be compassionate and caring towards people with HIV and AIDS, I was struck by the impact of his message. Watching with an extended Bhutanese family whose walls were covered with images of the fourth king, I was informed by a friend's father that the speech and the king's concern for the unfortunate showed his 'bodhisattva nature'. This is an important, if subtle, transformation. It arguably builds on the 'religious' lineage of the monarch, as well as raising him to an equally important 'spiritual' level as the Zhabdrung's reincarnation. Indeed, this religious pedigree was specifically highlighted in a newspaper report of the Crown Prince's meeting with the public in Lhuntse when he was described as the 'nineteenth generation' of Padmalingpa. The fifteenth century treasure finder (*terton*) Padmalingpa is arguably the most important Bhutanese religious figure, with the exception of the Zhabdrung, and his sons established various 'religious lineages' from which the Wangchuck dynasty is descended.[43]

The Zhabdrung's Legacy

The invocation of the Dual System in the Constitution demonstrates that it retains a saliency in contemporary Bhutan. In the background, the influences of the Zhabdrung and of Buddhism remain discernible—providing a comforting, if fragile, sense of continuity and shared meanings. However, the Constitution does not enshrine Buddhism as the State religion and specifically removes, for the first time in Bhutanese history, the political role of the Monk Body. The threads of continuity that run through Bhutanese philosophy and practice cannot mask the reality of change. The awareness that

[42] The fourth king abdicated in December 2006 and the Crown Prince became the fifth king.

[43] See, Michael Aris, *The Raven Crown*. Informants mentioned a prayer written by the current Je Khenpo that uses religious imagery in its praise of His Majesty Jigme Singye Wangchuck. Unfortunately, I was unable to locate a copy of the prayer though it appears to have been widely available.

familiar structures have outlived their time may come as a shock. Yet, perhaps it is in the new soil of change and radical breaks with the familiar that new concepts such as democracy and the rule of law can move from veneers to become embedded in local contexts in meaningful ways.

In my opinion, the Constitution provides a vision of Bhutan—especially with the removal of the Monk Body from the political process—that is quite distinct. Radical change does not necessarily mean a sudden event. Bhutan has been undergoing a steady, at times difficult, process of change. The images of Bhutan as a *be-yul* or Buddhist sanctuary underscore a desire to emphasize continuity, yet many of the structures and institutional frameworks hint at something still only being tentatively acknowledged—the Dual System and its influence have continued to determine the general perspective on Bhutanese society and State, even though the social fabric and, arguably, if admittedly quite slowly, the realities of political power have changed.

The Zhabdrung's political and legal frameworks have been transformed. Yet, from the period of unification in the early seventeenth century onwards, there have been sustained attempts to create a national culture with a set of values universally accepted (within Bhutan). These have been encapsulated in the concept of the Dual System as it emerged in Bhutan. These same values are now under pressure from the impact of urbanization and the emergence of new demands and desires by an educated middle class. The emergence of the modern nation-state of Bhutan reflects the close relationship between the political and the legal spheres. Law and the evolving legal framework have played a constitutive part in the creation of contemporary Bhutan. The 2008 Constitution encapsulates this relationship.

In this essay, I have attempted to suggest that the role of the Monk Body in Bhutan is undergoing a radical shift, though not as radical as some opponents of the government desire. Indeed, as I discussed earlier in this essay, even among Bhutanese who support the government there are privately expressed views that the Monk Body should no longer be supported by the State. We are aware that institutions can and do possess a certain tenacity, and in Bhutan the establishment of the monarchy in 1907 did not affect the Monk Body. The Monk Body was central to legitimatizing the new secular authority of the monarchy through the imagined and performative continuity of the Dual System naturalizing the transfer of the secular powers of the Desi and, I would argue, the religious prestige of the Zhabdrung to the new monarch. With the social and political transformations introduced by the third king, we arguably see an implicit shift—the Monk Body, with its emerging representation in the new political institutions, became openly able to comment on and influence laws and state policies.[44] Its presence in the new institutions and the ongoing control over the religious life of the country offered the ordinary Bhutanese a symbol of continuity with the Zhabdrung and the past during a period of major social transformation.

CONCLUSION: CONSTITUTION AS DEMOCRATIC FOUNDATION

This essay has approached constitutionalism, religion, and secularism in Bhutan with due reference to Bhutanese history and its religious and cultural identity. Bhutan in the early 1950s lacked the political and, more notably, the legal infrastructure that postcolonial states in South Asia either inherited or created on gaining independence. The move towards a recognizable modern constitution was slow. The majority of Bhutanese did not seek political reform or demand a constitution—a contrast to the popular movements in neighbouring Nepal in the 1950s and 1990. The impetus for the creation of the Constitution was from the fourth king. This approach reflects the top–down nature of reforms since the early 1950s and the major social, economic, and political changes introduced by the third king. In this essay, I have chosen to foreground a major, if potentially overlooked, change—the separation of church and state and the transformation of Buddhism

---

[44] See, Richard W. Whitecross, 'Buddhicisation of Bhutanese Law'. See also, Richard W. Whitecross, 'Transgressing the Law: Karma, Theft and Its Punishment', *Revues d'études Tibétaines,* (2008), Issue 13: 45–74; Richard W. Whitecross, 'Bhutan', in S. Tajic (ed.), *Countries at the Crossroads: A Survey of Democratic Governance* (Rowman & Littlefield Publishers, Inc.: Maryland, 2007).

from 'state religion' to 'spiritual heritage'. This disestablishment of Buddhism as the official State religion, as I have sought to outline here, marks a radical shift. Religions, including Buddhism, have been used and are used to promote particular nationalist or communal interests. As I touched upon briefly in my Introduction, the Bhutanese constitutional drafters chose, I believe, to explicitly avoid religion (Buddhism) being politicized and thereby used to divide Bhutanese society.

While other essays in this volume discuss conversion, religious laws, and communities, and reservations for specific minorities, I have only touched in passing on these themes. This is partly for the simple reason that they do not apply to Bhutan or that at present we must wait to see what cases arise that deal with conversion or, more specifically, the prohibition against proselytization. Rather, my essay is, as is Mara Malagodi's essay on Nepal in the present volume (Chapter 3), concerned with the move towards a participatory democracy in Bhutan. The disestablishment of Buddhism as the State religion and the exclusion of Buddhist religious figures from politics was arguably an important and necessary step towards creating a new civil space for political debate and dissent that minimized at least the relevancy of religion or religious tradition.

Unlike Nepal, Bhutan is still a fledgling democracy. The contestation of democracy in Nepal and its civil war have provided the Nepalese with a vocabulary and understanding of politics that is still emerging in Bhutan. However, Nepalese democracy is not a model that the Bhutanese will wish to follow. With the high level of university-educated Bhutanese studying in India and, more recently, in Thailand, both India and Thailand may prove to be role models that the Bhutanese will look towards. The Thai model of democratic constitutional monarchy, in 2010, looked tarnished, yet as the only other extant Buddhist monarchy, will continue to be an important model. It was to India that the Drafting Committee looked for advice on the Draft Constitution and with the ongoing transformation of the Bhutanese judiciary—with legally trained judges replacing those who had received no formal legal training—Indian constitutional law may be, as described by Jacobsohn and Shankar in this volume (Chapter 6), a 'looming presence'.

ANNEXES

Table 4A.1 Key Sections of the 2008 Constitution of Bhutan

Article No.	2008 Constitution of Bhutan[45]
2: The Institution of Monarchy	1. His Majesty, the Druk Gyalpo, is the Head of State and the symbol of unity of the kingdom and of the people of Bhutan. 2. The Chhoe-sid-nyi of Bhutan shall be unified in the person of the Druk Gyalpo who, as a Buddhist, shall be the upholder of the *Chhoe-sid*.
3: Spiritual Heritage	1. Buddhism is the spiritual heritage of Bhutan, which promotes, among others the principles and values of peace, non-violence, compassion, and tolerance. 2. [Bhutan is a country of Chhoe-sid and, in keeping with this tradition, (deleted in Second version published on 18th August 2005) and] the Druk Gyalpo is the protector of all religions. 3. It shall be the responsibility of religious institutions and personalities to promote the spiritual heritage of the country while also ensuring that religion remains separate from politics in Bhutan. Religious institutions and personalities shall remain above politics. 4. The Druk Gyalpo shall, on recommendation of the Four Lopons, appoint a learned and respected monk ordained in accordance with the Druk-lu (the tradition of the Drukpa Kagyu established by the Zhabdrung Ngawang Namgyal), blessed with the nine qualities of a spiritual master and accomplished in *ked-dzog*, as the Je Khenpo. 5. His Holiness the Je Khenpo shall, on the recommendation of the Dratshang Lhentshog, appoint monks blessed with the nine qualities of a spiritual master and accomplished in *ked-dzog* as the Four Lopons.

[45] Includes in italics sentences deleted from the first draft published on 25 March 2005.

	6. The member of the Dratshang Lhentshog shall comprise: (a) His Holiness the Je Khenpo as Chairman; (b) The Four Lopons of the Central Monk Body; and (c) The Secretary of the Dratshang Lhentshog who shall be a civil servant.
	7. The Zhung Dratshang and Rabdeys shall continue to receive adequate funds and other facilities from the State.
10: Parliament	6. At the commencement of each session of Parliament, the Druk Gyalpo shall be received in a joint sitting of Parliament with Chibdrel Ceremony and the session shall be opened with a *Zhug-drel-phunsum tshog pai ten drel*, and each session shall conclude with the *Tashi mon-lam*.
11: National Council	1. The National Council shall consist of twenty-five members comprising: (a) one member elected by the voters in each of the twenty Dzongkhags; and (b) five eminent persons nominated by the Druk Gyalpo. 3. All candidates from membership to the National Council shall neither belong to nor have affiliation to any political party.

Table 4A.2 Alternative Constitution Proposes by Exiled Opposition Groups

(Selected Articles from the alternative Draft Constitution launched by the National Front for Democracy in Bhutan on 17 July 2006, Mechi Bridge, border of Nepal and Bihar, India.)

Article No.	Alternative Draft
2: The Institution of Monarchy	1. His Majesty the Druk Gyalpo is the head of State and symbol of unity of the Kingdom and of the people of Bhutan.

(Cont'd)

Table 4A.2 (*Cont'd*)

Article No.	Alternative Draft
	2. Kanying-Zungdrel or co-existence of Kagyupa and Nyingmapa of the Mahayana Buddhism shall be unified in the person of the Druk Gyalpo who, as a Buddhist, shall be the upholder of the State religion, while other religions shall enjoy respective supremacy as a secular State and manage under respective trusts.
3: Spiritual Heritage	1. Buddhism is the spiritual heritage of Bhutan, which promotes, among others, the principles and values of peace, non-violence, compassion, and tolerance. All religions will have equivalence in Bhutan.
	2. Bhutan shall continue to be a Buddhist nation with Kanying Zungdrel existing in complete peace and harmony. The Druk Gyalpo shall be the protector of all religions.
	3. Bhutan shall respect secularism. All the religious institutions shall function under respective charity trusts.
	4. The Je Khenpo shall receive his *dar* from the Punakha macchen as per tradition.

CHAPTER FIVE

The Democratic State and Religious Pluralism

Comparative Constitutionalism and Constitutional Experiences of Sri Lanka

Deepika Udagama

INTRODUCTION

There is no denying that South Asia is one of the most colourful places on the earth. The colours come from the rich diversity of its peoples. The various hues added on by the multi-ethnic, multi-religious, multi-lingual dimensions of its peoples make for a beautiful mosaic, made up of the sum of its individual parts—the parts representing the diversity within the South Asian states. All too often, though, the mosaic is terribly fragmented. The task of keeping it all together, while retaining the integrity of the individual parts, is a huge challenge. The modern histories of the various South Asian countries bear witness to that.

The question then is, how do we keep it all together? As our countries modernize, embracing democracy, the rule of law, protection of human rights, and so on, answers to those challenges are sought through constitutional schemes. So, which constitutional scheme will deliver the magical answer? Can the South Asian constitutional experiences provide answers at all? Should we appeal to a larger overarching set of norms? The questions call for a major comparative study.

This essay, however, focuses on a less ambitious project. It intends to examine the postcolonial constitutional experiences of one South Asian nation—Sri Lanka—relating to religious pluralism, or the lack of it. Despite high social indicators, Sri Lanka, home to a multi-ethnic and multi-religious society, has had a troubled history in dealing with issues of pluralism. That troubled history exploded into a protracted secessionist war in 1983. The fault line of the majority–minority tension and the ensuing armed conflict has clearly been ethnicity, with the issue of language rights being one of the central grievances. Contrary to popular belief, religion has not figured as a factor informing the move for secession.

However, the constitutional provisions in both the Republican Constitutions of Sri Lanka (of 1972 and 1978), which accord to Buddhism—the religion of the bulk of majority Sinhalese—the foremost place, have been a sensitive issue among minority groups, and have certainly added to a larger sense of grievance arising from other issues. The sensitivities are particularly strong as the first republican constitution (1972) discarded the express provision for the protection of religious groups and other communities contained in the Independence Constitution (the Soulbury Constitution).

A more recent development that has aggravated nascent religious sensitivies is the violent opposition to activities of evangelical Christian groups and a consequential move to adopt an anti-conversion law that seeks to criminalize 'unethical' conversions. Interestingly, Buddhist and Hindu organizations have joined hands in pushing for this legislation fearing encroachment into their respective flocks by a 'common enemy'. The tension that surrounded this saga gave rise to fears of a religious fault line developing alongside the violent ethnic divide.

What could be the constitutional responses to these troubling developments? This essay will examine the jurisprudence of the Supreme Court of Sri Lanka on the various provisions relating to religion in the Independence Constitution and the two Republican Constitutions of 1972 and 1978. In recent years, in particular, the apex court has delivered contradictory judgments, some recognizing constitutional protection of religious pluralism, while others have adopted very restrictive views. The examination of those developments in light of comparative South Asian experiences and, at a broader level, of international human rights obligations will, it is hoped, highlight the constitutional challenges and, indeed, the reforms that ought to be put in place. Some thoughts on the vlaue of comparative constitutionalism, in the context of Sri Lanka's experiences that are discussed in the essay, will be presented in the concluding section.

RELIGIOUS FREEDOM: SOUTH ASIAN EXPERIENCES AND INTERNATIONAL HUMAN RIGHTS LAW PERSPECTIVES

All South Asian states have embraced democracy at present—at least notionally so. One of the major challenges facing democratic states is how to respect and ensure pluralism. The centrality accorded to the concept of the autonmous individual in liberal democratic theory necessarily requires a political environment which guarantees choices—choices not only relating to political thought, but also vis-à-vis cultural and social choices. Pluralism reigns when choices can be made freely and when the choices we make are recognized and respected on an equal footing. One of the most fundamental choices demanded by human society relates to the right of worship. Historically, and also at present times, those seeking freedom from religious persecution have catalysed political reform. That struggle has also deeply influenced the evolution of international human rights norms.

Modern constitutions in heterogenous societies have grappled with the question of how best to ensure religious pluralism, and continue to do so in view of new challenges. Even mature democracies have not adopted a uniform model, with some embracing secularism, while others still continue to recognize a State religion while assiduously providing constitutional guarantees of freedom of religion. In an era of heightened identity politics, the search for best practices and ideal models has become a difficult task.

Before moving on to examine the South Asian constitutional efforts in this regard, an assessment of international human rights norms is in order. They represent an overarching scheme of values that bind states, and as the Preamble to the Universal Declaration of Human Rights (1948)[1] so eloquently exhorts, amounts to a 'standard of achievement for all organs of society'. Today, it could be argued,

---

[1] General Assembly Resolution 217A(III) of 10 December 1948.

that the measure of constitutionalism is determined to a great extent by whether governance comports with universal human rights norms.

International Human Rights Law Perspectives

A thread that runs through all human rights debates and instruments is the Right to Equality and non-discrimination. While the concept of equality has wider connotations, the concept of non-discrimination entails prohibiting discrimination on recognized grounds ('suspect classifications', as US jurisprudence would have it). The United Nations Charter (1945) and all major international human rights instruments (including regional human rights instruments) oppose discrimination on the grounds of religion or belief. Note that the protection is afforded to non-believers as well.

Ensuring religious pluralism is a foundational principle of the United Nations. Promoting respect for human rights of all without discrimination on the basis of race, sex, language or religion is a principle that runs throughout the UN Charter (1945).[2] Provisions of the Universal Declaration of Human Rights (UDHR) (1948)[3], International Covenant on Civil and Political Rights (ICCPR) (1966)[4], and the UN Declaration on the Elimination of All Forms of Intolerance and of Discrimination Based on Religion or Belief (1981)[5] outline the core international human rights law norms on freedom of religion or belief. The UN Declaration on the Rights of Persons Belonging to National, Ethnic, Religious and Linguistic Minorities (1992)[6] articulates the group rights dimension of, *inter alia,* religious minorities.

The relevant UDHR and ICCPR provisions (Article 18 of each) recognize a broad guarantee of the 'right to freedom of thought, conscience and religion'. The right includes the right to adopt ('change' is used in the UDHR) a religion of one's choice and to

---

[2] See, Charter of the United Nations (1945) Articles 1(3), 13(1)(b), 56 read with 55(c), 62(2) and 76(c).

[3] See, note 1.

[4] General Assembly Resolution 2200 A(XXI) of 16 December 1966, entered into force on 23 March 1976.

[5] General Assembly Resolution 36/55 of 25 November 1981.

[6] General Assembly Resolution 47/135 of 18 December 1992.

engage in religious practices alone or in association with others. Religious activity in the form of teaching, practice, worship and observance are specifically mentioned as protected conduct. The right to thought, conscience and religion is absolute, meaning that no limitation can be imposed in enjoying these rights. Such rights also cannot be derogated from during periods of Emergency. However, the right of manifestation of religion or belief is circumscribed by the ICCPR when such limitations are prescribed by law and are necessary to protect public safety, order, health, morals, or the fundamental rights and freedoms of others. It also contains a stricture on the use of coercion that impedes the right to freely have or adopt a religion (Article 18(3)).

The Declaration on Religious Discrimination reiterates the same normative framework. It declares religious discrimination as 'an affront to human dignity' and a disavowal of the principles of the UN Charter. The significant contribution of the Declaration is the definition of 'intolerance and discrimination based on religion or belief'.[7] Further, it prohibits religious discrimination by both State and private parties. States are required to take legislative action to prevent discrimination and take 'all appropriate measures' to combat religious intolerance.

The above international instruments deal with religious freedom essentially as an individual right. The Declaration on Minorities focuses on the group rights dimensions, articulating rights of persons as members of a minority group. It stipulates both negative (for example, non-discrimination) and positive obligations (for example, creating favourable conditions for the enjoyment of rights of minorities) of States. It recognizes the need to permit minorities to effectively participate in decision-making concerning them, both nationally and regionally. It does so cautiously, adding that such participation shall not be incompatible with national legislation (Article 2(3)). The Declaration has been criticized for being minimalist. But it provides a framework within which the rights regime can be expanded.

[7] For the purposes of the present Declaration, the expression 'intolerance and discrimination based on religion or belief' means any distinction, exclusion, restriction, or preference based on religion or belief and having as its purpose or as its effect nullification or impairment of the recognition, enjoyment, or exercise of human rights and fundamental freedoms on an equal basis (Article 2.2).

Article 27 of the ICCPR which, unlike the Declarations, is legally binding on States Parties, declares: 'In those States in which ethnic, religious or linguistic minorities exist, persons belonging to such miniorities shall not be denied the right, in community with the other members of their group, to enjoy their own culture, to profess and practice their own religion, or to use their own language.'

Despite this normative framework, international law is silent on the type of constitutional arrangements or forms of State structures that ought to be put in place to ensure the protection of religious freedom, or for that matter, the larger issue of protecting minority rights. This is not surprising as international law does not prescribe national arrangements, permitting a 'margin of appreciation' in that regard. However, States cannot plead domestic laws as a defence for not fulfilling international obligations.[8] The expectation of international law is that States will fulfill their international obligations by taking appropriate action as they think fit.

It is significant that international human rights law does not reject the concept of State religion. Instead, what is sought to be achieved is religious freedom for all even where a State religion is recognized. The General Comment adopted by the UN Human Rights Committee (the treaty body established by the ICCPR to supervise its implementation) on freedom of thought, conscience, and religion authoritatively declares that position and delineates protection to be afforded to those who do not belong to the State religion.[9] The stipulated position of the Committee's interpretation clearly does

---

[8] Vienna Convention on the Law of Treaties (1969) Part III, http://untreaty.un.org/ilc/texts/instruments/english/conventions/1_1_1969.pdf (last accessed on 17 July 2012).

[9] The fact that a religion is recognized as a State religion or that it is established as official or traditional or that its followers comprise the majority of the population, shall not result in any impairment of the enjoyment of any of the rights under the Covenant [ICCPR] including Articles 18 and 27, nor in any discrimination against adherents to [sic] other religions or non-believers. In particular, certain measures discriminating against the latter, such as measures restricting eligibility for government service to members of the predominant religion or giving economic privileges to them or imposing special restrictions on the practice of other faiths, are not in accordance with the prohibition of discrimination based on religion or belief and the guarantee of equal protection under Article 26. (General Comment 22 adopted at the forty-eighth session of the UN Human Rights Committee (1993),

not require the separation of State and religion. This may come as a disappointment to committed secularists, including the author. It is certainly a tall order for any system of government which recognizes a State religion to pay heed to that feature and also to ensure that 'others' get to enjoy all their rights without hindrance. The thrust of the international normative framework is that irrespective of the State–religion nexus in a given system the State is obligated to recognize and protect the religious freedom of all (including non-believers) without discrimination.

South Asian experiences in this regard too, reflect diverse policies and diverse degrees of success, depending on the political history of each country and their social and cultural milieux.

South Asian Experiences

Many great religious traditions emerged from South Asia including Hinduism and Buddhism. The people of South Asia represent almost all the major religions in the world.

Libertarians would maintain that India has shown a great degree of political maturity by embracing secularism as a fundamental constitutional principle. In fact, through judicial fiat secularism is today considered an essential component of the basic structure of the constitution that cannot be changed except through political revolution. However, secularism is not without its critics among the Indian intelligentsia.[10]

Jawarharlal Nehru, the first prime minister of India, was a committed secularist. He idealized a secular constitutional order for the newly independent India. However, his vision of secularism was different to the 'wall of separation' theory adopted by US constitutional doctrine. He envisioned a State that would treat all religions equally. He took pains to explain that '[s]ome people think

---

para 9, http://www.unhchr.ch/tbs/doc.nsf/(Symbol)/9a30112c27d1167cc12563ed 004d8f15?Opendocument [last accessed on 17 July 2012].)

[10] See, T.N. Madan, 'Secularism in its Place', in Rajeev Bhargava (ed.), *Secularsim and Its Critics* (OUP: New Delhi, 1998), p. 297. See also, Ashis Nandy, 'The Politics of Secularism and the Recovery of Religious Toleration', in Rajeev Bhargava (ed.), *Secularsim and Its Critics*; Ashis Nandy, 'An Anti-Secular Manifesto', *Seminar*, (October 1985), 314: 1–12.

it [secularism] means something opposed to religion. That obviously is not correct. ... It is a state which honours all faiths equally and gives them equal opportunities.'[11]

Similarly, the founders of Pakistan and Bangladesh were both committed to the creation of secular political orders in the countries they helped create. However, the political trajectories of both countries eventually witnessed the adoption of Islam as the State religion, with the State–religion nexus becoming entrenched under military rule.

Despite Pakistan's founder and first Governor-General Muhammad Ali Jinnah's partiality toward secularism, political realities won the day.[12] The Preamble to the Constitution of the Islamic Republic of Pakistan (1956) refers to Jinnah's declaration that 'Pakistan would be a democratic State based on Islamic principles of social justice'. However, no State religion was recognized. All laws (barring personal laws of non-Muslims) had to conform with principles of Islam (Article 198). Religious freedom of all was recognized as a fundamental right (Article 18). This scheme was to change under the Constitution promulgated in 1973 wherein Islam was recognized as the State religion (Article 2). This move, however, was accompanied by strong guarantees of religious freedom for all (Articles 20–22). This trend of incremental strengthening of the State–religion nexus in Pakistan reached its zenith with the entrenchment of military rule in the country in the latter part of the 1970s under the military dictator Zia-ul-Haq when the Holy Qur'an and the Sunnah were declared the supreme law of the land.

The Constitution of the newly formed Bangladesh (1972) was cast in idealistic terms reflecting the revolutionary spirit of the new republic soon after its war of national liberation. 'Nationalism, socialism, democracy and secularism' were declared to be fundamental principles of state policy (Article 8(1)). However, the Fifth Amendment to the Constiution that sought to legitimize military decrees issued by the military regime of President Ziaur Rahman changed those ideals to 'absolute trust and faith in the Almighty Allah, nationalism, democracy and socialism meaning economic and soicial

[11] See, S. Gopal (ed.), *Jawaharlal Nehru: An Anthology* (OUP: Delhi, 1980), p. 330.

[12] Ayesha Jalal, *The Sole Spokesman: Jinnah, the Muslim League, and the Demand for Pakistan* (Cambridge University Press: Cambridge, 1985), p. 216.

justice'. A new clause, (Article 8(1A)), declares: '[a]bsolute trust and faith in the Almighty Allah shall be the basis of all actions'. It further introduced the expression '*Bismillah-Ar-Rahman-Ar-Rahim*' ('In the name of Allah, the Beneficent, the Merciful') just above the preamble to the Constitution.[13]

More recently, however, the Fifth Amendment was declared unconstitutional by the Appellate Division of the Supreme Court of Bangladesh. In a historic judgment,[14] a six-judge Bench, presided over by the Chief Justice, pronounced that the amendment was illegal and void *ab initio* as it amounted to an attempt to amend the constitution via military action. It is of significance that, although the Court condoned several provisions introduced through military decrees as necessary in the public interest, provisions of the Fifth Amendment that introduced a State religion were not condoned in that manner and were rejected. Thus, it appeared that the constitutional order would revert back to the initial secular framework. However, that was not to be. The Fifteenth Amendment to the Constitution, rushed through Parliament in July 2011 (in the absence of the boycotting opposition), has introduced a hybrid model recognizing both secularism as a fundamental principle of state policy and Islam as a State religion. How this model would work remains to be seen.[15]

It can be observed that gradually most countries in the region have settled for the adoption of a State religion, or have accorded primacy to a particular religion. The strength of legal guarantees of freedom of religion varies. The examination of those practices within the framework of international human rights is essential, in view of the growing convergence between international human rights obligations and constitutionalism.

Although South Asia is viewed as a prime theatre of communal conflict, that view belies a long history of coexistence among the

---

[13] In general see, Mahmudul Islam, *Constitutional Law of Bangladesh* (Mullick Brothers: Dhaka, 2008, 2nd Ed., reprint), Chapter I.

[14] *Khondker Delwar Hossain & Ors.* v. *Bangladesh Italian Marble Works Ltd., Dhaka and Ors.* (Appeal Nos. 1044 & 1045 of 2009), http://www.thedailystar.net/images/5thammendment.pdf (last accessed on 17 July 2012).

[15] See, commentary by N. M. Harun, *Fifteenth Amendment Introduces Fusion of Ideologies,* http://opinion.bdnews24.com/2011/07/07/fifteenth-amendment-intro-duces-fusion-of-ideologies/ (last accessed on 17 July 2012).

most esoteric of groups. Many scholars have referred to this tradition. T.N. Madan[16] and Ashis Nandy, for example, reject secularism as a modern and alien concept which has not worked well in India.[17] Nandy calls for reliance on the traditional practices of religious tolerance. Amartya Sen, too, acknowledges the long traditions of religious coexistence, but in a well-argued response,[18] takes the position that there is nothing 'modern' about secularism, if it is taken to mean 'symmetry of treatment' of all religious groups, and that secularism and traditional forms of tolerance are not contradictory. I agree with Amartya Sen. Secularism is not a rejection of religiosity in society; rather, it is a tool for ensuring the pluralist character of religiosity.

On the note of traditional tolerance, I recall the late Sri Lankan constitutional scholar Neelan Tiruchelvam exhorting his young protegés to visit the city of Kochin in Kerala which is a supreme testament to centuries of religious coexistence. Visiting the famed city later, I was amazed to discover more than mere tolerance of the 'other' on the part of the Hindu rulers of Kerala; what appeared was an open welcoming of religions as varied as Judaism and Syrian Orthodox Christianity with the granting of land to build their temples. They have coexisted with Hinduism, Islam, and other faiths for centuries.

South Asia has also witnessed the worst forms of religious intolerance and violence, as in the blood spilled during the Partition of India and pogroms witnessed in the various countries in the region. Amidst today's troubled politics of religion and ethnicity in South Asia, examples of coexistence of yore should not be permitted to fade away into the sepia hues of history. It is clear, however, that in addition to appealing to the good senses and traditions of the citizenry, the complexities of modern societies require a more formal foundation for respecting pluralism.

The modern constitutional schemes of South Asia vary regarding the treatment of religion. At present, only the constitutions of

[16] T.N. Madan, 'Secularism in its Place', p. 297.

[17] Ashis Nandy, 'The Politics of Secularism'. See also, Ashis Nandy, 'An Anti-Secular Manifesto'.

[18] Amartya Sen, 'Secularism and Its Discontents', in Rajeev Bhargava (ed.), *Secularsim and Its Critics*.

India[19] and Nepal (Interim Constitution, 2007)[20] recognize secular forms of government. For Nepal, it is a great leap from the previous constitution's (1990)[21] recognition of Nepal as a Hindu kingdom. The constitutions of Afghanistan (2004),[22] Bangladesh (1972),[23] Pakistan (1973),[24] and the Maldives (2008)[25] recognize Islam as the State religion. The Constitution of Sri Lanka (1978)[26] confers 'foremost place to Buddhism' (Article 9). It should also be noted that customary laws, some based on religion, continue to govern personal laws of South Asian nations, sometimes alongside secular general laws. Not a single country in the region has discarded customary laws in favour of a single uniform civil code.[27]

The new Constitution of Bhutan (2008)[28] has put in place an interesting system whereby Buddhism is recognized as the 'spiritual heritage of Bhutan'. The monarch has to be a Buddhist. However, the monarch is the protector of all religions in the country and separation of religion and politics has to be ensured (Article 3(3)). Freedom of thought, conscience, and religion is recognized towards all (Article 7). It could be best described as a hybrid system, which displays compatibility with the system envisaged in the ICCPR, if effectively implemented.

---

[19] http://lawmin.nic.in/coi/coiason29july08.pdf (last accessed on 17 July 2012).

[20] http://www.worldstatesmen.org/Nepal_Interim_Constitution2007.pdf (last accessed on 17 July 2012).

[21] http://www.nepaldemocracy.org/documents/national_laws/constitution1990.htm (last accessed on 17 July 2012).

[22] http://www.afghan-web.com/politics/current_constitution.html#chapterone (last accessed on 17 July 2012).

[23] http://www.banglaembassy.com.bh/Constitution.html (last accessed on 17 July 2012). See also, *Khondker Delwar Hossain & Ors.* v. *Bangladesh Italian Marble Works Ltd., Dhaka and Ors.*

[24] http://www.mofa.gov.pk/Publications/constitution.pdf (last accessed on 17 July 2012).

[25] http://www.presidencymaldives.gov.mv/Documents/ConstitutionOfMaldives.pdf (last accessed on 17 July 2012).

[26] http://www.priu.gov.lk/Cons/1978Constitution/1978ConstitutionWithoutAmendments.pdf (last accessed on 17 July 2012).

[27] Article 44 of the Indian Constitution declares as a directive principle of state policy that the State shall endeavour to secure a uniform civil code. This has not borne fruit yet.

[28] http://www.constitution.bt/html/constitution/glossary.htm (last accessed on 17 July 2012).

The principle of secularism was not included in the original text of the Indian Constitution. However, extensive provisions relating to freedom of religion were included in the original text (Articles 25–8) including provisions on minority rights (Articles 29–30). The principle of secularism as a feature characterizing the Indian State was added to the Preamble of the Constitution of India by the 42nd Amendment in 1976. Jain points out that it was an exercise in making explicit what was implicit in the Constitution.[29] In *Bommai* v. *Union of India*,[30] the Supreme Court held that the principle of secularism is a part of the basic structure of the Constitution. Again, as Jain points out, India's brand of secularism is not aloof from religion. It means that the State does not provide patronage to any particular religion: it is required to respect all religions and belief systems.[31] Article 28 imposes a stricture that wholly-State-funded schools cannot impart religious instructions. It has been interpreted to mean that the study of religions focussing on philosophy and values are not excluded whereas religious instructions are.[32] The State can regulate what are deemed secular matters of religious institutions (Article 25(2)(a)).

We will have to await the finalization of the ongoing Constitution-making process in Nepal to see how secularism develops there. Secularism in India continues to evolve despite scepticism on the part of some. Observed from outside, India's secular constitutional regime, despite its turns and twists, appears to be an attractive arrangement, especially in increasingly tumultuous times.

All South Asian countries, barring Bhutan,[33] have acceded to the ICCPR thereby undertaking binding international legal obligations on, *inter alia*, religious freedom. Maldives and Pakistan have entered reservations to ICCPR Article 18 (guarantee of freedom of thought, conscience, and religion) subjecting its application within their countries to the respective constitutional provisions.

---

[29] M.P. Jain, *Indian Constitutional Law,* 5th Ed. (LexisNexis Butterworths Wadhwa: Nagpur, 2009), p. 1201.

[30] AIR 1994 SC 1918; 1994 3 SCC 1.

[31] M.P. Jain, *Indian Constitutional Law,* pp. 1201–2.

[32] *Aruna Roy* v. *Union of India*, AIR 2002 SC 3176.

[33] For ratification record and reservations entered see, http://treaties.un.org/Pages/ViewDetails.aspx?src=TREATY&mtdsg_no=IV-4&chapter=4&lang=en (last accessed on 25 September 2011).

STATE AND RELIGION IN SRI LANKA

The Politics of Religion

Sri Lanka too has unfortunately fallen into the common trap of permitting excessive religious influence over politics and the politicization of religion. Ethno-religious identities that crystallized during colonial rule were further consolidated during the post-Independence period as a means of jockeying for political power and entitlements. The escalating ethno-religious schism between the Sinhala and the Tamils eventually culminated in a nearly three-decade-long fratricidal civil war in the northeast of the country. Those developments are in stark contrast to the centuries old tradition of coexistence and the reality of fluid identities among the various communities in Sri Lanka.

As an island nation situated in close proximity to busy sea routes, Sri Lanka has attracted many settlers and travellers over millennia. It also attracted three colonial powers in succession—the Portuguese (1505), the Dutch (1668), and the British (1796). All these phenomena have left a rich legacy of a multi-ethnic, multi-religious and multi-lingual population. Currently, the approximate percentage of population breakdown according to religion is Buddhist 76.7, Hindu 7.8, Muslim 8.5, Roman Catholic 6.1, and other Christian groups 0.9. The figures are according to the 2001 census which could not cover the districts affected by the armed conflict. Hence, the number of Hindus is reflected as less than adherents of Islam. It is also noteworthy that non-believers are not included in the breakdown.[34]

Today, most Sinhalese are Buddhist while most Tamils are of the Hindu faith. Both communities have small percentages of Christians of various denominations. However, this ethno-religious typology was not always so. It appears to be very much a construct of the historical mythology surrounding the formation of the nation. The *Mahavamsa*, the historical chronicle of the country, has been central to the idea that Lanka is the land of the Sinhalese who were chosen by the Buddha as guardians of Buddhism. The chronicle, written over many centuries by Buddhist monks, appears to have had the

[34] http://www.statistics.gov.lk/PopHouSat/PDF/Population/p9p9%20Religion.pdf (last accessed on 17 July 2012).

promotion of that idea as its core agenda and mission.[35] Although viewed with scepticism by historians and anthropologists as an elaborately embellished and romanticized construction of historical events to promote a self-serving goal of its writers, this central thesis of the *Mahavamsa* has had a powerful influence in shaping the self-identity of the majority Sinhala community.

According to the popular *Mahavamsa* account, the Sinhala were founded by the progeny of Prince Vijaya and his entourage, described as Indo-Aryans from north India, around fifth century BC. In the third century BC, the Sinhala King Devanam Piyatissa was converted to Buddhism by Arahat Mahinda, a kinsman of Emperor Asoka. Then onwards, Buddhism spread rapidly among the people and became the State religion with the unification of the country by the great Sinhala King Duttagamani (Dutu Gemunu) who defeated Elara, the Dravidian king who ruled the north. As de Silva points out, the duel between the two '...is dramatized as the central theme of the later chapters of the *Mahavamsa* as an epoch-making confrontation between the Sinhalese and the Tamils, and extolled as a holy war fought in the interests of Buddhism'.[36]

The Dravidian people from South India are often viewed as alien invaders who challenged the authority of Sinhala kings. The advent of Hinduism in the country much later is attributed to Dravidian settlers. Hence comes the typology of the Sinhala as protectors of Buddhism and Tamils (a generic term to describe all Dravidian groups) as adherents of Hinduism.

However, scholars have consistently pointed out the fallacy of this neat classification, noting that historically there were not only Sinhala Buddhists but also Tamil Buddhists, with shifting and overlapping ethno-religious identities.[37] Obeyesekere points out, for example, that King Kirti Sri Rajasinghe (1747–82), who interestingly was from Madurai in South India, served as one of the last kings of the Kandyan kingdom predominantly inhabited by the Sinhala. He was both a Buddhist and a Saivaite, and a speaker of Tamil, Telugu, and

---

[35] K. M. de Silva, *A History of Sri Lanka* (Vijitha Yapa: Colombo, 2005), pp. 6–8.

[36] Ibid., p. 16.

[37] Ibid.; G. Obeyesekere, 'Buddhism, Political Violence and the Dilemmas of Democracy in Sri Lanka', CSDS occasional paper (April 2009), pp. 14–16.

Sinhala. He initiated a great revival of Buddhism that lasted all the way up to the nineteenth century.[38]

This reality has been obfuscated not only by the historical account of the *Mahavamsa*, but also by a major Sinhala nationalist discourse that arose in the latter part of the nineteenth century in opposition to British colonial rule, which remains very influential among the Sinhala to this day. The discourse owes its origins to the movement launched by Anagarika Dharmapala in his effort to bring about a Buddhist cultural revival in the face of onslaughts on Buddhism by Christian missionaries and what he perceived as corrosive cultural influence of the West. The Anagarika's call for a Buddhist revival, however, ended up drawing a firm nexus between the Sinhala identity and Buddhism resulting in a strong articulation of Tamil 'otherness'.[39] As Obeysekere observes:[40] 'Dharmapala's reform entailed the notion of both Sinhala and Buddhism in opposition to Tamils as aliens. This oppositional dialectic could take the form of Sinhala versus Tamil in political discourse.'

It has to be noted, however, that the Tamil nationalist discourse which accompanied the militant separatist movement of the past several decades did not place emphasis on religion: rather, the objective of the Tamil nationalist project was the construction of the Tamil nation mostly along linguistic lines and gaining political recognition for it as such. Even though most Tamils are adherents of Hinduism, it is commonly believed that some of the major protagonists of Tamil nationalism were non-Hindus. Religion, therefore, has come into play not as the cause of tension between communities, but more in the form of a reluctant component of politically constructed ethno-religious identities. However, as we shall see below, the use of religion as an ethnic marker was to have serious constitutional and political ramifications under the two republican constitutions of Sri Lanka.

THE CONSTITUTIONAL FRAMEWORK

As pointed out above, the dividing line of the recent armed conflict in the northeast of the country is ethnicity, and not religion.

[38] Obeyesekere, 'Buddhism, Political Violence', p. 13 and endnote 8.

[39] H.L. Seneviratne, *The Works of Kings: The New Buddhism in Sri Lanka* (Chicago and London: University of Chicago Press, 1999), p. 26.

[40] Obeysekere, 'Buddhism, Political Violence', p. 37.

If religion mattered, it did so as a marker of ethno-nationalist identity as in Sinhala–Buddhist, Tamil–Hindu, or Muslim identity. Religious tensions did arise in the recent past, however, because of the opposition to activities of evangelical Christian groups by both Buddhist and Hindu religious organizations. The Buddhist groups included a political party, the Jathika Hela Urumaya, which was organized around an ideology of Sinhala–Buddhist nationalism. This rather unusual alliance pushed for the adoption of an anti-conversion law that would criminalize 'unethical' religious conversions. The alliance between the Buddhist and Hindu groups was significant in the context of the armed conflict in the northeast of the country. In this instance, it was apparent that the alliance viewed Christian evangelical activity as a common threat to its respective flocks.[41]

During the lengthy colonial experience of Sri Lanka, which spanned four and a half centuries, the local populace found converting to Christianity to be a quick path to obtaining patronage of the colonial authorities.[42] As was the case elsewhere in the Empire, the British played on the tensions among the various ethnic groups to their political advantage. By the time independence was on the horizon, the colonial authorities came to realize that the communal fissures within the native polity could prove to be incendiary.[43]

The Soulbury Constitution of Sri Lanka, which came into effect at independence in 1948, had a provision to safeguard the interests of persons belonging to the various communities and religious groups. Article 29(2) provided that no law shall be made prohibiting or restricting the free exercise of any religion or any legislation that discriminates against persons of any community or religion. Article 29(2)(c) specifically stipulated that no privilege or advantage could be conferred by law on persons of any religion or community that others were not entitled to; and Paragraph (d) assured that legislation could not interfere with any religious body except with the consent of

---

[41] See, report of UN Special Rapporteur on Freedom of Religion or Belief, Asma Jahangir, UN Doc. E/CN.4/2006/5/ Add. 3, http://daccess-dds-ny.un.org/doc/UNDOC/GEN/G05/166/64/PDF/G0516664.pdf?OpenElement (last accessed on 17 July 2012).

[42] K. Jayawardena, *Nobodies to Somebodies: The Rise of the Colonial Bourgeoisie in Sri Lanka* (Social Scientists' Association: Colombo, 2000), pp. 250–3.

[43] See, de Silva, *History of Sri Lanka*, pp. 531–53.

the governing authority of that body. Further, Article 29(3) stipulated that any law made in contravention of Clause (2) will be void to that extent. The necessary implication was the recognition of judicial review of legislation, a constitutional principle largely unfamiliar to the traditional British constitutional framework. The overall tenor of Article 29 suggested a secular constitutional framework.

This scheme was dramatically altered by the republican constitution adopted in 1972. The irony about the first autochthonous constitution was that, while it was adopted in the glorious republican spirit of vesting sovereignty in the people, its overall majoritarian bent, coupled with the elimination or dilution of checks and balances inherent in the Soulbury Constitution, further deepened the ethnic divide.[44] In fact, the Federal Party representing the interests of a large section of the Tamil population boycotted deliberations of the Constituent Assembly after a while. The remaining parties too failed to reach consensus on several key issues, and eventually the new Constitution was adopted by a divided vote of 119 to 16 with one abstention. [45]

From a minority rights point of view, the failure to include a provision comparable to the previous Article 29 was the major cause of discontent. That sense of grievance was amplified by the recognition of Sinhala as the only official language and the inclusion of Article 6 ('Buddhism Clause') which required that '[t]he Republic of Sri Lanka shall give to Buddhism the foremost place'.[46] All of this was compounded by the overall scheme of the Constitution that centralized power in the National State Assembly (in the name of people's power and parliamentary supremacy) and removed many checks and balances found in the Soulbury Constitution. One of the most problematic features was the removal of judicial review

[44] K. Loganathan, *Sri Lanka: Lost Opportunities* (CEPRA: Colombo, 1996), Chapter 3; de Silva, *History of Sri Lanka*, pp. 668–80.

[45] J.A.L. Cooray, *Constitutional and Administrative Law of Sri Lanka* (Sumathi Publishers: Colombo, 1995), pp. 59–95; Loganathan, *Lost Opportunities,* Chapter 3; Constituent Assembly of Sri Lanka, Official Report, Vol. 2, pp. 950–9.

[46] The Republic of Sri Lanka shall give to Buddhism the foremost place and accordingly it shall be the duty of the State to protect and foster Buddhism while assuring to all religions the rights granted by Section 18(1)(d) [freedom of religion clause]. —Article 6 of the 1972 Constitution of Sri Lanka.

of legislation. A small window of opportunity was given for pre-legislative review. A chapter on fundamental rights and freedoms was introduced. However, no specific constitutional remedy for violations of rights was recognized.

Colvin R. de Silva, widely recognized as the architect of the 1972 Constitution, was vehement in his denial that Article 6 made Buddhism the State religion. In the course of a public lecture fifteen years after the adoption of the Constitution, he made the startling revelation that the contested Article was a compromise reached to assuage the demands of hardline members of the Constituent Assembly that drafted the Constitution. He referred to a proposal made by a committee of the Constituent Assembly to include a provision to ensure that both the president and the prime minister be Buddhist or Sinhala Buddhist.

At de Silva's urging the committee members settled for the position that 'if you must work for religion, then Buddhism is in fact a religion which holds the foremost position in this country;' hence, it was not necessary to have the most powerful political offices in the country reflect the supremacy of Buddhism. It was that formula that eventually found its way into Article 6. He then went on to state that as a secularist, he would have been happy just to have the 'freedom of religion clause' (Article 18(1)(b)) in the Constitution, but observed that 'constitutions are made by Constituent Assemblies, they are not made by the Minister of Constitutional Affairs'. He was comfortable as long as a State religion was not established. He went on to assure, '[b]ut there is nothing here, and I repeat NOTHING, in Section 6 which in any manner infringes upon the rights of any religion in the country'.[47]

Another reason advanced by de Silva for moving away from the Article 29 formula of the Soulbury Constitution was scepticism about judicial review of legislation. Perhaps his socialist convictions caused him to recognize no authority over the legislature, the repository of people's sovereignty.

[W]hy then did we not bring Section 29 in that form into the 1972 Constitution? For the simple reason, as I said at the outset, if you put Section 29 in that form into the 1972 Constitution then Parliament's

[47] Colvin R. de Silva, *Safeguards for the Minorities in the 1972 Constitution* (A Young Socialist Publication: Colombo, 1987), pp. 9–17.

laws would become subject to decisions of the Supreme Court or other Courts of the land as to their validity. That was completely contrary not only to the principles of the Constitution, but also to the principles [sic] that people are sovereign.[48]

The unfortunate circumstances that led to the 1972 Constitution's inability to create a scheme that entrenched pluralism as a constitutional principle were accentuated by the reality that politicians of de Silva's caliber—avowed Leftists representing progressive viewpoints on minority rights—were then powerful coalition partners of the ruling United Front government. Somehow, apparently without much protest, powerful political ideals were compromised. Some ideals, such as the supremacy of the legislature, proved to be a misguided romanticization of republicanism that resulted in the dilution of democratic safeguards. The Tamil community, in particular, felt alienated from the new republic, and that sentiment, together with accumulated grievances, fuelled the violent political storm that engulfed the country for decades.

The second republican constitution adopted in 1978 on the whims of the United National Party headed by J.R. Jayawardena unfortunately perpetuated the ills of the 1972 Constitution and added some more in the form of the all-powerful executive presidency. Article 9 of the 1978 Constitution reproduced the contested Article 6 of the 1972 Constitution: 'The Republic of Sri Lanka shall give to Buddhism the foremost place and accordingly, it shall be the duty of the State to protect and foster the *Buddha Sasana*, while assuring to all religions the rights granted by Articles 10 and 14(1)(e).' The chapter on fundamental rights guarantees freedom of thought, conscience, and religion as an absolute right (Article 10): 'Every person is entitled to freedom of thought, conscience and religion, including the freedom to have or to adopt a religion or belief of his choice.' It is an entrenched clause that requires for its amendment a two-thirds majority in Parliament and a referendum (Article 83). A novel feature is the recognition of a specific constitutional remedy for infringement of fundamental rights (Articles 17 and 126). However, judicial review of legislation was once again done away with except the possibility of pre-legislative review of Bills. Furthermore, as

[48] Ibid., pp. 15–16.

per Article 16, all existing statutes, whether in compliance with fundamental rights or not, were to continue, permitting problematic customary personal laws to also continue.

Despite de Silva's assurance that the Buddhism clause in the 1972 Constitution did not establish a State religion, the tenor of the provision, and Article 9 of the 1978 Constitution that followed, were to have negative constitutional implications for religious freedom, as the discussion below on constitutional jurisprudence will establish.

Article 9 has had an impact at policy and institutional levels too. Since the late 1980s, successive governments have created ministerial portfolios on religious affairs. From time to time, there have been specific ministries to foster the *Buddha Sasana* and also to promote Muslim, Hindu, and Christian religious affairs. Sometimes, all religious affairs have been dealt with under one ministry. There are also separate governmental departments to deal with the affairs of the four major religions observed in Sri Lanka.

At present, there is a ministry of *Buddha Sasana* and Religious Affairs. According to the gazette notification that describes its duties and functions,[49] 'implementation of appropriate programmes and projects to protect and foster the *Buddha Sasana* as provided for in Article 9 of the Constitution, while ensuring to all religions the right granted by Articles 10 and 14(1)(e) of the Constitution' is a principal function. At the same time, the implementation and monitoring of programmes with respect to Hindu, Christian, and Islamic religious and cultural affairs is also stipulated as a function. A predominant number of other items on the list exclusively pertain to promoting and fostering Buddhism—for example, 'assisting the propagation of the *Buddha Dhamma*', 'administration of the *Buddha Sasana* fund', 'activities connected to international Buddhist centres'.

Similarly, the duties and functions of the Ministry of Higher Education contained in the same gazette include the following: 'higher education for Bhikkus in the relevant fields of study', 'promotion of Buddhist and Pali studies'. The Ministry of Education lists 'promotion of Buddhist and Pali studies in achievement of relevant Millenium Development Goals' and 'pirivena [Buddhist seminary] education and religious education at school level' as functions. There is no reference to educational activities pertaining to other religions in any of the lists.

---

[49] Gazette Extraordinary No. 1681/3 of 22 November 2010.

Constitutional Jurisprudence

Cases Relating to the Incorporation of Religious Bodies

A string of Supreme Court judgments delivered in quick succession between 2001 and 2003 has given rise to grave concern for the constitutional protection of religious freedom in Sri Lanka.

All three judgments stemmed from petitions challenging the constitutionality of legislative Bills which sought to incorporate charitable institutions set up by certain Christian denominations. The main bone of contention of the petitioners was that freedom of religion of non-Christians will be adversely affected by the establishment of Christian charitable bodies that would facilitate unethical conversions. All three petitions[50] were supported by the same counsel and the legal averments were more or less identical. In two of the cases, judgment was given in the absence of submissions defending the respective Bills. Significantly, in all three cases, the Attorney-General agreed with the submissions of the petitioners.

The first case[51] concerned the incorporation of an entity, 'Christian Sahanaye Doratuwa Prayer Centre'. Among its objectives were providing relief through prayer, assistance to secure jobs, and training of persons to engage in self-employment. It was those objectives that drew the ire of the petitioners. What was averred was that through such 'economic and commercial' activity, 'persons of another religion or belief who come to the prayer centre would be allured to adopt the religion of the prayer centre'. Such efforts, therefore, would amount to unethical conversions through allurement which would result in a violation of the rights of non-Christians to freely profess their religions. That would be a violation of Article 10 ('freedom of religion' clause). The Attorney-General agreed. No submissions had been made to defend the Bill.

In response, the Supreme Court made a distinction between the right to practise one's religion in association with others (Article 14(1)(c)) and the right to engage in an occupation, trade, business, or enterprise (Article 14(1)(g)). The latter, the Court pointed out, did not come within the ambit of religious freedom, and therefore,

---

[50] SC Special Determinations Nos. 2/2001, 2/2003, and 19/2003.

[51] SC Special Determination No. 2/2001, SC Minute of 24.05.2001, reproduced in *LST Review*, (2003), 14(191): pp. 21–5.

'[a] prayer centre that seeks special legislative recognition by way of incorporation cannot avail itself of these two freedoms together'. Doing so infringes others' right to freedom of religion under Article 10. The Court found that the Bill, therefore, had to be passed by a two-thirds majority in Parliament and be approved at a referendum.

With due respect to the Court, the reasoning of the judgment is very problematic. The Court proceeded on the assumption that charitable activities of religious bodies—it termed them as 'economic and commercial' activities—would necessarily result in conversions through allurements; or perhaps, the suggestion is that such mischief is inherent in Christian charitable bodies, if not in other religious bodies. The Court's position that charitable services relating to self-employment, vocational training, and the like cannot be viewed as religious practice is clearly based on such an assumption. Otherwise, there was no legal basis to reach the conclusion drawn by the Court.

The Court, presided over by the former Chief Justice Sarath Silva,[52] does not explain how it reached that assumption. The judgment refers to 'a significant body of material' relied on by the petitioner to establish the conversion of persons of one religion to another by allurement. However, the Court goes on to state that it is not necessary to examine the material 'which may be of social and political content but *does not have a direct bearing on the questions of law that arise for consideration*' (emphasis mine). In that case, what was the basis of the assumption that was foundational to the Court's findings? Would the Court have found that charitable activities of Buddhist, Hindu, Muslim, or others religions are similarly suspect?

In the second case,[53] the facts were almost identical to the first. The Court's approach was virtually the same. A significant feature of the case, though, was that the Bill was defended by an intervenient petitioner—the President of the New Wine Harvest Ministries, the body that sought incorporation by the impugned Bill. In submissions on behalf of the intervenient petitioner[54] it was pointed out that a number of religious bodies of Buddhist, Hindu, and Muslim faiths

[52] Chief Justice Sarath Silva is the chief patron of a prominent Buddhist temple in Colombo. He also appears regularly on television programmes to discuss Buddhist philosophy.

[53] SC Special Determination No.2/2003, SC Minute of 29.01.2003.

[54] Reproduced in *LST Review*, (2003), 14(191): 9.

had been previously successfully incorporated by Acts of Parliament when the incorporating laws had included as their objectives socio-economic activities that were not particularly confined to followers of the respective religion. For example, the Dharmavijaya Foundation Act No. 62 of 1979 includes the following general objectives: 'to promote the total development of man, both spiritually and physically, with the application of Buddhist principles to economic development and thereby establish a Dharmavijaya Samajaya [a society that champions Dharma]'.

The Court was not swayed by the argument that different treatment had been meted out to Christian bodies seeking incorporation. Its response (again delivered by former Chief Justice Sarath Silva) was that in exercising its jurisdiction to review Bills, the Court cannot examine the validity of past legislation, nor take their content as a standard of constitutional consistency. The Court appeared to be determined to stand its ground.

The third judgment under discussion was again delivered in a case in which the Supreme Court reviewed a Bill that sought to incorporate a religious institution through a Private Member's motion.[55] The religious institution—'Provincial of Teaching Sisters of the Holy Cross of the Third Order of Saint Francis of Menzingen of Lanka'—was based on Catholicism and had as its objectives, among others, the spread of knowledge of the Catholic faith, the conducting of educational activities, engaging in charity by serving in institutions such as hospitals and refugee camps, and the establishment of homes for the elders, orphanages, and the like.

The constitutionality of the Bill was challenged by a private party mainly on the basis that the stipulated objectives of the institution violated Article 10 of the Constitution, in that the objectives could give rise to situations of forcing those of other faiths to convert to Catholicism. As in the previous cases, it was argued that the institution, by engaging in religious teaching, educational activities, and working with the vulnerable, could force recipients to convert to the Catholic faith through allurements. While Article 10 of the Constitution *does* include the right to adopt a religion or belief, it

---

[55] SC Special Determination No. 19/2003, SC Minute of 25.07.2003, reproduced in *LST Review*, (2003), 14(191): 1–8.

was pointed out that the right had to be exercised through one's free choice. The scheme in the Bill, it was thought, would deprive vulnerable persons of that choice. The Sisters' Order was not notified of the proceedings and, therefore, had no opportunity of responding to the petition.

What was particularly significant in the 'Sisters of Saint Francis of Menzingen' case was that the Court unanimously accepted the argument that the Bill violated the Buddhism Clause (Article 9) of the Constitution as well. It was thought that the propagation of another faith, combined with altruistic activities, would impact negatively on Buddhism by converting its adherents through force and allurement:

> [W]hen there is no fundamental right to propagate [religion] [under the Sri Lanka Constitution of 1978], if efforts are taken to convert another person to one's own religion, such conduct could hinder the very existence of the *Buddha Sasana*. What is guaranteed under the Constitution is the manifestation, observance and practice of one's own religion and the propagation and spreading [of] Christianity as postulated in terms of clause 3 [of the Bill] would not be permissible as it would impair the very existence of Buddhism or the *Buddha Sasana*.[56]

Indeed, the implications of the Court's position could have far-reaching implications. It was almost as if Sri Lanka had become a theocracy with the propagation of 'other religions' being taboo. The Court simply assumes that the propagation of Christianity will necessarily 'impair the very existence of Buddhism'. Again, no reasons are adduced to justify such an assumption. If indeed unethical conversions were to be facilitated by these religious bodies, why did the Court not discuss the impact on non-Buddhist religious groups? After all, Article 9 itself requires freedom of religion to *all* religions. The judgment certainly is at variance with the assurances of de Silva that the constitutional Buddhism Clause would not impact on non-Buddhists in a discriminatory manner.

The Court, as in previous cases, did not refer to any empirical data or experiences that would have justified the position it took. The three petitions, as it were, seemed to be based on speculation and alarmism. As pointed out earlier, the Attorney-General on behalf of the State agreed with the petitioners that the Bills indeed were

[56] Ibid., p. 7.

in violation of religious freedom, and in the third case that the Bill in question violated the Buddhism clause as well. In all three cases the decisions were reached unanimously. It is also significant that the same senior counsel appeared on behalf of the petitioners in all three cases, perhaps pointing to a concerted effort to prevent the incorporation of such religious bodies. If the Church or adherents of Christianity did respond to the series of judgments in an aggressive manner, another frontier of division in an already divided nation would have opened up.

The Sisters' Order then went before the UN Human Rights Committee complaining of the refusal to incorporate their religious institution. This was made possible by Sri Lanka's ratification of the First Optional Protocol to the ICCPR which permitted individual communications (petitions) to the UN Committee. The Committee, empowered to examine communications and provide views and recommendations, opined that the Supreme Court's decision was in violation of Sri Lanka's obligations under the ICCPR—specifically, obligations under the freedom of religion clause (Article 18) and the equal protection of the law clause (Article 26). The Committee pointed out that Sri Lanka was under a legal obligation to provide a remedy to the religious order. [57]

With regard to the use of comparative law, the petitioners had consistently referred to the judgment in *Rev. Stainislaus* v. *The State of Madhya Pradesh*[58] where the Supreme Court of India upheld the constitutionality of the anti-conversion laws of the states of Madhya Pradesh and Orissa which criminalized religious conversions on the grounds of force, fraud, or allurement. Chief Justice Ray drew a distinction between converting of another to one's religion and the right to spread the tenets of one's religion: the former, he argued, was not protected as a fundamental right whereas the latter was. The act of conversion itself was considered to be a violation of the right to freedom of conscience of the converted.

The *Stainislaus* judgment has attracted serious criticism. H.M. Seervai, an authoritative Indian constitutional law scholar, points

[57] UN Doc. CCPR/C/85/D/1249/2004, http://daccess-dds-ny.un.org/doc/UNDOC/DER/G05/449/74/PDF/G0544974.pdf?OpenElement (last accessed on 17 July 2012).

[58] (1977) AIR SC 908.

out that the judgment has ignored the legislative history of the constitutional freedom of religion clause (Article 25) which intentionally included the right to 'propagate' religion recognizing it to be an essential feature of some religions. Further, he correctly points out that the right to adopt a religion of one's choice is an exercise of freedom of conscience rather than its negation. Conversion through force, fraud or allurement will be caught up in the constitutional limitations attaching to the practice of freedom of religion. Seervai calls for the overruling of the *Stainislaus* judgment arguing that the judgment is clearly wrong and has the potential of causing great 'public mischief'.[59]

The Supreme Court of Sri Lanka cited the *Stainislaus* judgment with approval in two of the cases discussed above[60] to support its stance against conversions. The Court was emphatic that unlike Article 25 of the Indian Constitution, Article 10 of the Sri Lanka Constitution did not recognize the right to 'propagate' religion and, therefore, would not attract constitutional protection. The Court made light of the fact that the right to manifest one's religion through teaching is guaranteed under Article 14(1)(e) of the Constitution of Sri Lanka. One could argue that the dividing line between teaching and propagation is thin at best. However, the Court did not explore that dimension.

It appears that the reference to, and use of, the *Stainislaus* judgment by the Sri Lanka Supreme Court was for the narrow purpose of giving expression to a limited reading of religious freedom under the Constitution.[61] In any event, one is hard put to understand the relevance of that judgment to the cases under consideration. The Bills that were under review did not necessitate a discussion on the constitutionality of religious conversions if not for the Court's own unsubstantiated assumption that teaching and socio-economic

[59] H.M. Seervai, *Constitutional Law of India*, 4th Ed., Vol. 2 (N.M. Tripathi Pvt. Ltd.: Bombay, 1993), pp. 1286–9.

[60] SC Special Determination No. 2/2003, SC Minute of 29.01.2003; SC Special Determination No. 19/2003, SC Minute of 25.07.2003, reproduced in *LST Review*, (2003), 14(191): 1–8.

[61] See also, Alexandra Owens, 'Protecting Freedom of and from Religion: Questioning Law's Ability to Protect Against Unethical Conversions in Sri Lanka', *Religion and Human Rights*, (2006), 1: 41.

activities of the Christian institutions sought to be incorporated would necessarily give rise to unethical religious conversions. This use of comparative constitutional jurisprudence for such narrow ends certainly does not bode well for the progressive development of the law.

Review of Bill Prohibiting Forcible Conversion of Religion

In 2004, the Supreme Court was presented with twenty-one petitions by members of the public challenging the constitutionality of a Private Member's Bill entitled 'Prohibition of Forcible Conversion of Religion'. The petitioners averred that various provisions of the Bill were in violation of religious freedom including the freedom to practice religion, the Right to Equality and non-discrimination, and, interestingly, Article 9 itself. The Bill[62] was presented by Reverend Omalpe Sobhitha Thero, Member of Parliament (MP), a Budddhist monk representing the Jathika Hela Urumaya. The preamble to the Bill suggests that it had the support of non-Buddhist sections as well:

> ...WHEREAS, the Buddhist and non-Buddhist are now under serious threat of forcible conversions and proselyzing [sic] by coercion or by allurement or by fraudulent means;
>
> AND WHEREAS, the Mahasanga [Buddhist clergy] and other religious leaders realizing the need to protect and promote religious harmony among all religions, historically enjoyed by the people of Sri Lanka....

It is common knowledge in Sri Lanka that Buddhist and Hindu organizations collaborated on this effort.

The Bill prohibited religious conversions 'directly or otherwise' through 'force or by allurement or by any fraudulent means' (Section 2). Punishment to those who contravene that provision was imprisonment up to five years and fine (Section 4(a)). Those who were found guilty of converting a minor, a woman or persons belonging to categories specified in a schedule would be subject to an enhanced term of imprisonment and fine. Further, it required that those who adopt a new religion and also those who facilitated or participated in a

---

[62] Published in Gazette of the Democratic Socialist Republic of Sri Lanka, Part II, 28 May 2004.

conversion ceremony should inform the administrative authorities of the area in which the adoption took place within a stipulated period (Section 3). Failure to do so would be punished with imprisonment of up to five years and imposition of a fine (Section 4(b)).

This effort to criminalize forced conversions ended up with a mixed reaction of the Supreme Court. The Court found[63] the requirement to report a religious conversion by the converted and those who facilitated or witnessed a conversion to be a restraint on their freedom of religion and thus violated Article 10 of the Constitution. The Court did not discuss the reasoning underlying the finding. Certain other clauses relating to procedure were found to be in violation of the equality clause. As Article 10 is an entrenched constitutional clause, the Court declared that the Bill should therefore be adopted by the constitutionally prescribed special procedure which included submitting the Bill to a referendum.

Criminalization of religious conversion by force and fraud and through allurement was not found to be unconstitutional, although the Court suggested amendments to narrowly tailor the definition of those terms to fit the objectives of the Bill.

The Court did not elaborate on the scope of Article 10; nor did it explore whether the concept of criminalization of religious conversions—other than through force and fraudulent acts which are already punishable under existing law—is disproportionate and, therefore, constitutionally offensive.

Particularly problematic was the criminalization of conversion through allurement. Allurement was defined in the Bill as an 'offer of any temptation in the form of any gift or gratification, grant of material benefit or grant of employment or promotion in employment' (Section 8(a)). Petitioners unsuccessfully argued that acts of benevolence and charity in obedience to gospel commands may be misconstrued as acts of allurement. The Court found that what is offensive is the 'willful engagement of a deceitful exercise to secure a conversion'.[64] It proposed that the definition of allurement in the Bill be amended to include the phrase 'for the purpose of converting a person from one religion to another'.[65]

---

[63] SC Determination Nos. 2–22/2004, SC Minute of 9.08. 2004.

[64] Ibid., p. 11.

[65] Ibid., p. 15.

The question remains, however, whether offering allurement even for the purpose of conversion should be criminalized. What if the recipient of such beneficence voluntarily changes religion irrespective of the motive of the giver? Offering allurement to change political opinion or loyalties is not penalized under the law except during election time. Why are religious conversions viewed more rigidly than, for example, change of political opinion or allegiances? The Court did not examine these issues. It is submitted, with due respect, that unless a nuanced approach is adopted in dealing with these important issues, the constitutional rights discourse will remain within very parochial confines.

What is significant for purposes of the present essay is that the Court cited *Kokkinakis* v. *Greece*,[66] a case decided by the European Court of Human Rights. There, the Court was presented with the issue of deciding on the compatibility of a conviction by Greek courts of a man for engaging in proselytism in violation of Greek law with the European Convention for the Protection of Human Rights and Fundamental Freedoms. Greece has ratified the Convention.

The Court found the Greek law in question to be in line with the requirements of Article 9 of the Convention (freedom of religion clause). It was stated that the State may have to intervene in manifestation of religion or belief in order to 'reconcile the interests of the various groups and ensure that everyone's beliefs are respected'. However, on examining the facts of the case, the Court found that the petitioner had been convicted of illegal proselytism in violation of the European Convention as there was no proof of him having coerced the complainant or of having exploited her naivety. The Court went on to point out that a balance must be struck between religious freedom and State intervention that are 'necessary in a democratic society'. Freedom of religion includes 'the right to convince one's neighbour, for example, through "teaching", failing which, moreover, "freedom to change one's religion or belief", enshrined in Article 9, would be likely to remain a dead letter'.

The Supreme Court used certain sections of the *Kokkinakis* judgment only to buttress its position that anti-conversion laws that outlaw proselytism through allurement or coercion are compatible

---

[66] 17 EHRR 397; 260-A Eur. Ct. H.R. (Series A).

with religious freedom. The manner in which the European Court sought to find a balance between a broad interpretation of religious freedom on the one hand and narrowly defined legitimate State intervention on the other were not examined. The use of international or comparative law in this utilitarian manner, without carefully examining jurisprudence in its entirety, certainly cannot enrich constitutional jurisprudence.

Consequent to the judgment of the Supreme Court, so far the Bill has not been presented to Parliament for adoption. Subsequently, a few months after the judgment another MP from the Jathika Hela Urumaya, Ven. Ellawala Medhananda Thero, presented a Private Member's Bill to make Buddhism the 'official religion' of the republic which was also declared unconstitutional.[67] A few months later, in February 2005, another draft of the anti-conversion law entitled 'Freedom of Religion Act', which had been endorsed by the Attorney-General as being constitutional, was presented to the Cabinet for its approval for presentation to Parliament by former Prime Minister Ratnasiri Wickramanayake in his capacity as the minister of *Buddha Sasana*. It appears that the enactment of the Bill has not been pursued.

The Nineteenth Amendment Judgment

In a positive turn, the Supreme Court found a move to introduce the concept of a State religion to be in violation of the basic tenets of the Constitution. In the review of a Bill entitled the 'Nineteenth Amendment to the Constitution', a unanimous judgment[68] of the Court found the idea of a State religion to be repugnant to guarantees of freedom of religion, the right to profess one's religion, and the Right to Equality and non-discrimination. Curiously, the judgment found language in the Bill that was very similar to Article 9 of the Constitution to be in violation of the constitutional equality clause.

Clause 9(3) (of the Bill) provides: 'The State shall foster, protect, patronize *Buddha Sasana* and promote good understanding and harmony among the followers of other forms of worship as well as

[67] See the next section here for a discussion on the Supreme Court judgment on the Nineteenth Amendment Bill.

[68] SC Determination No.32/2004, SC Minute of 17.12.2004.

encourage the application of religious principles to create virtue and develop quality of life.'

This clause, which enjoins the State to patronize the *Buddha Sasana* while ignoring other religions, was found to be inimical to the principle of equality which is enshrined in Article 12 of the Constitution.

As the judgments are brief and not elaborated on, it is very difficult to discern the judicial reasoning underlying the various approaches. For example, Justice T.B. Weerasuriya, who participated in the progressive Nineteenth Amendment judgment, also participated in one of the judgments which struck down a Bill to incorporate a religious institution accepting anti-conversion arguments.

Justice Tilakawardane, who wrote a separate opinion on the Nineteenth Amendment case, found support for her arguments against a State religion in Article 9 itself: 'The assurance given to the state by Chapter II [Article 9] of the Constitution is to give the foremost place to Buddhism, but it explicitly says that this must necessarily be balanced to include the assurance that there should not be any interference to the equality of all religions in the country.'[69]

She emphasized that the Sri Lankan Constitution creates a secular form of governance recognizing the multicultural and plural nature of society.[70]

Pronouncement that Sri Lanka Is a Secular State

In a subsequent judgment, Chief Justice Sarath Silva—he had earlier found the incorporation of certain religious institutions to be in violation of religious freedom because of the possibility of unethical conversions—too declared that Sri Lanka is a secular State. The declaration that 'it has to be firmly borne in mind that Sri Lanka is a secular State' came in a case in which the petitioners, trustees of a Muslim mosque, complained that the police had restricted the use of loudspeakers by the mosque in violation of their fundamental rights.[71] The loudspeakers had been used for performing the customary Islamic call to prayers.

---

[69] Ibid., concurring judgment of Tilakawardane, J., p. 1.

[70] Ibid., p. 2.

[71] *Trustees, Kapuwatta Mohideen Jumma Mosque* v. *OIC Weligama*, SC Application No.38/2005 (FR) SC Minute of 9.11.2007.

The Chief Justice went on to state that as Sri Lanka is a secular State, no religious group (in this instance, adherents of Islam) could have an advantage over others, especially with regard to the enforcement of environmental protection measures (in this instance to control noise pollution). The Chief Justice's declaration on secularism was based on the argument that under Article 3 of the 1978 Constitution of Sri Lanka, sovereignty lies in the people devoid of any distinction. The judgment does not elaborate on the nexus between equal sovereignty and secularism. There was also no reference to Article 9 (Buddhism clause).

Article 9 still continues to be a source of friction and will remain so either it is done away with in a future amendment, or there is an authoritative judgment which provides clarity and assurances to the 'other' religions.

CONCLUSIONS: THE VALUE OF COMPARATIVE CONSTITUTIONALISM

The Sri Lankan constitutional experience on the State–religion relationship has been confusing, unpredictable and whimsical at best. There is no certainty about the applicable constitutional principles as judicial interpretations and reasoning have varied from situation to situation. The end result is a very confused state of affairs regarding the relationship between religion and the State. The State is to give preference to the religion of the majority, yet it is considered to be secular. The concept of a State religion has been rejected, yet minority religious institutions are enjoined from engaging in religious activities for fear that they may be inimical to the majority religion.

Underpinning that uncertainty is the nebulousness regarding the scope and meaning of Article 9 of the 1978 Constitution. Despite the reassurances of the architect of the Constitution that it will not impinge on the rights of other religious groups, both constitutional jurisprudence and State policy have clearly recognized preferential position of Buddhism as *primus inter pares*. There is no gainsaying that a true Buddhist legacy, with its tenets of compassion and tolerance, will only shore up democracy in a country. But what is at issue here is how the politics of religion and State power mesh together to undermine equality and pluralism in society.

The jurisprudence of the Supreme Court of Sri Lanka on the State–religion nexus has drawn on Indian constitutional jurisprudence and supranational human rights jurisprudence. However, it is clear that such references have been made only selectively, more to buttress the Court's position than to explore new dimensions that would have aided in progressive development of the law that effectively acknowledges and protects religious diversity. As far as South Asian constitutional jurisprudence is concerned, it has to be admitted that the choices available to the Court are quite limited. It is doubtful that the Court would have resorted to jurisdictions which recognize a State religion—and that would cover most of the countries in the region. The new constitutional dispensations in Nepal and Bhutan are as yet unknown quantities. That only leaves Indian jurisprudence for reference. India's constitutional commitment to secularism as an element of its basic structure does not seem to fit in well, not only with the Sri Lankan constitutional scheme, but also with the judicial approaches to the State–religion nexus. If the Sri Lankan judiciary had properly appreciated the experiences of its Indian counterpart, quite possibly the three 'incorporation cases' may have been decided quite differently.

In contrast, Sri Lankan constitutional jurisprudence has very readily drawn on South Asian jurisprudence (almost exclusively on Indian case law) relating to certain other areas of fundamental rights protection. That is so particularly with regard to a wider reading of freedom of expression and equal protection of the law. One gets the sense that an expanded reading of those freedoms is normatively congruent with the thinking of the Sri Lankan judiciary. The New Doctrine on Equality developed by the Bhagwati Court has, after an initial hesitation, now become a staple feature in equality cases;[72] so also, judicial receptivity to the recognition of economic and social rights via the existing guarantees of civil and political rights.[73]

---

[72] D. Udagama, 'The Right to Equality: The New Frontier in Judicial Activism', in A.R.B. Amerasinghe and S. S. Wijeratne (eds), *Human Rights, Human Values and the Rule of Law* (Legal Aid Foundation: Colombo, 2003), p. 297.

[73] D. Udagama, 'Indivisibility of Human Rights as a Fundamental Principle of Constitutional Rule', in A.R.B. Amerasinghe and S.S. Wijeratne (eds), *Human*

However, as we have observed above, issues pertaining to identity have elicited judicial insularity.

One may conclude from the above discussion that, perhaps of all the constitutional tasks, ensuring pluralism in a fragmented polity is one of the most challenging ones. Establishing religious pluralism is perhaps one of the most arduous tasks. It seems to me that comparative constitutionalism can be very useful in strengthening rights, accountability of government and so on when there is a common value base shared between and among comparative jurisdictions. Comparative experiences and jurisprudence can be very useful to provide modalities and reasoning to be employed to achieve shared political ideals, or to catalyze thinking on those ideals that are thought to be sufficiently attractive to contemplate. Whether altogether new ideals can be created through the use of comparative constitutional jurisprudence remains, in my mind, questionable. In other words, the usefulness of comparative jurisprudence generally lies more in informing the exercise of the 'margin of appreciation'—as European human rights jurisprudence would have it—in regard to the implementation of a commonly accepted norm.

Constitutionalism itself is today measured against certain higher values. As a student of international law and as a human rights advocate in the mode of Falk's 'citizen pilgrims',[74] I would argue that today international human rights norms represent the 'higher values' that inform constitutionalism. Of course, the idea of universal norms has been contested, and will continue to be contested. But at a practical level, their appeal is obvious. The emotionally charged demands for constitutional orders that protect human rights and social justice articulated in the recent 'Arab Spring' protest movements in the Middle East bear witness to that. The cure for constitutional parochialism lies in the appeal to that higher normative order.

If Sri Lanka's constitutional discourse is captive to the limitations within its own Constitution and constitutional jurisprudence,

---

Rights: Theory to Practice (Legal Aid Commission, Sri Lanka, and Human Rights Commission, Sri Lanka: Colombo, 2005), p. 285.

[74] Richard Falk, *Achieving Human Rights* (Routledge: New York, 2009), pp. 202–7.

its international legal obligations to uphold people's rights—as internationally defined and recognized as relevant by the people—will have to trump those limitations at a normative level; that is a truism, both on legal and moral planes. Where comparative constitutional jurisprudence could effectively contribute is in providing the tools—the reasoning and the modalities—to achieve those ideals.

CHAPTER SIX

Constitutional Borrowing in South Asia

India, Sri Lanka, and Secular Constitutional Identity

Gary J. Jacobsohn and Shylashri Shankar

You can translate a word by a word, but behind the word is an idea, the thing which the word denotes, and this idea you cannot translate if it does not exist among the people in whose language you are translating.[1]

These are the thoughts of the great nineteenth century Bengali writer Bankim Chandra Chatterji, whose doubts about the transferability of ideas from one culture to another have found a contemporary echo in an increasingly voluble debate over the judicial application of foreign sources in constitutional adjudication. This debate has surfaced mainly in the United States, where disparagement of constitutional borrowing resonates deeply both politically and jurisprudentially, but in other places, too, the question of how permeable constitutional borders should be often evokes passionate contestation.

One such place is South Asia, and in this essay we pursue the question of cross-national uses of foreign law with reference to a subject that, perhaps more than any other in this region, generates sharply divergent views, namely, secularism. Specifically, we look at

---

[1] Quoted in T.N. Madan, 'Secularism in Its Place', in Rajeev Bhargava (ed.), *Secularism and Its Critics* (Oxford University Press: New Delhi, 1998), p. 308.

Indian constitutional law as a possible source for judicial borrowing and outcomes in Sri Lanka. That Indian jurisprudence would present judges in neighbouring South Asian countries with precedents and ideas for addressing their own Church–State issues is not surprising. Although, as we will detail, the constitutional status of religion in India is in various ways unique to that nation, its dominant position in the subcontinent—politically, economically, and militarily—ensures that the legal configuration of its spiritual and temporal domains will receive serious attention in non-Indian South Asian courts. In the case of Sri Lanka, the direct intervention of the larger nation in the internal constitutional affairs of its island neighbour creates the further likelihood that the Sri Lankan judiciary's close scrutiny of Indian constitutional approaches may have as much to do with political necessity as it does with jurisprudence.

Close scrutiny, however, need not result in decisions to emulate the scrutinized; indeed in South Asia, scepticism about the wisdom of doing so in matters related to secular constitutional development is well entrenched in the political and legal culture. More often than not, it is directed towards proposals rooted in a Western-style model of separation of the Church and the State that strikes local observers as out of synchronization with the realities of religion as experienced in the region. For example, the quote from Chatterji appears in an essay by T.N. Madan, who, along with Ashis Nandy, are the most prominent Indian critics of secular solutions imported from the West for application to the South Asian setting.[2] Even among many who find the critiques of Madan and Nandy too sweeping in their categorical rejection of the liberal secular world-view, there remains substantial doubt about the prospects for constitutional transplantation. Whatever the merits of this anti-modernist critique, it has enjoyed a respectful, and sometimes influential, hearing within Indian legal and scholarly communities.[3]

---

[2] Madan and Nandy embrace a Gandhian, anti-modernist suspicion of the State, which places them at odds with much of mainstream secular opinion in India. This also makes them much more sceptical of ideas imported from the West. For Nandy's views, see, for example, 'The Politics of Secularism and the Recovery of Religious Tolerance', *Alternatives*, (1988), Issue No. 13.

[3] See, for example, Amartya Sen, *The Argumentative Indian: Writings on Indian History, Culture and Identity* (Farrar, Straus, and Giroux: New York, 2005), pp. 312–15.

Our concern, however, is not with such long-distance borrowing, but with the sort that takes place among nations sharing a closer geographical proximity. While such proximity may suggest—particularly to the distant observer—greater incentives for cross-national constitutional appropriation, those closer to the scene and possessing a more refined sense of relevant political and cultural differences may, in contrast, find themselves impressed by the obstacles to successful legal transplantation.[4] Indeed, to the extent that fundamental concerns about the character of the polity are implicated in decisions about the use of foreign sources in constitutional adjudication, geographic contiguity should in principle be irrelevant to questions centering on the wisdom or advisability of constitutional borrowing.[5]

In Indian jurisprudence, concerns about the character of the polity receive constitutional articulation in the doctrinal language of 'basic structure'.[6] Thus, the Supreme Court has, invoking that designation, found a number of constitutional features of such importance

---

Sen differs sharply from Nandy and Madan but credits them with a 'plausible' diagnosis of the problem.

   [4] In this regard, it is worth reflecting on the American–Canadian constitutional relationship. See, for example, Seymour Martin Lipset, *Continental Divide: The Values and Institutions of the United States and Canada* (Routledge: New York, 1990).

   [5] Responding to criticism that the draft of the Indian Constitution borrowed heavily from other constitutions at the expense of India's indigenous village system, B.N. Rau (the author of the original draft) said:

> [S]o long as the borrowings have been adapted to India's peculiar circumstances, they cannot in themselves be said to constitute a defect.... To profit from the experience of other countries or from the past experience of one's own is the path of wisdom. There is another advantage in borrowing not only the substance but even the language of established constitutions; for we obtain in this way the benefit of the interpretation put upon the borrowed provisions by the courts of the countries of their origin and we thus avoid ambiguity or doubt.

   B.N. Rau, *India's Constitution in the Making* (Orient Longman: Bombay, 1960), p. 360.

   [6] The doctrine has been described in many works. See in particular, A. Lakshminath, *Basic Structure and Constitutional Amendments: Limitations and Justiciability* (Deep & Deep Publications: New Delhi, 2002); Paras Diwan and Peeyushi Diwan, *Amending Powers and Constitutional Amendment*, 2nd Ed. (Deep & Deep Publications: New Delhi, 1997); and Sudhir Krishnaswamy, *Democracy in India: A Study of The Basic Structure Doctrine* (Oxford University Press: New Delhi, 2008).

that it will challenge any action, including an amendment of the Constitution, which would threaten their existence. In several landmark decisions, it has justified its commitment to basic structure by asserting the Court's obligation to preserve the Constitution's transformative and ameliorative identity.[7] In this essay, we propose to consider the practice of constitutional borrowing in light of this commitment. Much as the defense of constitutional identity in India has structured the judicial response to the behaviour of non-judicial institutional actors, it can also function as a measure of the behaviour of courts themselves. Will the incorporation of foreign ideas and approaches into a nation's constitutional settlements materially threaten its constitutional identity? If it does, should that necessarily preclude borrowing? If a particular (basic) structural attribute (such as, secularism in India) is critical to a polity's constitutional identity, should courts in nations where that attribute is differently constituted (for example, Sri Lanka) pursue the indigenous orientation to the exclusion of the foreign? Or, to the extent that constitutional identities are at least in part mutable, is the judicial decision to seek instruction from the jurisprudence of another judiciary an appropriate way to re-constitute or reinforce a polity's identity?

To address these questions, we situate the debate over the use of foreign legal materials within the context of the Sri Lankan Supreme Court's consideration of Indian secularism jurisprudence. The centrepiece of our analysis is the Court's judgment in a landmark case in which the issue of secularism was positioned at the intersection of several subjects critical to comparative constitutional reflection on India and Sri Lanka: basic structure, federalism, and popular sovereignty. The case concerned a challenge to an amendment to the Constitution that provided for devolution of political power as a solution to Sri Lanka's destructive and debilitating ethnic conflict. Had there been no mention of India in the Court's several opinions, any informed observer would still have been mindful of the instrumental Indian role in inspiring the events that culminated in the litigation. But the opinions are rich in references to constitutional

---

[7] The major cases are discussed in Gary Jeffrey Jacobsohn, 'An Unconstitutional Constitution? A Comparative Perspective', *International Journal of Constitutional Law,* (2006), 4(3): 460–87.

jurisprudence from the mainland neighbour, and we will discuss their significance to the question at hand. Again, that question focuses on secularism, yet as we shall see, the invocations of Indian experience do not, for the most part, explicitly relate to that subject. This will permit us to emphasize that the problem of secularism, as well as the attendant issues connected to constitutional borrowing, cannot intelligibly be considered apart from some fundamental structural and philosophical issues that transcend the primary focus on religion and politics.

Of course, to make this argument, we first have to outline the various ways in which secularism in India and Sri Lanka is similarly and differently constituted. Some of these ways are obvious as textual matters, for example, the constitutionally entrenched principle of non-establishment in India as opposed to the explicit constitutional support for Buddhism in Sri Lanka. Others are to be found in the broader historical commitments of the two regimes, for example, their contrasting approaches to religiously-based social and economic inequalities. As part of this background we will consider several Church–State cases in which the Sri Lankan Supreme Court has been instructed in its judgments by the rulings of its Indian counterpart.

THE DEBATE OVER FOREIGN SOURCES

There is nothing new about cross-national constitutional borrowing. For centuries, constitutional designers and interpreters have looked beyond their shores to discover in the practices of other nations possible sources for emulation.[8] But with the increased trafficking in constitutional ideas that has accompanied the global judicialization of politics, the appropriateness of doing so—particularly as this relates to the activity of courts—has emerged in recent years as a contested issue. The controversy is particularly pronounced in the United States, where the Supreme Court is notable for having its judgments cited in other countries, but where judges have historically been reluctant to return the compliment.[9]

---

[8] A notable example from India is its borrowing of the idea of directive principles from Ireland.

[9] For a discussion of this controversy, see, Gary Jeffrey Jacobsohn, 'The Permeability of Constitutional Borders', *Texas Law Review*, (2004), 82: 1763–818.

Nearly fifty years ago, Indian legal scholar P.K. Tripathi anticipated some of the concerns about constitutional borrowing that today are commonly heard in the debate—on and off of the Court—in the United States.

> When a judge looks to foreign legal systems for analogies that shed light on any of the new cases before him, he is looking to legal material which he is absolutely free to reject unless it appeals to his reason. Appeal to one's reason, more often than not, amounts to a confirmation and a strengthening of one's own opinion rather than a shaping of that opinion…. Historical association, cognate nature of the two legal systems, analogy of legal institutions, a supposed need for uniformity, similarity or identity of language, and such other 'reasons' as may be advanced, seem to possess no compelling force of their own; any of them can be played against another; any of them could be preferred to another; and, of course, any of them could be cited in support of a decision where it happens to suit.[10]

For Tripathi, then, the flaw in the practice of citing foreign sources is that it exacerbates the problem of judicial discretion; it is an invitation to judicial opportunism.

More recently, American judge and scholar Richard Posner affirmed that this objection remains a continuing concern. 'If foreign decisions are freely citable, any judge wanting a supporting citation has only to troll deeply enough in the world's *corpus juris* to find it.'[11] Posner proceeds to connect this critique—let's call it the *opportunism objection*—to another that emphasizes cultural diversity. '[F]oreign decisions emerge from complex social, political, cultural, and historical backgrounds of which Supreme Court justices…are largely ignorant.'[12] Accordingly, the abuses associated with judicial

---

The scholarly literature on this subject is rapidly growing. A representative sample of contrasting views may be found in Roger P. Alford, 'In Search of a Theory for Constitutional Comparativism', *UCLA Law Review*, (2005), 52: 639–713; and Vicki C. Jackson, 'Constitutional Comparisons: Convergence, Resistance, Engagement', *Harvard Law Review*, (2005), 119(1): 109–28.

[10] P.K. Tripathi, 'Foreign Precedents and Constitutional Law', *Columbia Law Review*, (1957), 57: 319–46.

[11] Richard Posner, 'The Supreme Court: Foreword', *Harvard Law Review*, (2005), 119(31): 86.

[12] Ibid.

discretion are much more troubling when they are entwined in the confusion of cultural misapprehension.

Culture objection embodies two related concerns, both of which need to be examined within the South Asian context. The first implicates the question of competence, the second, of identity. Strategic judicial invocation of imported constitutional materials stands a good chance of proving unreliable in light of the presumed inability of judges to make the necessary functional translations between culture A and culture B.[13] The legally sacrosanct principle of *stare decisis* provides cover for opportunistic judicial selectivity, and the reward for manipulating homegrown precedents is often achievement of the judge's desired result. In the case of foreign precedents, however, the lack of familiarity with the cultural context within which those precedents are embedded can easily render unattainable the outcome sought by the uninformed judge. Such failures are arguably more likely to occur in areas of law where the issues under consideration are less amenable to the application of universal standards. For example, Vicki Jackson has argued that the benefits of cross-national borrowing are lower for adjudication of doctrinal questions of federalism than in the adjudication of individual rights issues.[14] Thus, 'federalism provisions of constitutions are often peculiarly the product of political compromise in historically situated moments, generally designed as a practical rather than a principled accommodation of competing interests'.[15] As we shall see, federalism and secularism are closely connected in India and Sri Lanka, and it will behoove us to consider whether these issues are too 'contingently located' for 'transnational understandings of those terms to emerge'.[16] The same might of course be asked of secularism itself.

In doing so, it will be necessary to situate these issues within a wider context of constitutional purpose and aspiration. The question of competent and effective translation (to say nothing of the concerns about legitimacy such borrowings might evoke) must distinguish

---

[13] On this point, see, Mark Tushnet, 'The Possibilities of Comparative Constitutional Law', *Yale Law Journal*, (1999), 108: 1225.

[14] Vicki C. Jackson, 'Narratives of Federalism: Of Continuities and Comparative Constitutional Experience', *Duke Law Journal*, (2001), 51: 223.

[15] Ibid., p. 273.

[16] Ibid., p. 274.

among the various constitutive commitments that might differentiate countries. This encourages what Sujit Choudhry has referred to as 'dialogical interpretation', that is to say, 'comparative jurisprudence [as]…an important stimulus to legal self-reflection'.[17] The result of this reflection could very well be rejection of the foreign precedent, but the judicial exercise may be heuristically valuable in clarifying and deepening the understanding of one's own constitutional condition.[18] As Choudhry's discussion (Chapter 2 in this volume) of the landmark *Naz Foundation* case cogently demonstrates, the application of foreign precedents can serve to highlight 'the ideals animating the adoption of the Indian Constitution' even when the judicial rationale for such usage is not expressly elaborated.[19]

Stated otherwise, the effort might serve to illuminate a nation's constitutional identity. For example, in Choudhry's account of the Delhi High Court's 2009 decision striking down, on constitutional grounds, a ban on consensual same-sex acts of adults in private, the Court's appropriation of foreign jurisprudence illustrates 'that there is a way to do comparative constitutional law seriously that not only acknowledges but also affirms the special place of the Indian Constitution in the modern Indian political identity'.[20] Indeed, the

[17] See, Sujit Choudhry, 'Globalization in Search of Justification', *Indiana Law Journal*, (1999), 74: 819–36. Seen in this light, there is nothing in principle that should lead one to expect that borrowing is a practice whose benefit is to be appreciated most by those with transformational constitutions. Indeed, to appreciate why one should endeavour to preserve, comparative jurisprudence may provide the most compelling answers.

[18] See, Kim Lane Scheppele, 'Aspirational and Aversive Constitutionalism: The Case for Studying Cross-constitutional Influence Through Negative Models', *International Journal of Constitutional Law*, (2003), 1(2): 296.

[19] See in this volume, Chapter 2 (Sujit Choudhry, 'How to Do Comparative Constitutional Law in India: *Naz Foundation*, Same Sex Rights, and Dialogical Interpretation').

[20] Choudhry, Chapter 2 in this volume: 'External legal sources were used as foil to constitutional self-reflection, and nourish and reframe the judges' reading of internal constitutional sources.' Choudhry's emphasis on 'the constitution as a dynamic, evolving instrument of social change' is consistent with the view taken in this essay on the essence of Indian constitutional identity. The Court manifestly intended its decision to be interpreted as a defense of an Indian constitutional identity that 'protects and celebrates diversity'. *Naz Foundation* v. *Government of India*, WP(C) No. 7455/2001 (2009), at para 80.

Supreme Court of India has confronted the problem of constitutional identity much more explicitly and directly than have the courts in most countries. In the years of wrestling with the recurring question of the unconstitutional constitutional amendment, the Court developed the basic structure doctrine, according to which specific features of the Constitution were deemed sufficiently fundamental to the integrity of the constitutional project as to warrant immunity from significant change. Underlying the basic structure jurisprudence is a preoccupation with constitutional identity. In *Kesavananda Bharati* v. *State of Kerala*, the leading Indian case on implicit substantive limits to constitutional revision, one of the judges concluded: 'One cannot legally use the Constitution to destroy itself.' He then added: 'The personality of the Constitution must remain unchanged.'[21] This emphasis became a recurring theme in Indian jurisprudence, as exemplified in *Minerva Mills Ltd.* v. *Union of India* with the injunction: '[T]he Constitution is a precious heritage; therefore you cannot destroy its identity.'[22]

CONSTITUTIONAL SECULARISM IN INDIA AND SRI LANKA

India

Much of the resistance to constitutional borrowing from the West is attributable to the well-founded perception that religion on the subcontinent is more deeply entrenched in the fabric of society than it is in the United States or in Europe. Although India (unlike its neighbours) shares a formal political and constitutional commitment with democracies in the West to State neutrality toward religions within its borders, a profoundly different view prevails on the possibility, let alone the desirability, of relegating the spiritual life to the private realm. Again, Bankim Chandra Chatterji expressed very well a sentiment that has continuing constitutional import and significance.

> With other peoples, religion is only a part of life; there are things religious, and there are things lay and secular.... To other peoples, their relations to God and to the spiritual world are things sharply distinguished from their

---

[21] *Kesavananda Bharati* v. *State of Kerala*, 1973 SC 1461 (1973), 1624.
[22] *Minerva Mills Ltd.* v. *Union of India*, AIR 1980 SC 1789, 1798.

relations to man and to the temporal world…. [In India the spiritual and temporal lives] are incapable of being so distinguished. They form one compact and harmonious whole, to separate which into component parts is to break the entire fabric.[23]

Thus, where faith and piety are widely and directly inscribed in routine social patterns, a viable constitutional approach to Church–State relations will require greater attention to the substance of religious belief than in places where social conditions bear a less theological imprint.

Indeed, from the very beginning of constitutional governance in independent India, official indifference to what transpired within the religious domain was never a plausible option. The Indian Constitution was adopted against a backdrop of sectarian violence that was only the latest chapter in a complex centuries old story of Hindu–Muslim relations on the Asian subcontinent. Much of that history had been marked by peaceful coexistence; nevertheless, the bloodbath that accompanied Partition reflected ancient contestations and ensured that the goal of communal harmony would be a priority in the constitution-making process. If not as urgent, then certainly as important, was the goal of social reconstruction, which could not be addressed without constitutional recognition of the State's interest in the 'essentials of religion'.[24] The depth of religion's penetration into a social structure that was by any reasonable standard grossly unjust, meant that the framers' hopes for a democratic polity would have to be accompanied by State intervention in the spiritual domain. The design for secularism in India required a creative balance between socio-economic reform that could limit religious options and political toleration of diverse religious practices and communal development.

---

[23] Quoted in Nirad C. Chaudhuri, *Hinduism: A Religion to Live* (Oxford University Press: New Delhi, 1979), p. 11.

[24] What this means is that justices in India often find it difficult to avoid what their counterparts in many other countries can, namely, an inquiry into theological issues so as to determine what exactly is integral to a given religion. For example, in an important early polygamy case, the opinion for the Court observed: '[I]t is rather difficult to accept that polygamy is an integral part of Hindu religion.' *State of Bombay* v. *Appa*, AIR Bombay 84, (1952), 86. In another case the Court similarly concluded that polygamy is not 'an essential part of the Hindu religion'. *Ram Prasad* v. *State of U.P.*, AIR Allahabad 411 (1957), 413.

This balance is inscribed in several constitutional provisions that express the limits and possibilities of secularism in India. Thus, the ameliorative aspiration of Indian secularism is embodied in Article 25, which, after providing for religious freedom, declares that the State shall not be prevented from 'regulating or restricting any economic, financial, political or other secular activity which may be associated with religious practice'. Additional provisions are designed to accommodate the other principal facet of Indian social reality, the entrenched character of communal affiliation. Under Article 26, religious denominations are granted the right to establish and maintain institutions for religious and charitable purposes, and the same right is extended to the creation and administration of religiously based educational structures in Article 30. Taken together, the ameliorative and communal provisions evince a constitutional purpose to address the social conditions of people long burdened by the inequities of religiously inspired hierarchies, while pursuing a vision of inter-group comity whose fulfillment necessitates caution in the pursuit of abstract justice.

The delicate balance of the Constitution's dual commitment to social reform and the integrity of group religious life is dramatically highlighted in the Supreme Court's repeated efforts to illuminate the State's obligation 'to secure for the citizens a uniform civil code throughout the territory of India'. This Article 44 commitment is located in the Directive Principles section of the Constitution, which means that its aspirational content falls short of creating an enforceable legal right. Nevertheless, the Court's interpretive interventions in regard to these matters have left a significant impression on the Indian political landscape. Its judgment in the *Shah Bano* case, in which a Muslim woman's claim to maintenance from her divorced husband was upheld over the objection that to do so would undermine Muslim personal law, precipitated a series of political actions—including the government's support of legislation to undo the decision—that (whatever the objective reality) became a rallying cry for many who seven years later participated in the destruction of the Babri Masjid (a mosque) in the city of Ayodhya. More recently, the principal opinion in *Sarla Mudgal* v. *Union of India*, a case concerning one of the ingenious ways in which Hindu men have tried to circumvent the ban on polygamous marriages, roiled political waters again by declaiming: 'When more than 80% of the citizens have already been brought under the codified personal law there is no justification whatsoever to keep in abeyance, any more, the introduction of "uniform civil code" for all citizens in the territory of India.'[25]

In a sense, the question as to the merits of this insistence on uniformity is what the debate over secularism in India is all about. The principle of *sarva dharma sambhava*, or equal treatment of religions, is widely accepted as the foundational premise of the nation's secular constitutional commitment, but its meaning has long been contestable. For some it means that 'no one religion should be given preferential status, or unique distinction, that no one religion should be accorded special privileges...for that would be a violation of the basic principles of democracy'.[26] Under this banner of constitutionally required state equidistance from all religions may be found people with very little in common politically, including Western-oriented constitutional liberals and many Hindu nationalists who have figured out that the enforcement of this principle may work in favour of the majority religion.[27]

Sri Lanka

Secularism in Sri Lanka is inextricably linked to the ethnic struggle between the majority Sinhalese (who are predominantly Buddhist) and minority Tamils for equality and even supremacy.[28] While the first

[25] *Sarla Mudgal* v. *Union of India*, AIR SC 1531 (1995), 1532.

[26] Justice A.M. Ahmadi, in *S. R. Bommai* v. *Union of India*, 3 SC 1 (1994), 76.

[27] Another version is less formalistic in its understanding of equality and arguably more reflective of the reality of Indian secularism as well as its normative presuppositions. As explicated by such theorists as Neera Chandhoke and Rajeev Bhargava, this depiction holds that the application of formal equality in a profoundly non-egalitarian society only insures that pervasive inequality will be reproduced. This leads, in Bhargava's account, to an endorsement of 'contextual secularism', which has at its core the 'strategy of principled distance'. Rajeev Bhargava, 'What is Secularism For?', in Rajeev Bhargava (ed.), *Secularism and its Critics*, p. 515.

[28] According to the 2001 Census (which does not include the violence affected districts in the north and the east), approximately 76.7 per cent of the 16.92 million Sri Lankans are Buddhist, 7.8 per cent Hindu, 6.1 per cent Christian (mainly Roman Catholics), and 8.5 per cent Muslim (mainly Sunnis). Christians live mainly in the west, with much of the east Muslim and north almost exclusively Hindu. Family

constitution in 1948 did not address the position of Buddhism and even incorporated specific minority safeguards, later constitutions omitted these safeguards and gave primacy to Buddhism while simultaneously mandating religious freedom for the minority Hindu, Muslim, and Christian groups. Since Independence, the Sri Lankan State grappled with maintaining the hegemony of Sinhalese Buddhist national identity without undermining other ethnic and religious identities. Buddhism was harnessed and politicized to respond to ethnic and linguistic differences, prompting commentators to liken it to Hindu nationalism in India. Sinhala Buddhist reality equated the ethnic community (Sinhalese) with religion (Theravada Buddhism), language (Sinhala), race (Aryan Sinhalese), and nation (Sri Lanka).[29] Sinhala nationalism emphasized the unitary nature of the State controlled by the Sinhala majority and rejected equal status for Tamil nationalism because of historically buttressed fears of Dravidian conquest.[30] Even the national flag, according to the Tamil minorities, represented the dominance of the Sinhalese community in the form of a lion with a sword.[31]

---

law is adjudicated by the customary law of each religious group with final appeal in a secular authority, the Supreme Court. Separate ministries in the government address religious affairs, namely, the Ministry of *Buddha Sasana*, the Department of Muslim Religious & Cultural Affairs, the Ministry of Hindu Religious Affairs, and the Ministry of Christian Affairs.

[29] D. Allen, 'Religious-Political Conflict in Sri Lanka: Philosophical Considerations,' in D. Allen (ed.), *Religion and Political Conflict in South Asia: India, Pakistan, Sri Lanka* (Greenwood Press: Westport, Connecticut, 1992). Allen warns against viewing Sinhala Buddhism as a monolithic entity, and cites studies that emphasize significant differences between popular and doctrinal/scriptural Buddhism, tradition, and modern revivalist Buddhism.

[30] See also, J. Uyangoda, 'The State and the Process of Devolution in Sri Lanka', in S. Bastian (ed.), *Devolution and Development in Sri Lanka* (ICES: Colombo, 1994); N. Tiruchelvam, 'Federalism and Diversity in Sri Lanka', in Yash Ghai (ed.), *Autonomy and Ethnicity* (Cambridge University Press: Cambridge, 2000), pp. 198–200.

[31] The flag has a lion with a sword facing two stripes in saffron and green symbolizing minorities. A Tamil senator, S.Nadesan, recorded his disapproval of the design in 1950: 'I regret that I am unable to agree to the majority decision of the National Flag Committee. In my view a national flag apart from giving an honoured place to all communities in the flag must be a *symbol of national unity*. ... [A]nyone viewing the design...cannot be blamed if he thinks that the minorities are given a place outside the Lion Flag.... Why then do we want to segregate the saffron and green strips which are provided to satisfy minority sentiments outside the borders

The majority–minority struggle played out in the citizenship and linguistic arenas. Immediately after Independence, the failure of legal challenges to three discriminatory pieces of legislation—the Citizenship Act, 1948, the Franchise Legislation, 1949—depriving Tamil plantation workers of Indian descent of franchise—and the Official Language Act, 1956—making Sinhalese the only official language—eroded the faith of the minorities in the institutions of the State.[32] These events trapped the State into correcting historical imbalances in education and employment for the Sinhalese at the expense of the Tamils and other minorities. Sovereignty was equated with unitarism and centralization, which soon found expression in the Sinhalization of administration, triggering militant secessionism of Tamils and an exodus of mixed race Europeans.[33] As Asanga Welikala points out, the formal constitutionalization of Sinhalese majoritarianism occurred in 1972.

The Constitution of 1972 discontinued the special protection accorded to minorities by Section 29 of the previous Constitution of 1947, expressly entrenched the unitary nature of republic, and impinged not only on the secular principle, but also trampled upon multicultural sensitivities by giving constitutional recognition to Buddhism as having a 'foremost' status in the state, entitling it to the latter's protection. It whittled down the principle of horizontal separation of powers at the centre and strengthened majoritarianism. In this way, Sri Lanka's first autochthonous constitution only served to aggravate ethno-political tensions by replicating the very constitutional anomalies at the heart of minority concerns.[34]

---

of the Lion Flag?' Report of the National Flag Committee, Parliamentary Series, Fourth Session of the First Parliament, No.5, 27 February 1951.

[32] *Mudanayake* v. *Sivagnasunderam; Kodikam Pillai* v. *Mudanayake* challenged the Citizenship Act No. 18, 1948 and the Franchise Act, 1949 depriving these Tamils of franchise. However the judges found the laws *intra vires*. *Kodeswaran* v. *Attorney General* challenged the Official Language Act, which required bureaucrats to pass language tests to qualify for promotion and increments. Again, judges refused to consider the constitutionality, and merely confined themselves to examining whether a public servant had the right to sue the crown for recovery of wages.

[33] James Manor, *The Expedient Utopian: Bandaranaike and Ceylon* (Cambridge University Press: Cambridge, 1989).

[34] Asanga Welikala, 'Towards Two Nations in One State', paper presented at the Institute of Federalism (University of Fribourg: Fribourg, 2002).

What was the place for ethnic and religious minorities, particularly the Hindu Tamils, within a Sri Lankan nation? To answer this question, let us turn to the Sri Lankan Constitution, which differs from India in three important ways that have implications for the practice of cross-border borrowing. First, the Constitutions—1948, and particularly 1972 and 1978 Constitutions—have been explicitly preservationist of a historical Sinhala project, unlike the ameliorative bent of the Indian counterpart.[35] The Preamble to the 1978 Constitution promised all citizens freedom, equality, justice, fundamental human rights, and an independent judiciary. Article 9, which was introduced in 1972 and continued in 1978, guaranteed the foremost place to Buddhism and made it the duty of the State to protect and foster the *Buddha Sasana*, while assuring to all religions the rights guaranteed by Articles 10 and 14(1)(a) and (e). Article 10 guaranteed the 'freedom of thought, conscience and religion, including the freedom to have or adopt a religion or belief of his choice,' and Article 14 allowed the freedom of worship, free expression (including religious expression), and the freedom singly or in groups in public or private to manifest one's religion or belief in worship, observance, practice, and teaching.[36] Other rights included the right to be treated equally by law and not to be discriminated against on religious grounds.[37] The Buddhist nature

[35] Jayadeva Uyangoda, 'Questions of Sri Lanka's Minority Rights', *Minority Protection in South Asia Series*, (2001), 2: 58–63. Uyangoda argues that any impulse for constitutional reform emanating from the Sinhalese political leadership was conceptualized not in terms of democratizing majority–minority relations within a pluralist framework, but as a way of giving juridical expression to the majority community's nationalist aspirations. A contrary view, as Udagama (Chapter 5 in the present volume) highlights, is that of Colin R. de Silva who maintained that Article 9 did not infringe on Article 10, but an analysis of court rulings by us and Udagama shows that the Supreme Court used Article 9 to narrowly interpret Article 10.

[36] *Jeevakaran* v. *Ratnasiri Wickremanayake and Others* (S.C. No. 623/96). The Hindu petitioner said that the Government's policy of removing a Hindu sacred day (Mahasivaratri) from the list of public holidays was a violation of freedom of religion, worship and equality (Article 12(2)). The judgment held that there was a clear distinction between infringement of a right, and 'not facilitating' a right. 'The essence of the freedom of worship is that the State (or even a private employer) must not prohibit or interfere with the citizen's practice of his religion, but is not bound to provide facilities for such practice.'

[37] Article 12 (which corresponds to the Indian Constitution's Article 14) forbids the State from denying to any person equality before the law, and equal protection

of the state meant that equal treatment of other religions could be sacrificed when Buddhism was under threat (which, as we shall see, occurred in the religious conversion cases).

Second, unlike India, the entire Constitution can be (and has been) amended or repealed by the legislature as long as two-thirds of parliamentarians (including those absent) vote for it, implying a view of the Constitution 'as a statute rather than as a special document'.[38] Some Articles were harder to amend and included the freedom of religion and worship, the pre-eminent position of Buddhism, and the commitment to the unitary nature of the state. They reflected the basic character of Sri Lankan constitutional identity. However, these 'entrenched' Articles are not similar to India's inviolable 'basic structure'.[39] Most judgments have permitted their repeal.[40]

Third, the notion that sovereignty is vested in the people and by implication in Parliament prevents judicial review and has profound implications for secularism and minority rights, since the Sinhalese majority can, in theory at least, design a new constitution abolishing secularism.[41]

These distinctions had an important impact on whether judges borrowed or did not borrow from Indian jurisprudence. The *Thirteenth Amendment* case and the cases concerning bigamy and

---

of the law. This Article guarantees equality among equals (that is, formal equality).

[38] Rohan Edrisinhe, 'Sri Lanka: Constitutions Without Constitutionalism: A Tale of Three and a Half Constitutions', Sri Lanka: Colombo (unpublished paper).

[39] Article 82(5) provided that a Bill to amend any provision of the Constitution or repeal and replace the Constitution required a two-thirds majority of all the members of Parliament voting for it, including those not present. Article 83 allowed for the amendment, repeal, and replacement of or inclusion of anything inconsistent with Articles 1, 2, 3, 6, 7, 8, 9, 10, and 11 or of Article 83 itself, if the number of votes cast in favour of it amounted to not less than two-thirds of the whole number of members of the House voting for it (including those not present) and the People approved it at a Referendum. Articles 1, 2, 3, 6, 7, 8, 9, 10, and 11 have been referred to as 'entrenched' Articles.

[40] In *Premalal Perera* v. *Weerasuriya*, they read Article 10 as 'entrenched', while in the *Thirteenth Amendment* judgment they permitted total amendment and repeal.

[41] However, the Court has the power to vet infringements of fundamental rights by executive and administrative actions. See also, R. Coomaraswamy, 'Devolution, the Law, and Judicial Construction', in S. Bastian (ed.), *Devolution and Development*; and R. Coomaraswamy, *Ideology and the Constitution: Essays on Constitutional Jurisprudence* (International Centre for Ethnic Studies: Colombo, 1996), Chapter 5.

conversion demonstrate the identity-reinforcing nature of Sri Lankan judicial borrowing, in which judges engaged in behaviour, best described as opportunistic cross-border borrowing, to preserve the unitary and Buddhist nature of Sri Lanka.

The *Thirteenth Amendment* Case

The Holding

The Thirteenth Amendment arose from the decentralization agreement negotiated under Indian auspices in the Indo–Sri Lankan accord of 1987. The agreement came after years of bloody conflict between a guerilla group, the Liberation Tigers of Tamil Eelam (LTTE), and the Sri Lankan government. The Sinhalese–Tamil ethnic relationship had followed a sequence of ethnic cohabitation (1948–56), autonomy (1956–72), soft separatism (1972–83), and ethnic conflict (1983–present).

The agreement's devolution of power to provincial councils necessitated changes to Article 2, which had 'entrenched' the unitary nature of the state. The shift towards federalism (and India's role in this development), and the perception that the reforms effectively eroded the sovereignty of the country, aroused violent protests from sections of Sinhalese society, in particular an armed insurgency led by the Janatha Vimukthi Peramuna (JVP). President J.R. Jayawardene needed the Supreme Court's approval for the constitutional amendment after Buddhist organizations challenged it in Court. It was then narrowly affirmed by a 5–4 margin.

The Thirteenth Amendment, which was roughly patterned on the Indian model of federalism, was designed to address two demands of the Tamil minority—equal language rights and greater autonomy. Article 18 was amended to include Tamil as an official language and English as a link language. A Provincial Councils Bill decentralized power to the provinces, thus seemingly undercutting the unitary basis of governance; although, as Edrisinhe points out, the reality was that the Amendment merely provided a veneer of devolution while retaining vast powers with the centre.[42] Not only did the Provincial Councils not have complete control over any subject,

---

[42] Interview, March 2006.

they could be abolished or their power curtailed by unilateral actions of the Central Parliament. The Amendment, which was piloted by President Jayawardene's party, was passed by a two-thirds majority in Parliament. It was challenged as a breach of Article 2 (unitary state), Article 3 (sovereignty of people), and Article 9 (pre-eminent position of Buddhism). The issue before the justices was whether the amendment was in fact a breach of the entrenched Articles.

All the justices agreed that the Thirteenth Amendment could not affect the pre-eminent position of Buddhism or the unitary nature of the state, which were the main elements of Sinhalese Sri Lankan constitutional identity. While the majority interpreted devolution within a unitary framework, the minority rejected the changes, insisting that their radical features required submission for popular approval through a referendum.[43] The majority viewed the bills as either ordinary legislation (needing a simple legislative majority) or constituent legislation (requiring a two-thirds majority), while the minority saw them as amendments necessitating Article 83's mandate of a two-third majority and follow-up referendum.

India's Looming Presence

In his dissent, Justice Wanasundera spoke of the *Thirteenth Amendment* case in a manner that possibly reflected a consensus not otherwise apparent in the substance of the decision's various opinions. He described it as 'the most critical, the most important and the most far-reaching [case] that had ever arisen in the history of our courts'.[44] What perhaps accounts for this assessment were the issues of identity that were debated by the members of the Court. Thus, the division among the justices implicated some of the most profound concerns that can be raised about a constitution: whether changes to it have transformed its identity into something very different from what it was.

---

[43] Four judges agreed that there was no need for a referendum since the nature of the pertinent changes was consistent with the Constitution. One judge agreed with that general assessment but said that the Thirteenth Amendment's adoption nevertheless required the referendum. Four judges dissented, arguing that both Bills required a referendum.

[44] *In re The Thirteenth Amendment to the Constitution and the Provincial Councils Bill*, 2 Sri L.R. 312 (1987), at 333.

In answering this question both the majority and minority were importantly influenced by Indian constitutional design and interpretation. On the key point—did the Thirteenth Amendment so decisively alter the Constitution's basic structure as to render it illegitimate?—the majority found the Indian experience inapposite and the minority held it essential to reaching the correct outcome in the case, namely, the invalidation of the constitutional changes. But on several inter-related issues, both sides drew upon the illumination from Indian experience in framing the constitutional questions and shaping their judicial responses.

The Court's opinion by Chief Justice Sharvananda concluded: '[T]here is no foundation for the contention that the basic features of the Constitution have been altered or destroyed by the proposed amendments. The Constitution will survive without any loss of identity despite the amendment. The basic structure or framework of the Constitution will continue intact in its integrity.'[45] His reason for thinking so was that Sri Lanka's unitary state would remain in place because devolution would not convert it into a federal or quasi-federal state. He characterized the unitary state as one possessing the supremacy of the Central Parliament and the absence of subsidiary sovereign bodies; while a federal state has coordinate authorities independent of each other. He read the Provincial Councils Bill as devolving rather than decentralizing power:

> The concept of devolution is used to mean the delegation of central government powers without the relinquishment of supremacy. Devolution may be legislative or administrative or both. It should be distinguished from 'decentralisation' which is a method whereby some central government powers of decision making are exercised by officials of the central government located in various regions.[46]

Interestingly, the judgment regarding the undiminished authority of the central government anticipates the Indian Supreme Court's ruling in that country's leading case on secularism, *S. R. Bommai v. Union of India* (3 SC 1, 1994). There, the Court upheld the President's authority, in the aftermath of the destruction of the Babri

---

[45] Ibid., at 329.
[46] Ibid., at 327.

Masjid in Ayodhya, to dismiss three elected state governments for failing to comply with the (secular) provisions of the Constitution. Because nothing in the Thirteenth Amendment reduces the power of

> ...the President to hold that a situation has arisen in which the administration of the Province cannot be carried out in accordance with the provisions of the Constitution and take over the functions and powers of the Provincial Council, there can be no gainsaying the fact that the President remains supreme or sovereign in the executive field and the Provincial Council is only a body subordinate to him.'[47]

Of course, in India, the President's power was exercised to affirm the Constitution's basic structure as a protection for a threatened religious minority, whereas the Court in Sri Lanka was in effect reassuring the Sinhalese majority that, appearances to the contrary notwithstanding, devolution would not interfere with the central government's ability to defend the State's Buddhist identity, which is to say, 'the Constitution will survive without any loss of identity'.

Oddly, given the finding that the entrenched provisions of the Constitution had not been violated, Chief Justice Sharvananda rejected the reliance by some (including the minority) on landmark Indian cases that affirm the Court's authority to declare amendments unconstitutional when they violate basic structure. His point would seem to be that even if you disagreed with the majority and believed with the minority that the Thirteenth Amendment ran afoul of entrenched Article requirements, there would still be no judicial warrant for nullifying a procedurally correct amendment to the Constitution. In so opining, the Justice was rejecting, as applicable to Sri Lanka, India's most distinctive contribution to world constitutional jurisprudence—the idea that a constitutional amendment could be unconstitutional, and further, that the Supreme Court had the authority to strike it down.

> [B]oth our Constitutions of 1972 and 1978 specifically provide for the amendment or repeal of any provision of the Constitution or to the repeal of the entire Constitution.... We are of the view that it would not be proper to be guided by concepts of 'Amendment' found in the Indian judgments.... Fundamental principles or basic features of the

[47] Ibid., at 323.

Constitution have to be found in…some provision or provisions of the Constitution and if the Constitution contemplates the repeal of any provision or provisions of the entire Constitution, there is no basis for the contention that some provisions which reflect fundamental principles or incorporate basic features are immune from amendment. Accordingly, we do not agree with the contention that some provisions of the Constitution are unamendable.[48]

In other countries (for example, Ireland), the amendability of all provisions of the constitution is often defended in accordance with a theory of popular sovereignty, which holds that the people must always retain the power to alter any part of their governing document. Hence the constitution, as was pointed out earlier, is treated more like ordinary law than as a sacred document. Yet it is in Justice Wanasundera's dissenting opinion that we find a popular sovereignty argument, invoked, however, to legitimate the nullification of the Thirteenth Amendment: '[O]ur Constitution, like the US Constitution and unlike the Indian or UK Constitutions, vests Sovereignty in the People and the organs of Government hold a mandate and are agents of the People.'[49] But if Sri Lankan constitutionalism is to be distinguished from India's on democratic grounds, that does not gainsay the fact that the Indian precedents on striking down constitutional amendments should be scrupulously followed in the present instance. Thus, the constitutional changes cannot be regarded as 'entrenching the basic features of the Constitution'.[50] '[T]he Thirteenth Amendment seeks to create an arrangement which is structurally in conflict with the structure of the Constitution and with its provisions both express and implied. The Bill therefore cannot be passed without at least a Referendum.'[51]

The referendum requirement (not present in India) was presumably the basis for the popular—and through it, parliamentary—sovereignty claim, but it is clear that for the minority, the threatening substance of the constitutional changes was the underlying cause for concern, which is why Indian cases such as *Kesavananda* and *Minerva Mills* were so attractive as touchstones for constitutional guidance.

[48] Ibid., at 329.
[49] Ibid., at 335.
[50] Ibid., at 336.
[51] Ibid., at 383.

The nature of the threat could be formulated in abstract structural terms as a radical transformation of a constitutionally mandated unitary system into a federal system whose decentralization of power represented a blatant transgression of constitutional design. But it was hard to conceal—not that any effort was made—the primordial essence of the alleged constitutional infirmity: the assault on the Buddhist and Sinhalese identity of the polity.

The majority had insisted, 'the Provincial Councils can place no impediment in the way of the State giving Buddhism the foremost place and protecting and fostering the *Buddha Sasana* in terms of Article 9 of the Constitution'.[52] To which Justice Wanasundera responded: '[T]he official recognition of the traditional homelands of the Tamils will toll the death knell of the Sinhala people in those Provinces.'[53] The reliance of this Justice on Indian jurisprudence is also an effort to avoid an unwanted Indian fate, namely the adoption of a 'two-nation theory', which, while it arguably serves the interests of the Tamils, would surely undermine the 'ideal of a Sri Lankan [read: Sinhalese Buddhist] nationality'. Reduced to its essentials, it is an argument that mirrors the rhetoric of Hindutva in India, where, according to its proponents, the content of Indian nationality should reflect the culture of the Hindu majority. In Sri Lanka, however, ethno-religious nationalism is sanctified by constitutional language that is nowhere to be found in its Indian counterpart.

Whatever the wisdom of constitutional devolution, power sharing, as Radhika Coomaraswamy has pointed out, 'has never been an important part of Sri Lanka's political tradition'.[54] The use of the referendum to resolve minority issues, she argues, is anti-democratic, as it inevitably spells the tyranny of the majority. The extent to which power sharing has been adopted within the Indian political context is a strongly contested matter.[55] Nevertheless, it is understandable

---

[52] Ibid., at 332.

[53] Ibid., at 337.

[54] R. Coomaraswamy, *Ideology and the Constitution*, p. 154.

[55] See, for example, the debate between Arend Lijphart and Paul Brass on the question of whether India qualifies as a consociational regime: Paul R. Brass, 'Ethnic Conflict in Multiethic Societies: The Consociational Solution and Its Critics', in Paul R. Brass, *Ethnicity and Nationalism: Theory and Comparison* (Sage: New Delhi, 1991), pp. 333–48.

why the Indian-inspired devolution formula incorporated in the
Thirteenth Amendment would be perceived by many as 'structurally
in conflict with the structure of the Constitution both expressed
and implied'.[56] The primacy of Buddhism in Sri Lankan identity
is explicitly expressed in the Constitution, and implicitly in the
structural attributes of constitutional design—mainly the unitary
state—the same foundational commitment will be found. As argued
by Justice Wanasundera:

> The Indian Constitution provides for a federal structure with a strong
> centre. The Indian proposals acceded to by us clearly indicate a shift in
> views, no doubt under pressure tilting the scales in favour of the Tamil
> demands for autonomy. In fact some of those proposals go beyond what
> is found in the Indian Constitution and is intended to give even a greater
> autonomy to the Provincial Council than that obtaining to the States in
> India. All the proposals of the Indian Government go to reinforce the
> position of Provincial Councils, extend its powers and entrench its legal
> structure.[57]

The constitutional changes in the Thirteenth Amendment
would, according to this view, decentralize power and not simply its
administration. Chief Justice Sharvananda had contended that under
the directive principles of state policy (Article 27(4) of the Constitution),
the terms of the altered document simply represented compliance with
the mandate to 'strengthen and broaden the democratic structure of
government and the democratic rights of the People by decentralizing
the administration and by affording all possible opportunities to the
People at every level in national life and in government'.[58] These
terms were neither a departure from the constitutional commitment
to a unitary state nor a threat to the continued predominance of the
Sinhalese majority. The Indian example shows that power can be
centralized while administration is decentralized.

In rejecting this assessment of what the legislature had done,
the Chief Justice's opinion also pointedly distinguished Sri Lankan
jurisprudence from Indian practice by relegating the directive
principles to a state of constitutional insignificance.

---

[56] *In re The Thirteenth Amendment,* p. 383.

[57] Ibid., p. 353.

[58] Ibid., p. 326.

While the Indian courts have leaned on these principles to resolve matters of doubt, I do not think they should have any controlling effect on any provision of the Constitution. These Directive Principles are really ethical or moral principles to guide the State. If any kind of legal importance is to be given to them, this would make the constitution unworkable.[59]

Thus, even if one disagreed with his interpretation of the directive principles, their irrelevance to constitutional decision-making meant that their application to the issues in this case is an improper exercise of judicial power. The judicial strategy of boldly stating a constitutional conclusion and then advancing a backup position that yields the same result, should there be resistance to the main finding, parallels the Sharvananda approach with regard to basic structure compliance and the Court's authority (or lack thereof) to declare an amendment unconstitutional.

What, then, can we say about cross-national borrowing in the *Thirteenth Amendment* case? There are at least several inter-related points to be made: (a) Both the majority and minority opinions addressed the constitutional issues in the case mainly in the light of indigenous sources. At key moments, however, foreign experience was injected into the discussion; on such occasions India was the only country that figured prominently in the decision-making of the Sri Lankan judges.[60] Although India had a significant role in the events that formed the backdrop to the case, the judicial deployment of constitutional law from that country appears unrelated to that history. (b) The appeal of Indian jurisprudence was entirely opportunistic and did not implicate core issues of constitutional identity. Here we can distinguish between positive and negative borrowing; thus, even when the invocation of Indian precedents was viewed as suggestive for the Sri Lankan case, it was never intended to constitute a source for emulation on any critical issues having to do with the secular identity of the state. (c) To the extent that the principal underlying issue concerned the question of whether and how an ethno/religious majority would maintain its position of political dominance within

[59] Ibid., p. 355.

[60] The majority has a very brief reference to the UK, but the opinion quickly concludes that the materials cited are of no relevance to the case at hand. See, ibid., p. 346.

the polity, the use of Indian sources did not evince any explicit acknowledgement of that issue. Rather, structural issues involving federalism and constitutional amendments were the focus of cross-national consideration. Although India's unique constitutional arrangements for the secular configuration of society is entwined in these structural matters, the Indian secular model did not overtly enter into the judicial debate in Sri Lanka.

It is, we think, significant that the *Thirteenth Amendment* justices, mindful of the salience of the case for issues of constitutional identity, never allude to the Indian constitutional approach to secularism. Far from evincing a deficit in comparative cultural/constitutional understanding, as suggested by Tripathi and Posner, the judicial silence more likely reflects an awareness of the very different constitutive premises underlying the two nations' respective identities. Both the majority and minority opinions were committed to preserving the national dominance of the Sinhalese Buddhist majority, and thus there was no strategic benefit for judges invoking Indian legal understandings of the constitutional status of the religious majority. The debate over whether the constitutional changes threatened the unitary nature of the state was less about that particular basic feature of constitutional design than it was about another, the ethno-republican character of Sri Lankan constitutionalism. Vicki Jackson's argument,[61] that constitutional provisions concerning federalism are typically 'the product of political compromises in historically situated moments', highlights their potential for opportunistic cross-national borrowing; thus their origin in practical rather than principled accommodation meant that core issues of identity could be submerged under the less contentious rubric of constitutional structure.

More specifically, the Sinhalese chosen people narrative in Sri Lanka parallels the Hindu version in India, but the latter is not a narrative inscribed in the Constitution. Nor in India is religion implicated in the federal division of constitutional power; as has often been told, that is a story whose theme is linguistic diversity. While it is a theme very relevant to the Thirteenth Amendment's provision for Tamil language rights, in India (except perhaps in Kashmir and Sikkim), unlike in Sri Lanka, language and religion are ascriptively

---

[61] Jackson, 'Narratives of Federalism'.

differentiated, which means that devolution issues are not inevitably freighted with religious significance. For example, the battlefield of federalism is not the main venue in India for the political struggle over Hindutva. When, therefore, judges in Sri Lanka cite the Indian federalism model either favourably or unfavourably, their references do not convey any attachment to one or the other side of the debate about secularism in India. In Jackson's account, the 'contingently located' quality of federalism limits its possibilities for constitutional borrowing, but that assumes that the objective of the exercise is either transplantation of the experience of one place to another or at least the achievement of the kind of legal self-reflection that can dialogically result from comparative jurisprudence. This concern, however, is much less weighty when, as in the appropriation of Indian sources by Sri Lankan judges in the *Thirteenth Amendment* case, the occasion for borrowing can be understood in purely opportunistic terms.

Selective Borrowing

In this final section, we discuss two cases of borrowing concerning issues related to bigamy and conversion in order to provide additional insight into the character of constitutional borrowing by Sri Lankan justices in matters pertaining to secularism. The justices in these cases were inclined to uphold an absolute right to freedom of religion as long as this did not have a negative impact on Buddhism. When the primacy of Buddhism was at stake, they borrowed selectively from Indian case law to support a result beneficial to the constitutionally favoured religion.

Bigamy

Can a Roman Catholic man married to one woman under a law that prohibited polygamy, marry a second woman after converting to Islam, without divorcing the first wife? This was the question in *Natalie Abeysundere* v. *Christopher Abeysundere and Another*.[62] Christopher Abeysundere and his first wife, both Roman Catholics, were married under the Marriage Registration Ordinance, which, among other things, made polygamy illegal. Subsequently, Christopher married

---

[62] SC Appeal No. 70/96, decided in October 1997.

Edirisinghe under the Muslim Marriage and Divorce Act. His first wife brought legal action against him on charges of bigamy, to which Christopher responded that he and Edirisinghe had embraced Islam before their second marriage. The Magistrate's court convicted Christopher for bigamy, but the ruling was reversed by the provincial High Court on the basis of a Privy Council precedent.[63] Subsequently, the Supreme Court reinstated the conviction and voided the second marriage, arguing that the defendant could not 'cast aside his antecedent statutory liabilities and obligations' incurred by his first marriage. The five justices interpreted the Marriage Registration Ordinance as requiring a statutory obligation on the part of Christopher and his first wife to remain in a monogamous relationship. In the judgment, the justices emphasized the public policy of Sri Lanka to support monogamy by citing an earlier Privy Council judgment, *King* v. *Perumal*:

> It is thus clear that, except in the case of Muhammadans, *polygamy is as obnoxious to the public policy of Ceylon as to that of European States....* In view of the circumstance that polygamy is *expressly prohibited* by the Municipal law of the Colony (except in the case of Muhammadans) I am clearly of opinion that a polygamous marriage between persons who are not Muhammadans is void in Ceylon.[64]

The judgment quoted extensively from the reasoning of the Indian Supreme Court in the *Sarla Mudgal* case, where the issue was whether a Hindu husband, married under Hindu law, could solemnize a second marriage by embracing Islam.[65] Describing the Indian case as one of 'decisive importance', the Court agreed with the Indian Justice Kuldip Singh, who had held that the second marriage would be void because of contractual obligations of monogamy under the first marriage. [66] 'In my

---

[63] In *Attorney General* v. *Reid*, the facts of the case were similar to the Abeysundere situation. The Privy Council ruled that in a country like Ceylon, there must be an inherent right in the inhabitants domiciled there to change their religion and personal law and contract a valid polygamous marriage if recognized by the laws of the country, notwithstanding an earlier marriage. Only a statute could abrogate inherent right.

[64] *King* v. *Perumal*, (1912) 14 NLR 496 (Full Bench).

[65] See in this volume, Chapter 8, where John Mansfield underscores the influence of *Sarla Mudgal* on Sri Lankan jurisprudence in regard to the issue of conversion.

[66] However, in a case dealing with the non-registration of marriage between a Buddhist and a Roman Catholic, the Supreme Court said that a customary marriage

view,' wrote the Chief Justice, 'the reasoning of Justice Kuldip Singh...
is cogent and valid, and is clearly applicable to the facts before us....'[67]

Of particular persuasive power were the Indian jurist's reflections on the family:

> Marriage is the very foundation of the civilized society. The relation once formed, the law steps in and binds the parties to various obligations and liabilities thereunder. Marriage is an institution in the maintenance of which the public at large is deeply interested. It is the foundation of the family and in turn of the society without which no civilization can exist.[68]

Where the Privy Council had gone wrong was in failing to appreciate that the family upon which so much depends was an exclusively monogamous structure.

But the invocation of *Sarla Mudgal* does not reveal what made that case so controversial in India. Justice Singh's opinion was notable as much for its passionate call for compliance with the unequivocal mandate of Article 44 to achieve a uniform civil code as for its ringing affirmation of the institution of marriage. Although it avoided the judicial excesses of theological exegesis that made the *Shah Bano* decision uniquely provocative, it out-distanced the earlier case in the urgency of its insistence on implementing the constitutionally prescribed directive of uniformity. 'There is no justification whatsoever in delaying indefinitely the introduction of a uniform personal law in the country.'[69] The Court, according to Justice Singh, should be actively engaged in seeing that the regime of personal laws came to an end.

> Inevitably, the role of the reformer has to be assumed by the Courts because, it is beyond the endurance of sensitive minds to allow injustice to be suffered when it is so palpable. But piecemeal attempts of Courts to bridge that gap between personal laws cannot take the place of a common Civil Code.[70]

---

could be proved and established for persons other than Kandyans. The onus of proving to the contrary rested on the person denying the validity of the marriage. *Gracia Catherine* v. *Wijegunawardene* S.C. No. 5/85.

[67] *Abeysundere*, at 200.
[68] *Abeysundere*, at 200.
[69] *Sarla Mudgal*, at 1538.
[70] *Sarla Mudgal*, at 1539.

As the Justice affirmed in an interview with the authors, a critical component in Indian constitutional identity is 'the power of judicial review given to the judiciary which gives it the authority to enforce the Directive Principles'.[71]

The Justice's opinion was criticized not only for its robust assertion of judicial power, but also for its majoritarian implication, which, fairly or unfairly, was interpreted by some as anti-Muslim. As one critic wrote, '[*Sarla Mudgal*] is not exactly a legal judgment but more of a political sermon on how the Muslim community should learn to behave and what ought to be its relationship to the Indian State'.[72] Hindus, Sikhs, Buddhists, and Jains had all accepted the priority of national unity over sectarian attachments to religious practices regarding marriage, succession, and like matters; 'other communities' [read: Muslims] needed to get on board.

These sentiments were *obiter dicta,* and thus the Sri Lankan Court was surely not remiss in ignoring them in its judgment in *Abeysundere*. Moreover, it is difficult to see what profit there would be in antagonizing the local Muslim community, whose exceptional legal status regarding plural marriages enjoyed long-standing recognition in Sri Lanka. It is, however, also clear that constitutional borrowing in this instance was consistent with support for an indigenous constitutional identity that has as one of its cardinal assumptions the primacy of the nation's majority community.[73] Here, the borrowing from Indian case law reflected substantive concerns about how another country facing similar issues involving clashes between personal laws had resolved the matter. It demonstrates judicious

---

[71] Interview, New Delhi, 15 June 2006.

[72] Madhu Kishwar, *Religion at the Service of Nationalism and Other Essays* (Oxford University Press: New Delhi, 1998).

[73] By saying that the borrowing was consistent with commitment to maintaining the primacy of this community, we do not suggest that it was so motivated. Indeed the Sinhalese Buddhist community was not directly involved in the case. The judges also drew upon a ruling in a Privy Council case (*King* v. *Perumal*) to show that monogamy and the prohibition against polygamy (except in the case of Muslims) were part of public policy and the law since 1847. Strict legal interpretation of marriage rather than deference to cultural norms is a recurring theme in the Court's jurisprudence even where the majority community is involved. See, for example, *Gracie* v. *Wijeguna Wardene*.

borrowing where the circumstances were such as not to impact the Buddhist nature of Sri Lankan identity.

In doing so, it is easy to see why the animating vision behind the Indian precedent might have appealed to the Sri Lankan Court. That vision is one of 'legal universalism', which, as defined by Susanne and Lloyd Rudolph, 'treats individuals as the basic unit of society and the state and imagines homogeneous citizens with uniform legal rights and obligations.'[74] This idea, of course, is a staple of political liberalism, but in contemporary India it has come to be associated as well with the communal interests of the Hindu majority—at least as those interests have been articulated by the advocates of Hindutva, who seek to equate Hinduism with Indian national identity. As we have seen in the *Thirteenth Amendment* case, a consensus on the Supreme Court is discernible in the broad acceptance of the primacy of Sinhalese Buddhism in Sri Lankan identity and the common judicial intention to defend the unitary state, which is the structural attribute of constitutional design most closely associated with that defense. Any judicial outcome that secures the philosophical underpinnings of the unitary state—and therefore the predominant position of the constitutionally favoured majority—is to be seen as welcome indeed. To be sure, most advocates of a uniform civil code for India—and this includes justices such as Kuldip Singh—are not motivated by ethno-nationalist concerns. But just as surely, their arguments provide appealing sources for constitutional borrowing by those who may be so motivated.

Conversion

There is very little doubt about the ethno-nationalist motivations of Sri Lankan justices in another area of intense secular disputation—conversion. In an important case (*Menzingen* judgment) concerning this vexed issue, the Supreme Court reiterated that the freedom to worship did not include the right to propagate. [75] 'In Sri Lanka, the Constitution

---

[74] Susanne Hoeber Rudolph and Lloyd I. Rudolph, 'Living with Difference in India: Legal Pluralism and Legal Universalism in Historical Context', in Gerald James Larson (ed.), *Religion and Law in Secular India* (Oxford University Press: New Delhi, 2001), p. 37.

[75] *Provincial of the Teaching Sisters of the Holy Cross of the Third Order of Saint Francis in Menzingen of Sri Lanka* (SC: 19/2003). See also, *In re Christian Sahanaye*

does not guarantee a fundamental right to 'propagate' religion as in Article 25(1) of the Indian Constitution. What is guaranteed here to every citizen is the fundamental right by Article 14(1)(e) to manifest, worship, observe, practice that citizen's religion or teaching'.[76]

The petitioners, who included the Attorney-General and members of a Buddhist nationalist party, challenged a Private Member's Bill allowing a Christian group to 'propagate a religion while taking advantage of the vulnerability of certain persons'.[77] The Bill sought to incorporate a Catholic Order for the objectives of spreading the tenets of Catholicism through the following: providing religious, educational, and vocational training to the youth; teaching in educational institutions; serving in medical establishments, among others. The petitioners contended that the preamble of the Bill read with Clause 3 'make provision not only to propagate the Catholic religion, but to allure persons of other religions by providing material and other benefits...and thereby converting them to the faith that is sought to be spread'.[78]

The petition used the Indian Supreme Court's judgment disallowing conversion (principally *Stainislaus* v. *State of Madhya Pradesh*) as the centrepiece of their argument.[79] In the *Stainislaus* judgment, the Indian Supreme Court considered the question of whether freedom of religion and the right to propagate included the right to convert.[80] Article 25, Clause 1 of the Indian Constitution states that 'subject to public order, morality and health and to the

---

Doratuwa Prayer Centre (Incorporation) Bill (SC Determination No. 2/2001); *In re New Wine Harvest Ministries (Incorporation) Bill* (SC Determination No. 2/2003).

[76] Supreme Court Determination No. 2/2001 cited by judges in the *Menzingen* judgment.

[77] *Menzingen*, SC Determination No. 19/2003, at 4.

[78] Ibid., at 3. See also, in this volume, Chapter 5 (Deepika Udagama, 'The Democratic State and Religious Pluralism: Comparative Constitutionalism and Constitutional Experiences of Sri Lanka').

[79] *Stainislaus* v. *State of Madhya Pradesh*, AIR 1977 SC 908 (challenging two state acts that regulated activity aimed at conversion on the grounds that they violated the right to propagate guaranteed by Article 25). See also, Asanga Welikala, *The Menzingen Determination and the Supreme Court: A Liberal Critique* (Centre for Policy Alternatives: Sri Lanka, 2003), p. 1, and H.M. Seervai, *Constitutional Law of India*, 4th Ed., (1993), pp. 1286–8 (criticizing Indian judges for disregarding propagation by persuasion).

[80] *Stainislaus* v. *State of Madhya Pradesh*, AIR 1977 SC 908.

other provisions of this Part, all persons are equally entitled to freedom of conscience and the right freely to profess, practice and propagate religion'.[81]

The Sri Lankan justices referred to India's Chief Justice's reasoning in the *Stainislaus* case to agree with the petitioner's argument. Chief Justice Ray had outlined the limits of the right to propagate set forth in India's Article 25(1). 'What the article grants is not the right to convert another person to one's own religion, but to transmit or spread one's religion by an exposition of its tenets.'[82] The judge said if a person converted another person to his religion by force (including threat of divine punishment or displeasure), fraud, or inducement (which may be a gift or gratification including intangible benefits), such an act would impinge on the guarantee of the right to freedom of conscience.

The Sri Lankan apex court followed suit and ruled that it was permissible for persons to practie, but not to propagate, their religion. As Udagama (Chapter 5 in this volume) points out, in earlier judgments, the court had held similar Bills to be in violation of Article 10 (freedom of thought, conscience, and religion), but in this one, they said that the Bill violated Article 9 as well.[83] In accepting the *Stainislaus* precedent as authoritative, the Sri Lankan judges noted that constitutional provisions on conversion in the island nation were more restrictive than in India. The Court pointed out that the omission of the word 'propagate' in Articles 10 and 14(1) (e) of the Sri Lankan Constitution (unlike the Indian Constitution) was deliberate.[84] Furthermore, as Buddhism was accorded a pre-eminent position by Article 9 of the Sri Lankan Constitution,[85] it

---

[81] Ibid. (quoting Indian Constitution, Article 25, Clause 1).

[82] Pratap Bhanu Mehta, 'Passion and Constraint: Courts and the Regulation of Religious Meaning', in Rajeev Bhargava (ed.), *Politics and Ethics of the Indian Constitution* (Oxford University Press: New Delhi, 2008), pp. 311, 318. Mehta points out that the distinction seems to turn largely on the motive of the speaker. See also, Mehta, note 78, p. 333.

[83] Udagama, Chapter 5 in this volume.

[84] *Menzingen*, SC Determination No. 19/2003 at 4. ('The Indian Constitution spells out the word 'propagate' in Article 25(1). Articles 10 and 14(1)(e) of our Constitution do not refer to the word 'propagate' and therefore, it could be said that the provisions in our Constitution are more restrictive than that of Article 25(1) of the Indian Constitution.')

[85] Ibid., at 6.

was unconstitutional for Christian organizations to incorporate proselytizing through '[the] spread [of] knowledge of [the] Catholic religion [and] to impart religious, educational and vocational training to youth'.[86] Clause 3 was seen as a threat to the very existence of Buddhism and Sri Lankan identity because it created 'a situation which combines the observance and practice of a religion or belief with activities which would provide material and other benefits to the inexperience[d], defenceless [sic] and vulnerable people to propagate a religion'.[87]

The judges also drew on a decision of the European Court of Human Rights, where three officers of the Greek Air Force, who were followers of the Pentecostal church, were convicted for proselytizing three airmen of a lesser rank.[88] The Sri Lankan Court said that '[a]n examination of Clauses 3(c), (d) and (e) indicate strong relationships that of teacher–student, nurse/doctor–patient, curator–refugee and that of guardian–minor' and hence 'the reasoning of the European Court to the susceptibility of subordinate officers to superiors should apply with greater force in the case at hand'.[89] Inducement and propagation were seen as synonymous and hence a threat to Buddhism: 'What is guaranteed under the Constitution is the manifestation, observance and practice of one's own religion and the propagation and spreading [of] Christianity as postulated in terms of Clause 3 would not be permissible as it would impair the very existence of Buddhism or the *Buddha Sasana*.'[90]

In accepting the *Stainislaus* precedent as authoritative, the Sri Lankan judges carefully noted that constitutional provisions on conversion in the island nation were more restrictive than in India. Thus, the Indian precedent resonates more powerfully in Sri Lanka because of the absence in the latter country of any obvious countervailing language to check the power of the state to restrict conversions. In effect the argument for constitutional borrowing came to this: if in India, where in theory at least the constitutional

---

[86] Ibid., at 4.

[87] Ibid., at 6.

[88] *Larissis* v. *Greece*, 1998-I Eur. Ct. H.R. 362 (1998) (noting that the three officer airmen were found guilty of proselytizing in the Permanent Air Force Court).

[89] *Menzingen*, SC Determination No. 19/2003 at 5.

[90] Ibid., at 7.

commitment to secularism required scrupulous impartiality in the conduct of the state towards the nation's different religions, conversion could be curtailed, then surely in Sri Lanka, a country whose Constitution grants pride of place to the majority religion, the argument against such curtailment must be that much weaker.

But in India the *Stainislaus* ruling is a much-contested decision, and precisely for the reasons that made it so appealing as a jurisprudential resource in Sri Lanka, namely, that it violates the basic precepts of Indian secularism. Indeed, in subsequent litigation, specifically a challenge to the constitutionality of the Bharatiya Janata Party–led government of Rajasthan's 2006 anti-conversion law, the Supreme Court was asked to overturn *Stainislaus*. While that has not yet occurred, in legal circles the precedent is widely seen as having been based on an incorrect understanding of the Indian constitutional mandate for Church–State relations, one best explained as an anomaly of the Emergency period and its regrettable distortion of the balance between public order and individual freedom.[91]

How, then, according to the legal challenge, is the ban against conversion offensive to secularism and the basic structure of the Indian Constitution? In strict constitutional terms the claim is that the protection of the right to 'freely…propagate religion' by Article 25 envisions more than just the ability to profess; it entails 'the right to persuade another to join one's faith'.[92] Thus, the protection is at least as much concerned with the freedom of conscience and belief as it is with free speech. In broader terms, however, the restriction on conversion must be seen against the backdrop of the Hindu nationalist challenge to the secular State. 'The threat to the Hindu religion from aggressive and manipulative proselytizing is one of the cornerstones of fundamentalist Hindu ideology.'[93] Tellingly, the absence in most

---

[91] This discussion is based on the observations of the Supreme Court advocates who are leading the challenge to the law. Rajeev Dhavan and Aparna Ray, 'Adding Insult to Injury: The Rajasthan Dharma Swatantrya Bill, 2006' (Public Interest Litigation Support and Research Centre: New Delhi, 2006).

[92] Ibid., p. 8.

[93] Ibid., p. 38. As Ronald W. Neufeldt has pointed out, proponents of this ideology opposed conversion as early as the debates at the Constituent Assembly. Notable in this regard was the opposition of Purushottamdis Tandon. Ronald W. Neufeldt, 'To Convert or Not to Convert: Legal and Political Dimensions of

anti-conversion enactments of any restriction upon re-conversion to Hinduism reveals the majoritarian impulse behind such efforts. As we reflect on the practice of constitutional borrowing in our two countries, the main distinction on conversion may very well be the non-apologetic way in which defenders of restrictive laws in Sri Lanka put their arguments forward as a defense of constitutional identity.

Thus, Welikala says of the *Menzingen* decision that invoking Article 9 for the first time, twenty-five years after its promulgation, legalized an exclusivist majoritarianism of the Sinhala Buddhists at the expense of pluralism and the rights of minorities.[94] Otherwise, if the Court had been concerned about protecting vulnerable citizens from induced conversion, the judges could have used Article 14 (1)(e), and left Article 9 well alone. The Court's invocation of constitutional identity is transparent: '[I]f efforts are taken to convert another person to one's own religion, such conduct could hinder the very existence of *Buddha Sasana*.'[95] Difficult to imagine is an Indian judge openly declaring a comparable sentiment, to the effect that the State's restriction on proselytizing for the purpose of seeking converts from the majority religion was a constitutional means to advance the end of ensuring the existence of Hinduism. The constitutional cultures of different regimes often dictate the kinds of rhetoric that are permissible in rendering judgments that implicate the core assumptions of identity.

As we have seen, a common criticism of constitutional borrowing is that, in their reliance on comparative materials, judges are often too open to such inspiration and guidance in the face of critical differences between the borrower and the borrowee in historical development and social conditions. The conversion case in Sri Lanka demonstrates why the merits of such criticism require case-by-case analysis. As in the *Thirteenth Amendment* case, the justices in *Menzingen* were cognizant of the distinctions in multicultural premises underlying the neighbouring polities. This is clear from their appreciation of the significance of the alternative linguistic approaches to proselytizing appearing in the two constitutions. *Stainislaus* was attractive to these justices precisely because it provided an opportunity to exploit those differences in the interests of

---

Conversion in Independent India', in Robert D. Baird (ed.), *Religion and Law in Independent India* (Manohar Publishers: New Delhi, 2005), p. 385.

[94] Welikala, *Menzingen Determination*.

[95] *Menzingen*, SC Determination No. 19/2003 at 5.

the local constitutional identity.[96] Interestingly, the Indian ruling became less attractive in legal circles in India, where it was increasingly seen as a constitutional anomaly that needed to be righted in the interests of the local constitutional identity. Our conclusion is that, far from evincing a deficit in comparative cultural/constitutional understanding on the part of the justices in Sri Lanka, the strategic calculations underlying the borrowing in this instance succeeded in part because of the earlier failure of the justices in India.

CONCLUSION

In *The Politics*, Aristotle asked: 'On what principle ought we to say that a State has retained its identity, or conversely, that it has lost its identity and become a different State?'[97] Answering that the identity of a State is inscribed in the substance of its constitution, Aristotle famously invoked a choral analogy to convey his idea that the consequence of fundamental constitutional transformation is a different identity for the State.[98] To be sure, the Aristotelian notion of a constitution is a more encompassing one than is generally imagined today, extending in the broadest sense to what we might understand as a 'way of life'. To the extent, however, that legal and social relations within polities are importantly influenced by their constitutions, the possible loss of identity attributable to constitutional transformation remains a phenomenon very much a part of our contemporary predicament.

One indication that this question of identity is quite relevant today is the debate over constitutional borrowing, in which, as we pointed out earlier, a principal objection to the practice is that it will compromise constitutional identity. Indeed, extended to its logical conclusion, the concern is that the exercise will culminate in precisely the sort of loss of identity contemplated by Aristotle. What we have

[96] Later reports suggest that one of the judges may not have appreciated the implications of using Article 9.

[97] Ernest Barker (ed. and trans.), *The Politics of Aristotle* (Oxford University Press: New York, 1962), p. 98.

[98] 'We may cite an analogy from the drama. We say that a chorus which appears at one time as a comic at another as a tragic chorus is not continuously the same, but alters its identity—and this in spite of the fact that the members often remain the same.' Ibid., p. 99.

seen in our analysis of several important cases involving cross-national uses of Indian decisions by Sri Lankan justices is that it is just as easy to view constitutional borrowing as part of a judicial strategy to reinforce critical components in the home country's constitutional identity.

In referring to the judicial borrowing in these cases as *opportunistic*, we therefore do not intend to equate such activity with *unprincipled* borrowing. The choices made by the Court—to borrow or not to borrow—were consistent with the larger judicial effort to secure the constitutional moorings upon which the identity of the Sri Lankan state was tethered. Foremost here is the preferred position of Sinhalese Buddhism. Thus, in the landmark *Thirteenth Amendment* case the justices' references to Indian jurisprudence were deployed in such a way as to affirm and support this foundational principle of Sri Lankan constitutional identity. While their attentiveness to Indian experience led them—both in the majority and in the minority—to reject much of this experience as a model for emulation, they clearly were adept at invoking just those structural features of Indian constitutional design that allowed them to advance their arguments for preserving the ethno-religious identity of the polity without acknowledging the very different ideological contexts within which these structural attributes are situated. So the borrowing by Sri Lankan justices was opportunistic in the sense that it was resourceful in its tendentious application of Indian constitutional materials, but principled to the extent that its advantage lay in potential reinforcement of essential— if controversial—regime principles.

As for the particular character of these principles, we have, with respect to the question of secularism, contrasted the preservative thrust of the Sri Lankan constitutional commitment with the corresponding transformative emphasis in India. While Christopher McCrudden's observation—that constitutional borrowing is much more likely to be practised by judiciaries in transformative regimes than in preservative ones[99]—may be true, we can now at least qualify this assertion with reference to the conservative aspirations of Sri

[99] Christopher McCrudden, 'A Common Law for Human Rights? Transnational Judicial Conversations on Constitutional Rights', *Oxford Journal of Legal Studies*, (2000), 20(4): 516–27.

Lankan constitutional identity.[100] If the appeal of comparative law is clear in the case of a court seeking to implement the social and political changes mandated by the constitution, judges animated by the contrary purpose of defending the constitutionally sanctified societal status quo may also have an incentive to look for guidance beyond their borders. The efforts to follow 'progressive' developments in other places may involve a more straightforward appropriation of foreign sources than we might expect in a setting where the principal object is to preserve what one already has. But as we have observed in the conversion case, the perceived threat posed by proselytizing to the status quo– the dominant position of the majority Sinhalese Buddhist community—can be effectively countered by selective citation of precedents from places where the opposite commitment lies at the core of constitutional identity. Particularly in the South Asian context, in which the Indian example and its oft-espoused affirmation of the principle of *sarva dharma sambhava* is, by dint of size alone, the most prominent model of secular constitutional development in the region, there may be considerable strategic advantage in defending unequal treatment with the help of jurisprudence extracted from this more egalitarian model.

Of course, we must in the end acknowledge that the practice of constitutional borrowing, like other judicial practices, cannot be readily reduced to any single motivation. In the conversion case, for example, there is evidence that, in addition to the explicitly stated desire to preserve the majoritarian cast of constitutional identity, judges may have had other objectives in mind, including one reflective of a specific hostility towards American missionary groups.[101] Such mixed motives are even clearer in the bigamy case, where the Indian Court's enthusiasm for legal uniformity arguably had attractive ethno-religious implications for Sri Lankan constitutional identity, but where, in the absence of any specific involvement by members

---

[100] See in this volume, Chapter 5 (Deepika Udagama, 'The Democratic State and Religious Pluralism'), for Udagama's argument that issues of identity have elicited judicial insularity.

[101] A former Supreme Court justice, who was also a Christian, made this point in an interview with one of the authors, Shylashri Shankar. See also, Chapter 5 in this volume, where Deepika Udagama highlights the problematic aspects of such a stance.

of the majority Buddhist community, the borrowing by the Sri Lankan justices was more likely dictated by a desire to follow the policy prescriptions of the Indian Court respecting the institution of marriage. That these prescriptions were also consistent with Buddhist views on monogamy as the only acceptable marital state for adherents of the religion is noteworthy;[102] hence the outcome in the case can, as in the other cases, be understood as identity-reinforcing. But not all identity-reinforcing outcomes explain constitutional borrowing, though, as we have seen, constitutional borrowing is often importantly a dialogical attempt by judges to resolve contentious issues by drawing on the experiences of other countries. Ultimately borrowing results from a mix of motives—opportunistic, self-reflective, and sometimes unreflective. Which one dominates may be less a function of judges themselves and more a function of the institutional balance between the executive and the judiciary.

---

[102] H.R. Perera, 'Buddhism in Sri Lanka: A Short History', in *The Wheel*, Publication No. 100 (Buddhist Publication Society: Kandy, Sri Lanka, 1966/1988).

CHAPTER SEVEN

Inheritance Unbound

The Politics of Personal Law Reform in Pakistan and India

Matthew J. Nelson

INTRODUCTION

This essay addresses the constitutional and political dimensions of formal legal change in Pakistan and India. The changes I address here have one chief characteristic. Above all, they involve a process of change with an explicitly 'religious' dimension: in effect, a process of changing ostensibly 'transcendent' or 'God-given' personal laws.

What are the constitutional and political conditions under which the content of such laws is made to change in Pakistan and India? What are the constitutional and political conditions that might intervene to stifle or restrict such change? Is it possible for ordinary legislators, in either country, to stand up and say, on any given day: 'Behold! Today the Laws of God have changed. Today we will write a new religious law?' This is, briefly stated, the question I address in the context of this essay.

I am particularly interested in the ways in which Pakistan's status as an 'Islamic' State (in effect, a State with a special constitutional commitment to the terms of Islamic law) might affect the process of religious-cum-legal change. Does the 'Islamic' status of Pakistan's Constitution constrain the process of (formal) legal change—with specific reference to the substance of ostensibly 'religious' personal laws—in any way?

Those with an interest in such questions often view the substantive terms of Islamic law, and especially State-based Islamic laws associated with specific types of formal *constitutional* protection, as somehow unusually 'inflexible' or 'fixed' (both for reasons of 'sacredness' and for specific 'constitutional' reasons). In the context of this essay, however, I take a closer look at this perspective, focusing specifically on the dynamics of religious-cum-political debate, religious-cum-legal flexibility, and ultimately, formal (and substantive) legal *change*.

Of course, neither Pakistan nor India is, as it were, constitutionally 'French', requiring a strict exclusion of religion from the legal affairs of the State. Neither is constitutionally 'American', requiring either a Jeffersonian wall of separation between religion, religious law, and the State (absent in India), or a firm commitment to religious non-establishment (absent in Pakistan). Both seek to engage and, in some sense, actively incorporate (within the State itself) the specific terms of 'religious' personal law. Both have courts with the power to interpret and enforce ostensibly 'God-given' laws. In fact, the difference between them simply lies in the fact that, over time, Pakistan has incorporated an explicit commitment to move beyond the 'equal status' approach adopted by India (according to which, by law, each religious tradition is supposed to be treated equally within a framework tied to specific notions of 'public order' and 'morality') in favour of what might be described as a 'special status' approach (according to which the State is constitutionally obliged to *privilege* the specific injunctions of Islam).[1]

Key similarities and important differences notwithstanding, I will pose the same set of questions for both Pakistan and India: Is it possible for the Pakistani legislature, facing explicit 'special status' conditions, to stand up and say on any given day, 'Behold!'? Is it possible for the Indian legislature, facing its own very different set of conditions, to stand up and say, 'Rejoice! Today the Laws of God have changed!'?

---

[1] See in this volume, Chapter 8 (John H. Mansfield, 'Religious Freedom in India and Pakistan: The Matter of Conversion').

The answer to this question is interesting. It is interesting, because, notwithstanding several important differences in each country, the answer seemed to remain more or less exactly the same in both countries for nearly sixty years (1947–2005). In fact, at a basic *constitutional* level, both countries articulated a pattern in which the postcolonial legislature *was* empowered to stand up and say, 'Behold!'. There was, in other words, no clearly enforceable constitutional proscription on such a proclamation in either country—a condition that remains in place even today.

At a specifically *political* level, however, both countries seemed to articulate a pattern in which this rather permissive constitutional position—by all accounts a position allowing almost unlimited space for reinterpretive religious-cum-legal reform—was taken up and put into practice only under very limited circumstances. In fact, the basic punchline of this essay lies in drawing attention to a *political* pattern in which this process of substantive religious-cum-legal reform was limited (in practice) to just two very specific contexts: first, a political context defined by military and/or non-military authoritarianism (for example, the military dictatorship of General Mohammad Ayub Khan in Pakistan or the Emergency led by Indira Gandhi in India); and, second, a political context defined by one-party dominant regimes in which the ruling party held, *on its own*, more than 60 per cent of the existing seats in the legislature.

Substantive religious-cum-legal reform, in other words, *is* constitutionally permitted in both countries. The terms of religious personal law are *not* (constitutionally) 'immutable'. (As John Mansfield notes in Chapter 8 of this volume, States have had an important role to play when it comes to the definition of personal religious practice in both countries.) And, yet, having said this, the political conditions under which each State has pushed for reform are revealing. Change has occurred, almost exclusively, in a political climate defined by a certain 'immunity' from the terms of multi-party (or cross-party) bargaining. Indeed, only *unrivalled* political elites have tended to be, legislatively, in a position to stand up and 'speak for God'.

Throughout, my focus is confined to just one area of religious-cum-legal reform: inheritance. In fact, the thrust of most debates regarding the general topic of inheritance, both in Pakistan and in India, has typically involved a specific set of concerns regarding the extent to which ordinary legislators might be in a position to 'add' new heirs to what many regarded as an already 'existing' and ostensibly 'sacred' list.

In India, among Hindus, married women tend to be excluded from the list of heirs outlined in the sacred Hindu *shastras*. And, as a result, political actors have frequently disagreed about the extent to which women might be 'added' to that 'existing' list of heirs—not simply as a matter of local practice or custom but rather as a matter of substantive and enforceable law.

The debate has, however, been more nuanced among Muslims in Pakistan, because within the Holy Qur'an women are already included in the list of so-called 'Qur'anic' heirs.[2] (They actually dominate that list.[3]) Notwithstanding efforts to enforce that list (against enduring notions of agnatic or all-male 'tribal custom'), therefore, the question of reform has largely moved beyond the question of adding individual women in favour of a more specific set of questions regarding the possibility of 'adding' orphaned grandchildren. In Qur'anic terms, many scholars insist that these grandchildren are excluded from the process of inheritance within their families by the 'early' death of their parents. And, yet, some reformers have attempted to 'correct' this anomaly even *within* the *suras* (verses) of the Holy Qur'an.[4] In fact, in some cases, they have taken it upon themselves to 'add' orphaned grandchildren to the list of sacred heirs by law.[5]

---

[2] See, Lucy Carroll, 'The Hanafi Law of Intestate Succession: A Simplified Approach', *Modern Asian Studies*, (1983), 17(4): 629–70; and 'The Ithna Ashari Law of Intestate Succession: An Introduction to Shia Law Applicable in South Asia', *Modern Asian Studies*, (1985), 19(1): 85–124.

[3] See, for example, verses 4:11, 4:12, and 4:176. Marmaduke Pickthall, *The Meaning of the Glorious Qur'an* (Taj Company Ltd.: Karachi, 1971), pp. 74, 75, 98.

[4] For a discussion of the Qur'an, later commentaries on the subject of Islamic inheritance, and the relationship between these commentaries and later effort to 'correct' the status of orphaned grandchildren, see, N.J. Coulson, *Succession in the Muslim Family* (Cambridge University Press: Cambridge, 1971).

[5] See, N.J. Coulson, 'Islamic Family Law: Progress in Pakistan', in J.N.D. Anderson (ed.), *Changing Law in Developing Countries* (George Allen & Unwin: London, 1963), pp. 240–57; J.N.D. Anderson, 'Recent Reforms in the Islamic Law of Inheritance', *International and Comparative Law Quarterly*, (1965), Issue 14: 349–65; Lucy Carroll, 'Succession of Orphaned Grandchildren in Pakistan: Conflicting

The question concerns the extent to which these legislative reformers, both in Pakistan and in India, might be in a position, both constitutionally and politically, to advance the reforms they desire.[6] In fact, the question concerns the circumstances within which ordinary legislators have actually found themselves in a position to stand up and say, 'Behold! Henceforth daughters shall be treated as equal members of every Hindu coparcenary'. Or, 'Hark! Orphaned grandchildren will henceforth be entitled to a specific share of every ancestral estate'.

THE POLITICS OF PERSONAL LAW REFORM IN PAKISTAN

Within the Islamic Republic of Pakistan one might expect the institutionalization of Islamic injunctions (within the Constitution) to introduce specific constraints on postcolonial patterns of independent legislative action. A special clause known as the Objectives Resolution (adopted in 1949 and added to the Constitution as a general preamble in 1956, before being elevated to the status of a substantive article—Article 2A— in 1985), for instance, states that 'the Muslims of Pakistan shall be enabled to order their lives in accordance with the fundamental principles and basic concepts of Islam'. In fact, further language embedded within the so-called directive principles goes on to note that specific steps, beginning with the establishment of a special institution known as the Council of Islamic Ideology, will be taken to ensure that (a) every law in Pakistan is brought into

---

Judgments on the Method of Calculation', *Islamic and Comparative Law Quarterly*, (1984), 4: 247–50; and, finally, Lucy Carroll, 'Orphaned Grandchildren in Islamic Law of Succession: Reform and Islamization in Pakistan', *Islamic Law and Society*, (1998), 5(3): 420–36.

[6] Before the promulgation of the Muslim Family Laws Ordinance (MFLO) in 1961, colonial and postcolonial efforts to engage Islamic laws of inheritance within the territories that formed a part of Pakistan did not address the task of 'substantive' reform. More often than not they simply took the question of substance for granted and sought to extend or restrict its application. See for example, the West Punjab Muslim Personal Law (Shariat) Application Act, 1948, the Northwest Frontier Province Muslim Personal Law (Shariat) Application Act, 1950, the Punjab Muslim Personal Law (Shariat) Application (Amendment) Act, 1951, and so on. See also, with reference to India as a whole, the Muslim Personal Law (Shariat) Application Act, 1937.

conformity with 'the injunctions of Islam as laid down in the Holy Quran and Sunnah' and, moreover, that (b) 'no law [will] be… enacted which is repugnant to such injunctions'.

Having established this Council of Islamic Ideology, however, the Constitution goes on to limit its role quite severely, noting in Article 230, for instance, that the work of this Council will be confined to providing 'advice' and 'recommendations' to the President, the National Assembly, the Provincial Assemblies, and so on. In fact, when General Ayub Khan intervened to 'add' orphaned grandchildren to the list of existing Qur'anic heirs in 1961, building directly on the work of a special Commission on Marriage and Family Laws with the promulgation of a bold new ordinance known as the Muslim Family Laws Ordinance (MFLO), the Council of Islamic Ideology was powerless to stop him.[7] Indeed, the Constitution did not *constrain* the process of reform. It merely provided a framework for ongoing (reform-oriented) *advice*.[8]

---

[7] In its push for reform, the Commission explained that 'if a person leaves a great deal of property and his father pre-deceased him, the grandfather gets the share that the father of the deceased would have got', adding that, [if] the right of representation is recognised by Muslim law among the *ascendants*,…it does not… seem logical…that the right of representation should not be recognised among the lineal *descendants* as well (emphasis added). Quoted in Lucy Carroll, 'The Pakistan Federal Shariat Court, Section 4 of the Muslim Family Laws Ordinance, and the Orphaned Grandchild', *Islamic Law and Society*, (2002), 9(1): 72 (fn7). 'The Islamic law of inheritance', they argued, 'cannot be irrational and inequitable'. Quoted in Carroll, 'Orphaned Grandchildren', (1998), p. 409 (fn1). Carroll, however, finds this analogy to the right of representation among ascendants 'unconvincing', because, she notes, 'the father's father takes in the absence of the father, not because he represents the father, but because in the absence of the father he is the nearest male agnatic ascendant', p. 411 (fn10). For further criticism, see, A.B.M. Sultanul Alam Chowdhury, 'The Problem of Representation in the Muslim Law of Inheritance', *Islamic Studies*, (1964), 3: 375–91.

[8] According to N.J. Coulson, the 'arbitrary and specious reasoning' of the Commission on Marriage and Family Laws 'demonstrated only the most superficial familiarity with Islamic legal history'. In fact, he argues, 'it is not surprising… that their proposals were condemned by their traditionalist colleague [Maulana Ehtisham-ul-Haq Thanvi] as an unwarranted interference by laymen in the realm of sacred law'. See 'Islamic Family Law', p. 247. Lucy Carroll adds that 'the claim on the part of a seven-member Commission containing three female members and only one representative of the *ulema* of a right to exercise *ijtehad* [that is, independent religious-cum-legal reasoning] and the promulgation of many of

In 1973, Prime Minister Zulfiqar Ali Bhutto promulgated an entirely new Constitution. But even then, the reforms introduced by General Ayub Khan remained firmly in place. The Constitution itself stated that Islam would be 'the State religion' (Article 2); but having said this, Bhutto ensured that the MFLO (1961) was carefully protected by a special constitutional provision known as the First Schedule.[9] In fact, he incorporated this First Schedule as a special ring-fence provision specifically to ensure that the MFLO would be shielded from any threat of malign judicial review—for example, on the grounds that its reform-oriented provisions regarding orphaned grandchildren were incompatible with 'a fundamental right' to some (countervailing) form of 'religious expression'. The constitutional status of Islam, in other words, was rendered explicit. But, even then, its reach did *not* extend to any *repeal* of existing religious-cum-legal 'reforms'.

General Zia-ul-Haq, for his part, launched his well-known 'Islamization' campaign with the construction of a parallel religious judiciary—first in conjunction with four so-called 'shariat benches' attached to each provincial High Court (1979) and then in conjunction with a new-fangled Federal Shariat Court (FSC) in Islamabad (1980).[10] Moving beyond the purely 'advisory' role of the Council of Islamic Ideology, these new courts, including the Shariat Appellate Bench of the Pakistan Supreme Court, were empowered to decide whether or not existing laws were in fact 'repugnant to the injunctions of Islam' and, if they were, to render them ineffective. But having

---

[their] recommendations as law by a martial law administration possessing neither Islamic nor democratic credentials…did not commend themselves to all sections of society. The *ulema* were particularly and predictably outspoken in their dissent'. Caroll, 'Orphaned Grandchildren', p. 436. See also, Tanzil-ur-Rahman, 'Succession Under Muslim Family Laws Ordinance 1961', *Pakistan Law Digest*, (1982), pp. 99–113.

[9] The First Schedule of the 1973 Constitution listed every law protected from the terms of Article 8, which stated that laws found to be inconsistent with fundamental rights protections would be considered legally 'null and void'. (In fact, by adding the MFLO and some 50–60 other laws to this Schedule, the Constitution freed the MFLO from any challenge on the basis of allegations regarding specific fundamental rights violations—for example, the right to profess or practise one's own religion.)

[10] See, Presidential Order No. 3 of 1979 (7 February 1979) and Presidential Order No. 1 of 1980 (27 May 1980).

established this parallel judiciary, Zia (somewhat surprisingly) went on to limit its scope, once again restricting it to the review of any law *except* (a) the Constitution itself and (b) 'Muslim personal law'. Indeed, by 1980, Jeffrey A. Redding argues that some had begun to ponder what might be described as the 'limited limitations' of Pakistan's existing constitutional architecture, noting that '[a] crafty parliament (or military authority)' should be able to legislate 'free from [any] fear that the Federal Shariat Court might intervene' simply by 'including [the word] "Muslim"' in the title of its legislation.[11] (After all, any law identified as a 'Muslim personal law' seemed to avoid any risk of judicial review.)

Even the Federal Shariat Court was slow in challenging this view. In the case of *Farishta* v. *Federation of Pakistan* (1980), for instance, the Shariat Appellate Bench of the Supreme Court simply reiterated—with specific reference to inheritance—that the MFLO was, in fact, completely immune to any form of judicial review on the part of Pakistan's shariat courts, adding, from a purely constitutional perspective, that Muslim personal laws were supposed to be reviewed by the (powerless) Council of Islamic Ideology.[12]

Even after the Preamble to the Constitution (a.k.a. the Objectives Resolution) was elevated from its position as a non-binding preamble to the status of a substantive Article 2A by virtue of an executive ordinance in 1985, the Supreme Court intervened in the case of *Hakim Khan* v. *The State* (1992) to declare that Article 2A was not a

---

[11] Jeffrey A. Redding, 'Constitutionalizing Islam: Theory and Pakistan', *Virginia Journal of International Law*, (2004), 44(759): 775.

[12] In *Farishta*, the Shariat Appellate Bench of the Supreme Court dismissed a decision rendered by the Shariat Bench of the Peshawar High Court. Agreeing with the government—the government of Zia-ul-Haq—the Court declared that, as per Article 203(b), the MFLO was *not* subject to the scrutiny of the Federal Shariat Court. In particular, the Court noted that Article 203(b) was designed to ensure that the jurisdiction of the FSC was limited to the review of 'ordinary' legislation (applying to all citizens) rather than any 'special' legislation known as Muslim personal law (applying only to Muslims). This 'Muslim-only' legislation would continue to be referred to the Council of Islamic Ideology. See, *Massamat Farishta* v. *Federation of Pakistan, Pakistan Law Digest*, (1980), Peshawar 47 (Shariat). See also, Lucy Carroll, 'Nizam-e-Islam: Processes and Conflicts in Pakistan's Programme of Islamisation, with Special Reference to the Position of Women', *Journal of Commonwealth and Comparative Politics*, (1982), 20: 57–95.

'supra-constitutional' provision that could be used to invalidate other (ostensibly un-Islamic) parts of the Constitution itself (for example, the Constitution's First Schedule).[13] And in *Kaneez Fatima* v. *Wali Mohammad* (1993), the Court returned to the same issue, noting that although Article 2A *could* be used to challenge the constitutional validity of an 'executive ordinance', it could *not* be used to strike down (a) other parts of the Constitution itself (following *Hakim Khan*) or, for that matter, (b) common pieces of routine legislation.[14] Indeed, following in the wake of *Kaneez Fatima* many came to believe that the courts were not in a position to import 'the principles of Islam' at all except to cater for special situations 'untended by express legislation'.[15]

Throughout the latter half of the twentieth century, in other words, the Federal Shariat Courts took up several cases designed to clarify the limits of the 'reformist' domain. But legally speaking, few limits emerged. In fact, a closer reading suggests that it was not the legislature's powers but its own that the Court was keen to check.

Finally, however, in the case of *Dr Mahmood-ur-Rahman Faisal* v. *Government of Pakistan* (1994), this pattern appeared to shift.[16] Stepping in to clarify the extent to which the terms of Muslim personal law were in fact 'excluded' from the possibility of review by the Federal Shariat Court, the Shariat Appellate Bench of the Pakistan Supreme Court explained that this 'exclusion' should not be taken to include the terms of Muslim personal law 'as a whole' (that is, Muslim personal law as it was said to apply to all Muslims in Pakistan). Instead, the Court declared, this exclusion was strictly limited to provisions that applied to a particular *sect* of Muslims. Only sectarian provisions, in other words, were 'excluded' from FSC-based patterns of religious-cum-legal 'review'.[17] (Of course,

---

[13] See, *Hakim Khan* v. *The State, PLD,* (1992) SC 585; see also, *The State* v. *Zia-ur-Rahman, PLD,* (1973) SC 49.

[14] See, *Kaneez Fatima* v. *Wali Mohammad, PLD,* (1993) SC 905.

[15] Salman Akram Raja, 'Islamisation of Laws in Pakistan', *South Asian Journal,* (2003), 2.

[16] See, *Dr Mahmood-ur-Rahman Faisal* v. *Government of Pakistan, PLD,* (1994) SC 507.

[17] Article 227 (pertaining to the Council of Islamic Ideology) was later amended to ensure that, in evaluating existing and proposed laws for repugnancy

Dr Mahmood-ur-Rahman Faisal did not intend to shield the MFLO from additional FSC-based scrutiny; but, with a few 'sectarian' adjustments, it could have done so very easily.[18] After all, Islamic laws of inheritance *are* routinely applied in 'sect-specific' ways[19]).

Precisely insofar as the MFLO was not seen as a 'sect-specific' law. However, it was in fact reviewed (as a law applying to 'all of the Muslims in Pakistan') in the famous case of *Allah Rakha* v. *Pakistan* (2000).[20] This case was a landmark. In fact, the Federal Shariat Court hastened to reject the inheritance provisions of the MFLO (Section 4) outright, arguing that, from a purely religious perspective, the ancestral share provided to orphaned grandchildren was simply 'un-Islamic'. Having said this, however, the Court did not go on to declare what the terms of Islamic law should be; instead it opted to leave this matter to the legislature, referring, by way of example, to the Egyptian Law of Bequests.[21] Indeed, it explained that

---

problems vis-à-vis the Qur'an and the Sunnah, the Council would define the terms 'Qur'an' and 'Sunnah' to mean 'the Qur'an and Sunnah as interpreted by [each] sect'. See, Presidential Order No. 14 of 1980 (18 September 1980). (Even here, however, the work of the Council was limited to the provision of non-binding advice.) For an extension of this point, see also, *Dr Amanat Ali* v. *Federation of Pakistan* (1983).

[18] 'Considering that intra-sect mobilization is...easier than pan-Muslim mobilization', notes Jeff Redding, 'the legislation of sectarian or communitarian law could eventually become more common than other forms of "Islamic" legislation'. And, 'if sectarian law proliferates', he notes, 'it is entirely possible the Shariat judicial system, as a result of its 1994 opinion, will encounter a future reduction in its jurisdiction....' Redding, 'Constitutionalizing Islam', p. 785.

[19] See, Lucy Carroll, 'The Hanafi Law'; Ibid., 'The Ithna Ashari Law'.

[20] See, *Allah Rakha* v. *The Federation of Pakistan*, PLD, (2000) FSC 1.

[21] In light of the fact that 'certain shares had been fixed by the Qur'an and therefore could not be modified', notes Fazlur Rahman, 'Egypt felt unable to assign a share of direct inheritance to the orphaned grandchildren and had recourse to the principle of mandatory will'. This principle was related to an injunction (2:180) encouraging wills that many jurists treated as 'abrogated' by the subsequent introduction of fixed shares. But in Egypt—and after 2000, in Pakistan as well— the 'mandatory will' appeared to be the preferred avenue of compromise between Qur'anic shares and contemporary notions of justice. Still, objections persisted. As Rahman explains, 'the Egyptian law...prescribes an inheritance share which is only veiled as mandatory will, since (1) the law, even if the propositus has made no will, presumes a will nevertheless, and (2) for the purpose of [measuring]...the amount to be given to the orphaned grandchild the share of the dead father "if he were alive"

the government of Pakistan should not be so bold as to 'add' any
new Qur'anic heirs, for example, by way of an 'executive ordinance';
instead, the ruling party should simply be encouraged to follow in
the footsteps of Egypt, Syria, Morocco, Kuwait, Jordan, Iraq, and
many others, introducing an ordinary piece of legislation assuming
the existence of a mandatory will to accomplish more or less exactly
the same thing.[22]

Of course, many continued to insist that the terms of Muslim
personal law were, somehow, fixed.[23] But over time, the judicial
record itself expressed a very different story. In fact, by the time the
Court announced its famous *Allah Rakha* decision, the record was
perfectly clear—a record of substantive religious-cum-legal reform
promulgated by a military dictator, protected by an elected prime
pinister, reinforced by a second military dictator, and then supported
by a vast array of superior religious and constitutional courts. Clearly,
the terms of religious-cum-legal 'reform' were not inconceivable. In
fact, the terms of 'reform' were already very well entrenched.[24]

The conditions within which 'reform' was possible, however, were
not determined (at least not exclusively) by the courts. More often

---

is [still] kept as a necessary point of reference'. See, Fazlur Rahman, 'A Survey of
Modernization of Muslim Family Law', *International Journal of Middle East Studies*,
(1980), 11(4): 464. Indeed, Lucy Carroll goes on to note that 'it would be difficult
to contend that [the 'obligatory bequest'] is founded in the Qur'an and the Sunnah
of the Prophet—as these have been traditionally interpreted for many centuries
past'. Carroll, 'Orphaned Grandchildren', (1998), p. 445.

[22] See, Egypt (1946), Syria (1953), Morocco (1958), Kuwait (1971), Jordan
(1976), and Iraq (1979). Additional strategies of a similar sort—mostly pertaining
to those who might wish to privilege certain heirs—were outlined by Lucy Carroll in
her article, 'Life Interests and the Inter-Generational Transfer of Property: Avoiding
the Law of Succession', *Islamic Law and Society*, (2001), 8(2): 245–86.

[23] See, Matthew J. Nelson, *In the Shadow of Shari'ah: Islam, Islamic Law, and
Democracy in Pakistan* (Columbia University Press: New York, 2010).

[24] For a comparative dimension, see, John R. Bowen, *Islam, Law, and Equality
in Indonesia: An Anthropology of Public Reasoning* (Cambridge University Press:
Cambridge, 2003) and 'Qur'an, Justice, Gender: Internal Debates in Indonesian
Islamic Jurisprudence', *History of Religions*, 38(1): 68–70, 72–8; Michael G.
Peletz, *Islamic Modern: Religious Courts and Cultural Politics in Malaysia* (Princeton
University Press: Princeton, 2002); and Mounira Charrad, *States and Women's Rights:
The Making of Postcolonial Tunisia, Algeria, and Morocco* (University of California
Press: Berkeley, 2002).

than not these conditions were tied to the content of local politics, with fragile coalitions remaining considerably more reserved than postcolonial dictators and one-party dominant regimes.

Looking back, for instance, we see that fragile coalition governments were often keen on extending the 'rhetoric' of Muslim personal law (for example, as a way to win political points) without, in any way, seeking to engage the rather more difficult task of 'substantive' religious-cum-legal reform: consider, for example, with respect to inheritance, specific efforts to extend the *application* of 'existing' shares for women—over and above, say, the prevailing terms of persistent 'tribal' customs (1948, 1950, 1951, and so on).

Following the military coup led by General Ayub Khan in 1958, however, we see something else entirely—something more 'substantive'. Again, the MFLO (1961) did not confine itself to the application of already 'existing' shares. Instead it completely *redefined* those shares. And of course it did so in the context of an almost untouchable (indeed an explicitly dictatorial) 'modernizing' postcolonial regime.[25]

Prime Minister Zulfiqar Ali Bhutto (1970–7) did not attempt to introduce any 'substantive' religious-cum-legal reforms, with one (possible) exception. This exception concerned his support for a special constitutional amendment (Article 260) excommunicating Pakistan's beleaguered Ahmedi minority. Yet even here it is essential to point out that, when this constitutional amendment was introduced in 1974, Bhutto's party—the Pakistan People's Party—did not hold more than 60 per cent of the existing seats in the legislature; in fact, they held only 59 per cent of those seats (a figure that amounted to nine times more seats than its nearest political competitor—the Pakistan Muslim League or Qayyum). Indeed, even if the promulgation of Article 260 *is* taken to represent a case of 'substantive' religious-cum-legal reform, it would not undermine the basic terms of my argument—an argument regarding the importance

---

[25] It is worth pointing out that in some ways Ayub Khan's promulgation of the MFLO was doubly untouchable owing to the existence of a Provisional Constitutional Order (PCO) creating vulnerable and compliant judges.

of political context and, especially, the value of a certain immunity from the exigencies of cross-party 'bargaining'.

The same pattern clearly re-emerged when General Zia-ul-Haq introduced his famous 'Islamization' campaign in 1979—a campaign characterized by a wide range of 'substantive' religious-cum-legal reforms concerning, for instance, marriage, divorce, taxation, rape, and the rules governing evidence in court. Again, each and every one of these reforms was promulgated by 'executive decree'. None emerged, by way of ordinary 'legislation', following the introduction of a (nominally elected) Parliament—that is, a nominally elected 'coalition' government— in the spring of 1985.

Again, the postcolonial history is clear. Although the terms of Muslim personal law were not closed off from the specific terms of reform (constitutionally), they were for the most part strictly set apart from any environment characterized by fragile 'coalition' governments. Whenever change has occurred, it has occurred in a context defined by (or akin to) 'dictatorship'.

The 1991 elections provided Prime Minister Nawaz Sharif with an absolute majority in the Pakistan National Assembly (51 per cent), and, shortly thereafter, Sharif introduced a bill known as the Enforcement of Shariat Bill. Given the size of Sharif's majority, however, this Bill did not involve any effort to amend the 'substance' of existing religious personal laws; instead, it simply aimed to extend the 'rhetoric' of those laws in a rather transparent bid to garner political support.[26] In fact, the extent of its (substantive) irrelevance was revealed in the mechanics of its final vote: among the religious parties in the National Assembly none rose to support (or oppose) the Bill; all of them simply abstained.

Six years later, however, in 1997, Sharif returned to power with a much larger majority (63 per cent), leading many to believe that he might take up the task of 'substantive' religious-cum-legal reform with somewhat greater vigour. But in the event he did not. Instead, he

---

[26] In the end this Enforcement of Shari'ah Act (1991) was passed by just 40 votes to 3. See, Christine Amjad Ali and Charles Amjad Ali, *The Legislative History of the Shariah Act* (Christian Study Centre: Rawalpindi, 1992). See also, Charles H. Kennedy, 'Repugnancy to Islam: Who Decides? Islam and Legal Reform in Pakistan', *The International and Comparative Law Quarterly*, (1992), 41(4): 769–87.

simply opted to pursue a constitutional amendment defining a more limited role for the army and, in the Fall of 1999, he was removed from power—this time in a military coup.[27]

Like General Ayub Khan and General Zia-ul-Haq before him, General Pervez Musharraf (1999–2008) seized upon the protections afforded by his own military 'dictatorship' to revisit the path of 'substantive' religious-cum-legal reform. In fact, Musharraf sought to amend the so-called Hudood Ordinances initially promulgated by General Zia-ul-Haq with an entirely new law known as the Protection of Women (Criminal Laws Amendment) Act (2006).[28] Separating 'religious' injunctions regarding 'adultery' from the language of 'rape' and placing any prosecution for the latter strictly within the (mundane) terms of Pakistan's existing criminal code, Musharraf's reforms were strongly opposed by an amalgam of religious parties known as the Muttahida Majlis-e-Amal (MMA) (although, in its purely 'advisory' capacity, the Council of Islamic Ideology supported them). In fact, the ruling party within Musharraf's own coalition (a party known as the Pakistan Muslim League-Quaid-e-Azam or PML-Q) actually joined the MMA in resisting this push for reform, forcing Musharraf to rely on several different 'opposition' parties to see his new law through. Indeed, without Musharraf, many noted that the prospects for reform were bleak. The support of a dictator was decisive.

Again and again, throughout the latter half of the twentieth century, the task of reform has fallen more or less exclusively to so-called 'progressive' dictators like General Pervez Musharraf in a tit-for-tat competition with ostensibly 'conservative' or 'reactionary'

---

[27] See, Babar Sattar, 'Pakistan: Return to Praetorianism', in Muthiah Alagappa (ed.), *Coercion and Governance: The Declining Political Role of the Military in Asia* (Stanford University Press: Stanford, 2001), pp. 385–412.

[28] Notwithstanding the demands of many human rights organizations, the Protection of Women (Criminal Laws Amendement) Act, 2006 did *not* repeal Zia's Hudood Ordinances. Instead, it retained the jurisdiction of this ordinance vis-à-vis the ostensibly 'religious' crime of 'adultery' (while, at the same time, making adultery a 'bailable offense' and abolishing both the death penalty and flogging for anyone who might be convicted).

Many religious scholars opposed these changes, arguing that every case of (consensual or non-consensual) 'extra-marital sexual intercourse' (including rape) should be treated in the same ('religious') terms.

dictators like General Zia-ul-Haq—both sides seeking to define and then, in due course, redefine the legal 'substance' of Islam. Clearly, the terms of Islamic law have not been closed off from the task of 'substantive' religious-cum-legal reform. But again, the conditions surrounding these reforms have remained quite far removed from the fragile coalition governments of the late 1940s, the early 1950s, the late 1980s, the early 1990s, and today. When change has occurred, it has occurred in a context defined by the benefits of bargaining 'immunity'. Only the 'immunized', it seems, are prepared to stand up and say, 'Behold!'

THE POLITICS OF PERSONAL LAW REFORM IN INDIA

The situation in India is, perhaps surprisingly, almost exactly the same. In fact, 'equal status' (secular) forms of constitutionalism notwithstanding (see John H. Mansfield, Chapter 5 in this volume), the only difference seems to lie in a basic tendency to replace the reform-oriented work of military authoritarian leaders like General Ayub Khan, General Zia-ul-Haq, or General Pervez Musharraf with the work of non-military authoritarian leaders and the leaders of one-party dominant regimes in which the ruling party enjoys a single-party majority of at last 60 per cent in the lower house of the legislature (that is, the Lok Sabha). The key to success for those with an interest in 'substantive' patterns of personal law reform, in other words, still flows from an ability to construct a political environment that is, for all intents and purposes, 'immune' to the inconveniences associated with cross-party legislative bargaining. (In his essay, Mansfield does not address this effort to redefine the substance of religious personal laws; instead, he considers cases in which individuals convert from one religion and, thus, one religious personal law to another.)

From a strictly constitutional perspective the terms of Indian secularism are remarkably ambivalent when it comes to the problem of 'substantive' religious-cum-legal reform. It could be that the Constitution's 'equal status' provisions amount to a recipe for equal-status safeguarding—that is, in some sense, a constitutional commitment to ensure that each religious tradition is 'equally protected' from the vagaries of State-based interference. But, of course, it could also be that India's 'equal status' provisions amount to a recipe for equivalent forms of (legislative or judicial) vulnerability; indeed, it may be that, together, the Indian Lok Sabha and the Indian Supreme Court are (constitutionally) responsible for bringing each tradition (including each tradition of religious personal law) into conformity with other constitutional norms—for example, the norm of gender equality (Articles 14 and 15).

Within the Indian Constitution, this impulse for equal-opportunity 'reform' is particularly evident within the so-called directive principles outlined in Articles 36–51 (including Article 44, which urges the State to reconcile its many different personal laws within what is commonly known as a 'uniform' civil code). Having said this, however, it is also clear that the special function of these directive principles is not at all unlike that of the directive principles we encountered in the case of Pakistan's Council of Islamic Ideology: on the one hand, 'directive principles' designed to promote a particular trajectory of reform (and thus, a particular 'constraint' on independent legislative action); and yet, on the other hand, a set of 'principles' that are themselves strictly 'advisory' (amounting to no immediately enforceable constitutional 'constraint' at all).

In India, just as much as Pakistan, those with an interest in the reform of religious personal law, and, especially, religious personal laws regarding inheritance, tend to confront specific questions regarding the extent to which new heirs might be 'added' to an already existing (and ostensibly sacred) list. Within the Mitakshara School of Hindu law traditionally prevailing in most parts of India (except Bengal), for instance, women are not regarded as full-fledged 'heirs'. In fact, within the Mitakshara School of law, their relationship with the ancestral property of their deceased male relatives is not defined by any specific form of 'ownership' rights at all; instead, it is defined by what is commonly known as a 'limited' lifetime estate— that is, an estate in which surviving widows, daughters, mothers, paternal grandmothers, and so on enjoy what is usually described as 'a usufructuary right of maintenance' until (a) their marriage or (b) their death. (With respect to an ancestral home or a piece of ancestral land, for example, these women will be 'maintained' either directly or via certain types of rental income; they will not be entitled to sell the land, or exchange it, or simply give it away.) In fact, among

Hindus in India, the challenge for would-be reformers typically lies in seeking to 'add' women to the list of those enjoying full-fledged legal 'ownership' rights to every 'ancestral' estate.[29]

Beginning in 1940 and then continuing after the independence of India in August 1947, the disinheritance of women was taken up with considerable vigour by a special committee known as the Hindu Law Committee.[30] The work of this committee was bitterly opposed by those who considered the existing terms of Hindu law to be utterly 'sacred' and, therefore, legally 'untouchable'. (As Reba Som explains, the members of this committee were plagued by 'a recurrent cry...that the Hindu *shastras* were hallowed by tradition', and, thus, that 'any attempt to tamper with them [would be] presumptuous

[29] The Hindu Law of Inheritance (Amendment) Act (1929) opened up colonial notions of Hindu law for reform. In particular, it declared that, in cases where a Hindu man died without any sons (or a surviving father), the right to inherit various forms of property *not associated with the Hindu coparcenary* (that is, the traditional body of 'agnatic' Hindu heirs) would include son's daughters, daughter's daughters, sisters, and sister's sons in preference to the man's surviving brothers. This adjustment did not affect the list of existing 'coparcenary' heirs; it simply elevated the Madras School of Mitakshara Hindu Law to the status of a national norm with respect to every other form of (non-coparcenary) property. In 1937, the British colonial State introduced a new law known as the Hindu Women's Right to Property Act (The Deshmukh Act), which aimed to provide Hindu widows with usufructuary access to a portion of the joint family estate once held by their deceased husbands—a portion equal to that inherited by each of her agnatic coparcenary sons. (Legally speaking, however, these women were not 'added' to the list of sacred heirs as full-fledged 'owners'. They were simply 'maintained' by a tiny portion of the 'share' once held by their husbands. And, alas, daughters were ignored altogether.)

[30] The authors of the first Hindu Law Committee report (1941) noted that 'Hindu law had kept in step with the requirements of society because of the efforts of the *smrtikaras*', that is, the authors of the *smrtis*, as well as various 'commentators'. But, insofar as 'such traditional authorities no longer existed', they noted that 'legislatures and the courts...[had a] responsibility [for] reinterpreting Hindu law to make it conform with the changed times'. See, Archana Parashar, *Women and Family Law Reform in India: Uniform Civil Code and Gender Equality* (Sage: New Delhi, 1992), p. 90. Still, Parashar explains that the members of this first Hindu Law Committee 'did not rely on the rules of interpretation...employed by [ancient] commentators. ... Instead they justified their proposals with a selective reliance on textual authority and...a recognition of changed conditions', always claiming to reflect 'the true intention of the *smrtis*' (p. 92); see also, pp. 98–101.

and undesirable'.)[31] But in due course this committee succeeded in putting forward a host of rather dramatic (and 'substantive') religious-cum-legal reforms.

Even after these reforms were tabled in 1948, they languished in the capital for more than eight years.[32] In fact, even after one of their chief architects, Constituent Assembly Chairman B.R. Ambedkar, unveiled India's new Constitution in 1950—a Constitution that left considerable room for such reforms—it was not until Prime Minister Jawaharlal Nehru emerged from India's first general elections in 1952 with a single-party majority amounting to 74 per cent of the existing Lok Sabha seats that the climate began to shift.[33]

In her account of this rather dramatic legal-cum-political development, Archana Parashar explains that within India, 'it was widely believed that, because…Congress [had] won the first general elections [with such a huge majority] it had acquired the mandate of the population for Hindu law reform'.[34] In fact, she notes, it was almost as if Nehru himself had secured the mantle of divine inspiration, announcing in the Hindu Succession Act, 1956—one of the four new Acts that came together to form India's 'reformed' Hindu Code—that, thenceforth, both Hindu sons and Hindu daughters

---

[31] Reba Som, 'Jawaharlal Nehru and the Hindu Code: A Victory of Symbol over Substance?', *Modern Asian Studies*, (1994), 28(1): 174.

[32] According to Archana Parashar, the 'reform of Hindu law was not taken up in response to public demand'. On the contrary, 'the State assumed…responsibility for reform on its own initiative' (p. 81). In fact, 'the authors of the second Hindu Law Committee [report] overtly assumed that the legislature had the right to decide what changes were needed…and when' (p. 85).

[33] Quoting Lok Sabha member R.K. Chahdhuri, Reba Som argues, 'without [Nehru], the [Hindu Succession Act]…would not have been passed at all' (p. 193).

[34] Parashar, *Women and Family Law Reform in India*, p. 88. See also, Som, 'Jawaharlal Nehru and the Hindu Code', p. 185. As Parashar points out, 'it is difficult to accept that at the time of first introducing the bills [in 1948] the government was not sure of its capacity to carry through some of the reform measures but succeeded in actually enacting them into law [only] after these proposals had been altered and made [even] more radical by the Joint Committee or by the Rajya Sabha' (for example, by including those governed by Mitakshara law within the ambit of the new legislation, despite earlier efforts to exclude this group) (p. 111). Clearly, the confidence needed to enact these reforms was delivered by the general election and, more specifically, Parashar explains, by the overwhelming size of the Congress Party majority.

would be entitled to an equal portion of the share ('ownership') once held by their deceased Hindu father.[35] Indeed, Nehru went even further, declaring that, for the first time ever, Hindu 'owners' would be entitled to create a will—a will that could of course be used to shift this new share for 'daughters' in favour of specific 'brothers'.[36]

Of course, the reach of this rather sweeping reform initiative was limited, particularly with respect to the all-important question of agricultural land, by the fact that the Indian Constitution continued to describe matters pertaining to land as a 'provincial' or 'state-level' subject. (See, for example, the so-called 'Concurrent List' outlined in the Seventh Schedule of the Indian Constitution.) But, even then, several states simply opted to repeat the experience first initiated in Delhi, using their own rather enormous state-level majorities to push Nehru's agenda forward.

In 1975, for instance, the Congress-led 'Ruling Front Alliance' in Kerala added the political immunities associated with Indira Gandhi's Emergency to its own overwhelming legislative majority—a majority amounting to 63 per cent of the seats in the Kerala State Assembly—to eradicate the persistence of any agnatic (all-male) 'Hindu coparcenary estates'.[37] Ten years later, the newly formed Telugu Desam Party in Andhra Pradesh used its powerful 69 per cent majority in the Andhra State Assembly to ensure that women throughout Andhra Pradesh

[35] Although the Act abolished the concept of a 'limited' lifetime estate, seeking to provide 'equal' rights for both sons and daughters in the property of their deceased father, the Act did not seek to eliminate the concept of an agnatic (all-male) 'coparcenary'. To illustrate: A father with three sons and a daughter would leave 1/4th to each son, as members of the agnatic coparcenary, with the final 1/4th—the father's own share—being divided into four 'equal' parts, including one part for each son and one part for the remaining daughter; each son = $1/4 + 1/16 = 15/16$; daughter = $1/16$.

[36] 'While the predominant effort was to justify [these] changes as being in consonance with the religious texts,' Parashar notes, *there was [really] no suggestion that the dharmasastras could not be modified by the legislature*' (emphasis added) (p. 96). See also, A. Gledhill, 'Constitutional and Legislative Development in the Indian Republic', *Bulletin of the School of Oriental and African Studies*, (1957), 20(1/3): 276; and Lucy Carroll, 'Daughter's Right of Inheritance in India: A Perspective on the Problem of Dowry', *Modern Asian Studies*, (1991), 25(4): 791–809.

[37] Because the tenure of Kerala's Ruling Front Alliance was extended three times during the Emergency, it remained in place when the Kerala Joint Hindu Family System (Abolition) Act, 1975 came into force on 1 December 1976.

would be treated as 'full' members of every Hindu 'coparcenary'.[38] Indeed, what set these moments of 'substantive' reform apart was not the political 'platform' of the ruling party ('national', 'regional', etc); what set them apart was the strength of the ruling party's majority.

In 1989, the Dravida Munnetra Kazhagam in Tamil Nadu captured 64 per cent of the seats in the Tamil Nadu State Assembly (following a year of President's Rule). And immediately thereafter, they repeated the work of their colleagues in Andhra Pradesh. Five years later, in 1994, similar reforms were undertaken under similar political circumstances in Karnataka, where the Congress Party held 79 per cent of the existing state-level seats, as well as in Maharashtra.[39] (It is, however, important to concede that, strictly speaking, the state-level majority in Maharashtra following the State Assembly elections of March 1990 amounted to slightly less than 50 per cent.[40] Still, few would disagree that the ruling Congress Party recovered quite dramatically after India's general elections in June 1991, securing 77 per cent of Maharashtra's 48 Lok Sabha seats; in fact, substantial victories in subsequent local *panchayat* and municipal corporation elections ensured that Maharashtra's state-level Congress Party was in a much stronger position when Maharashtra finally introduced its own Hindu Succession Amendment during the summer of 1994.)

Indeed, even when it came to the politically sensitive subject of Muslim personal law, India's efforts to pursue the path of 'substantive' religious-cum-legal reform followed more or less exactly the same pattern.

In 1973, for instance, Prime Minister Indira Gandhi simply ignored a pattern of elite *ulema*-based resistance when, armed with a single-party Lok Sabha majority of 66 per cent, she opted to revise the existing Criminal Procedure Code (Section 125) in

---

[38] In June 1985, the Telugu Desam Party used its overwhelming majority to abolish Andhra's Congress-dominated upper house (a.k.a. the Legislative Council), and, two months later, it went on to pass a new Hindu Succession (Andhra Pradesh Amendment) Act.

[39] See, the Hindu Succession (Tamil Nadu Amendment) Act, 1989, the Hindu Succession (Karnataka Amendment) Act, 1994, and the Hindu Succession (Maharashtra Amendment) Act, 1994.

[40] After the March 1990 Maharashtra State Assembly elections, the Congress Party held a total of 141 out of 288 seats (49 per cent).

an effort to ensure that all female divorcees throughout India—Muslim and non-Muslim alike—would be governed by the same law of maintenance (notwithstanding the presence of an entirely separate and, some argued, a constitutionally 'protected' Muslim personal law of divorce).[41] Indeed, when this issue resurfaced more than ten years later following the infamous *Shah Bano* decision in 1985, Prime Minister Rajiv Gandhi simply built on his own single-party majority—an unprecedented 76 per cent—to reframe the substance of Muslim personal law itself: 'Behold!', noted the Indian Supreme Court in its review of the entirely new Muslim Women's (Protection of Rights on Divorce) Act (1986) that emerged from this effort, Muslim divorcees would be entitled to receive a post-divorce allowance even beyond the traditional three-month period known as *iddat*.[42] And 'Lo!', this maintenance could be claimed from several

---

[41] Briefly stated, Indira Gandhi amended Section 125 of the revised Criminal Procedure Code to note that, for the purposes of claiming maintenance, the meaning of the word 'wife' should be taken to include both married and divorced wives. This did not introduce a change in terms of Muslim personal law per se, because, of course, the Criminal Procedure Code was a criminal law targeting all Indians without any special concern for their particular religious affiliations. But, even so, some Muslims objected on the basis that Muslim personal law contained its own (separate) provisions for the maintenance of divorced wives. Whereas Indira Gandhi sought to provide women (including divorced women) with a lifetime maintenance guarantee, for instance, some Muslims argued that in divorces initiated by husbands (known as 'triple *talak*'), Muslim men were obligated to maintain their divorced wives for a period of roughly three months, three menstrual, or three lunar cycles—a period known as *iddat*—and no more. And, in divorces initiated by wives (*khula*), they noted that husbands were not obligated to pay any maintenance at all; instead, divorced wives were generally expected to return the money they (should have) received at the time of their marriage—a sum described as *mehr*. In short, a law requiring husbands to maintain their divorced wives in perpetuity—and that too with an amount specified by a criminal judge—was regarded as anathema to traditional interpretations of Muslim personal law. The Constitution itself, many argued, allowed for a certain freedom of religious expression (including the preservation of religious personal laws subject to various notions of 'public order' and 'morality'), and, with this in mind, many insisted that Section 125 of the newly amended CrPC (1973) *should not apply to Muslims*. Still, Prime Minister Indira Gandhi simply built on the strength of her parliamentary majority, applying Section 125 to all citizens as a purely 'humanitarian' measure.

[42] In the case of *Mohammad Ahmed Khan* v. *Shah Bano*, (1985), 2 SCC 556, the Supreme Court noted that, as per Section 125 of the Criminal Procedure Code

different sources, including state-level *waqf* boards. And finally, 'Rejoice!' This provision was not limited to cases of *talaq* initiated by husbands. It applied to all divorces including so-called *khula* divorces initiated by Muslim wives.[43]

Of course, in the context of these reforms, Parashar noted that the government 'could have utilized…considerable scholarly opinion [noting] that it *is* possible and desirable to modify *some* aspects of… Islamic law *without* undermining [its] sacred nature' (emphasis added).[44] But, following in the footsteps of General Ayub Khan and his MFLO in Pakistan, the Supreme Court argued that Rajiv Gandhi did not bother. On the contrary, they noted that he simply responded to an appeal from local Muslims to clarify, in the context of *fresh legislation*, the 'substance' of Muslim personal law.[45]

(1973), destitute Muslim divorcees were entitled to receive a maintenance allowance from their husbands even beyond the period known as *iddat*. In fact, the Court reiterated the fact that Section 125 had been amended as a 'humanitarian' measure set apart from the specific terms of Muslim personal law (although, having done so, the Court went on to explain that, even if Section 125 had attempted to address the terms of Muslim personal law, it would have remained fully in keeping with the spirit of *shari'ah*). Needless to say, this effort to redefine the spirit of shari'ah prompted an intense political backlash, particularly on the part of the *ulema*, and especially, the Muslim Personal Law Board based in Delhi. In fact, the strength of this backlash led Muslim League General Secretary G.M. Banatwala to sponsor the bill that ultimately led to the promulgation of the Muslim Women's (Protection of Rights on Divorce) Act (1986).

[43] The Muslim Women's (Protection of Rights on Divorce) Act intended to 'protect' the rights of divorced Muslim women within the terms of Muslim personal law. In particular, it sought to embrace a modified interpretation of Hanafi Sunni jurisprudence and having done so, it sought to apply this interpretation to *all* Muslims (both Sunni *and* Shi'a) across India. In fact, even within this modified interpretation the Act explained that destitute Muslim divorcees would be entitled to file a claim for maintenance, not only from their ex-husbands, but also (for the first time) from other relatives, including their parents and their brothers, as well as state-level *waqf* boards.

[44] Parashar, *Women and Family Law Reform in India,* p. 186.

[45] The Muslim Women's (Protection of Rights on Divorce) Act, 1986, effectively reconstructed the substance of Muslim personal law to provide, in Section 3(1)(a), protections for destitute women similar to those granted by the Supreme Court in its *Shah Bano* decision. In fact, the nature of these protections was clarified in the case of *Daniel Latifi* v. *Union of India* (2001) 7 SCC 740, which, in upholding the Muslim Women's Act, 1986, explained that divorced Muslim women still enjoyed access to a 'reasonable and fair' level of maintenance even after the post-divorce

Throughout postcolonial India, the terms of 'substantive' religious-cum-legal reform have rarely occurred without the protections afforded by a climate of overwhelming political power. The Hindu Marriage (Amendment) Act, 1964, was introduced when Prime Minister Jawaharlal Nehru and the Congress Party controlled 73 per cent of the Lok Sabha seats; the Marriage Laws (Amendment) Act, 1976, was promulgated during Prime Minister Indira Gandhi's Emergency; the Commission of *Sati* (Prevention) Act, 1987, was passed when Rajiv Gandhi enjoyed a single-party majority of 76 per cent; and so on[46] (see Table 7.1). In fact, the only exception to this basic rule so far involves the recent promulgation of a new Hindu Succession (Amendment) Act by the Congress-led United Progressive Alliance (UPA) coalition that emerged in 2004—a coalition in which the Congress Party controlled the smallest number of Lok Sabha seats (just 27 per cent) ever held by a postcolonial ruling party.

Building on the combined efforts of several different civil society organizations, as well as—and, perhaps, especially—prior state-level reforms, this new Act (2005) introduced fully equal 'ownership' rights for Hindu sons and daughters (while, at the same time, allowing both to serve as the 'manager' of joint Hindu property).[47] And remarkably, it did so within the context of an extremely fragile coalition government. In fact, for the first time ever, the Indian government seemed to address the task of 'substantive' religious-cum-legal reform as a matter of routine civil society engagement and (above all) fragile *coalition* politics.

---

period known as *iddat*. In other words—owing to the rather innovative approach to maintenance enshrined in the Muslim Women's Act, 1986—women still enjoyed some access to a lifetime maintenance guarantee as outlined in Section 125 of the Criminal Procedure Code (1973).

[46] Parashar, *Women and Family Law Reform in India*, p. 272. The Marriage Laws (Amendment) Act, 1976, which provided additional grounds for the dissolution of marriage, such as divorce by 'mutual consent' and, somewhat later, Clause 21(a) in the Special Marriage (Amendment) Act, 1976 (according to which two Hindus married under this Act were made subject to the 'Hindu' Succession Act, 1956 rather than the 'Indian' Succession Act, 1925) were by far the most prominent examples. Indeed, the timing of these reforms in the context of Indira Gandhi's Emergency is telling.

[47] Some activists, such as Bina Agarwal, supported this change, even as they argued that the co-parcenary should have been abolished altogether. See, Bina Agarwal, 'Landmark Step to Gender Equality', *The Hindu*, 25 September 2005.

Table 7.1 Leading Party: Share of Lok Sabha Seats
(Government/Prime Minister)

Year	Share of Lok Sabha Seats (%)	Leading Party	Government	Prime Minister
1952*	74.4	Congress	Congress	Jawaharlal Nehru
1957*	75.1	Congress	Congress	Jawaharlal Nehru
1957*	75.1	Congress	Congress	Jawaharlal Nehru
1962*	73.1	Congress	Congress	Jawaharlal Nehru, Lal Bahadur Shastri
1967	54.4	Congress	Congress	Indira Gandhi
1971*	66.0	Congress	Congress	Indira Gandhi
Emergency: 1975–7				
1977	54.1	Janata Party	Janata Party	Morarji Desai, Charan Singh
1980*	66.7	Congress	Congress	Indira Gandhi
Assassination of Indira Gandhi: October 1984				
1984*	76.4	Congress	Congress	Rajiv Gandhi
1989	36.1	Congress	BJP-supported National Front	V.P. Singh, Chandra Shekhar
Assassination of Rajiv Gandhi: March 1991				
1991	44.8	Congress	Congress	P.V. Narasimha Rao
1996	29.5	BJP	Congress-supported United Front	H.D. Deve Gowda, I.K. Gujral

*Government with single-party majority above 60 per cent promulgates substantive religious personal law reform.

1998	33.4	BJP	BJP-led National Democratic Alliance	Atal Bihari Vajpayee
1999	33.4	BJP	BJP-led National Democratic Alliance	Atal Bihari Vajpayee
2004**	26.7	Congress	Congress-led United Progressive Alliance	Manmohan Singh
2009	37.9	Congress	Congress-led United Progressive Alliance	Manmohan Singh

**Government with single-party majority below 60 per cent promulgates substantive religious personal law reform.

CONCLUSION

The challenge, of course, lies in explaining why most coalition governments have felt themselves to be so much more thoroughly constrained than this initial UPA government in India (2004–9). Indeed, why is it that for so long, elected representatives have been so very subdued when faced with the prospect of *reforming* the religious-cum-legal landscape that surrounds them? Is the Hindu Succession (Amendment) Act, 2005, an *anomaly*? Or perhaps, as many reformers hope, an *arbiter* of future trends?

Clearly, specific 'constitutional' barriers are not sufficient to explain the inhibitions that I have highlighted in the context of this essay. On the contrary, neither India nor Pakistan harbours any relevant constitutional constraints. Neither harbours any special class of religious-cum-legal elites with any preemptive veto. And of course, as John H. Mansfield also stresses in his contribution to this volume, neither has attempted to erect a towering 'wall of separation' between religion, on the one hand, and the work of the legislature, on the other. In fact, from a purely 'constitutional' perspective, the most important question is really one regarding what can only be described as an apparent *inhibition*, on the part of several ruling coalitions, to *engage* the legally permissive environment that surrounds them. Is political negotiation or bargaining in a non-authoritarian multi-party coalition somehow more difficult when it comes to negotiations involving 'religion'? And if so, why? *Why are 'religious' laws, democratically, so much more difficult to reform?*

Constitutionally, existing attachments to religious personal law do not constrain the reach of democratic legislatures. In fact, in this sense, even 'special status' constitutions that privilege certain religious traditions cannot be said to depart (automatically) from the specific terms of democracy. And of course, drawing special attention to the power of history—for example, colonial history—it is simply impossible to suggest that the legacy of the colonial State might be sufficient to explain specific patterns of 'reformist' variation over time—not only between countries (Pakistan v. India) but also within them (Pakistan 1948 v. 1961; India 1948 v. 1956; and so on). On the contrary, like so many factors that stretch across these variations, the power of 'colonialism' is a 'constant'.

Even if prevailing constitutional and colonial arrangements fail to explain these patterns of variation, however, specific political arrangements do not: India under Prime Ministers Jawaharlal Nehru and Rajiv Gandhi and Pakistan under Generals Ayub Khan and Zia-ul-Haq pursued major 'substantive' reforms; Prime Ministers Benazir Bhutto and Narasimha Rao did not. If, however, fragile coalition governments like those of Benazir Bhutto and Narasimha Rao represent an increasingly common feature of the existing political landscape in South Asia—and I would argue they do— the question arises: *what are the implications of this coalition-based political landscape for the underlying possibility of (ongoing) religious-cum-legal reform?* Indeed, how does a history of reform set apart from the terms of cross-party bargaining interact with, *or challenge*, the outlook for reform in South Asia's postcolonial 'democracies'? Is the Hindu Succession (Amendment) Act, 2005 *an anomaly or an arbiter of* future trends?

When a well-known *mullah* by the name of Ehtisham-ul-Haq Thanvi rejected Ayub Khan's push to provide a legal defence for the inheritance rights of orphaned grandchildren, noting that, 'as a matter of principle, reference to public opinion on purely shariat questions amounts to trifling with…[the] shariat and ridiculing the religion',[48] he was not articulating the views of a lonely cleric. On the contrary, he was articulating an extremely widespread sense of political apprehension regarding the religious propriety of proactive religious-cum-legal reforms. He was, in fact, pushing back against the 'presumptuous' zeal of postcolonial reformers, articulating a popular attachment to the separation of religion, religious personal law, and modern 'democratic' politics.

When a Hindu Mahasabha member of India's Legislative Assembly asked, in 1955, 'what right…Prime Minister [Jawaharlal Nehru had] to initiate revolutionary bills which would shake the roots of Indian civilization shaped by a personal law which [had] stood the test of centuries', he was not articulating the views of a renegade Hindu 'extremist'.[49] He was, in fact, articulating a rather common pattern of formal (legal) hesitation—one that, at the time, reflected the views of his Congress Party colleague, the President of India, Rajendra Prasad.[50]

As David S. Powers noted, in 1998, in a special issue of *Islamic Law and Society* devoted to the Islamic law of inheritance, in 1998, it is essential to understand 'how Muslims have interpreted and, on occasion, reshaped and redefined the materials contained within the corpus of Islamic law'. In fact, he went out of his way to stress the extent to which Islamic law, 'like other legal systems', is 'a product of history'.[51] But the important question does not concern the power of history as such; rather, the most important question concerns the extent to which historically familiar processes of reinterpretation, redefinition, and reform have become so powerfully unfamiliar politically.[52] What are the implications of this political unfamiliarity for those with an interest in the relationship—indeed the special legal relationship—between 'religion' and 'democracy' today? Is it possible

[48] *Report of the Commission on Marriage and Family Laws* (Law Division, Government of Pakistan: Islamabad, 1963), p. 92.

[49] Som, 'Jawaharlal Nehru and the Hindu Code', p. 174.

[50] Ibid., p. 182.

[51] See, David Powers, 'The Islamic Inheritance System', *Islamic Law and Society*, (1998), 5(3): 290.

[52] Richly historicized processes of religious re-interpretation are often paired with a deep reluctance to define these processes as religiously (or politically) 'legitimate'. Indeed, those who seek to promote such processes are often seen as heretics.

to imagine a situation in which the processes that Powers described as historically and religiously 'normal' are, in fact, also politically 'normal' and, hence, politically accessible to those with an interest in reiterative patterns of religious debate, political negotiation, and, ultimately, 'democratic' religious-cum-legal reform?

Scholars have not yet had a chance to examine the bargaining processes that preceded the promulgation of India's Hindu Succession (Amendment) Act, 2005.[53] But when they do, several questions will merit their attention. These questions will concern the ways in which those involved in this process of reform managed to articulate a coherent 'religious' justification for their efforts. Did they succeed in bringing the terms of 'politics' and 'religion' together? And if they did, how exactly did they manage it? Did their efforts unfold within a 'religious' language of 'religious-cum-political reform'? And if so, what did that language sound like?

These are the questions that my project has raised so far: What does this language sound like? Is such a language possible? And if so, what are its preconditions?

---

[53] For a legal assessment of this law, see the work of Indian Law Commission Chairman, Justice A.R. Lakshmanan, 'Proposal to amend the Hindu Succession Act, 1956, as amended by Act 39 of 2005' (5 February 2008). See also, Agarwal, 'Landmark Step to Gender Equality'.

CHAPTER EIGHT

Religious Freedom in India and Pakistan
The Matter of Conversion

❧

John H. Mansfield

THE SITUATION IN INDIA

In 1995, in a case called *Sarla Mudgal* v. *Union of India*,[1] the Supreme Court of India held that when a Hindu man marries a Hindu woman under Hindu law, the man's conversion to Islam does not entitle him to marry a second Muslim wife, although Muslim law applicable in India permits it, nor is his first marriage to the Hindu woman dissolved by his conversion. If the first marriage is to be dissolved, it must be under Hindu law, if that is possible. The Court's judgment was in response to a number of writ petitions inviting the Court to restrain several husbands from marrying second wives and, in one case, a petition by a Muslim woman alleging that one of the husbands, after his conversion to Islam, had married her, but then had reverted to Hinduism. In that case the Muslim woman begged the Court to order the husband to maintain her. Although none of the cases before the Court involved a prosecution for bigamy, the Court expressly held that all husbands would be liable for the crime

---

[1] (1995) 3 SCC 635. See also, Chapter 6 in this volume ('Constitutional Borrowing in South Asia: India, Sri Lanka, and Secular Constitutional Identity'), where Jacobsohn and Shankar discuss the case, at footnote 25.

of bigamy. What other legal consequences followed from husbands' conversions and second marriages, the Court did not make clear.[2] In the course of its judgment, the Court suggested that the conversions were insincere and accomplished solely to escape the husbands' Hindu wives and obligations under Hindu law, although because of the looseness of the writ petition procedure, there seems to have been no opportunity to present evidence on this question.

In the opinions supporting the judgment, the unfairness to the Hindu wife in applying Muslim law either to dissolve her marriage or to allow a second wife is emphasized. After all, the opinions stated, she had married a Hindu by Hindu rites, fully expecting to live the life of a devout Hindu wife, and now she finds herself married to a Muslim, or not married at all, or that her husband has an additional wife. Her shock and disappointment can be appreciated. Still, had the Court reached the opposite result, the expectations of Hindu couples at the time of marriage would soon change and the possibility of conversion taken into account. Furthermore, the established rule is that when a person converts, succession to his estate will be governed by the law of his new religion, and this change of personal law will also defeat the expectations of those who would have inherited if the decedent had not converted.[3] Likewise, as several courts have pointed out, in a territorial-based law, a change of domicile might change the applicable law, whether of succession or of divorce.[4]

[2] Another Division Bench (two justices), composed of different Justices, followed *Sarla Mudgal* in *Lily Thomas* v. *Union of India*, (2000) SCC 225. The opinions in *Lily Thomas*, however, were more sensitive to the different legal consequences of declaring that the first marriage continued to subsist and that the second marriage was invalid. One of the opinions noted the claim of the convert that his right to religious freedom under Article 25 of the Indian Constitution would be violated if he was found guilty of bigamy, and rejected it. The same opinion suggested that a proper, progressive reading of Muslim law also would find the convert's second marriage to the Muslim woman invalid because of the subsisting Hindu marriage.

[3] See, *John Jiban Chandra Datta* v. *Abinash Chandra Sen*, (1939) ILR 2 Cal. 12, at 18.

[4] *Ayesha Bibi* v. *Subodh Chandra Chakrabarti*, (1945) ILR 2 Cal. 405, 418–9 *John Jiban Chandra Datta* v. *Abinash Chandra Sen*, (1939) ILR 2 Cal. 12, 18; *Khambatta* v. *Khambatta*, (1934) 59 ILR Bom. 278, 296. See also, the observation in *Dr. Abdur Rahim Undre* v. *Smt. Padma Abdur Rahim Undre*, (1982) AIR Bom. 341, 354: 'It cannot…be said that anybody has got a vested right in the matter of divorce. To say the least dissolution of marriage is not a part and parcel of the contract of marriage'.

The result in *Sarla Mudgal* is not explained by the application of either Hindu law or Muslim law, but by the application of the law of India, which evidently favours protecting the expectations of the first, the Hindu wife, as against any competing interest. What might be a competing interest? It is the interest of the person who has converted and embraced a new religion in living fully in accordance with his new religion, including having applied to himself its personal law, which he may consider part and parcel of his new religion. This value the Supreme Court did not discuss at all in *Sarla Mudgal*, nor did it recognize the conflict of interests or expound the principle that governed its choice.

There are a number of possible explanations for the result in *Sarla Mudgal*. The first might be the Court's concern to protect Hinduism from the inroads of Islam and Christianity, both of which are proselytizing religions interested in gaining new adherents, whereas Hinduism generally is non-proselytizing, except for modern movements of purification and reconversion. The frequent characterizations of the husbands, in one of the opinions in *Sarla Mudgal*, as 'apostates',[5] lends some credence to this theory. The same opinion manifests hostility towards the institution of polygamy,[6] although it is permitted to Muslims in India, suggesting another explanation for the Court's result. A third possible explanation is the desire to protect women, who in most of the recent cases have been the non-converting spouse,[7] and who are seen by the Court as especially vulnerable. However, in one of the litigated cases, as mentioned earlier, the petitioner was a Muslim woman who sought to be maintained after her husband reconverted to Hinduism, but it is not clear that the Court would provide her with a remedy. Furthermore, the Court expressly laid down a general rule that whichever spouse converts, whether it be the husband or the wife, the marriage can be dissolved only under the law of its celebration. A fourth possible explanation of *Sarla Mudgal* is a policy to make it difficult for Indians to convert from one religion to another, and so give teeth to Mahatma Gandhi's suggestion that conversion is a

[5] (1995) 3 SCC at 635, 639, 646–7.

[6] (1995) 3 SCC at 650.

[7] Though not in the older cases where the convert was often the wife. For example, *Crown* v. *Mussumat Gholam Fatima*, (1870) 5 Punjab Rec. 51.

positive evil.[8] If this is the policy, its tendency would be to confine people to the religion of their birth. Of course, through the general rule that the Court propounds—that you must get divorced under the law under which you were married—if the policy is as I just suggested, it would have a very uneven application. In the litigated cases, it might indeed be very difficult for the husbands to get divorced under Hindu law if their wives are not willing to cooperate. The same would be true of a conversion from Christianity to Islam. But, if we suppose the opposite, a conversion of a Muslim husband from Islam to Christianity, he would find it fairly simple to comply with the Muslim law and divorce his wife by issuing a *talaq*. Perhaps he would be well-advised to do this before his conversion.

Quite apart from the issue of divorce, if in the case of conversion from Hinduism to Islam one looks only to Hindu law, as J.D.M. Derrett had pointed out long ago,[9] the price of conversion is very high. Conversion gives grounds for divorce to the non-converting spouse; children of the convert cannot inherit from the latter's relations; the non-converting spouse may adopt without the consent of the convert; and the convert may lose the custody of his own children. These burdens on the freedom to change one's religion might be too much even for the *Sarla Mudgal* Court in its task of framing the law of India, law which must be the ultimate ground for decision even though the burdens are decreed by Hindu law.

Before Independence, the courts of British India struggled with the question *Sarla Mudgal* presents, for almost one hundred years. They struggled with it in a number of different contexts: prosecutions for bigamy, succession to the convert's estate, custody of the children of the first marriage, the legitimacy of children of the second marriage, efforts by an unconverted spouse to gain restoration of conjugal rights, and efforts by the converted spouse to gain custody of the unconverted spouse. In the early period, in the 1860s, courts seem to have rejected the *Sarla Mudgal* solution and emphasized the importance of freedom to change one's religion. In one of these early

---

[8] See, K.L. Seshagiri Rao, 'Conversion: A Hindu Gandhian Perspective', in C. Lamb and M.D. Bryant (eds), *Religious Conversion*, (Cassell: London, 1999), p. 136.

[9] J.D.M. Derrett, *Religion, Law and the State in India* (Free Press: New York, 1968), pp. 332–3.

cases, where a Hindu man had converted to Christianity, married a Christian woman, then reconverted to Hinduism and married a Hindu woman, his conviction for bigamy was quashed with the observation that a person must be equally free to become a Christian and to go back to Hinduism.[10]

After this early period, no clear pattern appears in the decisions of the high courts before Independence. A number of decisions could be classified as neutral with regard to the *Sarla Mudgal* question in the sense that they find no conflict between the personal laws involved. If one supposes that we are confronted with a Hindu marriage in which one spouse converts to Islam and then marries a Muslim, the decision is either that under Hindu law on account of the conversion the first marriage no longer subsists or under Muslim law the second marriage is invalid because of the failure to comply with some requirements of that law.[11] But other cases clearly line up for or against the *Sarla Mudgal* solution, and perhaps one could say that the authorities somewhat favour *Sarla Mudgal*.[12] In surveying this multitude of cases, there is a threshold question of critical importance which nowhere receives a clear answer: When is there a change of religion from a legal point of view? It would seem clear that this is a question that must be answered under the general

---

[10] Proceedings, 8 November 1866, Reports of Cases Decided in the High Court of Madras in 1866, 1867, and 1868, Appendix vii–ix (1868). See also, 4 Madras High Court Reports, Appendix iii (1868), following the 1866 decision.

[11] For example, *Imam Din* v. *Hasan Bibi*, (1906) 41 Punjab Rec. 309; *Abdul Ganj* v. *Azizul Haq*, (1911) 15 Calcutta LJ 263.

[12] A selection of pro-*Sarla* cases: *Crown* v. *Mussumat Gholam Fatima*, (1870) 5 Punjab Rec. 51; *Government* v. *Ganga*, (1880) 4 ILR Bom. 330; Administrator-General, (1886) 9 ILR Madras 466; *In re* Millard, 10 ILR Madras 218 (1887); *Jamna Devi* v. *Mul Raj*, (1907) 42 Punjab Rec. 198; *Emperor* v. *Lazar*, (1907) 30 ILR Cal. 550 (dictum); *Emperor* v. *Mt. Ruri*, AIR 1919 Lahore 389; *Noor Jehan Begum* v. *Eugene Tiscenko*, (1942) ILR 2 Cal. 165 (1941) (judgment of lower court); *Sayeda Khatoon* v. *M. Obadiah*, (1945) 49 CWN 745; *Robesa Khanum* v. *Khodudad Bomanji Irani*, (1946) 48 Bom. LR 864.

A selection of anti-*Sarla* cases in addition to those cited above for the early period: *Emperor* v. *Antony*, 8 Ind. Cases 572 (Mad. High Court, 1910); *Mussamat Nandi* v. *Crown*, (1920) 1 ILR Lahore 440; *Musst. Ayesha Bibi* v. *Bireshwar Ghosh Mazumdar*, (1929) 33 Cal. Wk. Notes clxxix; *John Jiban Chandra Datta* v. *Abinash Chandra Sen*, (1939) ILR 2 Cal. 12; *Ayesha Bibi* v. *Subodh Chandra Chakrabarti*, (1945) 2 ILR Cal. 405.

law of India and from its perspective, and that an answer cannot be found within the borders of any particular personal law. Some cases suggest that the depths of the putative convert's sincerity and real beliefs must be plumbed,[13] others require only a formal declaration with no concern for subjective motives.[14] For instance, in one case it is said that a conversion will be recognized even though the reason for the conversion was that the new religion had a superior social system or even that the motive for the conversion was to marry a particular person.[15] It is perhaps surprising that the answer to the question remains so obscure, since upon it could depend liability for the crime of bigamy.[16]

The cases over this long period make clear the weakness of the *Sarla Mudgal* opinions, because of the deficiencies of the writ petition process, in failing to distinguish the different legal effects of holding that the first marriage must be dissolved under the law of its celebration. These numerous cases involve prosecutions for bigamy, issues of succession to the convert's estate, rights of maintenance either of the first or the second wife, the legitimacy of the children of the second marriage and so on. One would expect that the particular legal consequences would influence the rule to be adopted. In the *Sarla Mudgal* case itself, I suppose it is clear that if the original Hindu wife simply went ahead after her husband's conversion and married another Hindu, she herself would be guilty of bigamy. To avoid criminal liability, she would have to go through a judicial procedure to divorce her husband, whereas perhaps she would not if the law of India had been interpreted to free the husband from the marital bond if he complied with Islamic law.

It may be suggested that if both spouses convert, the *Sarla Mudgal* rule should not apply: they should not have to get divorced under the

---

[13] *Dr. Abdur Rahim Undre* v. *Smt. Padma Abdur Rahim Undre*, (1982) AIR Bom. at 341, 358, 362.

[14] *Ghaus* v. *Fajji*, 29 Ind. Cases 857 (Chief Court of Punjab, 1915); *Ayesha Bibi* v. *Subodh Chandra Chakrabarti*, (1945) ILR 2 Cal. at 405, 414–15.

[15] *Ayesha Bibi* v. *Subodh Chandra Chakrabarti*, (1945) ILR 2 Cal. 405, 414–15. But in *Rakeya Bibi* v. *Anal Kumar Mukherji*, (1948) ILR 2 Cal. 119, it is stated that the conversion would not be 'genuine' if it was done simply to gain a legal right.

[16] Though under the rule of *Sarla Mudgal*, the question of whether there was a conversion will not arise.

law of their old religion.[17] Certainly in such a situation, the argument about the disappointed expectations of the wife and fairness due to her lose much of their force. Could it be argued that since both spouses converted, the original marriage had been changed into a marriage under the law of the new religion, even if there had been no formal ceremony? And what if a spouse renounces her old religion without adhering to another?[18] Under *Sarla Mudgal* it would seem clear she must get divorced under the law of her old religion. But if that solution is rejected, would she have any way to get divorced? Under the Special Marriage Act?[19]

In 1945, shortly before Independence, a dramatic conflict developed within the Calcutta High Court. In *Ayesha Bibi* v. *Subodh Chandra Chakrabarti*, Justice Ormond embraced an anti-*Sarla Mudgal* approach.[20] Two Hindus had married under Hindu law. The wife then converted to Islam and sought a declaration that her Hindu marriage was dissolved. The declaration was granted, the Court stressing the value of religious freedom. In the course of the judgment, an interesting subsidiary question was discussed: whether British India was an Islamic country—*Dar-ul-Islam*—or a non-Islamic country—*Dar-ul-Harb*.[21] The relevance of the question was that if India was an Islamic country, under Islamic law the wife had to ask her husband to convert to Islam and have him brought before a *kazi* (arguably a British Indian court), so that the *kazi* could ask the husband if he would convert, and decree the marriage dissolved if the husband did not accept Islam; whereas if India was not an Islamic country, the wife's conversion to Islam with an invitation to her husband to convert, without any judicial intervention, but with a specified waiting period, would suffice. The court ruled,

---

[17] For cases in which both spouses did convert, see, *Zuburdust Khan* v. *His Wife*, N.W.P. High Court Reports 370 (1870); *Gorbadhan Dass* v. *Jasdamori Dass*, 18 (1891) ILR Cal. 252; *Martha Samadhanam David* v. *Sudha*, (1950) AIR Mysore 26.

[18] See, *Mussammat Resham Bibi* v. *Khunda Bakhsh*, (1937) 19 ILR Lahore 277.

[19] Special Marriage Act, 3 of 1872, replaced by the Special Marriage Act, 1954.

[20] (1945) 2 ILR Cal. 405. Though perhaps the decision could be classified as neutral in the sense I referred to earlier, since the court believed its decision was not in conflict with any rights under the old religion.

[21] Ibid. at 422–3. The same question can be asked in case of present-day Pakistan.

contrary to an earlier case,[22] that India was not an Islamic country, notwithstanding the fact that its administration of Muslim law to Muslims, which was fortunate for the plaintiff-wife, since she had not instituted the sort of judicial proceeding Islamic law would have required in an Islamic country. In the same High Court the same year, Justice Lodge disagreed with Justice Ormond and adopted the *Sarla Mudgal* position. The case before Justice Lodge[23] involved two Jews who were married under Jewish law and then the wife converted to Islam. The Court declined to issue a declaration that the Jewish marriage was dissolved. A Special Bench was assembled to resolve the dispute for the Calcutta High Court, and it sided with Justice Lodge, holding that 'justice and right' would not be served by declaring that the marriage had been dissolved by the wife's conversion, and that it would be 'outrageous treatment' to tell the husband 'that he cannot retain his wife unless he forsakes his religion....'[24]

Shortly before Independence, the High Court of Bombay sided with Justice Lodge's view rather than Justice Ormond's, and it rested its decision expressly on 'justice and right', on the general law of India, rather than on any particular personal law.[25] In that case, the Court denied the request of a Parsi woman who had converted to Islam for a declaration that her earlier marriage to a Parsi had been dissolved by her conversion. In its judgment, the Court stated: 'It was difficult to see why the conversion of one party to a marriage should necessarily afford a ground for its dissolution. The bond that keeps a man and a woman happy in marriage is not exclusively the bond of religion'.[26] In this observation, the Court seems to have been influenced by its own idea that the purpose of marriage is happiness rather than some other objective, and that a difference of religion between the spouses is not a matter of great importance. The Court in *Sarla Mudgal* placed heavy reliance upon this decision of the Bombay High Court.[27]

---

[22] *In re Ram Kumari*, (1891) 18 ILR Cal. 264.

[23] *Sayeda Khatoon v. M. Obadiah*, (1945) 49 CWN 745.

[24] *Rakeya Bibi v. Anil Kumar Mukherji*, (1948) ILR 2 Cal. 119, 136.

[25] *Robasa Khanum v. Khodadad Bomanji Irani*, (1946) 48 Bom. LR 864.

[26] Ibid. at 878.

[27] (1995) 3 SCC at 642.

High Court decisions since Independence have followed the tradition of going both ways on the *Sarla Mudgal* issue. In one case, the *David* case,[28] a Hindu converted to Christianity, married a Christian woman, then both became Hindus and the husband took a second wife. (This was before polygamy among Hindus was prohibited.) The Court held that the husband was not guilty of bigamy. In another case with facts identical to *David*, except that the Christian wife had not converted to Hinduism,[29] the court followed the *David* case. While it expressed sympathy for the Christian wife, it asked what would be the situation of the Hindu wife if the Court declared her marriage invalid. In the last High Court decision before *Sarla Mudgal*, a Hindu converted to Christianity, married a Christian woman, reconverted to Hinduism and then married another, a Hindu wife. The Court held him guilty of bigamy.[30] This decision rebuts the suggestion made earlier that a reason for the *Sarla Mudgal* solution might be to protect Hinduism, since here it protects a Christian marriage.

In *Reid* v. *Reid*, a 1965 decision of the Privy Council on an appeal from Ceylon, a Christian man who had married a Christian woman converted to Islam and then took a second, Muslim wife. He was convicted of bigamy, but his conviction was reversed on appeal to the Supreme Court of Ceylon. The Privy Council affirmed the action of the Supreme Court, stating:

> [Their lordships] cannot agree that in a country such as Ceylon a Christian monogamous marriage prohibits for all time during the subsistence of that marriage a change of faith and of personal law on the part of a husband…. In their lordships' view, in such countries there must be an inherent right in the inhabitants domiciled there to change their religion and personal law and so contract a valid polygamous marriage….[31]

This decision, of course, was not binding on the courts of India, since it came after the Constitution of India was adopted and was on an appeal from Ceylon. In *Sarla Mudgal*, the Supreme Court of India cited the Privy Council's decision, but dismissed it for no stated

[28] *Martha Samadhanam David* v. *Sudha*, (1950) AIR Mysore 26.
[29] *Mrs A. Marthama* v. *A. Munuswamy*, (1951) AIR Mad. 888.
[30] *Kalanjiam Ammal* v. *Shanbagam*, (1989) Cr. LJ 405 (Madras).
[31] *Attorney-General of Ceylon* v. *Reid*, (1965) 1 All ER PC at 812,817.

reason. Such has been the influence of *Sarla Mudgal* that shortly after the judgment of the Supreme Court of India was handed down, the Supreme Court of Sri Lanka overruled *Reid* v. *Reid*, expressly relying on *Sarla Mudgal*.[32]

The rule laid down in *Sarla Mudgal* may be compared with the Caste Disabilities Removal Act, 1850.[33] That Act was adopted as a result of lobbying by Christian missionaries who wanted to make the lot of those converting from Hinduism and Islam to Christianity easier. The Act enabled converts to retain rights under their original personal law—such as rights of succession—notwithstanding their conversion. Thus, whereas in *Sarla Mudgal* the question was whether the convert should continue to be burdened with obligations deriving from his original personal law, under the Caste Disabilities Removal Act the convert could retain rights under the personal law of his now abandoned religion. He succeeded in continuing to be a Hindu so far as it was to his advantage, but in other respects could live according to his new faith. Of course the rule embodied in the Caste Disabilities Removal Act was religiously neutral: it did not matter whether you converted from Hinduism to Christianity or from Christianity to Hinduism: you retained whatever rights you had under your pre-conversion personal law.

If the Caste Disabilities Removal Act was neutral as among religions, the Converts' Marriage Dissolution Act, 1866,[34] which appears still to be in force in India but probably not in Pakistan, was not. It encouraged conversion to Christianity, and only to Christianity, by providing a judicial procedure through which the convert could have a marriage dissolved that had been celebrated under the law of another religion, if the unconverted spouse had repudiated or deserted the convert because of his conversion. Converts to Christianity from Islam were excepted from the Act on the theory that under Islamic law conversion automatically dissolved the marriage anyway, so there was no need for judicial intervention. But there was uncertainty as to whether conversion had that effect

---

[32] *Natalie Abeysundere* v. *Christopher Abeysundere*, Sup. Ct. Appeal No. 70/96 (16 December 1997).

[33] Act 21 of 1850.

[34] Act 21 of 1866.

under Hindu law, so legislation was necessary to permit the convert to remarry without fear of prosecution for bigamy. Thus, in the case of Hinduism, Western values were interposed to override arguable Hindu ideas, but at the same time ambivalence was shown towards this override by retaining certain rights of the unconverted spouse and the children. The Converts' Marriage Dissolution Act is a half-way house between the position of the Supreme Court of India in *Sarla Mudgal* and upholding the convert's right entirely to rid himself of his old religion: he is free to marry again without fear of prosecution, but certain obligations stemming from his old religion continue to burden him.[35]

THE SITUATION IN PAKISTAN

The law in Pakistan on the *Sarla Mudgal* issue is different from the law in India. In 1988 in a Federal Shariat Court case, two Christians had married under the Christian Marriage Act,[36] an act which both India and Pakistan have retained as the personal law for Christians. In the litigated case, *Mst. Zarina v. State*,[37] it was the wife who converted to Islam and then married a man who was himself a convert from Christianity to Islam. The unconverted Christian husband then filed a criminal complaint against his wife and her second husband for the crime of *zina*, sexual intercourse outside lawful marriage in violation

---

[35] The fascinating debates leading up to the passage of the Converts' Marriage Dissolution Act can be traced in the pages of the India Gazette for 1865–6. *India Gazette*, January–June, 1865, pp. 59–60; January–June, 1865 Supp. pp. 5–17; January–June, 1866, pp. 163–4; January–June, 1866 Supp. pp. 201–14. Sir Henry Maine, the Law Commissioner, was a strong proponent of the bill. Some Protestant ministers were supporters of the bill, no doubt to help converts, but also because they believed, relying on a passage in the Bible, that remarriage of a convert was authorized by Christianity. Other ministers opposed the bill, believing that this reading of the Bible was unwarranted and that Christianity required that the earlier marriage be honoured. Not only converts from Islam, but also converts from Judaism were excluded from the Act. This latter exclusion is not discussed in the debates, but perhaps is explained by a consensus among the ministers that Jewish marriage was due special respect. Interestingly, Roman Catholic canonical procedures were allowed to determine whether remarriage was permissible when the conversion was to Roman Catholicism.

[36] Act 15 of 1872.

[37] 40 PLD (1988) Federal Shariat Court 105.

of one of the Hudood Ordinances, promulgated during General Zia's regime.[38] This ordinance is applicable to all Pakistanis whether Muslims or belonging to religious minorities, even though its prohibition is based on Islamic law.[39] If the wife had not converted, she clearly would have been guilty of *zina*, since she had not obtained a divorce under the Divorce Act applicable to Christians.[40] The trial court convicted both defendants of the offense of *zina* and the wife additionally of the crime of bigamy. The Federal Shariat Court reversed the conviction, stating:

> The effect of conversion to Islam upon the character and status of the person so converted is that the convert renounces all his religious and personal law and immediately adopts the Muslim religion and personal law and is completely cut off from the past. He/she accepts a new mode of life and enters a new domain where his/her deeds, words and actions are governed by the law of his/her new religion and his/her future in all respects of life becomes amenable to Muslim law.[41]

Thus, the Shariat Court appeared to uphold the importance of freedom to change one's religion.[42] The Court paid no heed to the disappointed expectations of the Christian husband and focused entirely upon the freedom of the wife to change her religion. The Court appeared to derive its conclusion entirely from its understanding of Islamic law, both in regard to what it takes to become a Muslim and the legal consequences of conversion to Islam. We should not be surprised by this in view of the fact that the task of the Shariat Court is precisely to apply the law of Islam. There is ground for asserting that because of provisions in the Constitution of Pakistan and laws enacted under it, the most fundamental law in Pakistan is indeed Islamic law.[43] The fundamental law in India is, by way of contrast, secular.

---

[38] Offence of Zina (Enforcement of Hudood) Ordinance, 6 of 1979.

[39] See, *Mst. Saima* v. *State*, (2004) SD 928 (Lahore).

[40] Divorce Act, 4 of 1869. See also, *Mst. Saima* v. *State*, 2004 SD 928 (Lahore).

[41] *Mst. Zarina* v. *State*, 40 PLD (1988) FSC at 105, 109.

[42] See also, *Salamat Ali* v. *State*, (1989) P Cr. LJ 978 (FSC); *Afzal Masih* v. *State*, (2004) SD 1044 (FSC); *Tariq Masih* v. *State*, (2004) SD 443 (FSC).

[43] Constitution of Pakistan, Articles 2, 2(a), 31, 41, 203(d), 227; Penal Code Section 338(f). See, *Dr. M. Aslam Khaki* v. *Syed Muhammad Hashim*, PLD 2000 (1) SC 225, 406 (judgment of Justice Khalil-ur-Rehman Khan): 'every law to be framed by the Parliament has to conform to the injunctions of Islam....' The

It would seem that the same conclusion might be reached by a court in Pakistan if two people had married under the Special Marriage Act,[44] an act adopted for British India to enable those with no personal law, or those who had a personal law but wished to be rid of it, to get married. If one looks simply to the text of the Act, it requires that dissolution of a marriage created under the Act comply with the Divorce Act, 1869. But under the reasoning of the Shariat Court's decision in *Zarina*, which looked only to the Islamic law to determine under what conditions a pre-conversion marriage would be dissolved, there seems to be no basis for distinguishing between a pre-conversion marriage under Christian or Hindu law and a marriage under the Special Marriage Act.[45]

Suppose in *Zarina* a Muslim woman married to a Muslim man converts to Christianity and then marries a Christian. Conversion from Islam to either Christianity or Hinduism is almost unheard of these days in Pakistan,[46] although occasionally there are conversions from Islam to the Ahmadiyya faith,[47] which under the Constitution of Pakistan is not Islamic.[48] Of course, under the law applicable to Christians in Pakistan, the prior Muslim marriage would not be automatically dissolved by the conversion, but would require a judicial proceeding.[49] But leaving that aside, in a prosecution of the wife and her new Christian husband for *zina* or bigamy, would the court look exclusively to Christian law in judging the legal

---

particular question presented in this case was whether the taking of interest was repugnant to the injunctions of Islam. See also, *Allah Rakha* v. *Federation of Pakistan*, PLD 2000 FSC 1 (striking down provisions of Muslim Family Laws Ordinance allowing grandchildren to inherit from grandparents when parent had died before grandparents, and imposing conditions on divorce by *talaq*, both provisions found to be repugnant to injunctions of Islam).

[44] Act 3 of 1872. Still applicable in Pakistan.

[45] It may be noted that Muslims cannot be married under the Special Marriage Act, 1872, nor, for that matter, can Christians, Jews, or Parsis.

[46] But see, Human Rights Monitor, 2002–3, p. 97 (National Commission for Justice and Peace, Catholic Bishops Conference of Pakistan, 2003), mentioning one case of conversion to Christianity.

[47] See, *Pakistan: Insufficient Protection of Religious Minorities* 12–13 (Amnesty International, 2001).

[48] Article 260(3).

[49] Divorce Act, 1869. See also, *Salamat Ali* v. *State*, (1989) P Cr. LJ at 978, 979 (FSC).

effects of the conversion and subsequent marriage? The answer to this question would determine whether the policy underlying the *Zarina* decision is religiously neutral, supporting generally freedom to change religion, or is biased in favour of Islam. If the answer is no, the court would not look simply to Christian law, a divorce would have to be obtained under Muslim law either before the conversion or before the Christian marriage in order for the convert and her Christian husband to avoid conviction for *zina* with its horrendous consequences. Under the Dissolution of Muslim Marriages Act,[50] which governs the right of a Muslim wife to get a divorce and which is still applicable in Pakistan, conversion would not automatically dissolve the wife's Muslim marriage. If the *Zarina* case is biased in favour of conversions to Islam, and if among the reasons for the *Sarla Mudgal* decision in India is the protection of Hinduism from the depredations of Islam and Christianity, the laws in Pakistan and India regarding remarriage after conversion may not be entirely dissimilar. On the other hand, the Supreme Court's decision in *Sarla Mudgal*, as suggested earlier, may be based upon other policies.

I mentioned earlier the Caste Disabilities Removal Act, 1850. That Act in its original form is still in force in Pakistan. This means that conversion from one religion to another is made easier by the fact that the convert does not lose whatever rights he had under his old personal law. Thus, you can convert from Hinduism to Christianity without losing rights of succession under Hindu law, no matter how distasteful this might be from the perspective of Hindu law. But after Independence, Pakistan amended the act to prevent converts from Islam taking advantage of it.[51] Thus, if a person converts from Islam to Christianity or to any other religion, the consequences of the conversion will be determined entirely in accordance with Muslim personal law. The exclusion of converts from Islam from the benefits of the Caste Disabilities Removal Act is consistent with the *Zarina* decision, if the correct reading of that decision is that you can escape conviction for *zina* by converting to Islam, but usually not by converting away from Islam. If you convert away from Islam, additionally you would be deprived of any benefit you might have under Muslim personal law.

---

[50] Dissolution of Muslim Marriages Act, 8 of 1939.
[51] Caste Disabilities Removal (West Pakistan Amendment) Act, 10 of 1963.

In Pakistan in recent years, there has been a substantial number of conversions to Islam from other religions, notably from Christianity and Hinduism.[52] As mentioned earlier, there have been very few from Islam to Christianity and none to Hinduism that I am aware of. It is often said that conversion as such is not a crime in Pakistan.[53] Doubtless this is true with regard to conversion from one minority religion to another, but is it true for conversion away from Islam? Under the Blasphemy Laws that provide special protection for Islam,[54] it is a crime to defile the name of the Prophet, and what could be a greater insult to the Prophet or more injurious to the feelings of Muslims than to lose faith in the Prophet and to become an apostate from Islam? Conversions from Islam to the Ahmadiyya faith have been met with prosecutions for blasphemy or private violence accompanied by the state's failure to protect the convert.[55] Martin Lau has recently suggested that gaps in the Pakistan Penal Code might be filled by drawing upon Islamic law.[56] I am not competent to analyse the content of Islamic law, but it has recently been stated that the categories of apostasy and blasphemy are not clearly distinguished in that law.[57] A 1991 decision of the Shariat Court, which struck down as repugnant to Islam a sentence of life imprisonment for the crime of contempt of the Prophet, holding that under Islamic law only a death sentence was permissible, lends support to Lau's suggestion.[58] Conversion from Islam to another religion might be effective for the purpose of changing the convert's personal law— under the circumstances, both legal and factual, the applicable law of succession might be particularly relevant— but would not enable the

---

[52] Human Rights Monitor, 2000, p. 23 (National Commission for Justice and Peace, Catholic Bishops Conference of Pakistan).

[53] For example, see, Patrick Sookhdeo, *A People Betrayed: The Impact of Islamization on the Christian Community in Pakistan* (Isaac Publishing: Pewsey, Wiltshire, 2002), p. 267.

[54] Pakistan Penal Code, Subsections 295(b), 295(c), 298(a).

[55] See, Rasul Bakhsh Rais, 'Islamic Radicalism and Minorities in Pakistan', in C.H. Kennedy and R.B. Rais (eds), *Pakistan: 1995* (Westview Press: Boulder, Colorado), pp. 456, 462.

[56] Martin Lau, *The Role of Islam in the Legal System of Pakistan,* (Martinus Nijhoff: Leiden, 2006), p. 137.

[57] Sookhdeo, pp. 297–302.

[58] *Muhammad Ismail Qureshi* v. *Pakistan*, 43 PLD 1991 FSC at 10.

convert to escape the death penalty either under the law of Pakistan or apart from the law.

COMPARATIVE CONTEXT AND CONCLUSION

To return to India and to change the focus regarding conversion, some years ago, a number of Indian states enacted criminal legislation relating to conversion. These laws, motivated by fear of missionary activity by Muslims and Christians and by protectiveness toward Hinduism, made it a crime to procure conversion by force or fraud. One would have thought that the general criminal law was sufficient to deal with force and fraud, but the legislatures of these states thought that was not enough. To the extent that the new laws also criminalized procuring conversion by inducement, including holding out the hope of other-worldly benefits or threatening other-worldly punishments, they probably went beyond the existing criminal law. Nevertheless, the Supreme Court of India sustained the constitutionality of these new laws, notwithstanding the express protection in the Fundamental Rights section of the Constitution of India of the right to 'propagate' religion.[59] It was clearly understood at the time the Indian Constitution was adopted that both Islam and Christianity were proselytizing religions, even if Hinduism was not, and that the support of the minorities for the new Constitution was obtained by including in the general guarantee of religious freedom an express reference to the right to propagate. Still the Supreme Court upheld these state laws by finding in the fundamental right to religious freedom an interest in *not* being converted.[60] Emphasis on this negative freedom led to the Court's holding that a person interested in spreading a religious message would be protected by the Constitution only when he set forth his religion in a purely objective,

---

[59] Constitution of India, Article 25 (1); *Rev. Stainislaus* v. *State of Madhya Pradesh*, AIR 1977 SC 908. See, Jacobsohn and Shankar's discussion of this case in Chapter 6 in this volume, at note 79.

[60] The Supreme Court of Sri Lanka has also interpreted the religious freedom guarantee in its Constitution to include a right not to be converted by means of offering worldly advantages. Supreme Court Determination No. 2/2001; Supreme Court Special Determination No. 2/2003; Supreme Court Special Determination No. 19/2003.

academic way, without any intention to persuade another to change his beliefs.

In Pakistan we find no such general law regulating conversions. The reason is obvious: Islam is a proselytizing religion and no government of Pakistan would want to be seen to erect barriers in the way of this process. In addition, a criminal statute overtly burdening only conversion from Islam might be too blatant for any Pakistan government to embrace, especially if it is concerned with international opinion. Probably it has been thought that the blasphemy laws earlier referred to are enough to deter apostasy from Islam.

The somewhat technical legal questions I have been discussing relating to conversions and aspects of the personal laws that affect conversions, whose implications for religious freedom are not immediately apparent, must, of course, be placed in a wider context to appreciate their true significance.

The Indian Constitution declares India to be a secular state.[61] Nevertheless, in recent years, we have seen efforts by Indian governments to make it more of a Hindu state. Within the Constitution itself there is what I call the Hindu project: the Constitution authorizes the state to throw open Hindu temples to all classes and types of Hindus;[62] there is special assistance to Scheduled Castes;[63] there is authority to regulate Hindu endowments, which sometimes has been used to conform Hinduism to a particular model;[64] there is the Hindu Code, whose tendency is to eliminate diversities and to consolidate Hinduism into a single bloc.[65] On the administrative level, it is well-known that a Hindu coloration suffuses many government-supported public events. At the same time, there are provisions in the Constitution giving special protection to religious minorities,[66] although successive governments have failed to provide or been complicit in denying even ordinary protection to these minorities in a number of situations: Christians in Gujarat,

---

[61] Preamble to the Constitution.

[62] Article 25(2)(b).

[63] Article 15(4); Article 16(4).

[64] For example, *N. Adithayan* v. *Travancore Devaswom Bd.*, (2002), 8 SCC 106.

[65] Adopted in 1955–6, which covers various topics of the personal laws for Hindus.

[66] Article 29(1); Article 30.

Muslims in Mumbai, Sikhs in Delhi, the destruction of the Babri Masjid in Ayodhya. In any case, the unity of India is not in doubt, as it was fifty years ago, whether the basis for that unity is secular or tinged with Hinduism.

If we turn to Pakistan and consider the general conditions relating to religious freedom, including the right to convert, we find significant differences from India. In Pakistan, the trend over the last sixty years since Independence has been in the direction of increasing Islamization. The 'Objectives Resolution', which declares that 'Muslims shall be enabled to order their lives [in Pakistan]…in accordance with the teachings and requirements of Islam…', which began as a Preamble to the Constitution, was incorporated into the body of the Constitution in 1985.[67] The Hudood Ordinances, earlier referred to, based upon Islamic law although applicable to all, were introduced into the Penal Code during the Zia years, cheek by jowl with crimes drawn from English law. Shariat courts were created and given the task of determining which of the laws of Pakistan were repugnant to Islam. The Constitution was amended to pronounce authoritatively that Ahmadis are not Muslims. The Penal Code was changed to prohibit the Ahmadis from calling themselves Muslims, and indeed to prohibit them from proclaiming their faith in any effective way. There had already been in the Penal Code from the British period provisions prohibiting outraging of the religious feelings of any community,[68] but these were supplemented in Pakistan by additional provisions giving special protection to Islam.[69] In 1991, an act was passed making the Shari'ah the supreme law of Pakistan.[70] Since President Pervez Musharaf came to power in 1999, there has been a modest reversal of this trend in that separate electorates for the minorities, to which they objected because they thought it marginalized them in the political process, have been eliminated[71] and minority-owned educational institutions, which earlier had been nationalized, were returned to their original

[67] Article 2(a).

[68] For example, Pakistan Penal Code, Subsections 295, 295(a), 296.

[69] Pakistan Penal Code, Subsections 295(b), 295(c), 298(a).

[70] Enforcement of Shari'ah Act, 10 of 1991. But the act exempted 'any other law for the time being in force'.

[71] See, Rais, 'Islamic Radicalism', p. 464.

owners.[72] In spite of this modest reversal, the course of events in Pakistan has mainly contradicted the fundamental right of religious freedom contained in the Constitution of Pakistan.[73]

There has been ample documentation of both official complicity in the persecution of religious minorities and deliberate or negligent failure to protect them.[74] In addition, the condition of law in Pakistan, both constitutional and non-constitutional, has encouraged private activity discriminating against religious minorities. The fact is that there are few Hindus, Christians or Ahmadis in the higher administration, Christians are relegated to the most menial jobs, usually as sweepers, and the Hindus of Sind are poor agricultural labourers, constantly exposed to violence and threats of violence on account of their religion. Many of these Hindus have abandoned their property and fled to India. Many Ahmadis also have left Pakistan. As to conversion, a significant number of Christians and Hindus have been converted to Islam, if not by physical violence or threats of it, then as a result of their economic vulnerability.

The religious minorities—Christians, Hindus and Ahmadis—are a much smaller proportion of the population of Pakistan than the minorities—Christians, Muslims, Parsis—are of the population of India. The Christians in Pakistan are better organized to protect themselves than the Hindus, though either group, or both, when they act together, are relatively politically powerless.

The issue of religious freedom in Pakistan needs to be seen in the context of the struggle to determine the basis for Pakistan's identity and unity. Notwithstanding the provisions in the Constitution associating national identity with Islam, the emergence of Bangladesh made it clear that Islam alone was not enough to hold the country together in the face of ethnic, tribal and linguistic differences. The irony of this has not escaped observers, since the cry for a separate country called Pakistan was based on the idea that Muslims would

[72] Human Rights Monitor, 2002–3, p. 44 (National Commission for Justice and Peace, Catholic Bishops Conference of Pakistan, 2003).

[73] Article 20.

[74] See, Rais, 'Islamic Radicalism', p. 462; Human Rights Monitor, 2004 (National Commission for Justice and Peace, Catholic Bishops Conference of Pakistan, 2004); *Pakistan: Insufficient Protection of Religious Minorities* 14 (Amnesty International, 2001).

not be secure in a Hindu-dominated India. During the first period of national existence, there might have been a chance for Pakistan to evolve a secular basis for unity as India has done, notwithstanding the country's originating rationale, but as a consequence of the Islamization process sketched above, that possibility has now become extremely remote. Even within Islam, the well-recognized heterogeneous nature of South Asian Islam persists in Pakistan. Regional differences across Punjab, Baluchistan, Sind, the Northwest Frontier Province, tribal differences—the difference between the original Sindhis and those who came from India during Partition—support identities and loyalties other than to a united Pakistan. The significance of this is that the issue of religious freedom for the minorities receives a good deal less attention in Pakistan than it does in India, because of the numerous other issues that pose greater threats to Pakistan's survival as a nation. Thus, taking into account both the law and the facts in the two countries, religious minorities in Pakistan are substantially worse off than religious minorities in India both in regard to their freedom to practise their religion and in regard to their freedom to attract others to their faiths.

CHAPTER NINE

Pilate's Paramount Duty

Constitutional Reasonableness and the Restriction of Freedom of Expression and Assembly

T. John O'Dowd*

INTRODUCTION

Several contributions to this volume highlight the tensions that can arise in legal and political systems, and especially in constitutional courts, in South Asia, between receptiveness to the apparently universalizing influences of international human rights law and comparative constitutional law, on the one hand, and fidelity to the distinctive political, social, and cultural characteristics of the societies at hand. In particular, Gary Jeffrey Jacobsohn and Shylashri Shankar[1] examine the ambiguities of secularism as a constitutional concept in India and Sri Lanka, whilst Sujit Choudhry[2] considers how best to justify the citation of foreign and international precedents through the prism of the Delhi High Court's decision in *Naz Foundation v. Union of India.*[3] A somewhat different perspective

---

* My thanks are due to Gary J. Jacobsohn, John M. Mansfield, and Granville Austin for their valuable comments on the paper of which this chapter is an abbreviated and updated version.

[1] See in this volume, Chapter 6.

[2] See in this volume, Chapter 2.

[3] (2009) 160 DLT 277.

on the same issues may be brought to bear by returning to one of the classic clashes of conflicting arguments concerning the rationale and limits of freedom of expression within the liberal political tradition—that between John Stuart Mill and his supporters, and James Fitzjames Stephen.

The influence of the broad approach to the limitation of freedom of expression which those two nineteenth-century English thinkers set out can still be seen in constitutional doctrine and international human rights standards. On the one hand, Mill searched for some categorical principle that would restrict limitation of freedom of thought and discussion to cases in which some immediate and serious harm would result from its untrammelled exercise, without allowing the state the power to pass general judgment on the content of the expression under consideration. In contrast, Stephen argued that public authorities could not properly ignore the content of what was being communicated and its general tendency and that the substantial limits on the powers of the state to restrict expression, which he readily admitted were necessary, arose not from a fastidious, universal neutrality as to the value of what was being communicated, but from more pragmatic, though still abstract, considerations of the costs and benefits of censorship. In broad terms, the influence of Mill's approach can be seen in the First Amendment case law of the United States Supreme Court.[4] Stephen's approach, on the other hand, seems more in keeping with the case law of the European Court of Human Rights and with the way in which the Indian courts have dealt with freedom of expression.[5]

Apart from the resonances one may find in constitutional doctrine or international human rights law, the particular relevance to South Asia of the disagreement between these two nineteenth-century thinkers is that Stephen's arguments against Mill's thesis were significantly influenced by his experience in the Government of India. His view of the social, religious, and cultural realities in

---

[4] Compare Stephen's view with the refusal to import the 'clear and present danger' test into Indian law. See, J.F. Stephen (ed. R.J. White), *Liberty, Equality and Fraternity* (Cambridge University Press: Cambridge, 1967), pp. 68, 70–1; *State of Bihar v. K.K. Misra* (see, footnote 51).

[5] Adapting Mill's proposition: J.S. Mill, 'On Liberty', in *Three Essays* (Oxford University Press: London, 1975), p. 35.

the subcontinent sharpened his objections to the premises of Mill's argument for liberty of thought and discussion. In a very practical way, Stephen also left the imprint of these views behind him in India for, although he was largely content with the Indian Penal Code which Macauley had drafted, it fell to him to fill the gap which was left in it by the absence of an offence of sedition, a topic which remains controversial in the subcontinent to this day.

In his essay, Sujit Choudhry persuasively sets out the case for dialogic constitutionalism and situates the role of comparative jurisprudence within it:

> The first step is to use comparative jurisprudence as a means to identify important assumptions, both factual and normative, that underlie the interpreting court's own constitutional order.... By asking why foreign courts have reasoned a certain way, a court will ask itself why it reasons the way it does; comparative jurisprudence serves as an interpretive foil.[6]

In this essay, I propose to examine how the 'constitutional self-reflection' and 'heightened sense of legal self-awareness through interpretive confrontation and clarification' of which Choudhry speaks can also be furthered by reflecting on how it was that Indian conditions of life (as he understood them, at least) significantly shaped the case which Stephen made against Mill's argument in *On Liberty* and by examining how elements of the same basic outlook still run through the criminal legislation which the successor states maintain, the judicial interpretation of the Constitution of India, and the everyday, often banal administrative practice. In this way, one may hope to gain a deeper understanding of why it is that the Supreme Court of India, in particular, has consistently refused to be swayed by US First Amendment case law on the 'clear and present danger' test or the American abhorrence of prior restraints.[7] That is a phenomenon which invites a more sophisticated explanation than can be provided simply by the textual differences between the two constitutions. Even if it is undeniable that the view of the Supreme Court of India on these matters places it in the ranks of those who find Mill's arguments too abstract and simplistic and with those, such

---

[6] See in this volume, Chapter 2.

[7] For example, *Babulal Parate* v. *State of Maharashtra* (1961) SCR (3) 423.

as Stephen, who argue for a more pragmatic, contextual approach to freedom of expression, there is still a need to find some firm basis for the value of that freedom in constitutional adjudication, one that properly respects the democratic nature of the Constitution of India and the commitment to social transformation which it embodies.

This essay proposes, therefore, first, to briefly review how his experience in India shaped Stephen's objections to Mill's classic argument; second, to examine the legacy which the Indian Penal Code which Stephen so admired (and the Code of Criminal Procedure) has left in this area; third, to consider what the application of those provisions has been in practice (and particularly how the Supreme Court of India has sought to interpret them in accordance with the presumption of constitutionality) and, finally, to assess how far it is European human rights law, and the concept of a 'democratic society' which it embodies, to which Indian (and Pakistani and Bangladeshi) courts should appropriately turn for persuasive guidance as to what are reasonable restrictions on freedom of expression in this area.

SITTING ON A VOLCANO

Sir James Fitzjames Stephen's time in the government of British India was brief, but it clearly influenced his own political and social thought and the legacies he left for the legal systems of the Raj's successor states. His service in India (December 1869 to April 1872) as the Legal Member of the Viceroy's Council allowed Stephen to contribute to several aspects of the law that have been largely retained in the successor states.[8] Stephen had a hand in the final form of the Native Marriages Act, 1872 and the Indian Contracts Act, 1872 and prime responsibility for the Indian Evidence Act, 1872. He was also responsible for some modifications

---

[8] For Stephen's contribution to Indian criminal law and procedure, see, L. Stephen, *The Life of Sir James Fitzjames Stephen,* 2nd Ed. (Smith, Elder & Co.: London, 1895), pp. 266–71; J.A. Colaiaco, *James Fitzjames Stephen and the Crisis of Victorian Thought* (Macmillan: London, 1983), pp. 100–4; J. Hostettler, *Politics and Law in the Life of Sir James Fitzjames Stephen* (Barry Rose: Chichester, 1995), pp. 96–102; J. Roach, 'James Fitzjames Stephen (1829–94)', *Journal of the Royal Asiatic Society of Great Britain and Ireland,* (1956), 1/2: 1–16.

to the Indian Penal Code. To Macauley's Penal Code,[9] which was then almost a decade old, Stephen proposed only relatively modest revisions,[10] most controversially repairing the unintended omission of sedition.[11] He later commented that the 'offences relating to religion'[12]

> ...carry the principle of tolerating and protecting all religions equally whatever to a length which cannot be justified, and which might lead to horrible cruelty and persecution if the government of the country ever got into Hindoo or Mohammedan hands. ... [Section 298] would surely cover every attempt made to convince any one that his religious opinions are untrue. It is impossible to convince any one that he is in error upon religious subjects without causing him great pain if he really believes in his creed, and the act of addressing cogent and earnest arguments to him on the subject must of necessity involve a deliberate intention of wounding his feelings.[13]

As such opinions might suggest, a crucial aspect of the influence of India on Stephen's thought was his belief that the British in India—aware as they must be that 'they sat on a volcano'—had a mission to maintain peace and order against ever-present threats of inter-communal conflict, threats that were integral to the nature of the communities they governed. His long intellectual engagement with the form and purpose of criminal law helped shape this belief, but that the belief, once formulated, then played a role in Stephen's development of his ideas about the role of the criminal law in maintaining social peace and unity.

[9] See, D. Skuy, 'Macaulay and the Indian Penal Code of 1862: The Myth of the Inherent Superiority and Modernity of the English Legal System Compared to India's Legal System in the Nineteenth Century', *Modern Asian Studies*, (1998), 32(3):513–57.

[10] For Stephen, '[the Penal Code] bids fair to be the most lasting monument of its principal author...' (J.F. Stephen, *A History of the Criminal Law of England* (3 vols), (Macmillan: London, 1883), Vol. III, p. 299.) On Stephen's role in its revision, see, Stephen, *Life of Sir James Fitzjames Stephen*, pp. 266–7.

[11] Ibid., p. 267.

[12] Pakistan PC (Act 45 of 1860), Section 124(a). See, footnote 28.

[13] J.F. Stephen, *History of the Criminal Law*, pp. 312–3. Compare 'the pain occasioned by treating a man's opinions as false', in Stephen, *Liberty, Equality and Fraternity*, pp. 121–2.

Back in England, Stephen rapidly emerged as a significant and searching critic of the views which John Stuart Mill had set out in *On Liberty* roughly a decade before. The influence of his experiences in India was clearly evident in the critique he presented of Mill's arguments for liberty of thought and discussion. Indeed, Stephen started work on the articles that became his response to Mill—*Liberty, Equality and Fraternity*—while he was on his voyage home from India.[14] In particular, he drew on his Indian experience in responding to Mill's challenge to opponents of liberty of thought and discussion to defend the state's entitlement to repress what it regards as religious falsehood, without thereby justifying Pontius Pilate's judgment on Jesus of Nazareth.[15] Stephen was undismayed.

> Was Pilate right in crucifying Christ? I reply, Pilate's paramount duty was to preserve the peace in Palestine, to form the best judgment he could as to the means required for that purpose, and to act upon it when it was formed. Therefore, if and in so far as he believed, in good faith and on reasonable grounds, that what he did was necessary for the preservation of the peace of Palestine, he was right.[16]

Stephen saw a clear parallel with British rule in India.[17] Stephen certainly shared what Jacobsohn and Shankar refer to as 'the well-founded perception that religion on the subcontinent is more deeply entrenched in the fabric of society than it is in the United States or in Europe'.[18] For Stephen, any British officer in Punjab or the northwest provinces who, if faced by a Guru or Iman whose preaching was 'whatever might be the preacher's own personal intentions... calculated to disturb the public peace and produce mutiny and rebellion', failed to act as Pontius Pilate did would rightly be 'hanged as a rebel and a traitor'.[19] In the second edition of *Liberty, Equality*

---

[14] L. Stephen, *Life of Sir James Fitzjames Stephen,* p. 307.

[15] J.S. Mill, 'On Liberty', p. 35.

[16] Stephen, *Liberty, Equality and Fraternity*, p. 110.

[17] His comparison between the Pax Britannica and Pax Romana, Ibid., pp. 112–14, resembles his characterization of British law's effects in India: J.F. Stephen, *History of the Criminal Law*, pp. 344–5, cited in Hostettler, *Politics and Law* , p. 99. See also, Skuy, 'Macaulay and the Indian Penal Code', pp. 513–57.

[18] See in this volume, Chapter 6.

[19] Stephen, *Liberty, Equality and Fraternity,* pp. 115–16. Footnote omitted. See also, the comparison of Pilate to 'a Resident with a strong armed force under his

and Fraternity, Stephen expanded on this point, in answering John Morley's charge[20] that he had overlooked Mill's acknowledgement that 'opinions lose their immunity, when the circumstances in which they are expressed...constitute their expression a positive instigation to some mischievous act' and Mill's famous example relating to the circumstances in which stating 'that corn dealers are starvers of the poor' may justly be punished.[21]

> No doubt you may [throw the abetment of a crime into the form of the expression of an opinion.].... My argument upon Pilate's case is that the mere preaching of a religion which relates principally to matters of belief and self-regarding acts may, under circumstances, tend to disturb the existing social order. If in that case the representatives of the existing social order persecute the religion it appears to me that the question whether they are right or wrong depends on the comparative merits of the religion which is persecuted and the social order which persecutes. ... This is directly opposed to the whole of Mr. Mill's chapter....[22]

Stephen also made a great deal of Mill's concession that '[d]espotism is a legitimate mode of government in dealing with

---

orders and Runjeet Singh by his side' (Ibid., p. 113), the statement that 'Pilate and his successors must have known that they sat on a volcano long before the explosion came' (Ibid., p. 114), and the observation that Jewish leaders made 'complaints against the new religious reformer [that is, Jesus] curiously like those which orthodox Mahommedans make against Wahabee preachers, or orthodox Sikhs against Kookas (Ibid.).

[20] J. Morley, 'Mr. Mill's Doctrine of Liberty', *The Fortnightly Review*, (August 1873), 20: 234–56, reprinted in A. Pyle (ed.), *Liberty: Contemporary Responses to John Stuart Mill* (Thoemmes Press: Bristol, 1994), pp. 289–90.

[21] J.S. Mill, 'On Liberty', p. 69. See, G.J. Jacobsohn, *The Wheel of Law: India's Secularism in Comparative Constitutional Context* (Princeton University Press: Princeton, 2003), pp. 68–9; J.J. Ofseyer, 'First Amendment Law: Taking Liberties with John Stuart Mill', *Annual Survey of American Law*, (1999), pp. 410–14.

[22] Stephen, *Liberty, Equality and Fraternity*, p. 115. 'English legislation in India proceeds on the assumption that ['Mahommedanism' and 'Brahminism'] are false. If it did not, it would have to be founded on the Koran or the Institutes of Manu'. (Ibid, p. 91.) On his views on religion, social values, and the law in India, see, Stephen, *Life of Sir James Fitzjames Stephen*, pp. 259–66, 286–9; J.A. Colaiaco, *James Fitzjames Stephen and the Crisis of Victorian Thought* (Macmillan: London, 1983), pp. 112–19. For modern Hindu perspectives, see also, Arvind Sharma, *Hinduism and Human Rights: A Conceptual Approach* (Oxford University Press: Oxford, 2004), pp. 96–121.

barbarians, provided the end be their improvement and the means justified by actually effecting that end'; he passed over the comment that until 'mankind have become capable of being improved by free and equal discussion...there is nothing for them but implicit obedience to an Akbar or a Charlemagne'. [23]

PUBLIC TRANQUILITY

In assessing the present day application of provisions that can be related to Stephen's critique of Mill's argument for liberty of thought and discussion, I will concentrate on the Penal Codes, leaving aside other potentially relevant laws, whether on national security, terrorism,[24] or the conduct of elections[25] (including the extensive case law on the latter).[26] Though much altered since 1872, the Penal Code

[23] J.S. Mill, 'On Liberty', p. 16. See, Stephen, *Liberty, Equality and Fraternity* (Cambridge: Cambridge University Press, 1967), pp. 68, 70–1.

[24] For example, externment, preventive detention or the Customs Act, 1962, Section 11 (India). Banning importation of Salman Rushdie's *The Satanic Verses* into India in 1988 was the first official action against it anywhere: Michael M.J. Fischer and Mehdi Abedi, 'Bombay Talkies, the Word and the World: Salman Rushdie's Satanic Verses', *Cultural Anthropology*, (1990), 5(2): 107.

[25] For example, Representation of the People Act (RPA), 1951 (India) (Act 43 of 1951), Section 8(1)(a) (as substituted by Act 1 of 1989, Section 4) referring to offences under IPC Section 153(a) (see footnote 29) and Section 505(2) or RPA, 1951 Section 8(1)(i) (as substituted by Act 1 of 1989, Section 4). See also, the Cantonments Act 2006 (Act 41 of 2006), Subsection 29(3)(g), 30(2)(4). See also, the Protection of Civil Rights Act, 1955, Section 8(1)(b) (as substituted by Act 1 of 1989, Section 4) under the Places of Worship (Special Provisions) Act, 1991, Section 6: Section 8(1)(j) (as inserted by Act 42 of 1991, Section 8). See also, RPA, 1951, Section 123(3) (as substituted by Act 40 of 1961, Section 23), Section 123(3a) (as substituted by Act 40 of 1961, Section 23), and Section 123(3b) (as inserted by Act 3 of 1988, Section 19).

[26] For example, *Manohar Joshi* v. *Nitin Bhaurao Patil & Anr* AIR (1996) SC 796; *Ramakant Mayekar* v. *Smt. Celine D'Silva* AIR (1996) SC 826; *Prof. Ramchandra G. Kapse* v. *Haribansh Ramakbal Singh* AIR (1996) SC 817; *Dr. Das Rao Deshmukh* v. *Kamal Kishore Nanasahebkadam & Ors* AIR (1996) SC 391; *Dr. (Mrs.) Vimal* v. *Bhaguji & Ors* AIR (1995) SC 1836. See also, *Ebrahim Sulaiman Sait* v. *M.C. Muhammad & Anr.* (1980) SCR (1) 1148. For discussion, see, Jacobsohn, *The Wheel of Law* pp. 161–88; and S.P. Sathe, *Judicial Activism in India: Transgressing Boundaries and Enforcing Limits*, 2nd Ed. (Oxford University Press: New Delhi, 2002), pp. 182–91.

and the Code of Criminal Procedure to which Stephen contributed survive in India, Pakistan, Bangladesh, and Myanmar (Burma) in broadly similar forms. The offences introduced to the Indian Penal Code, in particular, since 1947 generally aim for a cohesive national identity, rather than simply maintenance of civil peace, but they also assume, as Stephen did, the criminal law's vital role in bringing to bear a paramount authority for the control of potentially explosive communal sensitivities and antagonisms. Broadly similar provisions exist in the Indian, Pakistani, and Bangladeshi Penal Codes, each of which is still derived from the Code with which Stephen was familiar and which he praised so highly.[27]

The Indian Penal Code contains offences of sedition,[28] of promoting enmity, hatred or ill-will between different groups on grounds such as religion, race, or language and doing acts prejudicial to the maintenance of harmony,[29] of making imputations or assertions prejudicial to national integration,[30] of committing deliberate and malicious acts, intended to outrage religious feelings of any class by insulting its religion or religious beliefs,[31] and of making statements conducive to public mischief.[32]

---

[27] For Stephen's praise of the Penal Code, see, footnote 10. Given the current legal and political situation in Myanmar, it is not proposed to include it in this survey.

[28] Section 124(a) (as substituted by Act 4 of 1898, Section 4, for the original Section 124(a) (inserted by Act 27 of 1870 Section 5 and adapted.)

[29] Section 153(a) (as substituted by Act 35 of 1969, Section 2, for Section 153A (inserted by Indian Penal Code Amendment Act, 1898 (Act 4 of 1898), Section 5) referring 'any person who by words either spoken or written, or by signs, or by visible representations or otherwise, promotes or attempts to promote, feelings of enmity or hatred between different classes....').

[30] Section 153(b) (as inserted by Act 31 of 1972, Section 2).

[31] Section 295(a) (as inserted by Criminal Law (Amendment) Act 1927 (Act 25 of 1927), Section 2).

[32] Section 505 (as substituted by Act 4 of 1898, Section 6). A new offence akin to sedition was added in 1969—making, publishing, or circulating any statement or report containing rumour or alarming news with intent to create or promote, or which is likely to create or promote, on grounds of religion, race, place of birth, residence, language, caste or community, or any other ground whatsoever, feelings of enmity, hatred or ill will between different religious, racial, language or regional groups, or castes or communities. Section 505(2) (as inserted by Criminal and Election Laws (Amendment) Act 1969 (Act 35 of 1969), Section 3). See also, the Protection of Civil Rights Act, 1955 (Act 22 of 1955), Section 7(1)(c) (incitement

Rioting and associated offences apart,[33] these crimes do not require imminent threat of harm but can embrace the 'mere preaching' that Stephen envisaged that the criminal law could legitimately prohibit, where a threat to public peace and order is sufficiently serious.[34] Section 298 is narrower, prohibiting words uttered or sounds made in the hearing of a person or gestures in the sight of a person or placing of any object in the sight of any person, with the deliberate intention to wound any person's religious feelings.[35]

In Pakistan, sedition (with adaptations),[36] deliberate and malicious acts, intended to outrage any class's religious feelings by insulting its religion or religious beliefs[37] and public mischief[38] are offences, as is promoting enmity, hatred, or ill-will between different groups on grounds of religion, race, place of birth, residence or language or doing acts prejudicial to maintenance of harmony.[39] In the context of forfeiture of publications under Section 99(a) of the Code of Criminal Procedure, the offence of promoting enmity has been applied to the promotion of enmity, hatred, or ill-will between different Muslim sects.[40]

---

to practice 'untouchability') and, especially Explanation II (as inserted by Act 106 of 1976, Section 9.) It is an offence to insult or attempt to insult, on the ground of 'untouchability', a member of a Scheduled Caste: Section 7(1)*(d)* (as inserted by Section 9, Ibid.); *M.A. Kuttappan* v. *E. Krishnan Nayanar & Anr.* (2004) INSC 129 (26 February 2004). See also Scheduled Castes and the Scheduled Tribes (Prevention of Atrocities) Act, 1989 (Act 33 of 1989), Section 3(1)(x).

[33] For example, Section 146 (rioting); Section 148 (rioting, armed with deadly weapon); Section 150 (hiring, or conniving at hiring, of persons to join unlawful assembly); Section 153 (wantonly giving provocation with intent to cause riot).

[34] See the texts accompanying footnotes 20–22.

[35] Section 298. The Pakistan and Bangladesh Penal Codes both retain this provision.

[36] Pakistan PC (Act 45 of 1860), Section 124(a). See also, footnote 28.

[37] Section 295(a). See also, footnote 31.

[38] Section 505. See also, footnote 32.

[39] Section 153(a) (as substituted by Criminal Law (Amendment) Act, 1973 (Act 6 of 1973, Section 2). Section 153(b) (as inserted by Act 31 of 1972, Section 2). See also, Section 153(b) (as substituted by Criminal Law (Amendment) Act 1973 (Act 6 of 1973), Section 2).

[40] For example, Maqbool Ahmed, 'Govt. Nullifies Fatwa against Inter-sect Marriages', *Daily Times* (Online Ed.) (3 August 2005), http://www.dailytimes.com.pk/default.asp?page=story_3-8-2005_pg7_35 (last accessed on 30 March 2011).

The Pakistan Penal Code makes special provision for the Islamic religion, reflecting the broader, gradual replacement of the Code by *shari'a* norms since the early 1980s.[41] As Mansfield points out in his essay, this is part of 'the trend over the almost sixty years since Independence...in the direction of increasing Islamization'.[42] It is an offence to willfully defile, damage, or desecrate a copy of the Holy Qur'an or of an extract from it or to use it in any derogatory manner or for any unlawful purpose (punishable by life imprisonment),[43] to defile in any manner the sacred name of the Holy Prophet Muhammad (punishable with death or imprisonment for life)[44] or to defile the sacred name of any wife, or members of the family of the Holy Prophet, or any of the righteous Caliphs or companions of the Holy Prophet (punishable with imprisonment for a term which may extend to three years, or with fine, or with both).[45] There are also offences concerning statements by persons (self-described as Ahmadis).[46] They may not describe themselves as Muslims nor preach or propagate their faith.[47]

Bangladesh has provisions similar to the Pakistani Code (as it stood in 1971)[48] and, in addition, the following offence:

505A. Prejudicial act by words etc. Whoever (*a*) by words either spoken or written, or by signs or by visible representations or otherwise does anything, or (*b*) makes, publishes or circulates any statement, rumour or report, which is likely to be prejudicial to the interests of the security of

---

[41] R. Peters, 'The Islamization of Criminal Law: A Comparative Analysis', *Die Welt des Islams* (n.s.) (1994), 34(2): 256–9); C.H. Kennedy, 'Islamization and Legal Reform in Pakistan, 1979–1989', *Pacific Affairs*, (1989), 63(1): 62–77.

[42] See in this volume, Chapter 8 (John M. Mansfield, 'Religious Freedom in India and Pakistan: The Matter of Conversion').

[43] Section 295(b) (inserted by Pakistan Penal Code (Amendment) Ordinance, I of 1982).

[44] Section 295(c) (inserted by Criminal Law (Amendment) Act 1986 (Act 111 of 1986), Section 2.

[45] Section 298(a) (inserted by Pakistan Penal Code (Second Amendment) Ordinance, XLIV of 1980).

[46] Section 298(b) (inserted by Anti-Islamic Activities of Quadiani Group, Lahori Group and Ahmadis (Prohibition and Punishment) Ordinance, XX of 1984).

[47] Section 298(c) (also inserted by the Ordinance of 1984).

[48] Bangladesh PC (Act 45 of 1860), Subsections 124(a), 153(a), 295(a), 505. Section 153(b) parallels the Pakistani Section 153(b) (see, footnote 39).

Bangladesh or public order or to the maintenance of friendly relations of Bangladesh with foreign states or to maintenance of supplies and services essential to the community, shall be punished with imprisonment for a term which may extend to seven years, or with fine, or with both.

The authorities in the three countries also often employ the Criminal Procedure Codes to prevent inflammatory use of free expression or assembly. In India, Section 144 is most significant.

Power to issue order in urgent cases of nuisance or apprehended danger.

(1) In cases where, in the opinion of a District Magistrate, a Sub-divisional Magistrate or any other Executive Magistrate specially empowered by the State Government in this behalf, there is sufficient ground for proceeding under this section and immediate prevention or speedy remedy is desirable, such Magistrate may, by a written order stating the material facts of the case and served in the manner provided by Section 134, direct any person to abstain from a certain act or to take certain order with respect to certain property in his possession or under his management, if such Magistrate considers that such direction is likely to prevent, or tends to prevent, obstruction, annoyance or injury to any person lawfully employed, or danger to human life, health or safety, or a disturbance of the public tranquillity, or a riot, of an affray.[49]

Such orders remain in force for up to two months.[50] If the state government considers it necessary for preventing danger to human life, health or safety, or riot or any affray, it may direct by notification that a magistrate's order remain in force for a specified further period (not exceeding six months.)[51] The Supreme Court struck down the government's previous power to extend a magistrate's order indefinitely.[52] In emergencies or where circumstances do not allow

---

[49] Code of Criminal Procedure (CCP), 1973 (Act 2 of 1974), Section 144(1). An executive magistrate is an administrative rather than a judicial officer, subordinate to the administrative head of the district.

[50] Repetitive orders would be an abuse: *Acharya Jagdishwaranand Avadhuta, etc.* v. *Commissioner of Police, Calcutta & Anr.* (1984) SCR (1) at 447, 462; *Babulal Parate* (footnote 95). See also, *Gulam Abbas & Ors.* v. *State of Uttar Pradesh & Ors* (1982) SCR (1) at 1077.

[51] Section144(4). Notification is 'an independent executive power'; the Government adopts the magistrate's order as its own: *State of Bihar & Ors* v. *K.K. Misra & Ors*, (1970) SCR (3) at 181, 195. On recission of orders, see, Subsections 144(5) and 144(6).

[52] CCP, 1898 (Act 5 of 1898), Section 144(6) empowered a state government to extend a Section 144 order for an unlimited period. Given 'no provision to make representation by the aggrieved party against the direction given by the Government;

service of a notice in due time, orders may be made *ex parte*.[53] On receiving an application for rescission of an order, the maker shall give the applicant an early opportunity to appear, either in person or by pleader, and to show cause against the order. If the magistrate (or the state government) wholly or partly rejects the application, he shall record the reasons in writing.[54]

The Pakistan[55] and the Bangladesh[56] Codes of Criminal Procedure broadly make similar provisions, without express limit on the prolongation of an order. In Pakistan, upon the abolition of the executive magistracy, the function vested in 'the *Zila Nazim* (District Mayor) upon the written recommendation of the District Superintendent of Police or Executive District Officer.'[57] In Bangladesh, the metropolitan areas have gradually been withdrawn from the charge of executive magistrates in this respect,[58] with equivalent powers, including the power to prohibit assemblies

---

no appeal or revision is provided against that direction and [that] the order made need not be of temporary nature' this was 'opposed to the fundamental principles of liberty and justice' and not a 'reasonable restriction'. *K.K. Misra*'s case (see, footnote 51) at 196.

[53] Section 141(2). Orders may be directed to a particular individual, or to persons residing in a particular place or area, or to the public generally, when frequenting or visiting a particular place or area: Section 144(3).

[54] Section 144(7).

[55] (Pakistan) CCP, 1898 Section 144 (as amended by Code of Criminal Procedure (Amendment) Ordinance 2001 (Ordinance XXXVII of 2001).) Orders shall not remain in force 'for more than two consecutive days and not more than seven days in a month'. There is no express limit on the length of time for which a Provincial Government directs that such an order should remain in force 'in cases of danger to human life, health or safety, or a likelihood of a riot or an affray'. (Section 144(6).)

[56] (Bangladesh) CCP, 1898, Section 144.

[57] Section 144(1) (as amended by Code of Criminal Procedure (Amendment) Ordinance 2001 (Ordinance XXXVII of 2001). See, *Devolution in Pakistan: Annex 2—Technical Considerations*, mimeo, Metro Manila: Asian Development Bank/DFID/World Bank, 2004; Mushtaq Ahmad Sukhera, Syed Mubashar Raza, Huma Chughtai, Muhammad Aslam Tareen, and Syed Tassaduq Hussain Bukhari, 'Police Reforms: Emerging Issues And Challenges', mimeo (National Institute of Public Administration: Lahore, 2003), pp. 29–32.

[58] See, (Bangladesh) CCP, 1898 Section 144(7) (as inserted by the Schedule to the Dacca Metropolitan Police (Amendment) Ordinance, 1976 (Ordinance LXIX of 1976) and amendment by Section 114 and Schedule III (Sr. No. 6(5)) of the Chittagong Metropolitan Police Ordinance, 1978 (Ordinance XLVIII of 1976).

and processions, being conferred on each metropolitan police commissioner.[59] With the separation of the executive magistracy from the judicial magistracy in Bangladesh, fresh provision has been made for the appointment of executive magistrates (including a district magistrate) for the metropolitan areas, as well as for each district.[60] This has since been confirmed by an Act of Parliament.[61]

The Criminal Procedure Codes give other powers ancillary to Penal Code prohibitions. In India, executive magistrates can require persons to show cause why they should not be ordered to execute a bond, with or without sureties, for their good behaviour for such period, not exceeding one year, as the magistrate thinks fit where, *inter alia*, that person is disseminating matter, publication of which is punishable under Sections 124(a), 153(a), 153(b), or 295(a).[62] Proceedings may be taken against the editor, proprietor, printer or publisher of a duly registered publication, but only by the order or under the authority of the state government or an officer empowered by it.[63] The other Codes make similar provisions.[64]

[59] See, Dhaka Metropolitan Police Ordinance, 1976 (Ordinance III of 1976) Section 4 (removing the DMA from the charge of any district magistrate); Section 29 (power of the police commissioner to prohibit assemblies or processions). See also, Section 28 (power to prohibit certain acts for the prevention of disorder). See also, the Chittagong Metropolitan Police Ordinance, 1978 (see, footnote 58) Subsections 4, 29, 30; the Khulna Metropolitan Ordinance, 1985 (Ordinance LII of 1985), Subsections 4, 29, 30.

[60] (Bangladesh) CCP, 1898, Section 10(1) (as substituted by Section 8 of the Code of Criminal Procedure (Amendment) Ordinance, 2007 (Ordinance No. 2 of 2007)). The separation of the judicial and executive branches of the magistracy was a belated implementation of a directive given by the Supreme Court in the *Masdar Hossain* case: *Secretary of the Ministry of Finance* v. *Masdar Hossain* (1999) 52 DLR (AD) 82.

[61] Code of Criminal Procedure (Amendment) Act, 2009 (Act 32 of 2009), Section 8. The Government may, under any law for the time in force, confer all or any of the powers of an executive magistrate in relation to a metropolitan area on the commissioner of police: CCP, Section 10(7) as inserted by Section 8 of Act 32 of 2009. See also, the amendment made (Ibid., Section 55) to CCP, Section 144(1).

[62] CCP, 1973 (Act 2 of 1973), Section 108(1).

[63] Section 108(2).

[64] (Pakistan) CCP, 1898, Section 108 (as amendment by the Code of Criminal Procedure (Amendment) Ordinance 2001, XXXVII of 2001) and by the Law Reforms Ordinance, XII of 1972); (Bangladesh) CCP, 1898, Section 108 (as amendment by the Bangladesh Laws (Revision And Declaration) Act, 1973 (Act

Indian state governments may declare forfeit books, newspapers, or other documents, which appear to them to contain any matter, publication of which is punishable under several sections of the Penal Code.[65] On application, the High Court of the state may set aside such a declaration.[66] Pakistan and Bangladesh have broadly similar—though in Pakistan and Bangladesh more extensive—provisions in their codes.[67]

GOD'S GIFT TO MANKIND[68]

In this section I deal mainly with the present-day operation of the Codes in the Union of India, where coexistence of Hindus

---

No. VIII of 1973), Section 3, Schedule II and by the Code of Criminal Procedure (Amendment) Ordinance, 2007 (Ordinance No. 2 of 2007), Section 40). See also, the Scheduled Castes and the Scheduled Tribes (Prevention of Atrocities) Act, 1989, Section 17(1) (India). The state government may make schemes specifying the manner in which officers referred to Section 17(1) shall take appropriate action as specified in such schemes, to prevent atrocities and to restore the feeling of security amongst the members of the Scheduled Castes and the Scheduled Tribes. The Communal Violence (Prevention, Control and Rehabilitation of Victims) Bill, 2010 (not yet enacted at the time of writing) proposes similar provisions in relation to communal violence.

[65] CCP, 1973 (Act 2 of 1973), Section 95(1). The relevant provisions are Subsections 124(a), 153(a), 153(b), 292, 293, and 295(a).

[66] Section 96.

[67] (Pakistan) CCP, 1898, Subsections 99(a–b), 99(d)–99(g) (as amendment by the Law Reforms Ordinance, XII of 1972 and the Anti-Islamic Activities of Quadiani Group, Lahori Group and Ahmadis (Prohibition and Punishment) Ordinance, XX of 1984); (Bangladesh) CCP, 1898, Subsections 99(a)–99(g) (as amendment by the Code of Criminal Procedure (Amendment) Act, 1991 (Act No. XVI of 1991) Subsections 3, 4, by the Bangladesh Laws (Revision and Declaration) Act, 1973 (Act No. VIII of 1973) Section 3, Schedule II and by the Code of Criminal Procedure (Amendment) Ordinance, 2007 (Ordinance No. 2 of 2007), Section 34. The Pakistani CCP is wider by embracing offences under Subsections 295(b), 295(c), and 298(a)–298(c), Pakistan PC (see, footnotes 43–7), and the Bangladeshi CCP by including publications that contain what appears to the government to be 'any matter which is defamatory to the President…, Prime Minister of the Government, the Speaker of Parliament…or any words or visible representations which incite, or which is likely to incite any person or class of persons to commit any cognisable offence'.

[68] 'Speech is God's gift to mankind.' *Life Insurance Corporation of India & Ors* v. *Prof. Manubhai D. Shah etc.* (1992) SCR (3) at 595, 605, Ahmadi, J.

and Muslims continue to the greatest extent, under an ostensibly secular regime. Furthermore, Stephen's expectations conflict most sharply with the reality of a parliamentary democracy in which, the Emergency apart, the criminal law has not generally suppressed political opposition in a manner seriously threatening the fairness of national elections.

Under Article 19(1) of the Constitution of India 'All citizens shall have the right...(a) to freedom of speech and expression; (b) to assemble peaceably and without arms[, and] (c) to form associations or unions....'[69] Subsections (2) to (4) prescribe limitations specific to each of these rights. Freedom of speech and expression shall not

> ...affect the operation of any existing law, or prevent the State from making any law, in so far as such law imposes reasonable restrictions on the exercise of the right conferred by the said sub-clause in the interests of the sovereignty and integrity of India, the security of the State, friendly relations with foreign States, public order, decency or morality, or in relation to contempt of court, defamation or incitement to an offence.[70]

The right to assemble peaceably and without arms shall not 'affect the operation of any existing law insofar as it imposes, or prevent the State from making any law imposing, in the interests of the sovereignty and integrity of India or public order, reasonable restrictions on the exercise of the right'.[71] The right to form associations and unions shall not

> ...affect the operation of any existing law in so far as it imposes, or prevent the State from making any law imposing, in the interests of the sovereignty and integrity of India or public order or morality, reasonable restrictions on the exercise of the right conferred by the said sub-clause.[72]

---

[69] Constitution of India, 1950 Article 19(1).

[70] Article 19(2) (as substituted by Constitution (First Amendment) Act, 1951, Section 3 (with retrospective effect)).

[71] Article 19(3) (as amendment by Constitution (Sixteenth Amendment) Act, 1963, Section 2).

[72] Article 19(4) (as amendment by Constitution (Sixteenth Amendment) Act, 1963, Section 2). Section 2 of the Act of 1963 inserted the words 'the sovereignty and integrity of India or'. Although not enforceable in any court, it is also every citizen's duty '...(e) to promote harmony and the spirit of common brotherhood amongst all the people of India transcending religious, linguistic and regional or

Pakistan[73] and Bangladesh[74] have similar constitutional provisions concerning these basic freedoms. The Pakistani provision also permitting reasonable restrictions on freedom of expression made by a 'law in the interest of the glory of Islam'. However, as Mansfield points out in his contribution to this volume, '[t]here is ground for asserting that because of provisions in the Constitution of Pakistan and laws enacted under it, the most fundamental law in Pakistan is indeed Islamic law'.[75] It is difficult to disagree with his further conclusion that 'the course of events in Pakistan has mainly contradicted the Fundamental Right of religious freedom contained in the Constitution of Pakistan.'[76]

---

sectional diversities; to renounce practices derogatory to the dignity of women;… (*h*) to develop the scientific temper, humanism and the spirit of inquiry and reform [and] (*i*) to safeguard public property and to abjure violence'. Article 51(a) (as inserted by Constitution (Forty-second Amendment) Act, 1976, Section 11). On the status of the fundamental duties, see, *AIIMS Students' Union* v. *AIIMS & Ors* (2002) 1 SCC 428. See also, *Sri Baragur Ramachandrappa & Ors* v. *State of Karnataka* (2007) SCR(5) 1086 (BP Singh & Harjit Singh Bedi, JJ).

[73] Constitution of Pakistan, 1973 Article 16 (right to assemble peacefully and without arms, subject to any reasonable restrictions imposed by law in the interest of public order); Article 17 (right to form associations or unions, subject to any reasonable restrictions imposed by law in the interest of sovereignty or integrity of Pakistan, public order or morality) (as amendment by Constitution (Fourth Amendment) Act, 1975 (Act 71 of 1975), Section 3); Article 19 (right to freedom of speech and expression, and freedom of the press, subject to any reasonable restrictions imposed by law in the interest of the glory of Islam or the integrity, security or defence of Pakistan or any part thereof, friendly relations with foreign States, public order, decency or morality, or in relation to contempt of court, commission of or incitement to an offence (as amendment by Constitution, Fourth Amendment) Act, 1975 (Act 71 of 1975), Section 4).

[74] Constitution of Bangladesh, 1972 Article 37 (right to assemble and to participate in public meetings and processions peacefully and without arms, subject to any reasonable restrictions imposed by law in the interests of public order health); Article 38 (right to form associations or unions, subject to any reasonable restrictions imposed by law in the interests of morality or public order) (as amendment by Second Proclamation Order No. III of 1976); Article 39(2) (right of every citizen of freedom of speech and expression and the freedom of the press, subject to any reasonable restrictions imposed by law in the interests of the security of the State, friendly relations with foreign states, public order, decency or morality, or in relation to contempt of court, defamation, or incitement to an offence.)

[75] See in this volume, Chapter 8.

[76] Ibid.

The Supreme Court of India's early decisions clearly favoured freedom of expression. Apart from libel, slander, and similar restrictions existing in 1950, a law restricting freedom of speech and expression could fall within Article 19(2) only if directed solely against the undermining of the security of the State or its overthrow, not merely because the restrictions were generally in the interests of public order.[77] A law purporting to authorize restrictions on a fundamental right in language wide enough to cover restrictions both within and outside the permissible limits, could not be upheld, even so far as applicable within those limits. Being not severable, the mere possibility of unconstitutional application made it wholly unconstitutional and void.[78] The Legislature (the same body that had adopted the Constitution) immediately amended Article 19(2), extending the grounds of restriction for freedom of expression and of speech.[79]

Some years later, the editor of a magazine devoted to cow protection, convicted of publishing a cartoon offensive to Muslims, challenged the validity of Section 295(a).[80] The Supreme Court upheld:

[I]f certain activities have a tendency to cause public disorder, a law penalising such activities as an offence cannot but be held to be a law imposing reasonable restriction 'in the interests of public order' although in some cases those activities may not actually lead to a breach of public order. ... S. 295A does not penalise any and every act of insult to or attempt to insult the religion or the religious beliefs of a class of citizens but it penalises only those acts of insults to or those varieties of attempts to insult the religion or the religious beliefs of a class of citizens, which are perpetrated with the deliberate and malicious intention of outraging the religious feelings of that class. ... It only punishes the aggravated form of insult to religion when it is perpetrated with the deliberate and malicious intention of outraging the religious feelings of that class. The calculated tendency of this aggravated form of insult is clearly to disrupt the public order and the section, which penalises such activities, is well

---

[77] *Romesh Thapar* v. *State of Madras* (1950) SCR 594, 602–3. See also, *Brij Bhushan & Anr.* v. *State of Delhi* (1950) SCR 605.

[78] *Romesh Thapar* v. *State of Madras*, 603.

[79] Article 19(2) (as substituted by Constitution (First Amendment) Act, 1951, Section 3 (with retrospective effect)).

[80] *Ramji Lal Modi* v. *State of Uttar Pradesh* (1957) SCR 860.

within the protection of clause (2) of Article 19 as being a law imposing reasonable restrictions on the exercise of the right to freedom of speech and expression....[81]

Some limits imposed by law 'in the interests of public order'—such as prohibiting any instigation to non-payment of taxes—have been held not to be 'reasonable restrictions'. This had no proximate connection or nexus with public order; the connection was far-fetched, hypothetical, problematical or too remote.[82] However, as I consider below, the Indian Supreme Court's approach differs significantly from US constitutional law on freedom of speech.[83]

Section 124(a) of the Penal Code is interpreted narrowly, to sustain its validity. According to *Kedar Nath Singh*, only acts involving intention or tendency to create disorder, or disturbance of law and order, or incitement to violence can be sedition.[84] The courts generally read Section 153(a) and cognate provisions just as restrictively. [85] However, in actual practice, there are serious reasons to be concerned about the ready resort to sedition charges in cases in which the requirements set out in *Kedar Nath* have not been satisfied.[86] The recent Binayak Sen case is only the most prominent example of such apparent misuse of the law.[87]

Sections 153(a) and 505(2) require *mens rea*[88] and another common element: feelings of enmity, hatred, or ill-will '*between different*' religious or racial or language or regional groups or castes and communities. 'Merely inciting the feeling of one community or group without any reference to any other community or group cannot

---

[81] Ibid., 867, Das, CJ. See also, *Virendra* v. *State of Punjab* (1958) SCR 308.

[82] *Superintendent, Central Prison, Fatehgarh* v. *Ram Manohar Lohia* (1960) SCR (2) 821.

[83] *S. Rangarajan etc* v. *P. Jagjivan Ram* (1989) SCR (2) 204, 212.

[84] *Kedar Nath Singh* v. *State of Bihar* AIR (1962) SC 955.

[85] *Ebrahim Sulaiman Sait* v. *M. C. Muhammad & Anor* AIR (1980) SC 354 (RPA, 1951 Section 123(3a)) reaffirmed in *Manzar Sayeed Khan* v. *State of Maharashtra & Anr* (2007) SCR(4) 907 (K.G. Balakrishnan, Lokeshwar Singh Panta and D.K. Jain, JJ).

[86] Siddharth Narrain, '"Disaffection" and the Law: The Chilling Effect of Sedition Laws in India', *Economic and Political Weekly*, XLVI(8): 33–7.

[87] See, 'Free Binayak Sen Campaign: Resist the Silent Emergency', http://www.binayaksen.net/ (last accessed on 30 March 2011).

[88] *Balwant Singh & Anor.* v. *State of Punjab* (1995) 3 SCC 214; *Bilal Ahmed Kaloo* (footnote 89).

attract either....'[89] Courts have treated prevention of enmity between different classes similarly[90] but, if publications do promote enmity, hatred and ill-will between, for example, Hindus and Muslims, on grounds of religion, it is no defence simply to present them as a political thesis or as historical truth.[91] The truth of facts stated is no defence to charges of electoral 'corrupt practices' by promoting enmity on religious grounds, if the effect is to promote feelings of enmity or hatred.[92]

Holding Section 144 of the Code of Criminal Procedure to be valid, the Supreme Court[93] stated:

> The gist of action...is the urgency of the situation, its efficacy in the likelihood of being able to prevent some harmful occurrences. As it is possible to act absolutely and even *ex parte* it is obvious that the emergency must be sudden and the consequences sufficiently grave. Without it, the exercise of power would have no justification. It is not an ordinary power flowing from administration but a power used in a judicial manner and which can stand further judicial scrutiny in the need for the exercise of the power, in its efficacy and in the extent of its application.
>
> . . .
>
> [T]here are sufficient safeguards available to person affected by the order and the restriction, therefore are reasonable. ... [S.] 144 is not unconstitutional if properly applied and the fact that it may be abused is no ground for striking it down. The remedy then is to question the exercise of power as being outside the grant of the law.[94]

Thus, '[US] doctrine that previous restraints on the exercise of fundamental rights are permissible only if there be a clear and present danger...cannot be imported...because the fundamental rights guaranteed under Art. 19(1)...are not absolute rights'.[95] However,

---

[89] *Bilal Ahmed Kaloo* v. *State of Andhra Pradesh* (1997) 7 SCC 431. See also, *Gopal Godse* v. *Union of India* (1970) 72 BLR 871.

[90] *Ramesh.s/o Chotalal Dalal* v. *Union of India* (1988) SCR (2) 1011.

[91] *Babu Rao Patel* v. *State of Delhi* (1980) SCR (2) 1082.

[92] *Ebrahim Sulaiman Sait* v. *M.C. Muhammad & Anr.* (1980) SCR (1) 1154.

[93] *Madhu Limaye* v. *Sub-divisional Magistrate, Monghyr & Ors* (1971) SCR (2) 711.

[94] Ibid., at 727, 729.

[95] *Babulal Parate* v. *State of Maharashtra* (1961) SCR (3) at 423, 425. In justifying Section 144, the Court observed: Public order has to be maintained in advance in order to ensure it and, therefore, it is competent to a legislature to pass a law

state governments can extend such orders for a limited period only, and after allowing representations by the aggrieved party or with some form of appeal or revision.[96]

The High Court may review Section 144 orders. The Karnataka High Court deemed unlawful an *ex parte* order preventing a Bajrang Dal[97] leader from entering a district where communal tensions were high following murder of Hindus by Muslims. There was no urgency justifying departing from the rules of natural justice and excluding him altogether was excessive; a specific prohibition on rallies and speeches would suffice.[98] However, the Supreme Court upheld a two-week prohibition on a Vishwa Hindu Parishad (VHP) leader, Praveen Bhai Togadia's entering a 'communally sensitive' district for the purpose of participating in any function.[99] Arijit Pasayat, J, emphasized both the magistrate's freedom of action under Section 144 and the principle of secularism:

> No person, however big he may assume or claim to be, should be allowed, irrespective of the position he may assume or claim to hold in public life, to either act in a manner or make speeches which would destroy secularism recognised by the Constitution. ... It means that (the) State should have no religion of its own and no one could proclaim to make the State have one such, or endeavour to create a theocratic State. Persons belonging to different religions live throughout the length and breadth of the country. Each person, whatever be his religion, must get an assurance from the State that he has the protection of law freely to profess, practice and propagate his religion and freedom of conscience.
>
> ...
>
> Quick decisions and swift as well as effective action necessitated in such cases may not justify or permit the authorities to give prior opportunity or consideration at length of the pros and cons. The imminent need

---

permitting an appropriate authority to take anticipatory action or place anticipatory restrictions upon particular kinds of acts in an Emergency for the purpose of maintaining public order. Ibid., at 437.

[96] *State of Bihar & Ors.* v. *K.K. Misra & Ors.* (1970) SCR (3) at 181, 195.

[97] Youth wing of the Vishwa Hindu Parishad (VHP), an organization espousing Hindutva ideology.

[98] *Pramod Muthalik* v. *District Magistrate, Davanagere* ILR (2003) KAR 1953, 1958–9 (K. Sreedhar Rao, J). The order did not set out, as required, all necessary details of the supporting facts and reasons.

[99] *State of Karnataka & Anr.* v. *Praveen Bhai Thogadia* (2004) SCR (3) 652 (Arijit Pasayat, Doraiswamy Raju, JJ).

to intervene instantly having regard to the sensitivity and perniciously perilous consequences it may result in, if not prevented forthwith, cannot be lost sight of.[100]

A wide range of behaviour prompts use of Section 144 to prevent 'obstruction, annoyance or injury to any person lawfully employed, or danger to human life, health or safety, or a disturbance of the public tranquillity'. In parts of India,[101] Pakistan[102] and Bangladesh[103] magistrates regularly prohibit gatherings of more than five persons around any examination hall or order similar preventive measures during the period of school examinations. A bandh also frequently elicits sweeping preventive measures, [104] as have protests

---

[100] Ibid., For other bans and restrictions on Thogadia under Section 144, see, 'Gujarat bars Togadia's march, blocks yatra', *The Times of India* (Online Ed.) (17 November 2002), http://timesofindia.indiatimes.com/cms.dll/html/uncomp/articleshow?artid=28502530 (last accessed on 30 March 2011); 'Togadia's visit: Police step up vigil', (Kerala) *The Hindu* (Online Ed.) (10 April 2004), http://www.hindu.com/2004/04/10/stories/2004041003300700.htm (last accessed on 30 March 2011); 'Togadia arrested for trying to walk into Kandhamal', *Deccan Herald* (Online Ed.) (19 March 2011), http://www.deccanherald.com/content/59004/togadia-arrested-trying-walk-kandhamal.html (last accessed on 30 March 2011).

[101] For example, 'Board action plan to ease pressure on examinees', *The Times of India* (Online Ed.) (Ahmedabad, 24 February 2005), http://timesofindia.indiatimes.com/articleshow/1031377.cms (last accessed on 30 March 2011); 'FATEHGARH Sahib: Section 144 imposed', *The Tribune, Chandigarh* (Online Ed.) (5 September 2005), http://www.tribuneindia.com/2005/20050905/region.htm (last accessed on 30 March 2011); 'Section 144 for 10th class exam', *The Hindu* (Online Ed.) (23 March 2009), http://www.hindu.com/2009/03/23/stories/2009032358740300.htm (last accessed on 30 March 2011).

[102] 'Nazim bans entry to exam centres', *The Nation* (Online Ed.) (10 May 2009), http://www.nation.com.pk/pakistan-news-newspaper-daily-english-online/Regional/Islamabad/10-May-2009/Nazim-bans-entry-to-exam-centres (last accessed on 30 March 2011) 'Section 144 imposed around [Rawalpindi] exam centers', *The News International* (Online Ed); (31 January 2011), http://www.thenews.com.pk/NewsDetail.aspx?ID=10389 (last accessed on 30 March 2011).

[103] For example, '2005 HSC exam begins today with reduced examinees', *Bangladesh Observer* (Online Ed.) (12 May 2005), http://www.bangladeshobserveronline.com/new/2005/05/12/district.htm (last accessed on 16 October 2006).

[104] For example, '[Indore] observes total bandh, several shrines damaged', *Hindustan Times* (Online Ed.) (7 July 2005); 'Tense after rape fury', *The Telegraph* (Calcutta) (6 August 2005), http://www.telegraphindia.com/1050806/asp/siliguri/story_5079397.asp (last accessed on 30 March 2011); 'Violence flares

against the Narmada Dam.[105] Section 144 sometimes applies in ways indirectly related to public order. Thus, magistrates may require landlords to furnish information about their tenants to the nearest police station [106] or impose sweeping restrictions to facilitate contested land surveys.[107]

State governments also frequently use Section 95 of the Code of Criminal Procedure. In 2003, the Communist Government of West Bengal banned Bangladeshi author Taslima Nasrin's autobiography, after the controversy surrounding her life and works in her homeland;[108] Rajasthan banned a proselytizing Christian publication which denigrated Hindu and Jain religious beliefs;[109] and Haryana, a book criticizing Mahatma Gandhi.[110] Maharashtra has banned

---

up again in Lalgarh', *The Hindu* (Online Ed.) (21 July 2009) http://www.hindu.com/2009/07/21/stories/2009072154610500.htm (last accessed on 30 March 2011).

[105] Amnesty International, *India: Persecuted for Challenging Injustice: Human Rights Defenders in India* (26 April 2000), ASA 20/008/2000, pp. 12–14, http://www.unhcr.org/refworld/docid/3b83b6ef0.html (last accessed on 30 March 2011); Balakrishnan Rajagopal, 'Limits of law in counter-hegemonic globalization: The Indian Supreme Court and the Narmada Valley struggle', *Leiden Journal of International Law,* (2005), 18(3): 360 (reprinted in B. de Souza Santos and C.A. Rodríguez-Garavito (eds), *Law and Globalization from Below: Towards a Cosmopolitan Legality* (Cambridge University Press: Cambridge, 2005), pp. 183–217.

[106] 'Ban orders till Nov. 13', *The Tribune, Chandigarh* (Online Ed.) (14 September 2005), http://www.tribuneindia.com/2005/20050914/punjab1.htm (last accessed on 11 June 2012).

[107] 'Ban orders imposed on 30 villages in Udupi taluk', *The Hindu* (Online Ed.) (10 August 2005), http://www.hindu.com/2005/08/10/stories/2005081004140300.htm (last accessed on 30 March 2011).

[108] 'Bengal bans Taslima's book', *The Hindu* (Online Ed.) (29 November 2003), http://www.hinduonnet.com/thehindu/2003/11/29/stories/2003112905441100.htm (last accessed 30 March 2011), an order subsequently set aside by the High Court: 'HC lifts ban on Taslima', *The Telegraph* (Calcutta) (23 September 2005), http://www.telegraphindia.com/1050923/asp/bengal/story_5274462.asp (last accessed on 30 March 2011).

[109] 'Saffron strike', *Frontline,* (8–21 April 2008), 23(7), http://www.hinduonnet.com/thehindu/fline/fl2307/stories/20060421004410600.htm (last accessed on 30 March 2011).

[110] 'Haryana Govt. orders seizure of book on Gandhi', *The Hindu* (Online Ed.), http://www.hindu.com/2006/09/09/stories/2006090915770500.htm (last accessed on 30 March 2011).

several works on Chhatrapati Shivaji,[111] although in the most prominent case, three years after it had been imposed, the Supreme Court quashed the prohibition, on the ground of lack of authorial intention to cause disorder or incite the people to violence.[112] Private parties may seek forfeiture of publications under the Code,[113] but attempts to censor through public interest litigation have thus far failed.[114]

The High Court must quash an order that does not set out the substance of the grounds on which it was made or if it is not satisfied, based on the grounds set out in the order only, that the publication concerned contained matter punishable under the relevant sections.[115] There have been several examples of forfeitures later set aside by the court; a special bench of the Calcutta High Court set aside the prohibition of Taslima Nasrin's *Dwikhondito*.[116] There are also cases upholding forfeitures on grounds of injury to religious feelings. The Supreme Court recently commented:

> India is a country with vast disparities in language, culture and religion and unwarranted and malicious criticism or interference in the faith of others cannot be accepted.
>
> . . .
>
> Section 95…is not violative of Art. 19(1)(a) of the Constitution, as the action taken thereunder is of a preventive nature and that a extremely

[111] 'Maharashtra bans another book on Shivaji, copies seized', *The Hindu* (Online Ed.), http://www.hindu.com/2006/01/11/stories/2006011105511300.htm (last accessed on 30 March 2011).

[112] *Manzar Sayeed Khan* v. *State of Maharashtra & Anr* (2007) SCR(4) 907 (K.G. Balakrishnan, Lokeshwar Singh Panta and D.K. Jain, JJ).

[113] 'Order on seizure of publicity material stayed', *The Hindu* (Online Ed.) (20 January 2005), http://www.hindu.com/2005/01/20/stories/2005012005600400.htm (last accessed 30 March 2011).

[114] For example, Chandmal Chopra's petition in the mid-1980s seeking to have the *Qu'ran* prohibited: *Chandmal Chopra* v. *State of West Bengal* (Calcutta High Court, 17 May 1985, Basak, CJ); Mody (1987) 945. See also, *Odyssey Communications Pvt. Ltd.* v. *Lokvidayan Sangathan* (1988) SCR Supl.(1) 486; *Ramesh s/o Chotalal Dalal* v. *Union of India* (1988) SCR (2) 1011.

[115] *Harnam Das* v. *State of Uttar Pradesh* (1962) SCR (2) 371; *Chinna Annamalai* v. *State of Tamil Nadu* AIR 1971 Madras 448 (FB).

[116] 'HC lifts ban on Taslima', *The Telegraph* (Calcutta) (23 September 2005), http://www.telegraphindia.com/1050923/asp/bengal/story_5274462.asp (last accessed on 30 March 2011).

efficacious remedy under Section 96...is available to an aggrieved party or person. It is significant, and it is clear from the very large number of judgments that have been cited before us, that most of the matters pertain to attacks on minorities or religious and social groups or individuals who are perceived as being prodigals or heretics and therefore unacceptable to the conservatives amongst the mainstream. It cannot ever be over-emphasized that India is a country with huge diversities in language and religion and the weaker amongst them must be shown extra care and consideration.[117]

THE ROLE OF COMPARATIVE LAW

The Supreme Court of India stresses that its approach differs significantly from US free speech law, so that First Amendment case law is no safe guide to interpreting Article 19(2).[118] This rests not merely on textual differences between the two constitutions, but on fundamentally different views of the relationship between freedom of expression and social order, views that can be traced back to Stephen, his response to the India he found, and the legacy he and his kind left in the subcontinent. Choudhry makes a broadly similar point in his essay when he points out how Mayo Moran's comparative analysis of the US and Canadian case law on 'hate speech' shows that the difference in approaches turns on divergent background assumptions about the nature of hate speech, the interests at stake in its regulation, and the nature of the state, which

---

[117] *Sri Baragur Ramachandrappa & Ors* v. *State of Karnataka* (2007) SCR(5) 1086 (BP Singh & Harjit Singh Bedi, JJ) upholding the forfeiture of the novel *Dharmakaarana*, on the ground of its offensive references to the twelfth-century religious figure Basaveshwara. In 2006, having registered a case under Subsections 153(a) and 295(a), the police in Delhi arrested Alok Tomar, of the Hindi-language magazine *Senior India*, and seized all copies of the relevant issue, arising from its re-publication of the *Jyllands Posten* cartoons that caused worldwide controversy over their depiction of the Prophet Muhammad. 'Magazine Editor held', *The Hindu* (Online Ed.) (23 February 2006), http://www.hindu.com/2006/02/23/stories/2006022317090900.htm (last accessed on 30 March 2011). See also, 'Journo Alok Tomar gets bail in cartoon case', *outlookindia.com* (2 March 2006), http://outlookindia.com/pti_news.asp?id=367587 (last accessed on 30 March 2011). Vijay Dixit, chairman of the publishing group had been arrested and bailed earlier: Ibid.

[118] For example, *K.A. Abbas* v. *Union of India* (1971) 2 SCR 446, 467; *S. Rangarajan etc.* v. *P. Jagjivan Ram* (1989) SCR (2) at 204, 212–13.

are exposed through constitutional comparison. In the American constitutional tradition, hate speech is regarded as a form of extreme political expression, whereas in Canada, it is the verbal manifestation of racial and religious discrimination.[119]

As Moran points out, the Canadian vision is of the State as the guarantor of a proper balance between the rights of those who assert their right to free expression and those who may suffer grave harm as a result.[120] There is a clear, if distant, connection here with Stephen's view, sharpened and confirmed by his experience of India, of the State's fundamental duty to guarantee social peace and order. However, where Stephen fails to provide guidance for modern circumstances is in his inability to account for the other role of the State to which Moran draws attention—as the guarantor of the values of a democratic society.[121]

In dealing with US First Amendment cases, the Indian courts' basis for self-awareness has clearly been (as Choudhry puts it) 'interpretive confrontation'. In these cases, Indian judges have confronted the intellectual legacy of John Stuart Mill and, in doing so, they have sharpened their awareness that there is no 'very simple principle' of liberty of thought and discussion such as exists in India (or in Pakistan or Bangladesh, for that matter). Indian judges have thus found a negative 'interpretive foil' by which they can gauge what freedom is *not* in a South Asian context. Where, then, might they find a positive stimulus for reflecting upon what that freedom *is*, in an Indian context?

Do James Fitzjames Stephen's ideas about liberty of thought and discussion—strongly influenced as they were by his Indian experience—continue to be relevant in the subcontinent? They clearly have some relevance, since much of the legislation that he and his kind introduced remains in force in the successor states. Have his views themselves any broader philosophical importance? He objected

---

[119] See in this volume, Chapter 2 (Sujit Choudhry, 'Comparative Constitutional Law in India'), citing M. Moran, 'Talking About Hate Speech: A Rhetorical Analysis of American and Canadian Approaches to the Regulation of Hate Speech', *Wisconsin Law Review*, (1994), 6: 1425–514.

[120] Ibid., 1488–9. See, *Sri Baragur Ramachandrappa & Ors v. State of Karnataka* 2007 SCR(5) 1086 (B.P. Singh & Harjit Singh Bedi, JJ).

[121] Ibid., 1489–91.

'rather to Mr Mill's theory than to his practical conclusions'[122] or 'the practice of modern Liberals'.[123] In that spirit, he set out 'how the question ought to be discussed' and 'in what cases is liberty good and in what cases is it bad?'

> Compulsion is bad: (1) When the object aimed at is bad. (2) When the object aimed at is good, but the compulsion employed is not calculated to obtain it. (3) When the object aimed at is good, and the compulsion employed is calculated to obtain it, but at too great an expense.[124]

This broadly foreshadows both the proportionality tests employed by the Supreme Court of Canada and the European Court of Human Rights and the 'reasonable restriction' test used by the Indian courts. Both systems reject, as Stephen did, the idea that there is some 'very simple principle...entitled to govern' the limits of freedom of expression[125] such as 'content (or viewpoint) neutrality' or a pithy maxim like Justice Powell's that '[u]nder the First Amendment there is no such thing as a false idea....'[126] Indian law does not insist, any more than Stephen did, upon a categorical distinction between throwing 'the abetment of a crime into the form of the expression of an opinion' and 'the mere preaching of a religion' or other doctrine.[127] Proximity or likelihood of the danger is certainly relevant; the Supreme Court once described a document as 'written in high-flown Bengali language and contain[ing] a good deal of demagogic claptrap with some pretence to poetic flourish.'[128] While such '[r]hetoric... might in conceivable circumstances inflame passions as, for example,

---

[122] Stephen, *Liberty, Equality and Fraternity,* p. 74.

[123] Ibid., p. 119.

[124] Ibid., p. 85.

[125] Adapting Mill's proposition: J.S. Mill, 'On Liberty', p. 14.

[126] *Ward* v. *Rock Against Racism*, 491 US 781 (1989); S.J. Heyman, 'Spheres of Autonomy: Reforming the Content Neutrality Doctrine in First Amendment Jurisprudence', *Wm. & Mary Bill of Rts. J.*, (2002), 10(3): 647–717; *Gertz* v. *Robert Welch, Inc.,* 418 US 323, 340. See, Jacobsohn, *Wheel of Law,* pp. 14–15, 180–5, arguing that 'viewpoint neutrality' is an inappropriate requirement in the context of Indian constitutionalism.

[127] Compare Stephen's view (see, the quotation at footnote 22) with refusal to import the 'clear and present danger' test into Indian law (see, the passage at footnote 95).

[128] *State of Bihar* v. *Shailabala Devi* (1952) SCR 654, 661 Mahajan, J.

if addressed to an excited mob' it must be proved that it did in fact infringe the prohibition of matters which 'incite to or encourage, or tend to incite to or encourage the commission of any offence of murder or any cognizable offence involving violence'.[129] Nevertheless, if the 'tendency' of words or other forms of expression is sufficiently clear, that may justify suppressing it 'in the interests of public order', even if cannot be shown that it has been or is likely to pose any 'clear and present danger' of disorder.[130] Although Stephen's criticisms of Mill are not, therefore, merely negative, to find adequate support for a positive principle of freedom of expression one still needs to draw on a body of precedents or a series of decisions that gives due weight to the values of a democratic society.

Canadian constitutional law is one possible source. The case law of the European Court of Human Rights is another. The Indian Supreme Court has occasionally referred to the case law of the European Convention in relation to freedom of expression.[131] However, the full potential for these to function as an 'interpretive foil' for Indian courts seems not to be fully appreciated. Though developed independently, the Strasbourg proportionality test has much in common with the Indian notion of 'reasonable restrictions'. In particular, the 'real and proximate' relation which the Indian courts seek between a law and a ground of restriction resembles the Strasbourg Court's 'relevancy' and 'sufficiency' criteria.[132] More generally, Indian judicial *dicta* are often reminiscent of the European touchstone of what is 'necessary in a democratic society'.[133] There would probably, indeed, not be a great deal to be gained by the Indian courts formalizing their

---

[129] Ibid., 663.

[130] *Ramji Lal Modi* v. *State of Uttar Pradesh* (1957) SCR 860 (see, footnote 81).

[131] *Reliance Petrochemicals Ltd.* v. *Proprietors of Indian Express Newspapers, Bombay Pvt. Ltd.* (1988) SCR Supl. (3) 212; *S Rangarajan etc.* v. *P. Jagjivan Ram* (1989) SCR (2) 204, 228–29; *Secretary, Ministry of Information & Broadcasting* v. *Cricket Association of Bengal & Anr.* (1995) AIR SC 1236.

[132] For example, compare *Superintendent, Central Prison, Fatehgarh* v. *Ram Manohar Lohia* (1960) SCR (2) 834–6 and *Observer and Guardian* v. *UK* (1992) 14 EHRR 153 para. 59.

[133] For example, 'the right to freedom of speech…is the very foundation of democratic way of life', *Superintendent, Central Prison, Fatehgarh* v. *Ram Manohar Lohia*, 837; 'in any set up, more so in a democratic set up like ours, dissemination of news and views for popular consumption is a must', *Life Insurance Corporation of India & Ors* v. *Prof. Manubhai D. Shah etc.* (1992) SCR (3) at 608, Ahmadi, J.

decision-making in terms of 'proportionality' since they anticipated the essential elements of that test by two decades or so.

What is the specific relevance of the Strasbourg case law in the current field? It allows national authorities a wide margin of appreciation to deal with the protection of morals and of religious sensitivities and so challenges to restrictions in these areas generally fail.[134] Even where the specific expression at issue does not seem offensive, the Court may uphold general measures designed to avoid religious discord.[135] Moreover, some forms of expression, such as Holocaust denial or incitement to hatred on grounds of race or religion may 'deflect Article 10 of the Convention from its real purpose by using his right to freedom of expression for ends which are contrary to the text and spirit of the Convention'[136] and be unprotected by Article 10, due to Article 17.[137] Even if the 'margin of appreciation' concept is inapplicable in India, each system is thus similarly disposed to accept broad restrictions on inflaming religious animosities and rivalries.

Both systems stress the importance of effective judicial review of decisions restricting freedom of expression, of fair procedures,[138] of not stifling legitimate criticism of parties and politicians and of allowing relevant and proportionate contributions to debates on matters of public interest, even ones of great sensitivity.[139] There is

---

[134] For example, *Otto-Preminger Institut* v. *Austria* (1994) 19 EHRR 34; *Wingrove* v. *UK* (1997) 24 EHRR 1; *Murphy* v. *Ireland* (2004) 38 EHRR 13.

[135] Ibid.

[136] For example, *Garaudy* v. *France* (Appl. No. 65831/01) admissibility decision of 24 June 2003 (Holocaust denial). See also, *Norwood* v. *UK* (Appl. No. 23131/03) admissibility decision of 16 November 2004 (stirring up hatred against Muslims); *Witsch* v. *Germany* (Appl. No. 7485/03) admissibility decision of 13 December 2005 (contesting Hitler and the NSDAP's responsibility for the murder of Jews).

[137] 'Nothing in [the] Convention may be interpreted as implying for any State, group or person any right to engage in any activity or perform any act aimed at the destruction of any of the rights and freedoms set forth herein or at their limitation to a greater extent than is provided for in the Convention.'

[138] Compare, for example, *Association Ekin* v. *France* (2002) 35 EHRR 35 or *Steel & Morris* v. *UK* (2005) 41 EHRR 403 with *State of Bihar & Ors* v. *K.K. Misra & Ors* (1970) SCR (3) 196.

[139] For example, *Oberschlick* v. *Austria (No. 2)* (1998) 25 EHRR 357; *Jerusalem* v. *Austria* (2003) 37 EHRR 25; *Feldek* v. *Slovakia* (Appl. No. 29032/95), judgment of 12 July 2001. Compare Arijit Pasayat J.'s *dicta* in *State of Karnataka & Anr.* v. *Praveen Bhai Togadia* (2004) SCR (3) 652 (Arijit Pasayat, Doraiswamy Raju, JJ);

more divergence over the issue of prior restraints—although both accept them in theory, the Indian courts seem much more tolerant of them in practice.[140]

Given the sensitivity of religion and related topics, South Asian lawyers and judges might profitably consider, generally, which sorts of limitation on public discussion of religious controversies are *not* acceptable in Strasbourg.[141] Thus, mere 'intransigent attitude towards and profound dissatisfaction with contemporary institutions...such as the principle of secularism and democracy' cannot automatically be deemed 'a call to violence or as hate speech based on religious intolerance' regardless of context. '[T]he mere fact of defending *sharia*, without calling for violence to establish it, is not "hate speech."'[142] If 'gratuitously offensive' expressions are as far as possible avoided, authors may contribute to discussions of questions of public interest by considering a particular religious doctrine's detrimental effects. A debate concerning the causes of the Holocaust may warrant attributing some responsibility to religious doctrines still held by the Roman Catholic Church. Restrictions on freedom of expression cannot be justified merely because believers are shocked and offended, not by gratuitously offensive or insulting expressions or by a deliberate incitement to hatred or disrespect, but simply due to the believers' repudiation of the criticism itself.[143] Similarly, a strongly worded criticism of the actions or statements of a religious leader was protected by Article 10, since it 'neither unduly interfered with the right of believers to express and exercise their religion, nor did it denigrate the content of their religious faith'.[144] The Convention thus protects vigorous criticism of Muslim beliefs, provided it does not

---

S. *Rangarajan etc.* v. *P. Jagjivan Ram* (1989) SCR (2) 204, 212; 'HC lifts ban on Taslima', *The Telegraph* (Calcutta) (23 September 2005), http://www.telegraphindia.com/1050923/asp/bengal/story_5274462.asp (last accessed on 30 March 2011).

[140] For example, compare *Superintendent, Central Prison, Fatehgarh* v. *Ram Manohar Lohia* (1960) SCR (2) 834–6 and *Observer and Guardian* v. *UK* (1992) 14 EHRR 153 para. 59.

[141] *Müslüm Gündüz* v. *Turkey* (Appl. No. 35071/97) judgment of 4 December 2003; *Giniewski* v. *France* (Appl. No. 64016/00) judgment of 31 January 2006; *Aydin Tatlav c Turquie* (*Requête no 50692/99*) *l'arrêt de 2 mai* 2006.

[142] *Müslüm Gündüz* v. *Turkey*, paras 48, 51.

[143] *Giniewski* v. *France*, paras 51, 52.

[144] *Klein* v. *Slovakia* (Appl. No. 72208/01) judgment of 31 October 2006, para 52.

insult believers as individuals or gratuitously attack sacred symbols. If one avoids such insults, Article 10 protects even highly caustic attacks on Islamic or other religious beliefs.[145] Conversely, the assertion of a religious belief which expressed in highly shocking, even offensive terms and which might reasonably be considered a manifestation of 'superstition, intolerance et obscurantism' (such as a claim that a major natural disaster was divine punishment of the speaker's religious adversaries) may well be protected by Article 10, provided that—when one considers it by the yardstick of the speaker's own religious conceptions—the statement does not incite to violence or to hatred against persons who are not members of the speaker's own religious community.[146]

Could India also profit from the European Court of Human Rights (ECHR) approach to the concept of secularism? As Jacobsohn and Shankar observe, it is not easy simply to transplant European concepts (themselves quite diverse) of the relationship between religion and the state to South Asia.[147] Perhaps the Indian, Pakistani, or Bangladeshi 'societal model cannot be considered compatible with the Convention system'. For example, if it were a European state, India's plurality of personal laws might violate the ECHR,[148] since 'private-law rules of religious inspiration...such as rules permitting

---

[145] *Aydin Tatlav c Turquie*, para 28.

[146] *Nur Radyo Ve Televizyon Yayinciliği AŞ c Turquie* (*Requête no* 6587/03) *l'arrêt de 27 novembre* 2007 *par* 30. The severity of the penalty (a suspension of a television station's right to broadcast for 180 days) was also a factor in this case. A violation of Article 10 was also found in the similar case of *Kutlular c Turquie* (*Requête no* 73715/01) *l'arrêt de 29 avril* 2008.

[147] See in this volume, Chapter 6.

[148] *Refah Partisi (Welfare Party) & Ors* v. *Turkey* (2003) 37 EHRR 1 par 119 (Grand Chamber). However, the personal law in India consists of 'rules laid down by the State', not 'static rules of law imposed by the religion concerned', and personal law covers a narrower field than there envisaged (excluding the criminal law, for example). The Chamber (Third Section) contemplated a system in which '*all* legal relationships' are potentially differentiated based on an individual's religion and a 'difference in treatment between individuals [occurs] in all fields of public and private law according to their religion or beliefs'. It seems likely, however, that even a more restricted system of personal law, such as India's would in a European state, impermissibly 'categorise everyone according to his religious beliefs and would allow him rights and freedoms not as an individual but according to his allegiance to a religious movement'. (See (2002) 35 EHRR 56 para 70.)

discrimination based on the gender of the parties concerned, as in polygamy and privileges for the male sex in matters of divorce and succession' are prejudicial to public order and democratic values for Convention purposes.[149]

Although European and South Asian political, social, and cultural circumstances may differ greatly, some principles similar to those of the Strasbourg case law are already to be found in Indian decisions, as in the Supreme Court's defence of the freedom to criticize caste-based preferences[150] or overturning the forfeiture of *Dwikhondito*.[151] A more systematic restatement of these principles by the Supreme Court, at some opportune moment, would be desirable. Reference to European decisions would help to draw out what is already latent in the existing case law and could offer some barrier to the ongoing abuse of the law of sedition.[152]

The Indian state also impinges on freedom of expression at lower levels. State governments use Section 95 in a largely opportunistic fashion, usually responding to particular groups (whether Muslims, OBCs, Marathi chauvinists, or whoever) who violently (often literally) oppose a work. Furthermore, the threat to freedom of expression often comes not from orchestrated state repression but from social and political violence or intimidation, often highly organized, by opponents of the views expressed. For example, although the prohibition on *Dwikhondito* may have been lifted by the Calcutta High Court, the author, Taslima Nasrin, who had resided in Kolkata since 2004, was the target of a campaign of violent protest (including threats to her life) by Indian Muslims.[153] Mass protests

---

[149] *Refah Partisi (Welfare Party) & Ors* v. *Turkey* (2003) 37 EHRR 1 para 128.

[150] *S. Rangarajan etc.* v. *P. Jagjivan Ram* (1989) SCR (2) 204, 212.

[151] 'HC lifts ban on Taslima', *The Telegraph* (Calcutta) (23 September 2005), http://www.telegraphindia.com/1050923/asp/bengal/story_5274462.asp (last accessed on 30 March 2011).

[152] Siddharth Narrain, '"Disaffection"' and the Law', pp. 33–7.

[153] 'Target Taslima: No room for critics in Islam?', *IBNLive* (10 August 2007), http://ibnlive.in.com/news/target-taslima-no-room-for-critics-in-islam/46563-3-single.html (last accessed on 30 March 2011); Special Correspondent 'Taslima roughed up in Hyderabad', *The Hindu* (Online Ed.) (10 August 2007), http://www.hindu.com/2007/08/10/stories/2007081058910100.htm (last accessed on 30 March 2011).

in Kolkata forced her to take refuge in New Delhi.[154] One national cabinet member publicly advised her to desist from publishing blasphemous statements directed at any religion.[155] The Minister for External Affairs made it clear that the Government of India was prepared to offer her shelter, but that it expected in return that she would 'refrain from activities and expressions that may hurt the sentiments of our people'.[156] After several months in close protective custody in New Delhi and despite agreeing to make amendments to the text of *Dwikhondito*,[157] Nasrin left India in March 2008 for medical treatment.[158] Despite making two brief return visits, she claimed that she had not been able to secure a visa or a renewed residence permit on conditions that she would find acceptable, as regards her freedom of movement within the country or her access

[154] Debashis Konar, 'Cops asked Taslima to leave city', *The Times of India* (Online Ed.) (22 November 2007), http://timesofindia.indiatimes.com/Cities/Kolkata-/Cops-asked-Taslima-to-leave-city/articleshow/2560494.cms (last accessed on 30 March 2011); Ramesh Randeep, 'Bangladeshi writer goes into hiding', *The Guardian* (London) (Online Ed.) (27 November 2007), http://www.guardian.co.uk/world/2007/nov/27/india.books (last accessed on 30 March 2011).

[155] 'Taslima must desist from blasphemous writing', *IBNLive* (25 November 2007), http://ibnlive.in.com/news/taslima-must-desist-from-blasphemous-writing/52989-3.html?from=search-relatedstories (last accessed on 30 March 2011).

[156] 'Taslima will continue to get shelter in India', *The Financial Express* (28 November 2007), http://www.financialexpress.com/news/taslima-will-continue-to-get-shelter-in-india/244429/ (last accessed on 30 March 2011).

[157] Arindam Sarkar, 'Taslima gives in, withdraws parts of her book', *The Hindustan Times* (30 November 2007), http://www.hindustantimes.com/storypage/storypage.aspx?id=debea49a-2bb0-4f7e-9f79-695ecc18df1e&&Headline=Taslima+gives+in,+withdraws+parts+of+her+book (last accessed on 30 March 2011); Kajari Bhattacharya, 'I've lost all creative freedom: Taslima', *The Statesman* (Online Ed.) (22 January 2008), http://www.thestatesman.net/index.php?option=com_content&view=article&id=219728:I%E2%80%99ve%20lost%20all%20creative%20freedom:%20Taslima%20&catid=35:page-one&from_page=search (last accessed 30 March 2011).

[158] 'Taslima leaves India for medical treatment abroad' (Kolkata) (19 March 2008), http://www.thaindian.com/newsportal/uncategorized/taslima-leaves-india-for-medical-treatment-abroad_10029172.html (last accessed 30 March 2011); '"Lonely" Taslima to return to Kolkata or Agartala', Agartala (IANS) (15 May 2008), http://newshopper.sulekha.com/lonely-taslima-to-return-to-kolkata-or-agartala_news_909103.htm (last accessed on 30 March 2011).

to the media.[159] However, it appeared that she had not given up her ambition to return to India and, specifically, to Kolkata.[160] Taslima returned to India in February 2010 and was given a further one-year extension of her visa.[161] However, in the absence of permanent residency her continued presence in India remains precarious.[162]

In present day India, violent protests and the compliance of governments with their demands are more insidious threats to freedom of expression than systematic and ideologically motivated censorship, directed from the Centre. The High Courts do belatedly intervene to curb the worst of such excesses. However, it is cause for concern that far-reaching curbs on freedom of expression and assembly under Section 144, which are quite frequent in certain regions, seem to be less often the subject of such judicial review. Widespread use of Section 144 reflects the executive magistracy's continuing role in maintaining public order at the district level

---

[159] 'Taslima returns to India; taken to undisclosed location', *The Times of India* (Online Ed.) (8 August 2008), http://timesofindia.indiatimes.com/India/Taslima-returns-to-India-taken-to-undisclosed-location/articleshow/3342467.cms (last accessed on 30 March 2011); 'Taslima returns to India; taken to undisclosed location', *The Times of India* (Online Ed.) (8 August 2008), http://timesofindia.indiatimes.com/India/Taslima-returns-to-India-taken-to-undisclosed-location/articleshow/3342467.cms (last accessed on 30 March 2011); 'I am living a life out of a suitcase: Taslima', *The Hindu* (Online Ed.) (6 January 2009), http://www.hindu.com/2009/01/06/stories/2009010659721400.htm (last accessed on 30 March 2011); 'Taslima barred from entering India till May 31', *Business Standard* (Online Ed.) (27 March 2009), http://www.business-standard.com/india/storypage.php?autono=57477&tp=on (last accessed on 30 March 2011); 'Taslima asked to come back later!' *Pune Mirror* (Online Ed.) (30 March 2009); http://www.punemirror.in/index.aspx?page=article&sectid=4&contentid=2009033020090330003311639320a2480d&sectxslt=&pageno=3 (last accessed on 30 March 2011).

[160] 'Taslima set for India in visa bid', *The Telegraph,* (Calcutta) (4 August 2009), http://www.telegraphindia.com/1090805/jsp/nation/story_11322767.jsp (last accessed on 30 March 2011).

[161] 'Taslima seeks permanent residency as Govt. extends visa', *The Hindu* (Online Ed.), 16 February 2010, http://www.thehindu.com/news/national/article107787.ece (last accessed on 10 September 2012).

[162] 'Birthday gift to Taslima, visa extended by one year', NDTV/*Press Trust of India*, 12 August 2010, http://www.ndtv.com/article/india/birthday-gift-to-taslima-visa-extended-by-one-year-44026 (last accessed on 10 September 2012).

and below; it will be interesting to see the longer-term results of its abolition in Pakistan.[163]

In this context, Sir James Fitzjames Stephen would have certainly sympathized with the 'man on the spot'[164] and reaffirmed the irrelevance to his task of 'modern sophisms' concerning freedom of expression. Would Stephen also consider his forebodings of 'horrible cruelty and persecution if the government of the country ever got into Hindoo or Mohammedan hands' as having been realized since 1947? Pakistani law now explicitly protects Islam and denies some the right to describe themselves as Muslims.[165] Although no similar changes have been made in the Penal Codes of India or Bangladesh, much depends on the application of the law at the lowest levels. What most separates Stephen's outlook from the present-day context of constitutional and human rights issues in South Asia is the practical value attached to democracy. Stephen has been described as 'the most severe antagonist of democracy during the second half of the nineteenth century' amongst English political thinkers.[166] He was strengthened in his protests against the inevitable march of democracy by 'analogies between India and England which ignored the profound differences in the culture and the history of the two countries'.[167] What he considered to be 'wildest romance', that 'every one...should be provided with a rateable share of the sovereign power in the shape of a vote, and that the result will be the direction of power by wisdom',[168] underpins constitutional democracy in South Asia and elsewhere.[169] Even so, however, are not opinions on democracy,

---

[163] See, the text accompanying footnote 57.

[164] Increasingly, the woman on the spot; as in the example given in: Ban orders till Nov. 13', *The Tribune, Chandigarh* (Online Ed.) (14 September 2005), http://www.tribuneindia.com/2005/20050914/punjab1.htm (last accessed on 11 June 2012).

[165] See, footnotes 41–7.

[166] Colaiaco, *James Fitzjames Stephen,* p. 153.

[167] Ibid. For Stephen's mature views on democracy, generally see, Ibid., 153–6, 194–9. For relevant passages in Stephen's own writings, see, Stephen, *Liberty, Equality and Fraternity*, pp. 174–8, 211–12.

[168] Ibid., p. 212.

[169] See footnote 133.

not so very different from Stephen's, often voiced at dinner parties in New Delhi, or Islamabad, or Dhaka?[170]

To conclude, for Stephen, the Codes enabled a 'handful of unsympathetic foreigners' to rule justly and firmly the 'many races, languages and creeds'. The foreigners have long departed. At the very least, Stephen might well conclude that these 'somewhat grim presents' the British made to the peoples of the sub-continent, even if 'little calculated to excite affection', are still 'eminently well calculated to protect peaceable men and to beat down wrongdoers, to extort respect, and to enforce obedience'.[171]

---

[170] See, for example, Thomas Blom Hansen, *The Saffron Wave: Democracy and Hindu Nationalism in Modern India* (Oxford University Press: New Delhi, 1999).

[171] J.F. Stephen, *History of the Criminal Law*, pp. 344–5. Interestingly, Narrain draws attention to the rhetorical inversion of 'affection' and 'disaffection' that Mahatma Gandhi employed in his speech from the dock when on trial for sedition in 1922: Narrain, '"Disaffection" and the Law', p. 34.

CHAPTER TEN

Constitutionalism and the Judiciary in Bangladesh

৵৶

*Ridwanul Hoque**

INTRODUCTION

The term 'constitutionalism' is open to many interpretations but refers generally to the idea of complete political accountability of those charged with public governance in meeting constitutional mandates such as the protection of fundamental rights, widening of public sphere in the governance system, and the realization of ideals of equality, justice, and human dignity. Constitutionalism also signifies 'the dynamic institutional and cultural framework and processes of constitutional governance beyond the mere text of a written constitution'.[1] These conceptualizations of constitutionalism envision the judiciary in any polity with a role to play in enforcing and achieving the goals of constitutionalism, a role that should be essentially 'beyond the text' of the constitution which it is charged to expound.

* For analyses in this essay, I have relied on two of my earlier works: R. Hoque, *Judicial Activism in Bangladesh: A Golden Mean Approach,* (Cambridge Scholars Publishing: Newcastle upon Tyne, 2011); R. Hoque, 'Bangladesh's Experience with Judicial Activism', *South Asian Journal,* (2010), 30: 25–43. I would like to thank Arun K. Thiruvengadam and Vikram Raghavan for their valuable comments on an earlier draft of this essay, but the usual disclaimer applies.
[1] Constitutionalist Abdullahi A. An-Naim in a personal communication with me in April 2008.

The role of the judiciary vis-à-vis constitutionalism as outlined above is, however, riddled with debates everywhere in the world, including in Bangladesh. The long-standing traditional view of the Court as 'the weakest' of state organs having no power to take any 'active resolution whatever'[2] tends to minimize the judicial role in achieving constitutionalism. Over the last fifty years or so, however, there has been a global expansion of judicial power[3] and a growing acknowledgement of the judges' unique social–constitutional competence to actively resolve issues of constitutionalism.[4] The global trend of extended judicial authority in enforcing constitutionalism[5] has been embraced by legal systems of the world in varying manifestations. The onus on the judges in transitional democracies or so-called third world countries is, however, thought to be relatively more vigorous than elsewhere.

In this essay, I seek to analyse the role of the judiciary in Bangladesh in promoting and enforcing principles of constitutionalism.[6] The purpose will be attained principally by attending to the question of how the Supreme Court of Bangladesh has construed and enforced the Constitution as a fundamental charter of social and

---

[2] Alexander Hamilton, 'The Federalist, No. 78: The Judiciary Department', in John Jay and C. Rossiter (ed.), *The Federalist Papers: Alexander Hamilton, James Madison* (Mentor: New York, 1778/1999), p. 433.

[3] C.N. Tate and Torbjörn Vallinder (eds), *The Global Expansion of Judicial Power* (New York University Press: New York, 1995).

[4] This essay does not cover the details of these debates, although analyses presented here stand informed of them. But see in this volume, Chapter 11 (Arun K. Thiruvengadam, 'Revisiting "The Role of the Judiciary in Plural Societies" (1987)'), that assesses debates about the 'proper' role of the Indian judiciary in public interest litigation.

[5] This is sometimes inappropriately called 'judicialization of politics'. See, Ran Hirschl, *Towards Juristocracy: The Origins and Consequences of the New Constitutionalism* (Harvard University Press: Cambridge, Mass.; London, 2004).

[6] The judiciary is but one institutional mechanism for constitutionalism. There are a number of statutory and publicly-funded agencies independent of the government, such as the Human Rights Commission and the Anti-corruption Commission, that are playing increasingly a vital role in promoting good governance. Analysing these societal organizations is beyond the scope of the current essay. But see, G. Rizvi, 'Holding the State Accountable: Building Institutions of Democratic Accountability', Barrister Ishtiaq Ahmed Memorial Lecture 2010 (Asiatic Society of Bangladesh: Dhaka, 12 December 2010).

political values. In order to set in proper perspective its role vis-à-vis constitutionalism, we first need to look at the historical background of Bangladeshi constitutionalism and also briefly at the constitutional position of the Court.

The very birth of Bangladesh in 1971, following the nine-month-long historic war of independence,[7] conveys its people's deep commitment towards the values of constitutionalism, who had long suffered the evils of military rule and social injustice. Ironically, however, except for brief interludes of constitutional governments, Bangladesh, for much of its history, has experienced authoritarian rule. Sadly, throughout the past years of the country, the situation of governmental unaccountability and impunity has often prevailed over the norms and ethos of constitutionalism, due mainly to constitutional manipulation by those in power.

Bangladesh's parliamentary democracy faced a tragic situation in 1974–5 when a State of Emergency (1974) was imposed[8] and a one-party presidential form of government was installed with assaults on many founding values of the nation such as the independence of the judiciary.[9] Most tragically, after the brutal assassination of the founder of the nation, the military intervened in 1975 and thwarted the Constitution, pushing the country to a long-drawn autocratic era (1975–90) until its democratic transition in 1991. Since then, Bangladesh has had democratic governments, with the exception of the recent two-year-long State of Emergency (2007–8) imposed

---

[7] After having declared its independence on 26 March 1971, Bangladesh (the then East Pakistan) formally attained nationhood on 16 December 1971 when the occupying West Pakistani forces surrendered. On Bangladesh's birth history, see, among others, C. Baxter, *Bangladesh: A New Nation in an Old Setting* (Westview Press: Boulder, Colorado; London, 1984) and R. Sisson and L. E. Rose, *War and Secession: Pakistan, India, and the Creation of Bangladesh* (University of California Press: Berkeley, LA; Oxford, 1990). For the international law perspective, see, S. Roy Chowdhury, *The Genesis of Bangladesh* (Asia Publishing House: New York, 1972) and M.R. Islam, *The Bangladesh Liberation Movement: International Legal Implications* (University Press Limited: Dhaka, 1987).

[8] See, Article 141(a) of the Constitution that, along with the preventive detention provisions (Article 33), was introduced through the Constitution (Second Amendment) Act, 1973.

[9] See, the Constitution (Fourth Amendment) Act, 1975 (making, for example, the Supreme Court judges removable without legal process).

by the then non-party caretaker government on the ground of a constitutional crisis.[10] It is against this background of the country's political history that the constitution-enforcing role of its Supreme Court has to be analysed. Also important for this analysis is an understanding of the constitutional normative framework concerning the principles of constitutionalism.

The Constitution of the People's Republic of Bangladesh (hereinafter 'the Constitution'), adopted on 4 November 1972 and given effect from 16 December 1972,[11] has been a revolutionary document based on the supreme sacrifices of the people who liberated Bangladesh.[12] In the context of decolonization of many nations from the late 1960s to early 1970s, it was desirable that the Constitution reaped benefits from the regime of international human rights and global principles of constitutionalism.[13] Predicated upon

[10] The 'non-party' caretaker government (CTG), a system which is now repealed through the 15th Amendment to the Constitution, used to take the charge of State governance following the dissolution of Parliament and for three months principally to oversee the general elections. The CTG-system was introduced through the 13th Amendment to the Constitution in 1996.

[11] Until then, the country was governed by the first basic constituent document, the Proclamation of Independence Order of 10 April 1971 (effective from 26 March 1971), and also by the Provisional Constitution of Bangladesh Order, 1972.

[12] The Constitution was drafted by a thirty-four member Constitution Drafting Committee of the Constituent Assembly comprising 403 members who were elected in the 1970 elections for provincial and central legislative assemblies of the then Pakistan. Starting in mid-April 1972, the drafting committee held more than seventy meetings and several public consultations, after which it finalized the Constitution by early October 1972. After adopting the Constitution (with signatures of Assembly members), the Constituent Assembly went into automatic dissolution. Kamal Hossain, the then law minister and the chairman of the Constitution Drafting Committee, oversaw the drafting process intensely, and he is reported to have borrowed from experiences of foreign constitutionalists. There is a paucity of literature on the history of Bangladesh's constitution-making. But see, Abul Fazl Huq, 'Constitution-making in Bangladesh', *Pacific Affairs*, (1973), 46(1): 59–76; S. Malik, 'Laws of Bangladesh', in A.M. Chowdhury and F. Alam (eds), *Bangladesh: On the Threshold of the Twenty-First Century* (Asiatic Society of Bangladesh: Dhaka, 2002), p. 434.

[13] The known sources of inspiration were the constitutions of the UK, USA, India, and Ireland. Bangladesh adopted the model of constitutionalism that was a mix of the colonial British and American traditions. Interestingly, the fundamental rights provisions of the Constitution relied upon the language of the International Bill of Rights, prominently of the Universal Declaration of Human Rights 1948.

the values of 'the rule of law', 'respect for fundamental human rights and freedom', socialism, and 'equality and justice', the Constitution is what Rizvi calls 'a most remarkable essay on liberal democratic constitutionalism, allowing for popular participation'[14] and inclusion of the marginalized.[15]

The Constitution entrenches the principle of constitutional supremacy (Article 7) and sets out the State goal of social justice. It thus not only provides for a bill of rights with a wide spectrum of fundamental rights but also draws a charter of State duties under the banner of 'Fundamental Principles of State Policy' (FPSPs).[16] The state-policy principles, although not judicially enforceable, provide the normative framework for the governance of the state and law-making.[17] Together with the fundamental rights, they provide 'a reservoir of legal resources' which can be drawn upon by the Court and other institutions of governance to bring about social change.[18] Notably, the Constitution uniquely places the Supreme Court as its guardian, proclaiming the latter's functional independence and ensuring its authority to enforce the Constitution as a normative imperative. Specifically, the High Court Division of the Supreme

[14] G. Rizvi, 'Democracy & Constitutionalism in South Asia: The Bangladesh Experience', the Ash Center for Democratic Governance and Innovation, Harvard University, http://www.innovations.harvard.edu/cache/documents/8644.pdf (last accessed on 25 October 2010), pp. 25–6.

[15] See, for example, Article 28, the equality clause, which enables affirmative State actions. The Constitution adheres to an equitable concept of equality, exempting affirmative State actions for any 'backward section' of citizens from unconstitutionality.

[16] These principles (Articles 8–25), which in effect embody social rights, imposed positive responsibilities on the State, among other things, to pursue a planned economy to secure citizens' basic amenities of life (Article 16).

[17] See, Article 8 of the Constitution. The insertion of these principles into the Constitution as non-enforceable social goals was influenced by similar Indian constitutional provisions on 'directive principles'. For the debate on the normativity of 'principles' of State policy, see, U. Baxi, 'Directive Principles and Sociology of Indian Law', *Journal of the Indian Law Institute*, (1969), 11(3): 245–72.

[18] K. Hossain, 'Interaction of Fundamental Principles of State Policy and Fundamental Rights', in S. Hossain, S. Malik, and B. Musa (eds), *Public Interest Litigation in South Asia: Rights in Search of Remedies* (University Press Limited: Dhaka, 1997), p. 43.

Court[19] is sufficiently empowered to enforce fundamental rights, both horizontally and vertically, through appropriate 'directions or orders',[20] and to enforce legal obligations.[21] The constitutional scheme as a whole clearly envisages a strong form of judicial review of constitutionality, which extends not only over administrative actions, as is sometimes naïvely claimed, but also over legislative acts[22] and constitutional amendments.[23]

It is in light of the above politico-legal context that the present essay develops its arguments by evaluating the Court's performance during several phases of the Bangladesh polity. As will be seen below, judges in Bangladesh at times shunned their responsibility of upholding justice during extra-constitutional and martial law regimes. Except for some notable exceptions, the Court remained exceedingly deferential to the executive and resorted to subjective interpretation of the Constitution. It is true that the judiciary, starting from not long after independence of the country, could not function in a democratic environment for quite a long time. The long absence of democracy had left strains not only on the country's constitutional governance but also on its apex court judges. Not surprisingly, therefore, the Bangladeshi judiciary began to follow active adjudication of constitutional issues only lately.

The judges, particularly during the democratic periods, have, however, largely attempted to create a ground for actions in furtherance

---

[19] Its other and the top division is the Appellate Division, which hears appeals from any order, judgment, and decree of the High Court Division. The Chief Justice of Bangladesh, with a wide range of constitutional administrative powers over the management of the Supreme Court, sits in the Appellate Division. The President appoints the Chief Justice and other judges who are appointed to a particular division. See, especially, Articles 95 and 98 of the Constitution.

[20] Article 102(1) of the Constitution, to be read with Article 44(1).

[21] Article 102(2) of the Constitution.

[22] Article 7 declares that any other law inconsistent with the Constitution shall be void, while Article 26 enjoins the State not to legislate in derogation of fundamental rights, providing that any law other than constitutional amendments (Articles 26(3), 142(2)) made inconsistently with these rights shall be void. It may be noted that the legality of this wholesale ouster of judicial review of constitutional amendments on the ground of breaching fundamental rights is doubtful in light of the basic structure doctrine, discussed in the section 'The Judiciary on Unconstitutional Constitutional Amendments: The Evolution of the 'Basic Structure Doctrine' later in this chapter.

[23] See, *Anwar Hossain Chowdhury,* (1989) BLD (AD) (Special) 1.

of constitutionalism. In a number of high profile cases, the Court has sought to locate the fundamental features of the Constitution within the broader polity and asserted its authority for their defence. As will be seen in this essay, there is a trend of liberal rights jurisprudence and of ameliorative judicial activism most visibly in the area of public interest litigation. What explains the Bangladeshi Court's over-passivity in some cases and assertion in others? Is it the political environment that made the Court ambivalent? Or, is it the judges' legal training, social background, or change in mindset to effectively achieve justice that helped them adopt a new role? The change in the Court's interpretive philosophy and role-perception in recent years can indeed be attributed to all these factors. As the following analysis will further reveal, apart from these factors, there are some external factors that also help to explain the ambivalent judicial role.

Although Bangladeshi judges have often attempted to maintain the specificity of their domestic constitution, they are being increasingly influenced by comparative public law developments elsewhere, notably in the comparable neighbouring jurisdictions.[24] Arguably, the monumental achievement of the Indian public interest jurisprudence has helped them transcend their perception of the traditional judicial role of applying 'the law' as it is. They have adopted a new role in public interest litigation which has, correspondingly, helped the people renew their faith in judicial agency. Also, the globalization process generally and the development of global human rights jurisprudence in particular have had a positive impact on the Court's changed role. Despite the Court's changing role, however, the judiciary has often failed in adequately standing up for the cause of justice, which, as I argue below, may be attributed to the concerned judges' fondness for strict legal positivism, prevailing political dynamics, and other internal and external factors concerning the judiciary.

---

[24] As the court decisions analysed here show, the influence of comparative public law on the apex court judges of Bangladesh has been more real than it appears. See, *Md. Masdar Hossain* v. *Secretary, Ministry of Finance*, (1998) 18 BLD (HCD) at 558. See also, 115. See further, Hoque, *Judicial Activism in Bangladesh*, pp. 237–44. For an instance of the Court's awareness as to the need for preserving the legal–cultural specificity while comparing, see, *Sajeda Parvin* v. *Bangladesh*, (1988) 40 DLR (AD) 178 at 183, refusing to borrow from the Indian Supreme Court's preventive detention jurisprudence which it found 'radically different'.

Following this introduction, the essay analyses the judicial role in the post-Independence era including the martial law periods, and then examines, in the section 'The Judiciary on Unconstitutional Constitutional Amendments', the judicially established landmark doctrine of basic structure. In the next two sections, the role of the judiciary after the new beginning of democracy in 1991, and during and after the 2007–8 Emergency, are assessed. The Court's role in the post-1991 democratic set-up has been viewed through the prism of two very spectacular areas of its action—the phenomenon of public interest litigation (PIL) and the principle of judicial independence. The concluding section refocuses on the idea that the judicial role is context-specific and by reiterating that, although a facilitative support structure is important for a justice-enhancive judicial role, the judges' willingness to remain vigilant and to apply 'the law' creatively may significantly help them achieve justice and protect constitutionalism.

THE JUDICIARY AND CONSTITUTIONALISM: THE FORMATIVE YEARS

The post-Independence judiciary in Bangladesh had an extremely short democratic period within which it had to consolidate its constitutional jurisprudence. The initial Supreme Court was not even granted judicial review that came with the formal adoption of the Constitution.[25] Understandably, therefore, the Court began to abandon, albeit slowly, strict literalism in favour of a legal spirit-based method of interpretation so as to ensure justice by overcoming procedural difficulties and technicalities.[26] Importantly, the Court broke away from retrogressive judicial decisions of erstwhile Pakistan but, in some instances, duly drew upon old decisions that were compatible with the Constitution, although, as we shall see below, pro-establishment decisions of the Pakistani Supreme Court did cast some measure of negative influence upon Bangladeshi judges.[27]

Throughout the democratic regime in the 1970s, the judges remained relatively vigilant against the executive's encroachment on

---

[25] See, Article 4 of the High Court of Bangladesh Order, 1972.

[26] *Kutubuddin* v. *Nurjahan*, (1973) 25 DLR (HCD) at 21.

[27] Upon its birth, Bangladesh inherited Pakistani and the pre-1947 British colonial laws in an adapted form. See, among others, Article 149 of the Constitution guaranteeing the continuity of 'all existing laws' which clearly include not only statutory laws but also judicial laws.

people's fundamental rights. In personal liberty cases, for example, the Court developed a self-awareness of its constitutional duty to safeguard the rights of 'any person', to uphold 'human dignity' and the ideals of a liberal society including the 'due process of law'.[28] In the now famous case of *A. T. Mridha* v. *The State* (1973)[29] concerning the legality of detention of the petitioner under a law that precluded Court challenges of actions taken thereunder, the Court made the bold pronouncement that its constitutional supervisory power could not be ousted by a sub-constitutional legislation.[30]

The benchmark decision during the formative years was *Kazi Mukhlesur Rahman* v. *Bangladesh* (1974).[31] In this case an advocate challenged the constitutionality of the Bangladesh–India Treaty of 16 May 1974 involving exchange of territories. The High Court Division turned down his petition on the ground of his having no 'standing'. On appeal, the Appellate Division took a broader view that 'the question of *locus standi* does not involve the court's jurisdiction',[32] thereby distinguishing 'standing' from 'justiciability'. The Court heard the petitioner as he was vindicating an important constitutional issue affecting the rights of the general public.[33] The decision represents one of the few leading cases that have introduced rights-based arguments in Bangladeshi judicial discourse, leading the Court to recognize the abstract or public interest judicial review as well as the reviewability of international treaties implicating constitutional rights.

During the period of extra-constitutional regimes (1975–90), the judiciary largely faced a crisis of existence. This long period is marked by judicial passivity and, in some cases, unjustifiable judicial abdication of the responsibility of pursuing justice. During this period, there was indeed a judicial oscillation between occasional

---

[28] *A. T. Mridha* v. *The State*, (1973) 25 DLR (HCD) at 335, 338. See another striking case: *Aruna Sen* v. *Bangladesh*, (1975) 27 DLR (HCD) at 12 (holding that detention of any person without observing constitutional processes is unlawful).

[29] (1973) 25 DLR (HCD) at 335.

[30] Ibid., at 350. The Appellate Division reversed this decision on a narrow technical ground in *Solicitor, Govt. of Bangladesh* v. *A. T. Mridha*, (1974) 26 DLR (AD) at 17.

[31] (1974) 26 DLR (AD) at 44 (known as the *Berubari* case).

[32] Ibid., at 52, *per* Sayem, CJ.

[33] Ibid., at 51–2.

preservation of authority and submission to the 'non-law',[34] that is, martial law. In an infamous decision in *Halima Khatun* v. *Bangladesh* (1978), Justice Munim glorified the martial law proclamation that conditioned, but not wholly suspended, the Constitution. The Court held that the Constitution 'lost its character as [the] supreme law of the country'.[35] In refusing to give remedy to the claimant who challenged appropriation of her property as an abandoned property, Justice Munim found a 'total ouster' of the Court's jurisdiction by the martial law, reasoning that as a judge it was his 'duty' 'to administer a "harsh" or even an unjust law'.[36] Although the Court later tried and sought to mete out minimum justice by way of interpreting the martial law regulations and other laws a little liberally,[37] its performances until the democratic restoration in 1991 remained largely regressive and deficient in justice-consciousness.

During the period before 1991, the singularly exceptional area of judicial protective activity was that of personal liberty. Following the Special Powers Act 1974 that provided for preventive detentions without trial, hundreds of thousands of people became victims of this arbitrary law. Moreover, the first martial law regime (1975–9) combined with Emergency coexisted with the Constitution, thus creating considerable confusion about judicial review. When approached by detainees, the Court took more or less a proactive interpretational approach to the harsh laws. There have been, however, instances of both evasion and creativity, with the Court travelling from mechanistic application of the law[38] to a relatively more liberal course of constitutional or legal interpretation.[39]

---

[34] Justice Rahman's phrase in *Anwar Hossain Chowdhury*, (1989) BLD (AD) (Special) 1 at 180.

[35] (1978) 30 DLR (AD) at 207, 210.

[36] Ibid. In *Sultan Ahmed* v. *Chief Election Commissioner*, (1978) 30 DLR (HCD) at 291, 296, the martial law was termed as 'the supreme law of the land'.

[37] See, for example, the dissenting opinion of Sobhan, J, in *State* v. *Joynal Abedin*, (1980) 32 DLR (AD) at 110, arguing for the availability of judicial review when martial law courts were *corum non judice* or acted beyond their constituting legislation.

[38] See, *Ahmed Nazir* v. *Bangladesh*, (1975) 27 DLR (HCD) at 199, 211 (Munim, J. quite quickly found a 'valid order' of detention, without engaging with the legal questions involved).

[39] In *Karnaphuli Rayon and Chemicals Ltd* v. *Bangladesh*, (1976) 28 DLR (AD) at 116, for example, the Appellate Division held that it had the power even to

In a long series of preventive detention cases where the Court held in favour of the detainees, it refused to adopt the Indian practice of 'subjective satisfaction test' but rather insisted that the government's decision to detain any person must pass judicial examination of objectivity.[40] By way of another example, in a significantly bold assertion of judicial authority, the Court in *Sahar Ali* v. *A.R. Chowdhury* (1980),[41] which concerned Section 30 of the Special Powers Act 1974 that barred 'any court' from revising any order or judgment of special tribunals established under this Act, famously held that its constitutional supervisory power could not be ousted. This welcome instance of judicial interpretive activism ultimately triggered legislative removal of the illegality.

Despite these few instances of upholding the principle of legality, the Bangladeshi judiciary, on the whole, abdicated its constitutional responsibility of protecting the rule of law during the martial law regimes and largely became a partner of usurpers of the Constitution.[42]

THE JUDICIARY ON UNCONSTITUTIONAL CONSTITUTIONAL AMENDMENTS: THE EVOLUTION OF THE 'BASIC STRUCTURE DOCTRINE'

There has been a heated debate as to whether the judiciary should be the final arbiter of any given constitution. It is often said that popular sovereignty finds its expression in the elected organ of the state, the legislature, and that judicial invalidation of any change to the constitution brought by the legislature would be illegitimate and an affront to popular sovereignty.[43] By contrast, opposing arguments are

---

modify the language used in a statute if the literal interpretation thereof leads to injustice.

[40] See, the leading case of *Abdul Latif Mirza* v. *Govt. of Bangladesh*, (1979) DLR (AD) at 1.

[41] (1980) 32 DLR (HCD) at 142. For similar decisions, see, *Lutfur Rahman* v. *Election Commissioner*, (1975) 27 DLR (HCD) at 278; *Humayun Kabir* v. *The State*, (1976) 28 DLR (HCD) at 259.

[42] See, S.H.R. Karzon and A.A. Faruque, 'Martial Law, Judiciary and Judges: Towards an Assessment of Judicial Interpretations', *Bangladesh Journal of Law*, (1999), 3(2): 181–210.

[43] See, among many works, Gary J. Jacobsohn, 'An Unconstitutional Constitution? A Comparative Perspective', *International Journal of Constitutional Law*, (2006), 4: 46–87.

often made in favour of judicial review of constitutional amendments for the sake of preserving the constitution itself. These debates entered Bangladeshi legal discourse in the late 1980s when in an epoch-making decision in *Anwar Hossain Chowdhury* v. *Bangladesh* (1989),[44] the apex court invalidated the 8th Amendment to the Constitution of Bangladesh, holding that Parliament's amendatory power is subject to un-alterability of 'basic structures' of the Constitution.

In entrenching the now famous 'basic structure doctrine',[45] the Appellate Division in this case held that Parliament's amending power under the Constitution is 'limited' in that this is a 'derivative' constituent power[46] and hence cannot be exercised to alter or destroy its 'basic structures'. The Court was seemingly motivated to uphold the greater public interest and the nation's founding mottos of constitutionalism and democracy.

The then military authority by various martial law regulations diffused the High Court Division into seven permanent benches, and later constitutionalized this change by amending Article 100 of the Constitution, the constitutionality of which was challenged by some lawyers. The petitioners successfully argued that the High Court Division's plenary judicial power over the whole Republic was part of the basic structure of the Constitution which was unalterable even by a constitutional amendment.[47] In a three-to-one majority judgment, the Court adopted a holistic mode of interpretation and concluded that Parliament with unlimited amending power is an anathema to constitutional supremacy, a basic pillar of the Constitution.

[44] (1989) BLD (AD) (Special) 1.

[45] The doctrine is now entrenched in India, Bangladesh, Nepal (in the 1990 Constitution), Sri Lanka (see, *Re 19th Amendment to the Constitution*, (2003) 4 LRC 290 (SC)), and Pakistan (see, *Al-Jehad Trust* v. *Federation of Pakistan*, PLD (1996) SC 324; *Zafar Ali Shah* v. *General Parvez Musharraf*, PLD (2000) SC 869; *Wasim Sajjad* v. *Pakistan*, PLD (2001) SC 233; *Sindh High Court Bar Association*, (2009), below note 150). Also notable is the South African Constitutional Court's indication that it might not consider valid an amendment radically restructuring the Constitution's 'fundamental premises' (*United Democratic Movement* v. *President*, (2003) 4 LRC 98 (CC)).

[46] (1989) BLD (AD) (Special) 1, *per* Ahmed and Chowdhury, JJ, at pp. 143, 83.

[47] See opinions of Chowdhury, Ahmed, and Rahman, JJ, ibid., at 83, 156–7, 174.

Despite its several shortcomings and ambivalence in the reasoning of the majority judges,[48] the *Eighth Amendment* decision continues to remain the boldest ever instance of judicial activism in pursuit of constitutionalism in the Bangladeshi polity. The judges, by and large, were alert to the need for protecting 'the fundamental aim' of society, that is, the rule-of-law–based governance, from destruction.[49] As it now appears, they sought to locate and preserve what leading Indian scholars have called 'stateness'[50] or 'self-identity'[51] of the State. In solidifying the basic constitutional premise and 'self-identity' of their nation, the judges predicated their reasoning upon comparative public law besides taking moral–legal guidance from their own Constitution.[52]

It seems that the Court's conclusion was greatly informed and influenced by the famous Indian decision in *Kesavananda Bharati v. State of Kerala* (1973) that first authoritatively established in the common law world the doctrine of inviolability of the 'basic structure' of the Constitution.[53] It seems that, but for this strong persuasive decision from a powerful neighbouring jurisdiction it would be extremely difficult, if not impossible, for the Bangladeshi Court to produce such a structurally radical decision. Like the *Kesavananda*

[48] Two majority judges, for example, took a highly controversial view that a constitutional amendment is not a 'law' within the meaning of Article 7(2) of the Constitution. See, (1989) BLD (AD) (Special) 1.

[49] See, (1989) BLD (AD) (Special) 1, at p. 160, *per* Rahman, J.

[50] See, R. Sudarshan, '"Stateness" and Democracy in India's Constitution', in Z. Hasan, E. Sridharan, and R. Sridarshan (eds), *India's Living Constitution: Ideas, Practices, Controversies* (Permanent Black: New Delhi, 2002), pp. 159–78.

[51] See in this volume, Chapter 6 (Gary Jacobsohn and Shylashri Shankar, 'Constitutional Borrowing in South Asia') and Chapter 2 (Sujit Choudhry, 'How to Do Comparative Constitutional Law').

[52] In an interesting study in Chapter 6 of this volume, Jacobsohn and Shankar have shown that the Indian judges' concerns about 'the character of the polity', that is, their willingness to defend the 'constitutional identity', have led not to the rejection but to learning from comparable foreign materials. The Bangladeshi judges' reliance in *Anwar Hosain Chowdhury* on the Indian case of *Kesavananda* seems to be motivated by a similar sense of preserving constitutional identity.

[53] (1973) 4 SCR 225. Fascinatingly, counsel Kamal Hossain in *Anwar Hossain Chowdhury*, at 168, traced the genesis of the notion of un-alterability of a 'fundamental feature of the Constitution' to a 1963 decision of the then Dhaka High Court in *M. Abdul Huq v. Fazlul Quader Chowdhury*, (1963) 15 DLR (Dacca) at 355 (affirmed in PLD (1963) SC 486).

Court, the majority judges in *Anwar Hossain Chowdhury* could not reach a consensus as to the features which should be considered basic structural pillars of the Constitution.[54] Interestingly, there grew a consensus that there should be some basic features beyond the reach of Parliament's amending power. Even the opposing counsel and the dissenting judge did not rule out the existence of certain structural pillars.[55]

There are criticisms, both academic and political, of the basic structure doctrine, which are largely grounded in the passion for public sovereignty and public participation in democracy. These accusations are mostly akin to general criticisms against judicial activism,[56] and they tend to ignore that the basic structure doctrine did not intend to put any clog on Parliament's constituent or legislative power, far less on the people's power. It simply erected a bulwark against the destruction of one or more of the basic features of the Constitution, preservation of which was very much intended by its framers. In his judgment, Justice S. Ahmed poignantly observed that people's sovereignty is susceptible to attack and denial under many devices by the holders of power. Aware of the political realities prevalent in society, the judge rightly thought that such a bar on Parliament's amending power is 'an effective guarantee against frequent amendments of the Constitution in sectarian and party interest'.[57]

Critics of the basic structure doctrine often ignore the reality that even most activist judges conform to the 'dictate of conscience'

---

[54] Nor was it perhaps necessary for them to provide an exhaustive check list on such a delicate issue. Rahman, J, took a pragmatic approach to the determination of basic structures of the Constitution, deferring the task to the future. He, however, considered the rule of law as one component (p. 174), while S. Ahmed, J. (p. 156) identified eight overlapping features as part of the basic structure, from popular sovereignty to judicial independence to fundamental rights.

[55] Afzal, J., the lone dissenting voice, conceded (pp. 212–13) that in the name of amendment 'the Constitution cannot be destroyed'.

[56] For a view that, by 'constitutional theory' the Court lacked power to invalidate the 8th Amendment, see, I. Omar and Z. Hossain, '*Coup d' etat*, Constitution and Legal Continuity', *Law and Our Rights, The Daily Star*, (17 and 28 September 2005), Issue Nos 207 and 208, Parts 1 and 2.

[57] *Anwar Hossain Chowdhury,* (1989) BLD (AD) (Special) 1 at 256, *per* Ahmed, J. See also the reasoning of Rahman, J., who thinks that the doctrine is needed to tackle the excessive majoritarianism in the legislature (p. 169).

and tend to defer to the representative organs of the state when deference is due while examining the constitutionality of a law or constitutional amendment.[58] In basic structure challenges, the apex court judges in Bangladesh have by and large shown due deference to other coordinate state organs, although the danger of misusing the doctrine is always there. To note an exception, the recent judicial invalidation of the 13th Amendment to the Constitution, that incorporated the caretaker government system, can be seen as an inappropriate application of the doctrine resulting from the Court's misreading of the Constitution improperly, excluding the specificities of local politics.[59]

In the historic case of *Bangladesh Italian Marble Works Ltd v. Bangladesh* (2005),[60] which has come to be known as the *5th Amendment* case, the High Court Division declared unconstitutional the Constitution (Fifth Amendment) Act that gave constitutional protection to the first martial law regime and its actions and laws. The Court termed the martial law regime and several changes brought into the Constitution by martial law a 'grave' constitutional wrong and held that these exercises destroyed several basic features of the Constitution. It held that 'martial law' is unknown to the Constitution, let alone its having the authority to enable changes

---

[58] See, for example, *Farida Akhter and Others* v. *Bangladesh*, (2007) 15 BLT (AD) at 206 (finding constitutional the reservation of seats for women in Parliament, an exception introduced in 1972). By contrast, judges have duly invoked and applied the doctrine for the preservation of constitutionalism. See, *Khondker Delwar Hossain* v. *Bangladesh Italian Marble Works Ltd.*, (2010) 62 DLR (AD) at 298 and *Siddique Ahmed* v. *Bangladesh*, (2011) 33 BLD (HCD) at 84 in which the Court declared unconstitutional respectively the 5th and the 7th Amendments that legitimized martial law. The doctrine was also relied on in *Ruhul Quddus* v. *Justice M.A. Aziz*, (2009) ((2000) 52 DLR (AD) 82 (judgment 2 December 1999)). See further, S.H.R. Karzon and A.A. Faruque, 'Martial Law Regimes: Critically Situating the Validity of the Fifth and Seventh Amendments', *Bangladesh Journal of Law*, (1998), 2(2): 152–92.

[59] *M. Saleem Ullah* v. *Bangladesh*, Appellate Division decision of 10 May 2011 (which is an appeal from *M. Saleem Ullah* v. *Bangladesh*, (2005) 57 DLR (HCD) 171 in which the High Court Division held that 'non-party caretaker government' did not breach any basic structure but rather strengthened democracy). The full judgment of the Appellate Division has been written a year after the interim/brief judgment, and, as of August 2012, has not been made public.

[60] (2006) BLT (Special) (HCD) 1 (judgment 29 August 2005).

to the Constitution.[61] There are some weaknesses in the Court's reasoning, especially in its stance of sustaining the legality of some changes and of rejecting the other changes to the Constitution brought about by martial law fiats. Undeniably, this decision, later endorsed by the Appellate Division,[62] is a bold assertion against unconstitutional usurpation of state powers and, arguably, had acted as a deterrent to a likely military takeover during or before the 2007 Emergency. The decision in the *5th Amendment* case seems to have compensated in some way for the Court's earlier failing to discard martial law. As seen above, the Court mostly surrendered its autonomy and judgment to the executive, a legacy that until this decision kept the Court's post-1990 activism under a cloud.[63] Inspired by the *5th Amendment* decisions, the High Court Division has most recently declared unconstitutional the 7th Constitutional Amendment that legitimized the second martial law regime.[64]

A NEW JUDICIAL ROLE AFTER DEMOCRATIC TRANSITION (1991–2006)

The emergence of a new constitutional environment after the fall of the autocratic regime in 1990 led to the renewal of public faith, both in constitutionalism and in the judiciary.[65] The post-1990 Court came to be increasingly activated by a growing critical section of the public with a diverse range of causes, most often espoused through PIL. The judges, too, seemed sensitized about the need for

---

[61] Compare the Pakistani case of *Sindh High Court Bar Association* (2009), footnote 151. For a note on the *5th Amendment* case, see, R. Hoque, 'On *Coup d' Etat,* Constitutionalism, and the Need to Break the Subtle Bondage with Alien Legal Thought: A Reply to Omar and Hossain', *Law and Our Rights, The Daily Star,* (29 October 2005), Issue No. 213.

[62] See, *Khondker Delwar Hossain,* footnote 58.

[63] In some cases, for example, the post-1990 Court refused to review the legality of actions by past martial law administrators on the unjustifiable ground that those were protected by constitutional amendments. See, *Abdur Rashid Sarker* v. *Bangladesh,* (1996) 48 DLR (AD) at 99; *Shah Mohammad* v. *Secretary to the President,* (1996) 1 BLC (HCD) at 8.

[64] *Siddique Ahmed* v. *Bangladesh,* (2011) 33 BLD (HCD) at 84.

[65] M.H. Rahman, 'The Role of the Judiciary in the Developing Societies: Maintaining a Balance', *Law and International Affairs,* (1988), 11(1–2): 1–10.

protecting the public interest and enforcing constitutional justice, especially for those who continued to remain underprivileged and discriminated against.[66] During the post-autocratic regime, one saw a wave of constitutional judicial activism in Bangladesh, marking a significant paradigm shift driven by creative judicial interpretation and inspired by the judges' self-realization about their past failings during martial law regimes.[67]

In this period, the Court has built on its rights-protective personal liberty jurisprudence. In particular, it has sought to constrain the irrational use of the prevention detention law, but with little success in stopping abuses of the detention laws. In *Bilkis Akhter Hossain* v. *Bangladesh* (1997),[68] for example, the High Court Division held the government liable in damages for arbitrary detention of some political leaders, an appeal against which has remained on the dock of the Appellate Division for the last fifteen years. At the level of protection of fundamental rights, there have also been many new developments, especially in the field of right to life and good governance. For example, initiatives have begun towards constructing a theory of constitutional tort to check abuses of public power,[69] alongside the development of what is now a mature trend of self-initiated (*suo motu*) judicial interventions often directed towards removing illegality from the country's criminal justice system.[70]

---

[66] For example, it made interventions in the area of gender equality. See, for example, *Shamima Sultana Seema* v. *Bangladesh*, (2005) 57 DLR (HCD) at 201, quashing the allocation of differentiated functions to women commissioners of a local government body elected for the 'reserved seats'.

[67] See, for example, the decision in *Bangladesh Italian Marble Works Ltd*, (2005), above footnote 60, in which the Court virtually admitted to its abdication of responsibility during the martial law regimes.

[68] (1997) 17 BLD (HCD) at 344.

[69] See, for example, *Mohammed Ali* v. *Bangladesh*, (2003) 23 BLD (HCD) 389, perhaps the only case to have ordered public law damages for unlawful searches.

[70] See the landmark, first ever *suo motu* decision in *State* v. *Deputy Commissioner, Satkhira*, (1993) 45 DLR (HCD) at 643 in which the High Court Division ordered the release of an unlawfully detained person who had languished in jail for twelve long years with bar fetters tied to his legs since he was first arrested at the age of nine. On *suo motu* judicial interventions, see, R. Hoque, '*Suo motu* Jurisdiction as a Tool of Activist Judging: A Survey of Relevant Issues and Constructing a Sensible Defence', *Chittagong University Journal of Law*, (2003), 8: 1–31.

The post-1990 judiciary became persistently critical of wanton misuses of the exercise of its power to arrest by the police and other forms of police brutalities and excesses,[71] although little could be achieved in terms of effecting a change in the government's behaviour.[72] In the most prominent case in this field, the Court in *BLAST & Others* v. *Bangladesh* (2003)[73] handed down a ground-breaking judgment issuing directions and guidelines with a view to stopping largely unchecked police brutalities and custodial deaths. The Court was activated by a public interest group that had long been seeking to combat unconstitutional police practices. In this case, the Court forcefully underlined the need to do away with existing legal inconsistencies and ensure conformity with constitutional safeguards against torture and unlawful arrest, and formulated certain strategies and policies to regulate the arresting power of the police under the widely-framed Section 54 of the Criminal Procedure Code as well as to condition the magistrates' power to remand an accused person to the police. Unfortunately, however, an appeal against this rights-enhancive decision has since remained pending before the Appellate Division.

Notably, the new-found judicial assertiveness has by and large preserved the institutional balance, by strategically engaging with other branches of government, particularly on issues of wider political ramifications.[74] Unlike its previous role,[75] the Court now seemed prepared to enter into a democratic dialogue with the representative organ of the State, while at times remaining essentially passive on complex political issues such as the legality of *hartal* (political

---

[71] See, for example, *Saifuzzaman* v. *State*, (2004) 56 DLR (HCD) at 324.

[72] Both lack of further strong judicial vigilance and the executive's defiance of court decisions are responsible for this.

[73] (2003) 23 BLD (HCD) at 115.

[74] See, for example, *Najmul Huda, MP* v. *Secretary, Cabinet Division*, (1997) 2 BLC (HCD) at 414 (holding as justiciable the legality of a technocrat minister's speech on a matter unrelated to his portfolio).

[75] See, for example, *M/S Dulichand Omraolal* v. *Bangladesh*, (1981) 1 BLD (AD) at 1, 7, in which the Court shied away from the issue of legitimacy of Yahya Khan's regime, terming it as a 'political question', and thus ignoring even the Pakistani decision in *Asma Jilani* v. *Punjab*, PLD (1972) SC at 139 adjudging General Yahya's military rule as unconstitutional.

strikes).[76] In the first-ever constitutional reference by the President,[77] the Appellate Division refused to relinquish its advisory jurisdiction regarding the issue of the legality of long-drawn boycotting of Parliament, an exercise of which was argued by the opponents to have the effect of dragging the Court into politics. The Court advised the President that boycotting of Parliament by opposition members for a consecutive period of ninety days rendered their seats vacant.[78] By doing so, the Court clearly refused to uncritically accept the American doctrine of political question,[79] thereby showing its willingness to intervene in furtherance of the cause of constitutionalism.[80]

The strategy of cautious or what can be called passive judicial activism was perhaps most strikingly exercised in a 1992 decision in *Kudrat-E-Elahi Panir* v. *Bangladesh*[81] which concerned local-level governance. In this case, the petitioner challenged a law which abolished a local government unit, arguing that the law breached the constitutional mandate (Articles 9, 11, and 59–60) for elected local government bodies at every administrative unit. The petitioner's argument was also built around a few fundamental constitutional principles of State policy that sought to entrench democracy in the polity. The Appellate Division refused to strike down the law, reasoning that the legislature could pass such a law abolishing any particular tier of local government, and observed that it lacked authority to enforce the principles of state policy.

[76] In *Khondaker Modarresh Elahi* v. *Bangladesh*, (2001) 21 BLD (HCD) at 352, 375, the Court thought that the 'political issue' of *hartal* (strikes) 'should in all fairness be decided by the politicians'.

[77] *Constitutional Reference No. 1 of 1995 by the President* (1995) III BLT (Spl.) at 159.

[78] Article 67(1)(b) of the Constitution provides that if any Member of Parliament remains 'absent' from Parliament for such a period his or her seat would become vacant.

[79] In *Presidential Constitutional Reference No. 1,* above footnote 77, Afzal, CJ held: 'There is no magic in the phrase "political question". While maintaining judicial restraint the Court…can pronounce on an issue which may be dubbed as a political question.' (p. 173).

[80] See another decision of the High Court Division (2 November 2008) in *M.A. Mannan* v. *Bangladesh*, (2008), holding that it could go beyond the doctrine of political question so as to adjudicate politics-inspired constitutional issues such as the delimitation of constituencies.

[81] (1992) 44 DLR (AD) at 319.

In a trend-setting judgment, however, the Court set out to further the constitutional mandate for participatory local-level democracy. It held that the government had an obligation to make all existing local government laws compatible with the Constitution, and ordered elections to the existing local bodies within six months, bearing in mind the principle of special representation of women enshrined in Article 9 of the Constitution. This type of technical enforcement of non-justiciable fundamental principles of State policy signifies strategic judicial activism, launching a creative dialogue with the executive and the legislature. In a mixed response to this decision, the legislature thereafter enacted laws providing for election to city corporations with the provision of special representation of women.

Although the Court has not clearly articulated this, it has sought to craft a public law model of judicial review underpinned by 'pragmatic policy judgments'.[82] This expansion has taken place both within and beyond the sphere of public interest jurisprudence. In some decisions the Court resorted to the common law doctrine of public trust in order to remind the duty-bearers of the state that the powers they exercise are a trust reposed by the general public on them.[83] An early expression of this awareness by the Court was in *Kudrat-E-Elahi Panir* v. *Bangladesh* (1992),[84] in which the Appellate Division held that the President's satisfaction as to the existence of justifying circumstances warranting promulgation of an ordinance is not beyond the scope of judicial review. This holding was a breakthrough in the history of constitutional jurisprudence in that the President's ordinance-making power in Bangladesh has been a potential source of violence

---

[82] D.M. Driesen, 'Standing for Nothing: The Paradox of Demanding Concrete Context for Formalist Adjudication', *Cornell Law Review*, (2004), 89(4): 890.

[83] See, *BLAST* v. *Bangladesh*, (2008) 60 DLR (HCD) 176 (judgment 27 April 2006) (directing a government department to realize within six months a huge amount of arrear telephone bills from some 427 members of Parliament). The public trust doctrine was applied, for example, in *M. Saleem Ullah* v. *Bangladesh*, (2005) 57 DLR (HCD) at 171, and *Motiar Rahman* v. *Govt. of Bangladesh*, (2005) 57 DLR (HCD) at 327. The doctrine has also been invoked in other South Asian jurisdictions to ensure fair exercise of public power. See, for example, the Sri Lankan decision in *Premachandra* v. *Major Montague Jayawickrema*, (1994) 2 Sri LR at 90.

[84] (1992) 44 DLR (AD) at 319.

to constitutional democracy.[85] Following the above dictum, the High Court Division in the first-ever decision of its type in *Pirjada Syed Shariatullah* v. *Bangladesh* (2009)[86] invalidated an ordinance for not having been necessitated by circumstances. As the Court reasoned, the President's ordinance-making power must closely conform to the Constitution.[87]

Judicial review has been extended to new areas such as executive leverage concerning foreign relations and governmental inactions impinging on fundamental rights, and to legal issues implicating policy decisions where the wider concerns of constitutionalism have been found to be at stake.[88] For example, when legal issues involving the government's energy policy reached its docket, the Court went as far as to bar the government from exporting gas until the disposal of the case(s).[89] Similarly, in *Abdul Gafur* v. *Secretary, Ministry of Foreign Affairs* (1997), the Court invoked the constitutional legal protection clause (Article 31) and the constitutional right to life (Article 32) while imposing on the foreign office a positive duty to initiate diplomatic efforts to track and repatriate a female child trafficking victim later found detained in Kolkata.[90]

On a negative note, the Court can be critiqued for not extending the enforcement of fundamental rights horizontally. The public law style of adjudication demands the piercing of the narrow divide between private and public activity when the enforcement of public

---

[85] M. H Rahman, 'Our Experience with Constitutionalism', *Bangladesh Journal of Law*, (1988), 2(2): 126.

[86] (2009) 61 (DLR) (HCD) 647.

[87] Invalidating the Muslim Marriages and Divorces (Registration) (Amendment) Ordinance 2008, on the ground that its promulgation was not indispensable for the discharge of the caretaker government's duties.

[88] Interestingly, the Court shies away from recognizing that it can engage with policy issues. See, *Younus Mia* v. *Ministry of Public Works*, (1993) 45 DLR (HCD) at 498; *Dr Mohiuddin Farooque* v. *Bangladesh*, (1998) 50 DLR (HCD) at 84, 97 (there should be no judicial say regarding policy matters).

[89] See, for example, *Shah Mohammad Hannan* v. *Bangladesh,* Writ Petition (WP) No. 2052/1998 (interim order of 5 December 2001).

[90] (1997) 17 BLD (HCD) at 453. In another case, *Ain o Salish Kendra* v. *Bangladesh* (WP No. 6409/ 2008), the Court issued a *rule* asking the government to explain why the failing of the concerned ministries to ensure safe migration of workers should not be considered a breach of legal duty.

responsibilities and constitutional values are in question. By this standard, the Bangladeshi Court has been failing effectively to enforce constitutional rights and ethos against private individuals or entities.[91] The Court's reluctance to apply fundamental rights horizontally, although there is some measure of indirect horizontality, does not quite match either the letter or the spirit of Article 102(1) of the Constitution that makes fundamental rights enforceable against 'any person'.

Alongside the above-mentioned trend of judicial defence of constitutionalism, the Bangladeshi Court has sometimes revealed its close attachment to rigid Anglo-American legal notions, un-conducive for justice in the local context. For instance, the Court in a number of cases refused to invalidate laws only because they were harsh and arbitrary.[92] A more telling example of judicial indifference with damaging effects on judicial craftsmanship in achieving standards of constitutionalism is the case of *State* v. *Sukur Ali* (2004).[93] In this case, the High Court Division confirmed a death conviction imposed on a minor boy for the offence of rape and murder, reasoning that despite its will, it could not defy the language of the concerned special statute that provided for the mandatory death penalty for 'any person' guilty of the offence.[94] This is a questionable interpretation of the law which the Appellate Division later endorsed. It is submitted that the decisions of the two Courts fall far behind the norms and spirit of the Constitution.[95]

---

[91] In *Anwar Hossain* v. *Mainul Hosein*, (2006) 58 DLR (AD) at 229, the Appellate Division refused to enforce fundamental rights against private individuals, overruling the High Court Division in *Mainul Hosein* v. *Anwar Hossain*, (2006) 58 DLR (HCD) at 117, 157.

[92] *Bangladesh Krishi Bank* v. *Meghna Enterprise*, (1998) 50 DLR (AD) at 194. See also, *Bangladesh Retd. Govt. Employees' Welfare Association* v. *Bangladesh*, (1999) 51 DLR (AD) at 121 (the Court would not strike down a law as being shocking to conscience unless it clearly violates the Constitution).

[93] (2004) 9 BLC (HCD) at 238.

[94] See, Section 6(2) of the Suppression of Violence against Women and Children (Special Provisions) Act 1995 (the Act was later repealed in 2000).

[95] See further, R. Hoque, 'Criminal Law and the Constitution: The Relationship Revisited', *Bangladesh Journal of Law*, (November 2007), Special Issue: 45–78. See, however, *The State* v. *Md. Roushan Mondal Hashem*, (2007) 4 LG (HCD) at 12, rejecting the fallacious argument made in *Sukur Ali*.

Ironically, this kind of deplorable judicial escapism lent an impetus to the ongoing legal activism by civil-society members. In *BLAST* v. *Bangladesh* (2010),[96] a legal provision that was relied on for awarding a death sentence to a minor boy was challenged in 2005 by citing its incompatibility with the principle of constitutional supremacy and the fundamental right to life. The High Court Division in its 2010 judgment declared the concerned legal provision unconstitutional for prescribing the mandatory death penalty for the offence of 'rape and murder', but without altering or nullifying the death sentence already awarded to the minor offender.[97] The Court was probably concerned with prospective invalidation of the impugned law and, arguably, followed legal technicalities, leaving the issue for the Appellate Division. It seems that this cautiousness actually disguises studious avoidance of the issue of unjustness of the death penalty already awarded to the minor convict.

Public Interest Litigation and Constitutionalism

Following the hard-earned entrenchment of public interest litigation into the country's legal system in 1996,[98] PIL has since been increasingly used as a tool for achieving constitutionalism through litigation. The opening up of PIL, which has achieved both practical achievements and normative social impact, was the fruit of a sustained pressure of comparative developments elsewhere, particularly in

[96] (2010) 30 BLD (HCD) at 194.

[97] The Court drew insights from the Indian case of *Mithu* v. *State of Punjab*, (1983) 2 SCC at 277, invalidating Section 303 of the Indian Penal Code 1860 for prescribing mandatory death penalty for a convict for murder serving life imprisonment. An appeal has been made against the High Court Division's decision, and it seems that Sukur Ali, who has been in death row for the last eleven years, will have to wait further.

[98] See, *Dr. Mohiuddin Farooque* v. *Bangladesh*, (1997) 17 BLD (AD) at 1 (granting, for the first time, standing to an organization to challenge a flood action project). Unlike in India, the PIL movement in Bangladesh had not been steered by the judges. Rather, the activist lawyers needed to work hard to make the judiciary break away from the colonial jurisprudential inhibitions. On PIL, see generally, N. Ahmed, *Public Interest Litigation in Bangladesh: Constitutional Issues and Remedies* (BLAST: Dhaka, 1999); R. Hoque, 'Taking Justice Seriously: Judicial Public Interest and Constitutional Activism in Bangladesh', *Contemporary South Asia*, (2006), 15 (4): 399–422.

India,[99] although it was based on the Court's autochthonous style of constitutional interpretation fed by the dynamics of constitutional values such as 'justice' and the rule of law.

Starting off with collective rights and environmental justice, the Court in PIL cases has shown activism vis-à-vis a wide array of issues such as child health, protection of the homeless (slum dwellers), preservation of public parks or rivers, and public health[100] and hygiene. In some cases of a mixed genre, combining political rights claims and greater constitutional principles, the Court zealously guarded judicial independence; sought to promote electoral political culture[101] and ensure grassroot-level participation in democracy; acted to stop police brutalities; attempted to prevent sexual harassment at workplaces and educational institutions; checked corruption by state executives; and protected the rights of vulnerable people.

Interestingly, environmental justice seems to have drawn the Court's most intensive attention. In a long series of cases, the Court has proactively indulged in exercises directed towards the protection of the environment, mostly by issuing innovative remedies such as obliging the concerned government agency to make rolling reports of progress or by binding the government with specific positive obligations or by framing 'obligatory' guidelines. For example, a recent court action resulted in a string of government actions towards improving the conditions of four exceedingly polluted rivers surrounding Dhaka.[102]

---

[99] On cross-national influences in the development of PIL in South Asia, see, Arun. K. Thiruvengadam, 'In Pursuit of "the Common Illumination of Our house": Trans-judicial Influence and the Origins of PIL Jurisprudence in South Asia', *Indian Journal of Constitutional Law*, (2008), 2: 68–103.

[100] See, for example, *Prof. Nurul Islam and Others* v. *Bangladesh*, (2000) 52 DLR (HCD) at 413 (imposing a ban on advertisements of cigarettes in furtherance of the general public's 'right to life').

[101] See, for example, *Abdul Momen Chowdhury and Others* v. *Election Commission*, WP No. 2561 of 2005 (binding the Election Commission to require all electoral candidates to furnish information on eight counts covering issues such as their past criminal records), and *Kazi Mamnur Rashid* v. *Bangladesh*, (2009) 61 DLR (HCD) at 433 (underlining the government's duty to make the Election Commission 'independent').

[102] *Human Rights and Peace for Bangladesh* v. *Bangladesh*, (2009) 14 BLC (HCD) 759. (Affirmed in *City Sugar Industries* v. *HRPB*, (2010) 62 DLR (AD) at 428.)

Like the environmental PIL cases, most PILs in the initial stage focused on the goal of social justice, attempting to enforce what can be called collective or socio-economic rights through enforcing statutory duties or/and constitutional rights, notably the 'right to life'.[103] While judicial social rights activism in Bangladesh remains rudimentary and lags well behind activist instances, particularly of the Indian Court, the volume of constitutionalism-inspired PIL cases has increased significantly in recent times. The Court in these cases seems to have become attuned to the need for upholding the supremacy of the constitution and enacting justice vis-à-vis myriad forms of un-constitutionalism. For example, in a famous action, the Court invalidated the governmental permission granted to a foreign private company to construct a container-terminal at the Chittagong Port on the ground of non-transparency in public decision-making.[104] In some other notable actions, the Court invalidated a 'local government law' that undermined the principle of representative governance;[105] directed the government to establish special courts in the Chittagong Hill Tracts region for the protection of women and children;[106] voided a provision of mandatory death penalty;[107] and required the police on one occasion to submit to it fortnightly reports of the investigation concerning the 2007 terrorist attacks that killed many including two judges.[108]

Also notably, the judges in PIL cases have been increasingly undertaking lawmaking or policy-setting exercises with renewed enthusiasm. This has been a major shift in the Court's jurisprudence which, although it is often justified in terms of constitutional imperatives, is arguably driven by the post-Emergency (2007–8) democratic changes in the polity. As briefly covered below, the post-Emergency judiciary in Bangladesh has engaged itself in regaining

---

[103] See, for example, *Rabia Bhuiyan, MP* v. *Secretary, Ministry of LGRD and Others*, (2007) 59 DLR (AD) 176 (establishing the right to safe drinking water).

[104] *Engineer Mahmud-ul Islam* v. *Govt. of Bangladesh*, (2003) 23 BLD (HCD) at 80.

[105] *BLAST* v. *Bangladesh*, (2008) 60 DLR (HCD) at 234 (judgment 2 August 2005).

[106] *BLAST* v. *Secretary, Ministry of Law, Justice and Parliamentary Affairs*, (2009) 61 DLR (HCD) at 109 (judgment 24 February 2008).

[107] *BLAST* v. *Bangladesh*, (2010) 30 BLD (HCD) at 194.

[108] *Z.I. Khan Panna* v. *Bangladesh*, WP No. 8621 of 2005.

public confidence and rebuilding its image, showing 'new activism' in both ordinary and PIL cases, which has correspondingly enlivened the hitherto feeble social and legal activism.

A good example of the Court's new activism is its decision in a PIL against the government's inactions over the rampant incidents of sexual harassment of women. The Court in *BNWLA* v. *Bangladesh* (2009)[109] found that, despite constitutional mandates for gender equality and the equal legal protection for all, there was virtually no law to effectively prevent and punish sexual harassment of women. The Court issued detailed guidelines 'in the nature of law', binding the employers and educational institutions to follow them in preventing and suppressing sexual harassment of women until 'effective legislation' is made.[110] The formulation of the guidelines is akin to a legislative statute, and they largely resemble the guidelines against sexual harassment that the Indian Supreme Court issued in *Vishaka* v. *State of Rajasthan* (1979).[111]

The Court rationalized such radical adjudicative legislation by placing its reasoning on the Bangladeshi Constitution's basic premises such as 'equality' and 'protection' guarantees, although the major impetus and the ground of legitimacy for such action came from comparative foreign judicial decisions and certain international human rights instruments. In *BNWLA* and other leading PIL cases we actually find comparative law in action. The Court's all-out reliance on *Vishaka*,[112] although this was not made clear in the judgment, showcases how closely Indian PIL developments have influenced PIL jurisprudence in Bangladesh. This has been through a mode that Sujit Choudhry calls the 'dialogical' use of comparative public law,[113] although in a peculiarly Bangladeshi fashion, by which

---

[109] (2009) 14 BLC (HCD) at 694.

[110] (2009) 14 BLC (HCD) at 694, 706. A similar type of activism is also discernible in other areas of violation of rights. See, for example, *State* v. *Metropolitan Police Commissioner, Khulna*, (2008) 60 DLR (HCD) at 660 (issuing a number of guidelines to protect the rights of children in conflict with the law and recommending the domestication of the Convention of the Rights of the Child 1989, which Bangladesh has ratified).

[111] AIR 1997 SC 3011.

[112] Ibid.

[113] See in this volume, Chapter 2 (Sujit Choudhry, 'How to Do Comparative Constitutional Law'). See also, S. Choudhry, 'Globalization in Search of Justification:

the Court has attempted both to sharpen its reasoning and to draw justificatory force from the neighbouring jurisdiction with a similar legal culture.[114]

The above does not, however, lead to the conclusion that PIL-based judicial activism is free of imperfections. The Court's preparedness in PILs to be vigilant against injustices or the violation of citizens' rights does not seem to be sufficiently robust, coherent, and pragmatic.[115] While the Court has shown disproportionately active engagement with cases concerning its independence, it has not, for example, yet authoritatively established the jurisprudence of public law compensation for gross constitutional breaches including misfeasance in public offices. Nor has it adopted an adequately cooperative mode of adjudication in PILs, by involving public officials in implementation processes. Despite these limitations, however, PIL continues to help the willing and perceptive judges achieve goals of justice and constitutionalism.

The Judiciary on the Principle of Judicial Independence: Masdar Hossain and Beyond

While judicial protection of constitutionalism largely depends on the existence of an active and independent judiciary, perceptive judges may well navigate prevalent social and constitutional factors to attain and maintain judicial autonomy. The judiciary in Bangladesh has in a long series of cases shown its activism in protecting the independence

---

Toward a Theory of Comparative Constitutional Interpretation', *Indiana L.J.*, (1999), 74(3): 819–92.

[114] I consider the judges' style of using comparative law to be of a peculiarly Bangladeshi type because they seldom articulate the method and purposes of comparison. In most cases, one has to exercise considerable labour to determine whether the Court's use of foreign materials is for better reasoning or merely for the purpose of judgmental beautification. For an exceptionally articulate use of comparative law, see, *Md. Masdar Hossain* v. *Secretary, Ministry of Finance*, (1998) 18 BLD (HCD) at 558, 108. See also, the case of *Sajeda Parvin* (Article 4 of the High Court of Bangladesh Order, 1972).

[115] This observation fits in the facts of the case of *Ain o Salish Kendra* v. *Bangladesh*, (2007) 15 BLT (HCD) at 48 in which case the Court held that restraining a prisoner in bar fetters following the law is not unconstitutional. But see the pathbreaking decision in *BLAST* v. *Bangladesh*, (2003), above footnote 73.

of judiciary, which it adjudged as a basic pillar of the Constitution in the famous case of *Anwar Hossain Chowdhury*, discussed above. Following that decision, in an abstract judicial review in 1999,[116] a lawyer successfully challenged the constitutionality of appointing the Chief Metropolitan Magistrate of Dhaka without consulting the Supreme Court as per the Constitution's mandate.[117] In another PIL, the Court prevented an utterly politically-biased judge from performing judicial functions.[118]

Judicial decisions on the question of autonomy of the judges and the judiciary abound,[119] of which I now analyse the most prominent case of *Secretary, Ministry of Finance* v. *Md. Masdar Hossain and Others* (1999).[120] In *Masdar Hossain,* the Appellate Division, largely agreeing with the High Court Division,[121] issued some directives concerning judicial independence for 'forthwith' implementation by the executive. Despite several constitutional provisions providing for judicial independence, independence of Bangladesh's lower judiciary had long remained a matter of serious concern. Magistrates exercising judicial functions were indeed officers of the executive organ of the state, while judges in the 'judicial service', although they were not members of the executive, used to be appointed and were controlled by the administration. These issues of judicial independence came

[116] *M. Idrisur Rahman* v. *Shahiduddin Ahmed*, (1999) 19 BLD (HCD) at 291; *Bangladesh* v. *M. Idrisur Rahman*, (1999) 19 BLD (AD) at 203.

[117] See, for example, *Dr. Shahdeen Malik* v. *Bangladesh*, WP No. 2088 of 2005, in which the petitioner challenged, and gained an interim injunction against the government's attempt to transfer five assistant judges in disregard of the Supreme Court's opinion given earlier. See also, *Dr. Shahdeen Malik* v. *Bangladesh*, WP No. 11736 of 2006, challenging the constitutionality of appointing judicial officers to the civil service.

[118] *Khairul Alam Pipul* v. *Bangladesh*, WP No. 1171 of 2006 (Orders of 13 and 27 February 2006). (While still in office, the concerned judge declared in 2006 that he would run in the imminent general elections; the disputed judge later resigned.)

[119] See, for example, *Ruhul Quddus* v. *Justice M.A. Aziz*, (2009) 60 DLR (HCD) at 511, holding that appointing a sitting judge as the chief election commissioner breaches the principle of judicial independence. For quite an opposite view, see the earlier decision in *Shamsul Huq Chy* v. *Justice Md. Abdur Rouf,* (1997) 49 DLR (HCD) at 176.

[120] (2000) 52 DLR (AD) at 82 (judgment 2 December 1999).

[121] *Md. Masdar Hossain* v. *Secretary, Ministry of Finance*, (1998) 18 BLD (HCD) at 558.

to be the central theme of the judgment in this class-action lawsuit by some 223 judges challenging the withdrawal by the government of some of their financial benefits. Speaking for the Court, Justice Kamal reiterated that judicial independence is a basic pillar of the Constitution and hence cannot be 'demolished, whittled down, curtailed or diminished in any manner'.[122]

In a well-argued judgment buttressed by comparative constitutional law decisions from other comparable courts,[123] the Court found the executive and legislative organs to have committed a 'constitutional deviation' from obligations regarding independence of the judiciary.[124] It, therefore, set out to undertake a constitution-reinforcing role, ultimately directing the government to take necessary steps towards framing Presidential 'Rules' regulating appointments of lower court judges and magistrates and their posting, promotion, discipline, and pay or allowances; establishing a Judicial Service Commission to recommend recruitments to the judicial service and a Judicial Pay Commission; and ensuring the Supreme Court's financial autonomy.[125]

Following its verdict, the Court adopted the role of post-decision monitoring, kept the case open as a continuous *mandamus* for any consequential directive and through several strategies made the government fully implement its directives. Since November 2007, by virtue of the enactment of a new law, the magistrates were separated from the executive organ of the state and put under the governance of the Supreme Court.

The *Masdar Hossain* case led critics to raise questions about the propriety of the Court's intervention as well as about its lawmaking exercises. In its judgment, the Court offered largely reasoned responses to these common objections, virtually claiming

---

[122] *Masdar Hossain*, at 103.

[123] The Court relied on Indian, Pakistani, and Canadian decisions. In this case, the Court followed the engagement and dialogical models of comparative law uses, while remaining informed of the imperatives of its own constitution and the legal culture. See in this volume, Chapter 6 (Gary Jacobsohn and Shylashri Shankar, 'Constitutional Borrowing in South Asia'), where the authors analyse this style from the Indian and Sri Lankan perspectives.

[124] *Masdar Hossain*, at 108.

[125] Ibid., at 109.

that its activism was not un-contextual, but rather was in defence of the Constitution.[126] Interestingly, the more practical question as to whether the Court, under the garb of a constitution-reinforcing role, was not serving its own purposes has not so far been raised in Bangladesh.[127] As mentioned above, judicial activism over the issues of judicial autonomy has been more frequent and robust than over other tenets of constitutionalism including the protection of fundamental rights.[128] This scenario may make one think whether Bangladeshi judges have sometimes not made subjective use of their powers and the law to improve their own service conditions.[129]

Significantly, the rationale of the *Masdar Hossain* judgment was carried further forward in other cases. In one such post–*Masdar Hossain* instance, for example, the Appellate Division held that, despite the absence of a posited duty upon the President to consult the Chief Justice while appointing other justices, the practice of such consultation has turned out to be a binding constitutional convention and that the Chief Justice's opinion upon the executive's proposal of judicial appointments has primacy.[130]

---

[126] The Court (Ibid., at 160) reasoned that it can issue necessary directions to bring Parliament or the executive back to the constitutional path when they breach the Constitution. Also, it relied on the Pakistani decision in *Govt. of Sindh* v. *Sharaf Faridi*, PLD (1994) SC 105, to impose a positive obligation on the State to separate the lower judiciary.

[127] I sincerely thank Arun K. Thiruvengadam for leading me to make out this point. I have elsewhere discussed the role of judges' personal background factors in their judgments. See, R. Hoque, *Judicial Activism in Bangladesh*, especially chapters 4 and 8.

[128] Take, for example, the case of judicial failing in taking any significant action against the continuing gross violation of constitutional rights arising from custodial deaths, shootouts, or forced disappearances by law-enforcing agencies.

[129] This is, however, not to de-recognize the judicial role in ensuring procedural justice for people in other services.

[130] *Bangladesh* v. *Idrisur Rahman*, (2010) 7 LG (AD) at 137, 143 (affirming *Idrisur Rahman* v. *Secretary, Ministry of Law, Justice and Parliamentary Affairs*, (2009) 61 DLR (HCD) at 523). This is to note that the recently (July 2011) amended Article 95(1) of the Constitution now provides that the Supreme Court judges shall be appointed 'after consultation with the Chief Justice'. To note further, regarding the President's duty (Article 16) to consult the Supreme Court while controlling and disciplining the members of the lower judiciary, the *Masdar Hossain* Court (*Masdar*

THE 2007 EMERGENCY, THE POST EMERGENCY DEMOCRATIC REGIMES, AND THE JUDICIARY[131]

The 2007 Emergency, although it brought about certain judicial and politico-legal reforms, effectively clipped the constitutional rights and the protective role of the courts. In this context, the role of the Bangladeshi Supreme Court was undoubtedly critical both for the country's constitutional future and for public participation in governance. However, during the Emergency, the judiciary suffered a severe crisis of public confidence, with negative impact on its role as the protector of the Constitution. A quick review of the performance of the Supreme Court will reveal that while its High Court Division largely asserted self-confidence vis-à-vis the overbearing government, the Appellate Division often displayed undue deference to the executive.

Following the proclamation of Emergency, the President issued in quick time the Emergency Ordinance and the Emergency Power Rules, 2007, which, in their combined operation, suspended the enforcement of constitutional fundamental rights, created certain special offences, authorized the trial of certain offences under the new Emergency rules, and postponed the right of accused people to seek bail and challenge proceedings in a court of law.

In the context of these sweeping actions, I now turn to the role the higher judiciary played in protecting the norms of constitutionalism. In a significant, early Emergency-period decision, the High Court Division in *Moyezuddin Sikder* v. *State* (2007)[132] held that its inherent and wider constitutional authority to grant bail to the accused cannot be foreclosed by law even during the State of a National Emergency. A provision in the Emergency Powers Rules (EPR), 2007, provided that no person accused of an offence subjected to the EPR would be entitled to petition 'any court or tribunal' for bail. Based on a dynamic interpretation of the text, the Court held

---

Hossain, at 109) held that the views of the Supreme Court in this regard 'shall have primacy over those of the Executive'.

   [131] Analyses made in this section have drawn on arguments I have made earlier. See, R. Hoque, 'The Recent Emergency and the Politics of the Judiciary in Bangladesh', *National University of Juridical Science Law Review*, (2009), 2(2): 183–204.

   [132] (2007) 59 DLR (HCD) at 287 (judgment of 22 April 2007).

that the term 'any court' in the concerned rule was not intended to include the Supreme Court, inasmuch as no law can oust its constitutional supervisory jurisdiction. In this decision, the principle of rule of law was thus upheld against the prerogatives of an all-powerful Emergency-government. Unfortunately, however, the Appellate Division in *Moyezuddin Sikder* v. *State* (2008)[133] overruled the High Court Division's decision on a narrow interpretation of the law, quickly finding a 'manifest' legislative intention to oust the High Court Division's jurisdiction to grant bail in EPR-cases.[134]

In the case of *Bangladesh* v. *Sheikh Hasina* (2008),[135] a case that portrays the judges' usual dilemma during emergencies, the Appellate Division held that the trial of certain criminal offences by retrospectively applying procedural rules, if not the substantive law, was not unconstitutional. Earlier, the High Court Division significantly found that the relevant Emergency rules did not clearly authorize such retrospective trials and held that even retrospective operation of criminal procedural law is unconstitutional.[136] Drawing on rights-based reasoning, it further held that the ousting, by the EPR, of its power to grant bail was incompatible with the constitutional right to life and the guarantee of equal legal protection despite the fact that the 'Emergency law' postponed the right to judicially enforce fundamental rights.[137] These arguments were, not surprisingly, overturned by the Appellate Division.

There had been some measure of court-based legal activism during the Emergency. It needs to be noted that the Supreme Court's public interest jurisprudence played a major role in changing the way the people and civil society perceived the judicial role. Although public interest litigation grounded on constitutional rights arguments

---

[133] (2008) 60 DLR (AD) at 82.

[134] Ibid., at 88. Compare this with *Afzalul Abedin and Others* v. *Government of Bangladesh and Others*, (2003) 8 BLC (HCD) at 601, 643, which held that the denial in law of the accused's right to seek bail is a breach of due process.

[135] (2008) 60 DLR (AD) at 90.

[136] (2008) 13 BLC (HCD) at 121.

[137] Ibid., at 144–5. (This reasoning resembles the Pakistani SC's view in *Sardar Farooq Ahmed Khan Leghari and Others* v. *Federation of Pakistan*, PLD (1999) SC 57, 76, that despite the ousting of the Court's jurisdiction by the Emergency law, the Court can examine the compatibility of any executive action with the Constitution/statute.)

stalled due to the operation of Emergency law, public-spirited citizens or 'interested' politicians repeatedly invoked the operative part of the constitutional remedial clause to secure justice vis-à-vis actions of the government.[138] Although the Court took much time in appreciating that its power of judicial review on the ground of breach of legality was not foreclosed, there emerged some significant public interest actions seeking to place limitations on Emergency powers.

In *Advocate Sultana Kamal and Others* v. *Bangladesh* (2008),[139] three concerned citizens challenged the constitutionality of certain provisions of the Emergency Powers Ordinance (EPO) and Rules (EPR), without challenging the legality of the Emergency itself. In its judgment delivered just a few days before the Emergency was lifted, the High Court Division voided certain provisions of these statutes that precluded judicial review of any Emergency-decisions and curtailed the judicial power of senior courts to grant bails, hear appeals against interim court orders, and suspend sentences. The Court stressed that the provisions under challenge were an affront to the principles of justice and the due process of law.[140] Interestingly, although it stopped short of striking down the Emergency as unconstitutional, the Court observed that, under the Constitution, Emergency cannot continue for an indefinite period.[141] An appeal against the decision in *Advocate Sultana Kamal* has since remained pending in the Appellate Division which in its interim order stayed the judgment's efficacy.

Full-fledged constitutionality challenges to the 2007 Emergency went to the Court only during the waning days of the Emergency. In *M. Asafuddowla and Others* v. *Bangladesh* (2008),[142] constitutional provisions enabling the President to declare a State of Emergency generally and particularly to postpone the enforcement of constitutional

---

[138] Although the right to enforce fundamental rights under Article 102(1) of the Constitution was suspended, judicial review of 'legality' of other issues under Article 102(2) remained unaffected.

[139] (2009) 14 BLC (HCD) at 141 (judgment of 4 December 2008).

[140] Ibid., at 198.

[141] Ibid., at 189–90.

[142] Writ Petition of 24 November 2008. See also, another earlier challenge, *M. Saleem Ullah and Others* v. *Bangladesh*, (2008) WP No. 5033 of 2008.

rights were challenged.[143] The Court issued a *rule* calling for explanations from the government, but the case was not heard due to the withdrawal of the Emergency.

Alongside the PILs, the 2007 Emergency saw other ordinary constitutional cases with significant implications for constitutionalism and, strategically, for the future exercise of Emergency powers. The Court, however, seemed to be more confident in exercising activism regarding issues that did not directly concern the legality or efficacy of the Emergency regime. In *Md. Idrisrur Rahman* v. *Bangladesh* (2008),[144] for example, the High Court Division adjudged unconstitutional the Supreme Judicial Commission Ordinance 2008 on the ground that the Ordinance breached the constitutional principle of judicial independence by providing for a Commission the majority of whose members hailed from outside of the judiciary. In another important decision, the Court declared the Contempt of Court Ordinance, 2008 unconstitutional not only for violating the principle of judicial independence but also for not being within the President's constitutional power to make such a constitutive ordinance during the caretaker government's tenure.[145]

The above brings into sharp focus the proper judicial role during an Emergency. The traditional constitutional-legal theories often refute a role for the Court in helping the troubled nation to restore democracy.[146] The 'conventional view'[147] of the Court's role during an Emergency, from across the world, is that the judiciaries lack

---

[143] Indeed, the petitioners challenged the Constitution (2nd Amendment) Act 1973 that made provisions for Emergency.

[144] WP No. 3228 of 2008.

[145] *Md. Shamsul Hoque and Another* v. *Bangladesh*, WP of 2008 (judgment of 24 July 2008).

[146] On this, from the perspective of emergencies, see, D. Dyzenhaus, 'The State of Emergency in Legal Theory', in V.V. Ramraj, M. Hor, and K. Roach (eds), *Global Anti-terrorism Law and Policy* (Cambridge University Press: Cambridge, 2005), pp. 65–88.; T. Ginsburg and T. Mustafa (eds), *Rule by Law: The Politics of Courts in Authoritarian Regimes* (Cambridge University Press: Cambridge, 2008); V.V. Ramraj and Arun K. Thiruvengadam (eds), *Emergency Powers in Asia: Exploring the Limits of Legality* (Cambridge University Press: Cambridge, 2009).

[147] This expression has been drawn from Arun. K. Thiruvengadam, 'Asian Judiciaries and Emergency Powers: Reasons for Optimism?', in Ramraj and Thiruvengadam (eds), *Emergency Powers in Asia*, pp. 466–94.

capacity to prevent executive excesses in times of Emergency and that the judicial protection of rights in such times appears more elusive than real.[148]

In an important recent study on Asian Emergency-time judiciaries, Arun K. Thiruvengadam has argued that Asian judiciaries have by and large made a remarkable shift in their approach to judicial review of Emergency powers, by adopting a robust rather than a conventional stance.[149] This author has, however, argued that, despite this marked shift in judicial review approaches, whether a particular judiciary would actively review Emergency powers ultimately depends on mainly internal facilitative or supportive societal factors. Seen in light of this important insight, it is clear that, in deciding the cases concerning Emergency the two Divisions of the Supreme Court of Bangladesh took largely differing approaches—the High Court Division took a dynamic interpretive role vis-à-vis the Emergency laws while the Appellate Division mostly embraced legal formalism and uncritically deferred to the executive. Glancing through the above cases one gets the sense that the Appellate Division almost always displayed a policy preference for not interfering with the executive, although it is unclear whether it maintained strategic silence or abandoned its autonomy to the external political pressure arising from the Emergency.

Admittedly, the Emergency regime of the recent past created an atmosphere of fear and humiliation for the apex court judges who had to work in a situation of virtual non-independence lacking supporting factors such as judicial freedom and a rule-of-law–based government.[150] Nevertheless, given that the High Court Division tried

---

[148] See, B. Ackerman, 'The Emergency Constitution', *Yale Law Journal*, (2004), No. 113: 1029–91 (claiming that judges can do nothing better than they have done in the past during an Emergency, and urging for new constitutional concepts to better protect civil rights during such crises). See also, M.P. Singh, 'The Impact of Emergency on Fundamental Rights in India', *International Journal of Legal Research*, (1966), 1: 207.

[149] Thiruvengadam, 'Asian Judiciaries and Emergency Powers'.

[150] The regime-change everywhere has often impinged upon law, courts, and judicial elites. See, J.J. Schmidhauser, 'The Impact of Political Change upon Law, Courts and Judicial Elites', *International Political Science Review*, (1999), 13(3): 223–33; S. Shankar, *Scaling Justice: India's Supreme Court, Anti-terror Laws and Social Rights* (Oxford University Press: New Delhi, 2008), chapters 1–2.

to follow an intense form of judicial review, the pertinent question is how one should evaluate the legal reasoning that underlies the Appellate Division's excessive deference. It seems that, on the whole, the Bangladeshi judiciary's role during the Emergency in enforcing constitutionalism was a mixed bag of unconventional stances and the taking of traditional, deferential paths. As the interpretive techniques of the Appellate Division show, in addition to the atmosphere of judicial subjugation, the spill-over impact of past restrictive jurisprudence, and the background factors that often influence the judges' minds, it is the Appellate Division's legal formalism that is in part responsible for its deplorable silence during the Emergency.

Following the post-Emergency installation of a new democratic government in 2009, the Bangladeshi apex court seems to be increasingly acting in order to overcome the crisis of public confidence it incurred during the Emergency. This post-Emergency period can to some extent be likened to that of India that gave birth to the most powerful and activist court in the world and also to Pakistani Supreme Court's post-Emergency (from 2008 onwards) activism.[151] As seen above, the Supreme Court in recent times has been issuing activist judgments in the protection of fundamental rights and the principles of constitutionalism, often issuing novel remedies and making policy suggestions. For example, it is in this period that the Appellate Division has confirmed the High Court Division's invalidation of the 5th Amendment to the Constitution that constitutionalized a martial law regime. Also, unlike earlier *suo motu* interventions solely in the area of criminal injustice, the High Court Division has been increasingly acting on its own in other areas of constitutionalism by issuing *mandamus* and prohibitive orders.[152] Also worth mentioning

[151] For example, in *Sindh High Court Bar Association through Its Secretary* v. *Federation of Pakistan,* Constitutional Petitions 8 and 9 of 2009, the Supreme Court declared unconstitutional the imposition of Emergency by the then President on 3 November 2007, and held, unprecedentedly, that 'no validation, affirmation or adoption of unconstitutional...acts of a usurper of power could be made by... Parliament'. This arguably comes very close to establishing the 'doctrine of basic structure'.

[152] See, for example, *Government of Bangladesh* v. *Ministry of Home Affairs and Others,* (2008) 16 BLT (HCD) 264 (directing the installation of speed governors in all vehicles to prevent deaths from accidents), and *Seema Zahur* v. *State,* Crim. Misc.

is the new Court's emerging attempts in recent PILs towards crafting a cooperative model of judicial review, notably creating therein a role for experts and government agencies.

CONCLUSION

In this essay my aim has been to show how judges in Bangladesh have promoted and protected the cause of constitutionalism through active resolution of constitutional issues, based on globally informed but locally grounded interpretations of the constitution. The judiciary in Bangladesh, although it has not yet become what is called the 'good governance court',[153] has by and large earned some commendable achievements in enforcing constitutional justice. It would be too much, however, to claim that its role vis-à-vis constitutionalism is beyond question.

As discussed above, the judiciary under the guise of a theory of judicial self-restraint largely abdicated its responsibility during the martial law regimes and difficult political situations. On the other hand, while there has been a noticeable positive change in its rights and constitutionalism jurisprudence during the democratic era, the Bangladeshi judiciary arguably remained in the grip of strict legal positivism even during such phases. Bangladeshi judicial activism has indeed oscillated along with democratic phases in the country, and is increasingly becoming robust, particularly in the post-Emergency (2007–8) period. In addition to political dynamics, both internal and external factors concerning the judiciary, including the perception of the judicial role nourished and sustained by the judges, can be said to have contributed to these developments that are often riddled with ambivalences.

It is argued that, in the context of prevalent socio-political situations and the chances of imbalance of State powers in Bangladesh, the need for judicial vigilance for the protection of justice and good

---

Rule (*suo motu*) No. 10541/2008 (freeing a dumb woman victim from unlawful incarceration in prison).

[153] The term has recently been used by Nick Robinson to appreciate the role of the Supreme Court of India in promoting good governance. See, N. Robinson, 'Expanding Judiciaries: India and the Rise of the Good Governance Court', *Washington University Global Studies Law Review*, (2009), 8(1): 1–69.

governance is ever-present. The call is more earnest when the rights of the people as well as the higher norms of constitutionalism become handmaidens of any over-bearing government. The above analyses of the judicial role in achieving and protecting constitutionalism show that, while structural and political factors may retard the realization of this judicial role, a willing and able judiciary steeped in the values of rule of law, justice, and human welfare may effectively respond to this call by overcoming any systemic inhibitions, and prohibitive legal and doctrinal boundaries.

CHAPTER ELEVEN

Revisiting *The Role of the Judiciary in Plural Societies (1987)*

A Quarter-Century Retrospective on Public Interest Litigation in India and the Global South

୬ଡ଼ଡ଼

*Arun K. Thiruvengadam**

INTRODUCTION

The principal purpose of this essay is to revisit a classic work in the field of comparative public interest law, in relation to its conclusions on the potential of Public Interest Litigation (PIL) for countries in the global South. Published in 1987, *The Role of the Judiciary in Plural Societies* (hereinafter, *ROJ*) comprises a selection of academic papers presented at two workshops held in Surajkund, India and Eldoret, Kenya in August 1983 and February 1985 respectively. The volume was co-edited by the Sri Lankan academic activists Neelan Tiruchelvam and Radhika Coomaraswamy, and addressed the role of judiciaries in aiding public interest law movements in five countries across Asia and Africa. It serves as an excellent example of early comparative constitutional scholarship in Asia and Africa,

* This essay has benefited from presentations at: the 'Judicial Nineties' conference organized by the Alternative Law Forum, Bangalore in 2008; the inaugural LASSNET conference held in January 2009; and the Singapore conference in July 2009 that gave rise to this volume. In addition to those who participated actively at these presentations, thanks are due to the following for constructive criticism and comments: Sujit Choudhry, Varun Gauri, Madhav Khosla, Vikram Raghavan, and Ronojoy Sen. The usual caveat applies.

with contributions from constitutional scholars, judges, and activists drawn from several jurisdictions. All the contributors to the volume can broadly be described as progressives.[1] The final recommendation adopted in the second workshop—the volume lists the adopted recommendations in its conclusion—sums up the consensus among the various contributors to the volume: 'Judicial activism, encouraged by social action litigation [or PIL], inspired by constitutional values, may be regarded as a vital human technology for social change in impoverished societies.'[2]

This essay proposes to revisit this thesis by providing both a descriptive and a normative argument. The descriptive argument is based on the experience of PIL in India in the quarter-century since the volume was published. It is important to emphasize the limited nature of the descriptive argument, because it focuses only on one nation. Nevertheless, since the Indian experience of PIL was, as we shall see, the primary driving force behind the recommendation of the *ROJ*, studying it closely does have implications for countries in the global South. However, whether the lessons of the Indian experience are applicable generally even in South Asia is an issue beyond the scope of this essay.

---

[1] It may be necessary to offer some clarifications on terminology. The term 'progressive' means different things in different countries. In some countries it refers to right-wing conservatives. Without seeking to provide a comprehensive definition, I use the term to indicate people who favour the use of state policies to redistribute societal wealth in order to meet the basic needs of people and foster their inherent capabilities. Progressives need to be distinguished from 'liberals', at least as used in the American sense. Liberals have a fear of the state and emphasize negative liberties as a way of preventing the state from encroaching upon their freedoms. They tend to view the private realm, free from state interference, as the realm of freedom. Progressives, by contrast, view the private realm, which is shielded from state protection, as a realm of oppression and domination. They are in favour of strong state policies because they see governmental power as having more potential than harmful effect. Here, I have drawn sharper contrasts for the purpose of definitional clarity; in reality, liberals and progressives have more in common, and it is possible that the intermediate categories of liberal-progressives or progressive-liberals have more adherents. In adopting this distinction I follow, Linda McClain and James Fleming, 'Constitutionalism, Judicial Review and Progressive Change', *Texas Law Review*, (2005), 81: 433, 441.

[2] 'The Judiciary in Plural Societies: Some Conclusions', in Neelan Tiruchelvam and Radhika Coomaraswamy (eds), *The Role of the Judiciary in Plural Societies* (Frances Pinter: London, 1987), p. 186.

In the quarter-century since the publication of *ROJ*, many of the aspirations expressed by the contributors for the development of PIL did bear fruit, at least in India in particular and in South Asia more generally. Yet, paradoxically, one finds that in the early part of the twenty-first century, PIL in India has come in for harsh criticism from, of all people, progressives. Indeed, progressives in contemporary South Asian jurisdictions seem far less convinced that judicial activism is as much an unqualified human good as these contributors believed it to be. The first task of this essay is to explain how and why this has happened. The descriptive analysis raises concerns about the correctness of the normative vision offered by the contributors. Normatively, the argument is that the experience of a quarter-century of judicial activism in India demonstrates that a faith in the exclusive power of judiciaries to bring about social reform is misplaced, and must be substituted by a more nuanced and sophisticated account of the role that judiciaries can play towards achieving social justice in contemporary India, and by extension, in other societies of the global South.

The structure of this essay is this: Following this Introduction, the second section ('Overview of *ROJ*: Its Principal Themes and Conclusions') provides a brief overview and summary of the contributions and findings of *ROJ*. The third section ('The Transformation of PIL in India (1970s–2000)') summarizes developments in PIL in India from the outset, focusing on the experiences of the two decades since the publication of the book. This descriptive survey seeks to cover the growing discontent among progressives over PIL, and the reasons for such a trend. 'The Progressive Conception of the Judicial Role in Contemporary India', the fourth section, sets out the normative argument of the essay, which urges a reconsideration of the conclusions of *ROJ* and seeks to reformulate the appropriate role of judges in deciding PIL cases in contemporary India. The conclusion seeks to draw out comparative lessons from the terrain covered in the essay.

OVERVIEW OF *ROJ*: ITS PRINCIPAL THEMES AND CONCLUSIONS

As explained by Neelan Tiruchelvam in its Introduction, *ROJ* contained 'eight case studies on five plural societies in Asia and Africa'[3]

---

[3] Neelan Tiruchelvam, 'Introduction', in *ROJ*, p. xxi.

(India, Mozambique, the Philippines, Sri Lanka, and Tanzania) and sought to draw conclusions about the role that the judiciary can play in resolving common problems of poverty and ethnic conflict in these and other developing societies.

Re-reading the book nearly a quarter-century after its publication, one is struck by the influence of erstwhile trends and mindsets on its contents. As we will see in the short history of PIL in India in the next section, the mid-80s were a time when PIL was enjoying great popularity among progressive lawyers, judges, and academics, and the volume reflects this amply, as will be evident from some representative quotations that follow.

Tiruchelvam concludes his introduction to the volume by asserting that the experience of PIL in India 'has renewed faith in the potential of the Court as the custodian of the public conscience, and in the empowerment of ethnic minorities and tribals who are ordinarily excluded from the political arena.' In the first essay that follows Tiruchelvam's introduction, Coomaraswamy exhorts judges in developing countries to adopt more robust roles because of her belief that '[o]nly an imaginative judiciary with an instinctive sense of justice will be able to transcend the forces of social divisiveness and deliver judgments which will be respected by all sections of society'.[4]

This instrumental role of the judiciary is both reinforced and expanded in the contributions of the two Indians to the volume, Justice P.N. Bhagwati and Upendra Baxi, who are widely acknowledged to be critical actors in the founding and establishment of PIL in India. Indeed, the volume features two articles by Baxi. In one of them, he exhorts judges to become 'activist'. For him, an activist judge is a judge who is aware that she wields enormous executive and legislative power in her role as a judge and this power and discretion have to be used *militantly* for the promotion of constitutional values.[5]

In the second article, Baxi offered a more restrained and nuanced perspective, acknowledging that PIL was not without problems.

---

[4] Radhika Coomaraswamy, 'Towards an Engaged Judiciary', in *ROJ*, p. 16.

[5] Upendra Baxi, 'On the Shame of Not Being an Activist: Thoughts on Judicial Activism', in *ROJ*, p. 172. The same article appeared in the Indian Bar Review in 1984, and was probably written in the early 1980s.

Here he specifically noted that despite encouraging signs, the crucial phase of PIL in India between 1980 and 1982 had shown that its use had continued apace with the judiciary making 'constitutional compromises' which 'create new sources of anxiety'.[6] He also conceded that the movement in its early years could be viewed as having achieved 'relatively minor exercises in class-transcendence'. Yet, this nuance gets drowned out in the overall message of the article, which celebrates early successes in PIL cases and exhorts other judges in the Indian Supreme Court to convert to the cause.[7]

This theme is repeated in the other essays that seek to draw lessons from PIL in India for other developing countries. The two essays on Tanzania[8] detail how the judiciary in Tanzania had struggled to establish its legitimacy in the face of strong executive action that sought to curb judicial power. The author of one of these essays concluded that judges in Tanzania should seek to emulate the methods and tools of PIL evolved by judges in India.[9] Similarly, the essays on the Sri Lankan judiciary—by H.L. De Silva and Radhika Coomaraswamy—detail how the courts in that country had avoided their constitutional role in protecting fundamental rights. Coomaraswamy's conclusion once again shows an appreciation of the dangers of overly strong reliance on judiciaries:

> Activism with regard to a developing country is no simple matter. Nor is it often a matter of choice. Scholars have always warned that in defining the role of the judiciary, one must not go beyond the practical limitation of man and material. Enough consideration must be given to matters of

[6] Baxi, 'Taking Suffering Seriously: Social Action Litigation', in *ROJ*, p. 32. This piece has appeared in print in different versions, the earliest of which was in the *Delhi Law Review* in 1979.

[7] For a more detailed critique of Baxi's conceptions of the judicial role and of his idea of 'judicial activism', see, Madhav Khosla, 'Addressing Judicial Activism in the Indian Supreme Court: Towards an Evolved Debate', *Hasting Int'l & Comp. L. Rev.*, (2009), 55: 60–71 (analysing several of Baxi's works and asserting that his conception of 'judicial activism' has shifted over time and is analytically flawed in some respects).

[8] M.K.B. Wambali and C.M. Peter, 'The Judiciary in Context: The Case of Tanzania', in *ROJ*, pp. 131–45; R.H. Kisange, 'The Legal Profession: Pluralism and Public Interest Litigation in Tanzania', in *ROJ*, pp. 145–55.

[9] Kisange, 'The Legal Profession', p. 151.

judicial administration. Judicial activism can only be successful if it is combined with a pragmatic assessment of judicial capabilities.[10]

Nevertheless, Coomaraswamy went on to assert that 'issues of administration, time and cost cannot in themselves be seen as justification for the abdication of constitutional duties' and endorsed a robust role for judiciaries in protecting constitutional values in 'a multi-ethnic, multi-religious developing society'.

In its concluding section, the volume sets out the recommendations adopted at the Suraj Kund and Eldoret conferences. Given what has been described here so far, it should not come as a surprise that the contributors concluded that the need of the hour was for strong, robust judiciaries to exercise their powers of judicial review to uphold constitutional values in pluralist developing societies. The language of the resolutions is vivid and striking. The following three specific recommendations reveal an ambitious view of the role of the judiciary:

> 11. Judicial activism, far from being a threat to national security or the development of the nation-state, is imperative for the attainment of [liberal democratic and constitutional] objectives.
>
> ... 14. Judicial activism can be an important strategy to overcome all forms of oppression, exploitation, impoverishment, unjustifiable on any model of societal development in Asia and Africa. Since the majority of human beings in most African societies are among the impoverished and exploited, there is an urgent need for judicial activism in providing amelioration of such impoverishment and exploitation.
>
> ...18. Judicial activism, encouraged by social action litigation, inspired by constitutional values, may be regarded as a vital human technology for social change in impoverished societies.[11]

My principal argument in this essay is that this view of the role of the judiciary is deeply problematic. First, the presumption here appears to be that only 'activist' judges can provide deliverance from the many social ills that afflict countries in the developing world. While several contributors recognize the important role played by other social actors such as grassroot movements, social organizations, lawyers, and citizen clients, they are not given sufficient importance

---

[10] Radhika Coomaraswamy, 'The Sri Lankan Judiciary and Fundamental Rights: A Realist Critique', in *ROJ*, p. 128.

[11] *ROJ*, pp. 185–6.

in the final recommendations. The most significant actors for bringing about the necessary social change are 'activist' judges. Second, the task of interpreting and promoting constitutional values is also presumed to be straightforward, and entirely free from either complexity or problems of balancing and choice among competing priorities. The suggestion is that the texts of the constitutions at issue inexorably point to progressive ends, ignoring the reality that there can be several conflicting interpretations around which constitutional values are to be prioritized and, more importantly, how they are to be achieved. As we will see in the following section, this faith in the power of judges to bring about radical social change was misplaced, even in India, where PIL saw its greatest advances and achievements.

THE TRANSFORMATION OF PIL IN INDIA (1970S–2000)

This section seeks to analyse changes in trends of PIL in India. However, before turning to PIL, it sets out the background context which led to its emergence in the first place.

In the first few decades after Independence, the general perception of the Indian judiciary, including among progressives, was that it was acting as an impediment to much-needed social reforms (including land reforms and other forms of social redistribution). There were heated constitutional battles between the legislature and the executive on the one hand, and the judiciary on the other, and it was generally thought that in these contests, the judiciary sided with the more powerful sections of society (with the legislature presumably representing the interests of the downtrodden sections). The judiciary in general, and the Supreme Court in particular, reached a low point during the Emergency (1975–7), when the Supreme Court was seen as having capitulated under the strains of Indira Gandhi's excesses, and as having failed, despite having constitutional authority behind it, to act as a bulwark against the tyranny of a populist leader-turned-dictator. In holding in the *Habeas Corpus* case that preventive detention laws were immune from judicial review, the Supreme Court was widely perceived to have abandoned its role as the guardian of the Constitution.[12] This, combined with its earlier

---

[12] *A.D.M. Jabalpur* v. *Shiv Kant Shukla*, AIR 1976 SC 1207.

tendency to rule against the interests of weaker sections of Indian society, has given rise to an abiding scepticism towards the judiciary among sections of the progressive community. As we shall see, this lingering scepticism has manifested itself in the progressive critique of PIL as it has evolved since the 1990s.

The transformation of the judiciary in India, from being one of the most reviled institutions within India to one of its most revered, owes much to the phenomenon of PIL. Though this concept was more readily identified with the American civil rights movement and the activism of the Warren Court in the US in the sixties, judges in India adapted and modified American public interest law strategies in innovative ways to fashion its own PIL jurisprudence. Beginning in the mid- to late-1970s, and 'spurred on by an inchoate alliance of social activists, lawyers, journalists, and academics',[13] some judges of the Supreme Court began to entertain a series of PIL cases. As a result, the Court moved away from its traditional emphasis on civil and political rights, and began focusing on social rights cases, as well as cases involving the civil and political rights of the most oppressed sections of society. There is a near consensus among close observers of the Court on the view that the forms of judicial activism exhibited in PIL cases are to be understood as the Court's efforts to retrieve a degree of legitimacy after the collapse of its credibility during the Emergency.[14]

The Supreme Court's 1978 decision in *Maneka Gandhi* v. *Union of India*[15] is generally regarded as having secured a vital breakthrough, which set the stage for later decisions involving the enforcement of social

---

[13] This is how Rajeev Dhavan describes the beginning of the PIL movement. Rajeev Dhavan, 'The Republic of India: The Constitution as the Situs of Struggle: India's Constitution Fory Years On', in Lawrence W. Beer (ed.), *Constitutional Systems in Late Twentieth Century Asia* (University of Washington Press: Seattle, 1992), p. 383. For the account of one of the main actors in this movement, see, Baxi, 'Taking Suffering Seriously', in *ROJ*.

[14] See generally, Upendra Baxi, *The Indian Supreme Court and Politics* (Eastern Book Co: Lucknow, 1980), pp. 122–3, 233–45 (explaining how the Supreme Court's judicial activism in the post-Emergency phase was an attempt to 'bury its emergency past' and describing the steps taken in the area of rights of prisoners); S.P. Sathe, *Judicial Activism in India* (Oxford University Press: New Delhi, 2002); Jamie Cassels, 'Judicial Activism and Public Interest Litigation in India: Attempting the Impossible', *American Journal of Comparative Law*, (1989), 37: 495, 511.

[15] AIR 1978 SC 597.

rights. In this case, the Court held that Article 21 of the Constitution, which guarantees to every person the right to life, must be read expansively. The Court insisted that the traditional understanding of this provision, which had interpreted it as guaranteeing only freedom from personal restraint, was misplaced. The right to life, according to the Court, would include a variety of rights that add meaning to the right to life of an individual, and to the blossoming of her personality. In later years, the Court read several of the directive principles (which are located in the non-justiciable Part IV of the Constitution) into this expansive understanding of the right to life, and argued that to have a meaningful 'life', Indians would have to be guaranteed several of the social rights. More importantly, the Court began to hold that it was the duty of the government to implement these social rights. For instance, in one case, it held that the right to life in Article 21 also encompasses 'the bare necessities of life such as adequate nutrition, clothing and shelter and facilities for reading, writing and expressing oneself in diverse forms'.[16] In this manner (which has been described by one South African judge as 'smuggling social and economic rights in through the back door'[17]), the Supreme Court has sought to override the textual hurdle of Article 37 of the Constitution which specifically states that the directive principles are not judicially enforceable.

Between the late 1970s and now, the Supreme Court's decisions in PIL cases have enabled it to engage with virtually every significant issue of public life in India.[18] In a series of cases decided during the 1980s and early 1990s, the Supreme Court broke new ground by judicially creating rights to livelihood and housing,[19] health,[20] and

---

[16] *Francis Coralie Mullin* v. *Administrator, Union Territory of Delhi*, AIR 1981 SC 746.

[17] Justice Albie Sachs, 'Social and Economic Rights: Can They Be Made Justiciable', *S.M.U.L. Rev.*, (2000), 1384.

[18] See generally, Sangeeta Ahuja, *People, Law and Justice: A Case Book of Public Interest Litigation* (Orient Longman: Delhi, 1997). For a survey of the various issues tackled by the Court under its PIL jurisdiction, see generally, Ashok H. Desai and S. Muralidhar, 'Public Interest Litigation: Potential and Problems', in B.N. Kirpal, Ashok H. Desai, Gopal Subramanian, Rajeev Dhavan, and Raju Ramachandran (eds), *Supreme but not Infallible* (Oxford University Press: New Delhi, 2000), pp. 159–92.

[19] *Olga Tellis* v. *Bombay Municipal Corporation*, AIR 1985 SC 180.

[20] *Parmanand Katara* v. *Union of India*, AIR 1989 SC 2039; *Paschim Banga Khet Mazdoor Samiti* v. *State of West Bengal*, AIR 1996 SC 2426.

education[21] for Indians, and by issuing orders designed to implement these rights.

Since the fourth section of this essay focuses on the procedural mechanisms used in PIL cases, it is necessary to get a sense of the great innovations achieved by the PIL jurisdiction. The following have been identified as the distinctive and innovative procedural features of the PIL experience in its early phase by its leading academic and judicial analysts:[22] (1) epistolary jurisdiction (consisting of relaxing the traditional rules of *locus standi* to enable disadvantaged groups to approach courts by sending postcards, and enabling others to represent them in Court); (2) 'creeping'[23] jurisdiction (where the Courts sought to make long-term improvements to public administration by keeping cases pending and issuing interim directions and orders); (3) the appointment of socio-legal commissions of inquiry to assist the Court in ascertaining facts and deciding upon solutions; and (4) the evolution of new remedies.

In its early stages, the Court's focus in PIL cases was on very specific causes, almost all of which affected constituencies that were particularly disempowered, owing to a host of different causal factors. Indeed, the Court cited the fact that most of such constituencies would not have ready access to justice, to justify its admittedly adventurous steps to improve their situation. Thus, for instance, a number of these early cases (especially those involving Justice V.R. Krishna Iyer, who had a particular interest in ameliorating prison conditions having undergone incarceration himself) focused on the rights of prisoners. Clearly, prisoners were a category of citizens who were severely constrained in being able to pursue the rights that were due to them. The Supreme Court held, for instance, that those charged with criminal offences had positive rights to legal aid[24] and speedy trial:[25] On the negative side, prisoners were held to have constitutional rights against the following: solitary confinement,[26]

[21] *Unnikrishnan* v. *State of Bihar,* (1993) 1 SCC 645.
[22] Baxi, 'Taking Suffering Seriously', in *ROJ.*
[23] Baxi, ibid., p. 122.
[24] *M.H. Hoskot* v. *State of Maharashtra*, MANU/SC/0119/1978.
[25] *Hussainara Khatoon* v. *Home Secretary, State of Bihar*, MANU/SC/0084/1980.
[26] *Sunil Batra* v. *Delhi Administration*, MANU/SC/0184/1978.

bar fetters,[27] handcuffing,[28] delayed execution,[29] custodial violence:[30] and public hanging.[31]

Other groups whose causes were addressed in early PIL cases were the following: migrant labourers,[32] pavement dwellers,[33] children,[34] and mentally ill persons.[35] All of these groups fit the general category of cases that were the focus of the early phase of PIL cases, as each of these groups faced special difficulties in espousing its grievances through the regular channels of democratic politics.[36]

In recent scholarship on PIL, a consistent theme has been the transformation of PIL from the time of its inception in the late 1970s, to its evolution during the 1980s, to the causes it embraced in the 1990s, and eventually to the first decade of this century. This argument focuses on the changes in PIL that accompanied broader change brought about by India's embrace of policies of economic liberalization in the early 1990s. Thus, Aditya Nigam argues that PIL in the 1990s began reflecting the wider ideologies of 'neo-liberalism' and 'corporate capitalism' and emerged as 'the champion of the new order'.[37] Nivedita Menon's analysis confirms this assessment by undertaking a survey of cases decided by the Supreme Court in the 1990s which, according to her, 'have a clear logic and are

---

[27] *Charles Sobhraj* v. *Supt. Central Jail*, MANU/SC/0070/1978.

[28] *Prem Shankar Shukla* v. *Delhi Administration*, MANU/SC/0084/1980.

[29] *T.V. Vatheeswaran* v. *State of T.N.*, MANU/SC/0383/1983.

[30] *Sheela Barse* v. *State of Maharashtra*, MANU/SC/0382/1983.

[31] *A.G. of India* v. *Lachma Devi*, MANU/SC/0059/1985.

[32] *Bandhua Mukti Morcha* v. *Union of India*, AIR 1984 SC 802.

[33] *Olga Tellis* v. *Bombay* v. *Municipality*, AIR 1985 SC 180.

[34] *Lakshmikant Pandey* v. *Union of India*, AIR 1984 SC 469.

[35] *Upendra Baxi* v. *State of Uttar Pradesh*, 1983 2 SCC 308.

[36] Though the Supreme Court did not cite this as authority, its broad theoretical justification for PIL in the early phase fits well within the justification that the American constitutional scholar John Hart Ely had advanced for an expansive (or activist) judicial role. According to Ely, courts in general (and the Warren Court in particular, whose decisions he cited to support his theory) would be justified in going outside the normal boundaries of judicial review to espouse the cause of groups in society whose interests could not be protected through the majoritarian processes of ordinary democratic politics. John Hart Ely, *Democracy and Distrust: A Theory of Judicial Review* (Harvard University Press: Boston, 1980).

[37] Aditya Nigam, 'Embedded Judiciary or, the Judicial State of Exception', paper presented at the ALF conference on the Judicial Nineties, 2008.

remarkably consistent in terms of their outcome [which inevitably is]: Environment trumps People, Development trumps Environment'.[38] Going a step further than Nigam, she asserts that rather than being complicit with the neo-liberal project, 'the judiciary and the Law *are* the neo-liberal project'.[39]

This assessment, while somewhat extreme in its denunciation of the judicial role since the 1990s, does not fully capture developments in PIL during that period. It is nevertheless correct in alluding to the shift in the content and character of PIL during the 1990s. To illustrate briefly what these changes entailed, we may refer to a comprehensive survey of PIL cases that were decided during the period 1997–8. In the conclusion of the survey, S. Muralidhar presciently observed: 'The cases that were taken up for detailed consideration by the courts reflected a perceptible shift to issues concerning governance.'[40] This was the period during which the Supreme Court became proactive in its efforts towards: (1) cleaning up the political process by focusing on corruption at the highest levels of the political set-up in the *Hawala* case[41] and the *Fodder Scam* case;[42] (2) solving the chaotic traffic and pollution in Delhi;[43] (3) cleaning up the Taj and its surrounding area;[44] (4) regulating the disposal of hazardous waste;[45] (5) regulating the manufacture and sale of pesticides;[46] (6) addressing the issues of sexual harassment[47] and

---

[38] Nivedita Menon, 'Environment and the Will to Rule: The Supreme Court and Public Interest Litigation in the Nineties', paper presented at the ALF conference on the Judicial Nineties, 2008.

[39] Ibid.

[40] S. Muralidhar, 'Public Interest Litigation', *Annual Survey of Indian Law*, (1997–98), 33–34: 525. More recently, the term 'good governance' has come to be used to describe the issues courts have tackled in PIL cases since the 1990s. See generally, Nick Robinson, 'Expanding Judiciaries: India and the Rise of the Good Governance Court', *Washington University Global Studies Law Review*, (2009), 8: 1–69.

[41] *Vineet Narain* v. *Union of India*, (1998) 1 SCC 226.

[42] *Union of India* v. *Sushil Kumar Modi*, (1997) 4 SCC 770.

[43] *Suo Moto* proceedings in Re: Delhi Transport Department, (1998) 9 SCC 250.

[44] *M.C. Mehta* v. *Union of India*, (1998) 9 SCC 381; (1998) 9 SCC 711; (1998) 8 SCC 711.

[45] *Research Foundation for Science and Technology* v. *Union of India*, (1997) 5 SCALE 495.

[46] *Dr Ashok* v. *Union of India*, (1997) 5 SCC 10.

[47] *Vishaka* v. *Union of India*, (1997) 6 SCC 241.

female foeticide;[48] and (7) regulating the collection and distribution of blood by blood banks.[49]

Owing to constraints of space, this essay primarily relies on the scholarly work of Usha Ramathan to document the changing nature of PIL during the mid-1990s. Ramanathan describes the original constituency of PIL as being that proportion of the Indian population which was 'caught in the throes of severe disenfranchisement, dispossession and rightlessness' and includes within this category 'the bonded labourer, the incarcerated undertrial, the labouring child, migrant labour, and women in custodial institutions'.[50] In her telling, PIL cases across the 1980s and into the 1990s began to focus on a vast range of issues, most of which centred on issues affecting the middle classes in India, as opposed to the marginalized sections. Ramanathan states that in this new phase, which emerged more clearly in the 1990s, the Supreme Court had to balance competing interests, and gradually began to turn away from protecting the interests of the original constituencies of PIL. Ramanathan therefore argues that 'the constituency on whose behalf the enhancement of judicial power' had been justified in the first phase of PIL 'began to emerge as the casualty of that exercise of power' in the new phase of PIL that appeared in the 1990s.[51] More recently, Rakesh Shukla

---

[48] *Chetna* v. *Union of India*, (1998) 2 SCC 158.

[49] *Common Cause* v. *Union of India*, (1998) 2 SCC 367.

[50] Usha Ramanathan, 'Of Judicial Power', *Frontline*, (16–29 March 2002), 19(6), http://www.frontlineonnet.com/fl1906/19060300.htm (last accessed on 11 July 2012).

[51] Ramanathan has expanded upon her critique in several pieces. See generally, Usha Ramanathan, 'Displacement and Law', *Economic and Political Weekly* (*EPW*), (15 June 1996), 31(24); 'Demolition Drive', *EPW*, (2 July 2005), 40(27), and Ibid., 'Illegality and the Urban Poor', *EPW*, (22 July 2006), 41(29). Her critique is endorsed, with variations to the main argument, by other progressive scholars. See generally, Prashant Bhushan, 'Supreme Court and PIL: Changing Perspectives under Liberalisation', *EPW*, (1 May 2004), 39(18); Bhushan, 'Misplaced Priorities and Class Bias of the Judiciary', *EPW*, (4 April 2009), 44(14). Surya Deva, 'Globalization and its Impact on the Realization of Human Rights: Indian Perspective on a Global Canvas', in C. Raj Kumar and K. Chockalingam (eds), *Human Rights, Justice and Constitutional Empowerment* (Oxford University Press: New Delhi, 2007), pp. 237–63; and Balakrishnan Rajagopal, 'Judicial Governance and the Ideology of Human Rights: Reflections from a Social Movement Perspective', in Raj Kumar and Chockalingam, (2007), pp. 200–36.

has reached a similar conclusion after examining a body of case law relating to civil liberties, slum clearance, and labour rights, all of which directly affect the conditions of the poor in India: 'From the beginnings of PIL as pro-poor and trying to effectuate the rights of the exploited, it is increasingly taking *a diametrically opposite direction.*'[52]

In support of their arguments, the critics of PIL cite several significant decisions which can be classified under three categories.[53] One category of cases includes three cases: *Narmada Bachao Andolan* v. *Union of India*,[54] *N.D. Dayal* v. *Union of India*,[55] and *Tata Housing Development Company* v. *Goa Foundation*[56]—all of which involved the displacement of thousands of people as a result of large dam projects that were ultimately endorsed by the Supreme Court on the view that these projects were pursuing broader goals of development. A second set of cases which have been consistently cited for their neglect of the concerns of migrant workers and other marginalized groups while upholding the right to environment is the series of orders passed in the long-running *M.C. Mehta* v. *Union of India* (1985) case[57] that

---

[52] Rakesh Sharma, 'Rights of the Poor: An Overview of Supreme Court', *EPW* (2 September 2006), 41(35).

[53] These categories fit well into the three-pronged categorization employed by Sandra Fredman in similarly describing areas where PIL has been criticized for regressive decisions in the areas of 'urban development, protection of the environment, and dam development'. Sandra Fredman, *Human Rights Transformed: Positive Rights and Positive Duties* (Oxford University Press: Oxford, 2008), p. 142.

[54] (2000) 10 SCC 664. Here the Supreme Court allowed the Sardar Sarovar project that created one of the world's largest dams to proceed even though a comprehensive environment appraisal had not been conducted. In addition, this affected thousands of tribals and other disempowered groups of people who were forcibly relocated without adequate rehabilitation efforts or compensation.

[55] (2003) 7 SCALE 54. Again, the Court approved of a large dam project by dispensing with the requirement of an environmental impact assessment programme, and by ignoring an expert committee report which pointed to serious environmental problems.

[56] (2003) 7 SCALE 589. In this case, the Supreme Court approved a housing project that was to come up on forest land. Its order, according to Bhushan, effectively deprived hundreds of poor fishermen of their livelihood.

[57] AIR 1996 SC 2231; MANU/SC/1181/1996. The original case was initiated in 1985, but has had several offshoots over the years. Several of the orders issued by the Supreme Court over the last two decades have been helpfully catalogued and

oversaw the relocation of thousands of polluting industries outside of the limits of the city of Delhi. The third category of cases involves those where courts have prioritized the interests of modernizing elites and upper classes over those of weaker sections. This includes cases such as *Almitra Patel* v. *Union of India*,[58] where the Supreme Court ordered the demolition of slums and unauthorized structures set up by migrant workers and the poor. Even if these cases are few in number, one has to recall that the impact of each of these cases was typically felt on a large section of the population, and in that sense, each case had a potentially huge impact.

A more comprehensive study is that conducted by Varun Gauri, who has attempted to empirically test the claims of the critics of PIL in a systematic way.[59] He studied the entire set of PIL cases decided by the Supreme Court over a ten-year period between 1997 and 2007. Gauri concluded that his findings are 'consistent with the claim that judicial receptivity in the Supreme Court to Fundamental Rights claims made on behalf of the poor and excluded individuals has declined in recent years'. His data shows 'not only a decline in the win rate for marginalized individuals but a simultaneous increase in the win rate for advantaged individuals'. He concludes that his findings 'constitute a prima facie validation of the of the concern that judicial attitudes are less favorably inclined to the claims of the poor than they used to be, either as the exclusive result of new judicial interpretations or, more likely, in conjunction with changes in the political and legislative climate'.[60]

As Gauri concedes, the ambiguous manner in which the Supreme Court Registry classifies PIL cases creates difficulties in making definitive determinations about trends in these cases. Also, the specific methodological choices made by Gauri in seeking to conduct his study may also be open to debate, especially the

---

reproduced at http://www.elaw.org/resources/regional.asp?region=Asia (last accessed on 12 July 2012). (See the cases listed as '*M.C. Mehta* v. *Union of India*'.)

[58] (2000) 2 SCC 166; MANU/SC/2767/2000.

[59] Varun Gauri, *Public Interest Litigation in India: Overreaching or Underachieving?* World Bank Policy Research Working Paper No. 5109 (November 2009), http://papers.ssrn.com/sol3/papers.cfm?abstract_id=1503803 (last accessed on 5 December 2009).

[60] Ibid., p. 13.

factors he uses to assess success rates of the categories he terms as 'marginalized', 'disadvantaged', and 'advantaged.' It cannot be doubted, however, that Gauri's study is an important step towards making quantitative assessments of the PIL jurisprudence of the Supreme Court.

It would appear that a number of public interest organizations and NGOs have, for some time now, acted in a way which shows an appreciation of the conclusions reached by Gauri. This is confirmed by Jayanth Krishnan who argues, based on an extensive survey of seventy-three prominent NGOs and social advocacy groups, that the changed reality is leading to a situation where the most prominent social advocacy groups tend to avoid litigation as a deliberate strategy.[61] Krishnan explains that groups like the PUDR (People's Union for Democratic Reforms) have become disenchanted with the slow pace and inconsistent progress of PILs, and prefer to focus on alternative strategies, such as grassroots political mobilization. For several other groups (Krishnan specifically identifies the Centre for Law and the Environment, Conservazone, Lokayan, the National Federation of Women, Saheli, and the National Alliance of Women), the costs and institutional focus required for mounting and sustaining long-drawn PIL campaigns have caused them to avoid using them altogether. Overall, Krishnan emphasizes that social groups are beginning to shy away from using PILs in their strategies. Krishnan's findings are reiterated by more recent studies of aspects of PIL, with the empirical study by Gauri providing a solid empirical base for this conclusion.[62]

For these reasons, this essay supports the view advanced by a number of progressive scholars that the Indian Supreme Court has, in a process that began in the 1990s and has continued across the 2000s, transformed the nature of PIL, turning away, in several cases, from concerns it embraced in its original phase.

[61] Jayanth Krishnan, 'Social Policy Advocacy and the Role of the Courts in India', *American Asian Review*, (2003), 21: 91–124.

[62] See generally, Shylashri Shankar and Pratap Mehta, 'Courts and Socioeconomic Rights in India', in Varun Gauri and Daniel Brinks (eds), *Courting Social Justice: Judicial Enforcement of Social and Economic Rights in the Developing World* (Cambridge University Press: Cambridge, 2008) and Varun Gauri, 'Public Interest Litigation in India', p. 12.

THE PROGRESSIVE CONCEPTION OF THE JUDICIAL ROLE IN CONTEMPORARY INDIA

In this section, the focus is upon the following question: what should progressives do, when faced with an increasingly bleak situation where judges on the Indian Supreme Court have turned their back on at least some of the central progressive causes and concerns of the original phase of PIL?

Nigam and Menon do not offer direct prescriptions on the way forward. There are, however, hints about where they think the focus of progressives should lie. Both are extremely critical of the vast powers taken upon themselves by judges, and express deep concerns about the extent of this power. Nigam focuses on an extra-judicial speech delivered by Justice Ruma Pal to express surprise at the self-perception of Supreme Court judges as the ultimate interpreters and arbiters of constitutional text and values.[63] Menon is equally critical of the power wielded by the Supreme Court in cases involving environmental issues, and concludes by noting that more recently, the poor have 'militantly claimed spaces and livelihoods and spaces as their own'. At another point in her conclusion, she observes that 'the spectacularly successful campaign' against Special Economic Zones in Goa relied not on 'carefully drafted PILs or a thoughtful judiciary' but on '*militant* political mobilization'.[64] Although this is only an interpretation of their silence on this issue, both Nigam and Menon would probably counsel progressives to abandon the site of judicial intervention and focus instead on militant political mobilization.

Krishnan's study suggests that a number of social organizations and advocacy groups have already acted upon this advice. The argument of this essay is that this is an alarming trend and needs to be reversed. What is the alternative? Some progressives have implicitly suggested that what is required is a return to the original phase of PIL. In essence, they could be seen as demanding that a new generation of

[63] Nigam, 'Embedded Judiciary', 2008. The reference is to the following speech: Justice Ruma Pal, 'Judicial Oversight or Overreach: The Role of the Judiciary in Modern India', Centre for Advanced Study of India, University of Pennsylvania, CASI Working Paper Series, Number 08-03, March 2008.

[64] Menon,'Environment', 2008. (Emphasis added.)

judges in the mould of Justices V.R. Krishna Iyer, P.N. Bhagwati, O. Chinappa Reddy and D.A. Desai be appointed to redeem the potential of PIL for progressive causes. In my view, such a view is both unrealistic and problematic.

The contemporary situation which is characterized by excessive and overweening judicial power, where judges adopt 'command-and-control' strategies in PIL cases, may well be a direct result of the exhortations offered by the generation of progressive scholars who sought to influence and shape the discourse of PIL in its founding era. Looking at some of the landmark scholarly literature from the 1980s, one finds an astonishingly instrumental vision advanced for the judiciary. This is what is reflected in *ROJ* as a whole, the details of which we have examined in the second section of this essay.

Many judges of the Indian Supreme Court, having taken these messages to heart, began to flex their muscles, particularly in the 1990s, when the weakened political executive had no choice but to tolerate such judicial adventurism. Part of the problem was also the fact that the judges favoured by progressives (referred to more recently by Baxi as the Four Musketeers)[65] had retired, and were replaced by other judges who did not always share the same judicial philosophy or values. Baxi once referred to the evolution of PIL in India as 'at best an "establishment revolution"'.[66] The story of PIL in the 1990s seems to be consistent with the historical storyline of the weak records of other establishment-led revolutions.

When Aditya Nigam, writing in 2008, asks how Supreme Court judges came to believe that they wield untrammelled authority when deciding PIL cases, at least part of the answer can be tracked to progressive scholarship in the 1980s, including strands represented in *ROJ*, which counselled judges to believe that they were all-powerful and fully justified in incorporating their own understanding of the values of the Constitution into their decisions. So, when Justice B.N. Kirpal equates encroachers with pickpockets in a judgment

---

[65] Upendra Baxi, 'The Promise and Peril of Transcendental Jurisprudence: Justice Krishna Iyer's Combat with the Production of Rightlessness in India', in Raj Kumar and Chockalingam, (2007), pp. 3–25. The reference is to Justices V.R. Krishna Iyer, P.N. Bhagwati, O. Chinappa Reddy and D.A. Desai.

[66] Baxi, 'Taking Suffering Seriously', in *ROJ*, p. 49.

of the Supreme Court,[67] he is merely incorporating his own value judgments into the task of adjudication—and is thus directly acting on the questionable advice offered by progressive writings in the 1980s. The deification of activist judges by progressives seems, albeit with the benefit of hindsight, a mistake.

Progressive scholars and judges do not seem, while offering this advice, to exhibit a genuine belief in the values of constitutionalism and the rule of law. In adopting such an instrumental view of the task of judging, they seem to be unconcerned with maintaining the institutional credibility and neutrality of judges, to enable them to speak authoritatively while deploying the language of constitutionalism and the rule of law. Much of the initial criticism by some judges of the Supreme Court was indeed directed at the potential harm such nakedly ideological actions would cause to the credibility of the Supreme Court.[68] Progressive scholars were quick to dismiss these valid criticisms as being outdated and regressive, but in doing so, ignored the sensible pleas made to focus on a credible conception of the judicial role for handling PIL. In his more recent writings, Baxi too has been critical of the attitude of the judiciary in PIL cases. He has argued that from the 1990s onwards, the judiciary has trampled over the rights of labour and other marginalized sections in seeking to pursue policies that favour globalization and multinational capital.[69]

The argument of this essay is that in charting strategies for the future, progressives should avoid making the same mistake, and must instead advocate a role for judges where they can justifiably lend support to PILs without appearing to act in partisan or ideologically motivated ways. The first move in this regard is a negative one, where the emphasis is on what progressive judges should *not* do in

---

[67] *Almitra Patel* v. *Union of India*, MANU/SC/2767/2000 at para 14.

[68] See, for instance, the criticisms voiced by Justices Tulazpurkar and Hidayatullah during the initial stage of the development of PIL, pointing to several troubling aspects of the phenomenon. V.D. Tulzapurkar, 'Judiciary: Attacks and Survival', AIR 1983 (Journal) 9–18; and M. Hidayatullah, 'Highways and Bye-lanes of Justice', (1984) 2 SCC 1–7.

[69] Upendra Baxi, 'The Avatars of Indian Judicial Activism', in S. Verma and Kusum Kumar (eds), *Fifty Years of the Supreme Court of India: Its Grasp and Reach* (Oxford University Press: New Delhi, 2000).

PIL cases. In many PIL cases, judges seek to dominate the agenda of the proceedings, and adopt 'command-and-control'[70] measures, where they mimic bureaucracies by laying down fixed and specific rules, which prescribe the inputs and operating procedures of the institutions they seek to regulate.

By way of illustration, this essay focuses on three examples drawn from different eras of PIL cases. One can see symptoms of this tendency in the early 1980s' PIL that sought to regulate inter-country adoption of children, where detailed orders were issued to the authorities to solve the problem.[71] Although the Court did seek to solicit participation from NGOs and government agencies dealing with the issue of inter-country adoption, its final order reads like a legislative enactment, complete with the setting of age limits and precise procedures for conducting specified tasks. It was unclear exactly how the Court obtained the background information to base its definitive conclusions upon. The inflexibility of the rule-like 'guidelines' laid down by the Court later led to problems of implementation and confusion, because the case was finally decided by the order, and no authority could approach the Court for clarifications or modifications of the final judicial order. A more recent example of a PIL where the Court exercised an extraordinary degree of overweening control over the proceedings is the 1997 *Hawala* case (*Vineet Narain* v. *Union of India*).[72] To recall, the PIL was brought by two journalists and two lawyers, seeking investigation by the Central Bureau of Investigation (CBI) on details of illegal payments made by way of *hawala* transactions (that is, through an alternative remittance system that operates outside of traditional banking or financial channels) to several politicians for favours in the award of government contracts. Over a period of two years, the Court (especially after the case began to be heard by a bench headed by Justice J.S. Verma) adopted a posture that has been described by a sympathetic observer as 'dynamic, fearless and dominating'.[73] As Muralidhar describes it, the Court's actions

---

[70] I borrow this terminology from Charles F. Sabel and William H. Simon, 'Destabilization Rights: How Public Law Litigation Succeeds', *Harvard Law Review*, (2004), 117: 1016, 1019.

[71] *Lakshmikant Pandey* v. *Union of India*, AIR 1984 SC 469.

[72] (1998) 1 SCC 226.

[73] S. Muralidhar, 'Public Interest Litigation'.

achieved many things, including infusing investigatory authorities like the Central Bureau of Investigation (CBI) with autonomy and insulating them from executive interference. Yet, in the process of doing so, the Court displaced the actual petitioners, and appointed a senior advocate as *amicus curiae* to assist the Court. At the same time, intervention in the proceedings by everyone else was shut out, while some of the hearings were held in-camera, shutting out the public. Muralidhar, whose credentials as a PIL litigant and an astute and insightful chronicler of its development are impeccable, is critical of these aspects of the case, which 'defeat[] the very purpose of the jurisdiction', 'deprive[] public-spirited petitioners of their right to espouse a public cause', and render the participation of other organs of the State redundant. These criticisms echo those made by others about the overweening attitude of Court-appointed *amicus curiae*, committees, and the judges themselves.

The final example is the *Almitra Patel* (2000) case which dealt with the complex issue of solid management waste in Indian cities, and is referred to in the second section of the present essay. The details of the case, relying in particular upon interviews with the principal petitioner, and detailing its winding route have been recently reviewed by Rajamani.[74] Her narrative lays out how the PIL was initiated in 1998, and, while it was being heard by a bench presided over by Chief Justice Verma, focused initially upon measures to handle municipal solid waste. Sometime in 2000, when Justice B.N. Kirpal became the presiding judge, he turned the focus of the PIL to slum clearance. This resulted in the order where he expressed his view equating encroachers with pickpockets, which social activists found objectionable. The petitioner, Almitra Patel, expresses mystification at the turn the PIL took, and explains that she was not in favour of this decision.[75] As Rajamani explains, such an attitude on the part of the judges to exclude PIL petitioners even in cases where they had knowledgeable inputs to contribute, is 'representative of public interest environmental litigation in general'.[76]

---

[74] Lavanya Rajamani, 'Public Interest Environmental Litigation in India: Exploring Issues of Access, Participation, Equity, Effectiveness and Sustainability', *Journal of Environmental Law*, (2007), 19(3): 296–8.

[75] Ibid., p. 302.

[76] Ibid., p. 301.

This essay argues that progressives should critique such modes of adjudication and urge judges to abandon the 'command-and-control' strategies that are currently on display. Judges should instead be encouraged to adopt a far more modest, *facilitative role*, where the focus is on the citizens who suffer, the social movements who organize their interests, and the lawyers who represent them. This will help to avoid some of the problems related to domineering judges, individual lawyer-dominated agendas, and idiosyncratic judicial preferences that have plagued PIL in more recent times. Elsewhere,[77] I have elaborated about what such a facilitative role would entail in its details. Due to constraints of space, I only outline the broad details of that conception here.

Judges in India gain legitimacy for their extravagant actions in PIL cases from the fact that they are seen as making up for the deficiencies of the elected branches. Indeed, in several PILs, the Court has consciously sought to act as a deliberative forum for policy-making, and has used the judicial process to solicit—even mandate—responses from all wings of government. In doing so, it has taken several steps. For instance, it has reached beyond the central government to seek responses from state governments on issues that affect them and has required all ministries potentially affected by its decisions to provide their considered inputs. This essay argues that in exercising jurisdiction under PIL, judges should continue to be sensitive to the need to focus upon filling the deliberative gap, rather than seeking to impose their own subjective choices upon the judicial process. They must remember that their primary role should be to *facilitate* the reaching of sound policy decisions in cases that come up before them.

This facilitative role can be enhanced by a change in mindset which eschews the domineering methods noted in the examples above. What is required, instead, is a much more decentralized form of intervention, where the emphasis is on enabling all possible stakeholders to contribute meaningful inputs. Such inputs should be used to design flexible rules that are capable of responding to changing—and sometimes unpredictable or hostile—circumstances

---

[77] For a more detailed description of this conception and its details, see, Arun K. Thiruvengadam, 'Evaluating Criticisms of Contemporary Public Interest Litigation: A Progressive Conception of the Role of the Indian Judge', draft presented at the LASSNET conference, 2009.

on the ground. Throughout this process, the emphasis should be on making every stage of the judicial process transparent.[78]

How is this process to work in practice? Here, the attempt is to sketch out the broad details of the process. Although the progressive critics analysed in the second section of this essay have focused on the changing nature of PIL, this essay argues that at one level, the basic nature of PIL has not changed. Both in the early and later phases of PIL, the essential responsibility that judges have sought to take on is the difficult task of institutional reform, which is exacerbated by the problem of widespread governmental inaction in India. In the early phase, the institutions that were the subject of PIL's focus were prisons, mental hospitals, children's homes, and so on. During its 'governance' phase, the focus of PIL has been on institutions such as the police and investigatory agencies, environmental regulatory authorities, and schools. So, typically, courts are required to confront the problem of sick, failing, or recalcitrant institutions in PIL cases.

At a primary level, the Court should seek to ascertain whether the public institution in question 'is failing to satisfy minimum standards of adequate performance' and whether 'it is substantially immune from conventional political mechanisms of correction'.[79] Once the Court concludes that the institution is failing on these counts, it should initiate 'a process of supervised negotiation and deliberation among the parties and other stakeholders'.[80] Arguably, this is exactly what the Indian Supreme Court has done in a variety of PILs, such as the ongoing PILs dealing with the Right to Food[81] and the Police Reform[82] cases. In order to ensure that all stakeholders have opportunities to participate in the court hearings, the Supreme Court has resorted to methods such as taking out full-page advertisements in newspapers outlining the details of the PIL and soliciting

---

[78] My normative views are influenced by the experimentalist modes of intervention that have been reconstructed by Sabel and Simon after studying successful recent examples of public law litigation in the US. See, Sabel and Simon, 'Destabilization Rights'.

[79] Sabel and Simon, 'Destabilization Rights', p. 1062.

[80] Ibid.

[81] *PUCL* v. *Union of India*, (2006) 13 SCALE 399.

[82] *Prakash Singh* v. *Union of India*, (2006) 8 SCC 1.

participation from affected or interested individuals; issuing notice to the Advocates General of the various states on issues where the Court perceives that they may be affected or have contributions to make; and involving policy making bodies that, by virtue of their expertise, would have valuable insights into the problems being tackled in the institution before the Court.[83]

Once all the relevant stakeholders are before the Court, they should be encouraged to negotiate between themselves, under the aegis of the Court, on steps that can be taken to remedy the identified problem. While consensus should be the goal, the Court will have to decide upon a proposal which comes closest to an agreeable remedial regime. Although reaching a consensus will not be possible in all cases, having it set as a goal 'prevents premature closure and reinforces the threshold commitment of openness and mutual respect'.[84]

When the Court issues its order, it should avoid decreeing matters finally. As experience from tackling troubled institutions in previous PILs shows, in remedying institutional problems, it is best to adopt provisional measures which incorporate a process of reassessment and revision, while always allowing those with an interest in the institution to participate fully. Once again, the Court must strictly adhere to the value of transparency in setting out its interim orders and assigning responsibility for implementation to various agencies

---

[83] In an illuminating piece examining the use of expert bodies and social science evidence by the Supreme Court, T.K. Naveen commends this trend, but emphasizes the need to 'think through the role of such expert bodies and their composition, especially so since these bodies ought to aspire for neutrality'. In his view,

> [w]hat need to be evolved are guidelines for a judge using such appreciation and evaluation of such evidence; approaches that might be appropriate in the acceptance of such social science data as evidence, to not take it as absolute truth assertions, reminders to interrogate such data relentlessly before using it; mandatory opportunity to all parties concerned as well as the general public to respond to such data adduced as evidence; and systematic record of such social science facts and their appreciation so that [this record] can be evaluated in subsequent cases.

T.K. Naveen, 'Use of "Social Science Evidence" in Constitutional Courts: Concerns for Judicial Process in India', *Journal of the Indian Law Institute*, (2005). Naveen's recommendations fit well with the conception set out here, as they emphasize the same values of participation and transparency in the judicial process.

[84] Sabel and Simon, 'Destabilization Rights', p. 1068.

or individuals. This would necessarily mean, therefore, that the prominent, peremptory role given to *amicus curiae* (which became a familiar feature in PIL cases under Chief Justice Verma in the mid-to-late 1990s, and is a practice that has continued since) must be curtailed. Similarly, the practice of Court-appointed committees conducting hearings—as if they are substitutes for the Supreme Court itself (a practice that is constitutionally indefensible)—must also end. If participation, rather than final determination, is seen as a value in itself, the Court will be able to halt criticisms about the more problematic aspects of PIL. On issues of monitoring and compliance, the Court should, as it has increasingly done in PIL cases since the early 1990s, fix dates of hearing at regular intervals to monitor the progress of its provisional rulings. In invoking its power of contempt to ensure compliance, the Court must be more sagacious and avoid instances such as in some cases in the past which seem to be the product of frustration rather than 'reasoned elaboration'.

Progressives also need to attend to other worrying features of contemporary PIL. We have already noted the disturbing findings of a group of scholars that public interest organizations and social organizations have begun to abandon the route of PIL. This trend makes sense if we take account of the contemporary PIL scene, which is dominated by lawyers and assorted individuals who file PILs quite often with no direct connection to the clients or causes they seek to represent. This is followed by a 'top–down' process employed by the judges who subsequently hear the case and decide on its future development with inputs from 'experts' and 'court-appointed *amici*' who, once again, have very little direct contact with affected interests.

In his provocative study of PIL in India, Charlès Epp concludes that the Indian case offers a paradox: despite having one of the most activist courts in the world, which is also the most supportive of egalitarian and procedural rights, India has been 'unable to develop a sustained agenda' on rights. He argues that this is primarily because 'the Indian support structure for legal mobilization—the complex of financial, legal and organizational resources necessary for appellate litigation—remains weak and fragmented'.[85]

---

[85] Charles Epp, *The Rights Revolution: Lawyers, Activists and Supreme Courts in Comparative Perspective* (University of Chicago Press: Chicago, 1998).

In her extremely insightful and more recent study of PIL in India, Sandra Fredman provides a vision for PIL similar to the one outlined in this essay, emphasizing the roles of 'facilitation and coordination' that judges can play in enhancing deliberative democracy by encouraging 'governments to listen and interact with civil society'.[86] She reminds judges that '[u]ltimately, courts cannot supplant either political activism or the legislative process'. 'Nor can courts,' she continues, 'make good the failings of executive government, whether the latter are due to incompetence, lack of resources, or lack of political will'.[87] Fredman's solution is to emphasize the idea of a 'social conversation', (a term she borrows from Baxi), which 'de-centres the judicial role itself, portraying litigation not as a transfer of hierarchical power to the court, but as a trigger for democratic interaction between judges, government actors, and different social and political groups'.[88]

If PIL is to truly become a vehicle for addressing concerns of the marginalized in Indian society, its future will have to be crafted for it to be able to do so effectively and meaningfully. It is imperative that progressives focus on strengthening the network of social organizations that can build grounded and bottom–up litigation strategies, which seek to genuinely represent the concerns of the actual clients in PIL cases. Arguably, the recent Right to Food PIL represents one example of such a trend.[89] Such instances provide hope that with robust grassroots and civil society movements providing the ballast, judges will feel obliged to adopt more modest roles by deferring to the greater credibility and representational capacity enjoyed by a strengthened support structure.

CONCLUSION

Judicial activism is at once a peril and a promise, an assurance of solidarity for the depressed classes...as well as a site of betrayal. ... Courts are, at the

---

[86] Fredman, *Human Rights Transformed*, p. 125.

[87] Ibid.

[88] Ibid., p. 133.

[89] For a discussion of the facts of the case and the strategies adopted by the civil society groups that led the campaign, and for an assessment of the achievements of the litigation, see generally, Fredman, *Human Rights Transformed*, pp. 130–3; Lauren Birchfield and Jessica Corsi, 'Between Starvation and Globalization: Realising the Right to Food in India', *Michigan Journal of International Law*, (2010), 31: 691–764.

end of the day, never an instrument of total societal revolution: they are at best...instruments of piecemeal social engineering...never a substitute for direct political action.

— Upendra Baxi[90]

This bleak prognosis asserted by Baxi in 2000 sits oddly with his far more enthusiastic view expressed in *ROJ*. Indeed, Baxi's current views are more in line with the critical views on PIL expressed by Nigam and Menon more recently. The descriptive argument of this essay strove to demonstrate the dramatic transformation in the nature and content of PIL in the intervening years.

The normative argument of the essay does not find fault with the motives of scholars like Upendra Baxi, who has, for over six decades, indefatigably promoted the cause of the impoverished in India and across the global South.[91] It has focused, instead, on the view, amply reflected in the contributions to *ROJ*, that the main drivers for social change in countries in the global South ought to be judges and sensitized judiciaries. The normative argument advanced here is that the judiciary should reformulate its role in PIL by giving up the 'command-and-control' methods that have led to some of the gravest problems of contemporary PIL jurisprudence, including those where the judiciary has spurned the interests of the original constituency of PIL. My argument is that the judiciary should focus instead on being an ally to strong civil society groups and movements in their attempt to make the processes of Indian democracy more participatory, inclusive, and effective in pursuing the developmental goals enshrined in the Constitution.

This essay has focused exclusively on the Indian experience with PIL. What lessons does it offer for other countries in South Asia, or across the global South? When *ROJ* was published in 1987, PIL was almost exclusively an Indian phenomenon within South Asia. Since then, other judiciaries in South Asia—notably those in Pakistan and

---

[90] Baxi, 'The Avatars of Indian Judicial Activism', pp. 161–4.

[91] For particularly insightful examples from his vast body of work on these issues, see generally, Upendra Baxi, 'Introduction', in Upendra Baxi (ed.), *Law and Poverty: Critical Essays* (N.M. Tripathi: Bombay, 1988) and Upendra Baxi, *The Future of Human Rights*, 2nd Ed. (Oxford University Press: New Delhi, 2006).

Bangladesh—have experimented with PIL jurisdiction.[92] While the contemporary judiciaries in these nations have continued with PIL jurisdiction, echoes of the progressive critique of Indian PIL are to be found in the academic and public commentary in Pakistan and Bangladesh criticizing similar trends of 'command-and-control' strategies by their respective judiciaries.[93] It would, therefore, seem that the lessons suggested here would have broader application for the role of judiciaries in South Asia.

Moving beyond South Asia, the normative account offered in this essay has significant parallels with the lessons drawn by social activists and rights groups in contemporary Africa.[94] One such successful campaign was led by the South African AIDS NGO, the Treatment Action Campaign (TAC). In 2002, TAC successfully litigated in the courts to thwart the South African government's opposition to distributing a free drug that would significantly reduce mother–child transmission of AIDS. However, as a recent study of TAC's organizational strategy notes, its methods present a sharp contrast to the classic rights model practised by the American civil rights organizations of the twentieth century.[95] The campaign's successful constitutional litigation, culminating in the decision in its favour

[92] See generally, Arun K. Thiruvengadam, 'In Pursuit of the Common Illumination of Our House?: Trans-judicial Influence and the Origins of PIL Jurisprudence in South Asia', *Indian Journal of Constitutional Law*, (2008), 2: 67–103.

[93] See, for instance, Human Rights Commission of Pakistan, 'Public Interest Litigation: Scope and Problems', report of an HRCP seminar (28 March 2010), http://www.hrcp-web.org/pdf/Public%20Interest%20Letigation%20-%20 HRCP%20seminar%20report.pdf (last accessed on 18 September 2011), criticizing the tendency of judges to issue excessive *suo moto* orders while exercising PIL jurisdiction in Pakistan, and urging judges to focus on issues where the public interest arises strongly; and Ridwanul Hoque, *Judicial Activism in Bangladesh: A Golden Mean Approach* (Cambridge Scholars Publishing: Newcastle upon Tyne, 2011), suggesting a normative framework for the future of PIL in Bangladesh which is broadly similar to the one outlined here.

[94] See generally, Lucie E. White and Jeremy Perlman, *Stones of Hope: How African Activists Reclaim Human Rights to Challenge Global Poverty* (Stanford University Press: Stanford, California, 2011).

[95] William Forbath, Zackie Achmat, Geoff Budlender, and Mark Heywood, 'Cultural Transformation, Deep Institutional Reform and ESR Practice: South Africa's Treatment Action Campaign', in White and Perlman, *Stones of Hope*, pp. 86–7.

in the case of *Minister of Health* v. *Treatment Action Campaign*,[96] played a 'subordinate, supporting role' to its overall goal of building itself 'into an oppositionist movement in the national polity, with strategies directed at protesting, challenging and changing state policy, and enlisting and collaborating with allies in the state and party apparatus' in other national organizations such as trade unions. This is because TAC did not make court victories the object of its multi-faceted campaigns and did not assert that courts should be the central arena for initiating or shaping pro-poor state policies. Instead, it 'used litigation in the service of many-sided strategies to open up policy-making processes, to reshape programs and policies in democratic and pro-poor decisions, and to prod governments to implement them'.[97] Such a vision also enables judges to set defensible and legitimate boundaries to their own contributions to the development of public interest law and the attainment of social and economic justice across the global South.

---

[96] (2002) 5 SA 721 (CC).
[97] Forbath et al., 'Cultural Transformation', p. 87.

Afterword

So, what does it matter? Why bother with comparative constitutionalism? What legitimacy do the pronouncements of judges and legislators in other jurisdictions have, to influence the development of constitutional law in one's own nation? Is not jurisdictionalism the anchor for the legitimacy of unelected judges holding and exercising the large governmental powers of deciding constitutional conflicts? Is it not safer to stick steadfastly to local constitutional decisions, in charting the path forward for the governance of a sovereign people? Are there not dangers of regression to a new form of intellectual colonialism, in borrowing constitutional ideas from beyond the border? Don't we have enough to do analysing and encouraging national constitutionalism, without troubling our minds about the problems faced by judges in neighbouring and other countries, in accordance with their different constitutional charters?

Anyway, what is a retired Australian judge doing writing an Afterword to this book which has deliberately chosen to focus its attention on developments in constitutional law in South Asia? Is this 'South Asia' anything more than a repackaging of the old imperial paradigm of the subcontinent? The jewel in the British crown, when it held sway over (or greatly influenced) all the lands mentioned in this book: India, Pakistan, Bangladesh, Sri Lanka, Burma, and also Nepal and Bhutan?

I acknowledge the legitimacy of all of these questions. They, or like questions, are not ignored in this book. As the editors have explained, the manuscript grew out of conferences of constitutional lawyers held in London in 2006 and in Singapore in 2009. The participants could have chosen a different configuration of national constitutions to study. They could have extended their perspective to Malaysia, Singapore, the Maldives, even perhaps Mauritius. At a pinch, they could have thrown the net vigorously and picked up Papua New Guinea, Solomon Islands, Fiji; even maybe Australia and New Zealand. After all each of these countries has a constitutional law. Each has developed its legal system after the model derived from the British in or immediately after the colonial times. Each continues to utilize the English language, at least for constitutional and legal discourse. Each espouses the rule of law, independent courts, and uncorrupted judges.

The wider the net is cast, the hazier the focus of the emerging picture. It is like the lens of a camera. To get the sharpest image, we need to narrow the focus. Narrowing it to the identified lands of South Asia still results in a study that addresses the governance of a third of humanity. And whilst they share the commonalities of language and legal tradition with many others, the culture and historical legacy of South Asia afford deep attitudinal and societal links that makes the investigation specifically fruitful and promising.

I can only assume that the honour of writing this Afterword has fallen to me because of my many travels in the lands described in these chapters. And the desire of the editors to have an outsider (but a sympathetic one) who can look at the topics that are reviewed with dispassion and a certain distance. Perhaps an outsider will see linkages that those closer to the centre themselves miss or take too much for granted.

Comparative constitutionalism is a relatively new and controversial subject. Political scientists, historians, and governmental experts have long familiarized themselves with the way constitutional law operates in other lands. Yet, until recently, lawyers were not much interested in the topic. In part, this was because, in imperial times, the commonalities were largely those imposed by the metropolitan power—such as the century and more of appeals to the Judicial Committee of the Privy Council in London and the instructions given to the viceroys about the need for protection of imperial political and commercial interests. In part, it was the principle of jurisdiction that demanded most of the attention of the newly emerging scholars of national constitutional laws. They had enough on their plates, analysing and contributing to the elaboration of their national constitutional charters. The doings of constitutional judges and scholars in other lands, even neighbours, were not sufficiently relevant to engage a lot of time and attention. In part, there was probably a hierarchy of attitudes of indifference, mixed with disdain, for the way others approached constitutional law: with its mixture of political values and social aspiration that, inevitably, would differ from one country to another. Why would a judge or a scholar in the Indian legal system, for example, be interested in the way others tackled problems arising under their own constitutions, with their different texts, books, and learning?

It is perhaps significant that one of the first efforts at comparative constitutionalism in Asia was undertaken by the Australian National University in Canberra in 1960. The resulting dialogue was chaired by the retired Chief Justice of the High Court of Australia, Sir John Latham. It was a one-off event. Perhaps in 1960, even that distinguished jurist and former politician considered that comparative constitutionalism involved 'teaching' the newly independent nations of Asia how to observe British constitutional principles: elected parliaments; responsible ministers; a skilled and uncorrupted civil service; and independent judges with a distinctively modest role. It is the danger of revisiting these perceptions of comparative constitutionalism that gives rise to an occasional measure of scepticism and hesitation, given voice in several chapters of this book. If the commonalities of the constitutional arrangements of most of the countries were little more than the link they once shared with imperial Britain, this would produce a questioning attitude about the value to be added by such a discourse. So what are the distinctly 'South Asian' characteristics to be gleaned from comparing constitutional developments that have happened to each other?

Clearly, there are some common themes in the constitutional law and practice of South Asian countries that are likely to be peculiar to them or at least not of great moment in other lands that share the same general legal and constitutional traditions. Thus, there is the problem of apostasy and the demand of a person born into a family of one religion to convert to another religion, or the problem of renouncing religion altogether. These represent a challenge to the legal order that would hardly, if ever, arise in other parts of the world, such as Australia, Britain, Canada, or New Zealand. There the right to change religious allegiance or to join the growing numbers of citizens who reject religion altogether, hardly raise an eyebrow. Still, as cases described in this book (and the *Lina*

Joy case before the Federal Court of Malaysia[1]) show, this can be an acute issue in several countries of Asia where religious, geographical, and political concerns can sometimes trump the individual's right to freedom of religion.

Racial, ethnic, and cultural divisions now arise, in different guises, in most constitutional regimes throughout the world. However, the passions that they often engender in circumstances of communal conflict attract much attention in this book and for obvious reasons. Reconciling the deeply felt beliefs of differing religions and the secular principle of equality and freedom of religion is never easy. Even in supposedly fully secular societies, the emerging differences can sometimes sharpen serious hostilities. We have seen an instance of this in Australia in recent times. Although a rather limited, weak provision in the Australian Constitution upholds religious freedom,[2] it was the furious lobbying of religious organizations and their threats of retaliation to elected Parliaments who defied their will that recently produced the defeat in the Australian Federal Parliament of a proposed amendment to the *Marriage Act*, 1961 (Aust.), designed to open up marriages to same-sex couples.[3] This became a 'wedge' issue in politics, despite the evidence of repeated opinion polls that show that 70 per cent of the Australian population favoured the reform. Only one-third of present marriages in Australia are now actually conducted with religious rites.

Comparative constitutionalism in many Western countries today include debates over such issues as the constitutional principle of equality and the right to marry, and the constitutional principle according respect to deeply held religious beliefs.[4] This may not be an attribute of constitutionalism that has yet reached South Asia, although reports suggest that the question may be lapping at the

---

[1] *Lina Joy* v. *Majlis Agama Islam Wilayah Persekutuan*, (2007) 3 CLJ 557; M.D. Kirby, 'Fundamental Human Rights and Religious Apostasy', *Griffith Law Review*, (2008), 17: 151.

[2] Australian Constitution, Section 116.

[3] *The Marriage (Amendment) Bills* 2012 (Aust.) were defeated in the Australian Parliament: House of Representatives, 19 September 2012, Senate, 20 September 2012.

[4] *Minister of Home Affairs* v. *Fourie*, (2005) ZACC 19; *Halpern* v. *Canada* (A-G) (2003) 65 OR (3d) 161 (CA); *Perry et al.* v. *Schwarzenegger et al.*, (2010) 3:09-cv-02292.

doors of courts in Nepal. Still, the extent to which constitutional ideas and challenges nowadays jump borders and turn up in what would once have been the most unexpected places can be seen in the stimulating chapter about the *Naz Foundation* case in India.[5] In that case, the Delhi High Court (Shah CJ and Muralidhar J) upheld the challenge to Section 377 of the Indian Penal Code, insofar as it purported to criminalize adult, consensual, private sexual conduct in India. Many countries which, like India and others in South Asia, inherited anti-sodomy criminal laws from the period of British rule, have witnessed their legislative repeal in recent years. But in other countries with the same history, legislative fear and inaction has led to constitutional challenges before the courts. Those challenges have been upheld in constitutional litigation in the United States of America,[6] South Africa,[7] and in human rights challenges in Northern Ireland,[8] the Republic of Ireland,[9] Cyprus,[10] and Australia[11].

These constitutional cases, decided outside South Asia, naturally became a focus of the activities of local civil society organizations. *Pro bono* advocacy and court challenges have arisen in several countries. Ultimately, they have reached the courts of India. Some critics, hearkening to jurisdictionalism, suggest that they are completely irrelevant to the differing language, history, and cultural and spiritual circumstances of India. In India, the stigmatization of homosexuals was more akin to the humiliating diminution of the rights of dalits, by reference to their caste.[12] Against the background of a worldwide recognition of the irrationality of criminalizing adult, consensual, private conduct, it would have been astonishing had the judges of the Delhi High Court ignored these legal developments, happening in other countries with similar legal systems at the same time.

[5] *Naz Foundation* v. *Delhi and Ors.*, (2009) 4 LRC 838 (HC Delhi).

[6] *Lawrence* v. *Texas*, (2003) 539 US 558, reversing *Bowers* v. *Hardwick*, (1986) 478 US 186.

[7] *National Coalition for Gay and Lesbian Equality* v. *Minister of Justice* (SAF), (1998) 3 LRC 648.

[8] *Dudgeon* v. *United Kingdom*, (1982) 4 EHRR 149.

[9] *Norris* v. *Ireland*, (1991) 13 EHRR 186.

[10] *Modinos* v. *Cyprus*, (1994) 16 EHRR 485.

[11] *Toonen* v *Australia*, (1994) 1 Int Hum Rits Reports 97 (No. 3).

[12] Indian Constitution, Article 15 (2) (Prohibition of discrimination on grounds of religion, race, caste, sex or place of birth).

So this is how, in the world of today, constitutional developments arrive in one country, often at about the same time as they arise in others. This sharing and dialogue is not, of course, confined to geographical regions—whether within Europe, the Americas, Africa, or South Asia. But when the cases arise, it is very hard today to suggest that judges, addressing similar problems, must totally ignore what has been written by highly intelligent judges in courts of great distinction in neighbouring or far-off lands, faced with analogous problems. Of course, each judge must observe fidelity to his or her own national law. On some occasions, the national law is relevantly different in text or context, permitting or requiring a differing outcome.[13] Nonetheless, experience teaches the merit of studying what others have written in their own constitutional settings and then making proper allowance for the differences of text, context, and values. The availability of legal materials today is so much greater than it was for our forebears. Reading the approaches to common problems elsewhere, at the very least, helps a national judge to see the problems in a wider context; to hearken to the arguments of principle and policy that are properly raised; and to tick all the boxes of domestic relevance so as to make sure that no aspect of the problem has been overlooked or unappreciated.

The decision of the Delhi High Court in the *Naz Foundation* case was appealed to the Supreme Court of India, although not by the Union of India. The appeal has been argued and stands for judgment. In due course the Supreme Court will decide. But I did not perceive in the Delhi High Court's reason an illicit use of foreign constitutionalism. Rather, I saw at work a process that is widespread and beneficial in constitutional law today. It is an invocation of transnational jurisprudence to identify the broad constitutional context of the problem in hand, and resort to the national constitutional text and governing doctrine to provide the ultimate resolution of the problem for decision. Every other learned discipline in the world today approaches issues in this way. The law need not be different or immune from global perspectives.

In Australia, with one of the oldest national constitutions, relatively impervious to formal amendment, the highest court has been well versed in comparative constitutionalism, from the very start. This was, in part, because of professional habits of comparison, discursive opinions,

---

[13] *Banana* v. *State*, (1999) 1 LRC 120 (Zimbabwe SC). This decision differentiated the texts of the Zimbabwean and South African Constitutions in respect of protection of sexual orientation.

and analogous reasoning derived from the shared traditions of the English judges. But it partly arose out of the adoption of the federal principle and the early discovery of the utility of looking to the United States, and to Canadian and, later, Indian, courts to clarify problems arising under Australia's own constitutional document.[14]

In recent years, there has been a sharp debate over whether judges are justified in searching for analogies and comparisons from other countries and from the Universal Principles of Human Rights while undertaking the task of constitutional adjudication.[15] The limits of constitutional comparison are well understood. So are the special duties of fidelity to the national law and the avoidance of the dangers of misuse of foreign comparisons.[16] Just the same, Australian judges today look beyond their own borders to cast light on the meaning and operation of the national constitution. In a recent Australian case, the issue arose as to whether an attempt by Parliament to deprive all prisoners of the right (and duty) to vote in federal elections was incompatible with the text and implications of the Australian Constitution. In reaching an affirmative conclusion on that issue, the majority of the High Court of Australia[17] referred to a constitutional decision in Canada[18] and a decision of the European Court of Human Rights, seen as relevant by analogy.[19] The foreign decisions were not binding. They were not determinative. They did not control the Australian decision. But neither were they irrelevant. They represented useful background. Context. A review of values and issues. To ask lawyers and judges to ignore such considerations, in the age of the Internet, is both undesirable and futile.

That is why this book is so timely. It is looking at the linkages of constitutionalism in a region of the world of growing significance, both in economic and legal terms. The rule of law is the alternative

---

[14] M.D. Kirby, 'The Supreme Court of India and Australian Law', in B.N. Kirpal et al. (eds), *Supreme but not Infallible: Essays in Honour of the Supreme Court of India* (Oxford University Press: New Delhi, 2000), pp. 66, 76–9.

[15] *Mabo* v. *Queensland* (No. 2), (1992) 175 CLR 1 at 42; *Al-Kateb* v. *Godwin*, (2004) 219 CLR 562 at 589 (63), per McHugh J; cf at 617 (152), per Kirby J.

[16] *Public Service Board of NSW* v. *Osmond*, (1986) 159 CLR 656 at 668, per Gibbs CJ.

[17] *Roach* v. *Electoral Commissioner*, (2007) 233 CLR 162 at 177–9 (13)–(19), per Gleeson CJ and at 203–4 (100) per Gummow, Kirby, and Crennan JJ; cf at 220 (163) per Hayne J and at 224–5 (181), per Heydon J.

[18] *Sauvé* v. *The Queen*, (2002) 3 SCR 519 (SC–Canada).

[19] *Hirst* v. *United Kingdom* (No. 2) (2005) 42 EHRR 41.

to the rule of power, of families, of guns, of influence, of corruption. It is in the common interests of the people of the world to strengthen constitutionalism. With it comes individual freedom, fundamental human rights, and economic equality. The prospects for the future are good. We can all learn from each other. South Asia can broaden the lens of constitutionalism elsewhere so that we appreciate the role of comparative constitutionalism for the human species, for the lives of other animals and for the whole complex wonder of the biosphere.

I pay respect to the honorands of this volume. Neelan Tiruchelvam has been there since Creation. Upendra Baxi, then the youngest tutor at the Sydney University Law School, even taught me in the 1960s in my Master of Laws course, nearly fifty years ago. For their gifts of intellect, heart, leadership, and wisdom, I offer a grateful pupil's praise and thanks.

Sydney
November 2012

The Hon. Michael Kirby, AC CMG
Justice of the High Court of Australia
(1996–2009)

Index

Abdul Gafur v. *Secretary, Ministry of Foreign Affairs,* 323
Acharya, Nilamber, 103, 106
active nihilism, 34
Adhikari, K.L., 106
Adhikari, Prime Minister Man Mohan, 107
Adhikari, R., 106
adjudicative leadership, 37
Advocate Sultana Kamal and Others v. *Bangladesh,* 335
Afghanistan
    Constitution (1923), 27
    Constitution (2004), 155
    Taliban regime, 34
African constitutionalisms, 31, 34
Ahmadiyya religious communities, 27
Allah Rakha v. *Pakistan,* 228
Almitra Patel v. *Union of India,* 355
Ambedkar, Bhim Rao, 36, 236
American constitutional doctrine, 67–8, 70
    Equal Protection Clause, 80
    Establishment Clause case law, 66
    privacy constitutional doctrine, 74
American judges, 184, 186
anal intercourse, criminal prohibitions on, 52–4, 73–5, 80. *See also Naz Foundation* v. *Union of India*

Anglo-Nepali War (1814–16), 87
anti-blasphemy law, 27
anti-conversion law, 146, 160, 169, 171–4, 213–14
anti-sedition law, 29, 269, 271, 275, 275n32, 276, 285, 298
Anti-Untouchability Act, 1955, 79
Anuj Garg v. *Hotel Association of India,* 50
Aristotle, 9
Ariyaratne, 36
articulate consistency, notion of, 71
Asian constitutionalism, 5
Attorney-General of Ceylon v. *Reid,* 255n31
Austin, Granville, 26, 29, 31, 75, 77
Australian National University, 5
autonmous individual, concept of, 147
Ayesha Bibi v. *Subodh Chandra Chakrabarti,* 253

Balakrishnan, Chief Justice, 55
Banaras Hindu University's Law Faculty, 6
Bangladesh
    Bangladeshi judges, 304, 308–10, 315–18, 327, 329–32, 334, 338
    'Basic Structure Doctrine', 313–18

Codes of Criminal Procedure, 277–9
conceptualizations of constitutionalism, 303–4
Constitution of, 152, 155
Constitution of the People's Republic of Bangladesh, 306, 306n12
democratic transition (1991–2006), 318–25
expression 'Bismillah-Ar-Rahman-Ar-Rahim', 153
fundamental principles of state policy (Article 8(1)), 152
'Fundamental Principles of State Policy' (FPSPs), 307
judicial protection of constitutionalism, 329–32
judiciary, 20, 304, 304n6, 308–13
Judiciary on Unconstitutional Constitutional Amendments, 310
religious freedom, 152–3
right of every citizen of freedom of speech and expression and the freedom of the press, 283n74
right to assemble and to participate in public meetings and processions, 283n74
right to form associations or unions, 283n74
Shari'a-based constitutionalisms, 27
State of Emergency (1974), 305
State of Emergency (2007–8), 305, 333–9
state powers in, 20
suo motu interventions, 338
Bangladesh v. Sheikh Hasina, 334

Baxi, Upendra, 6, 14–15, 22, 344, 358–9, 366–7
Bhagwati, P.N., 177, 344, 358
Bhattarai, Prime Minister Krishna P., 97, 103
Bhutan. See also Draft Constitution of Bhutan; Monk Body of Bhutan
abolition of position of Desi, 121
administrative system based on Western models, 122
Bhutan State Congress Party, 122
Buddhism, role of, 17, 116–17, 126–7
Christian missionary in, 135–6
codification of traditional laws, 122
2008 Constitution, 142–3, 155
constitutional history, 16–17
constitution-making and constitutional processes in, 21
democracy, 141
drafting of Constitution, 128–32
Druk Kagyu tradition, 119–21
Druk National Congress Party (DNC), 127
dual system, 119–21
Dzongkha as the official language, role of, 122–3
Five-Year Plans, 121
forms of governance, 29
'Glorious Drukpa' (Pelden Drukpa), 123
Je Khenpos, role of, 125–6, 132–3
law code, 123, 123n16
minority languages and ethnic groups, 136
modernization of, 121–4

monastic community, role of,
121
National Assembly, 125–6
national identity, 1950s, 123
Nyingma tradition, 119
regional governors of Paro,
Daganna, and Jakar, 120
religion, role of, 17, 116–17
representatives of the Central
Monk Body, 124–8
Royal Advisory Council (*Lodey
Tshogdey*), 124–5
sacral monarchy, 137–8
secularism, 134
secular nature of, 118–19
separation of Church and
State, 132–6
social reforms under
Wangchuck, 121
Tenzin Chogyel's law code,
120
Zhabdrung, influences of,
138–40
Bhutto, Prime Minister Zulfiqar
Ali, 225, 230
Bickel, Alexander, 57
bigamy, issues related to, 205–9
Bilkis Akhter Hossain v.
Bangladesh, 319
BLAST & Others v. *Bangladesh*,
320, 325
Bodo/NDFB (National
Democratic Front for
Bodoland), 128n28
Bommai v. *Union of India*, 156
Bowers v. *Hardwick*, 52
British East India Company, 88
British Indian Independence Act,
29
Brudner, Alan, 57
Buchanan, James M., 38
Buddhism
in Bhutan, 17, 88, 128–40
in Sri Lanka, 18

Burma, 5
Constitution, 1947, 35n14

Canadian constitutional doctrine,
67–8
Chatterji, Bankim Chandra, 180
Chicago Theory of Government,
42
Choudhry, Sujit, 12–13, 15, 21,
187, 269
Church–State issues, 181, 184
Western-style model of
separation, 181
citizen's interpretation of
constitutionalism(s), 37–8
Code Napoléon, 89
colonial constitutionalism, 28–9
Queen Victoria's 1858
Proclamation, 28
in SAC, 28
The Commonwealth in Asia, 3
Company Raj, 28
comparative constitutionalism,
field of, 9–14, 371–2
case of *Naz Foundation,* 15
Choudhry's criticism, 12–13,
15
'dialogic' model of, 15
dominant players, 11
foundational debate, 12
'functionalist' approach, 11
Hirschl's views, 13
'identity-affirming' character
of dialogical mode, 15
as a judicial tool, 17
reasoning by analogy, 71–2
relationship between allied
disciplines and, 12
rise of modern, 10
role of, 291–302
separation of organized
religion from the state,
16–17
Sri Lanka, 176–9

textual similarities between
other constitutions, 15–16
as a judicial tool, 10
'universalist' approach, 11
use of empirical methods,
13–14
Conrad, Dieter, 6
Constitutional Court of South
Africa, 51
constitutional democracy, 5
constitutionalism-to-come, era of,
25
constitutional nihilisms (CN),
33–6
Constitutionalism in Asia, 5
constitution-making, 7
con-theory, 33
conversion, issues related to,
209–15
Coomaraswamy, Radhika, 3, 20,
201, 341, 345–6
critical legal theory, 12
cross-national constitutional
appropriation, 17–18, 182,
184–8
bigamy, issues related to,
205–9
conversion, issues related to,
209–15
culture objection, 186
debate in the United States,
185
flaw in the practice of citing
foreign sources, 185
opportunism objection, 185
principle of *stare decisis,* 186
problem of constitutional
identity, 188
secular constitutional
development, 188–96
Thirteenth Amendment,
196–205, 209
Crown v. *Mussumat Gholam
Fatima,* 249n7

cultural nationalism, 56, 72,
76
universalist response to, 73

Dalai Lamas of Tibet, 120
decision costs, 39n20
Declaration on Minorities, 149
Declaration on Religious
Discrimination, 149
Derrett, Duncan, 4
Derrida, Jacques, 38
Deuba, Prime Minister Sher
Bahadur, 107
Dharmapala, Anagarika, 159
dialogical model of comparative
constitutional interpretation,
63–82
directive principles of state policy,
31, 92, 202
District Registrar and Collector v.
Canara Bank, 48
Dominion of Ceylon's 1948
'Soulbury' Constitution, 3
Dr. Mohiuddin Farooque v.
Bangladesh, 325n98
Draft Constitution of Bhutan,
128–40
alternative, 143–4
Article 3(3), 133
Article 3(5), 133
Article 10(6), 133
Article 10(1)(b), 133
Articles 2(2) and 3(2), 130–1,
133, 135
Chibdrel Ceremony, 133
2008 Constitution, 142–3
as democratic foundation,
140–1
Drafting Committee, 128–9
driglam namzha or code of
etiquette, 133
dual system, 130
issue of equal status for all
religions, 134–6

Je Khenpos, role of, 125–6,
132–3
judiciary, 134
kasho and *kaydon*, 137
king's role, 130
National Council, 130
opening statement, 130
Preamble, 129
public debates, 130–2
reference to Buddhist heritage
and the Druk Kagyu
tradition, 130–1, 135
role of the Central Monk
Body, 129
sacral monarchy, 137–8
secularism, 134–6
separation of Church and
State, 132–6
Zhabdrung's political and legal
frameworks, 138–40
Dr Mahmood-ur-Rahman Faisal
v. *Government of Pakistan,*
227–8
Druk Kagyu order, 119–21
Drukpa Kagyu monastic
community, 121
Dudgeon v. *United Kingdoms,* 52
Du Plessis v. *De Klerk,* 65
Duttagamani, Sinhala King (Dutu
Gemunu), 158
Dworkin, Ronald, 71
dzong (fortress/monastery) of
Bhutan, 120

economic integration in South
Asia, 2
economies of scale, 40
Edrsinha, Rohan, 7
efficiency test, 40
Egyptian Law of Bequests, 228,
228n21
Eisenstadt v. *Baird,* 53
*The Endurance of National
Constitutions,* 14

Euro–American constitutional
models, 29
Euro–American 'Enlightenment',
38
European Court of Human Rights
(ECHR), 51, 293–4, 297
European Human Rights law, 270
external costs, 39n20

Farishta v. *Federation of Pakistan,*
226, 226n12
freedom of expression
Article 19(1) of the
Constitution of India, 282
Criminal Procedure Codes,
India, 278
John Stuart Mill *vs* James
Fitzjames Stephen, 268–70
in Sri Lanka, 194–5
Freedom of Religion Act, 174
Frontier Crimes Regulation
(FCR), 28

Gandhi, Mohandas, 36, 38
Gandhi, Prime Minister Indira,
238, 241
Gandhi, Prime Minister Rajiv,
239
German constitutional law, 70
Gledhill, Alan, 4
Goldsworthy, Jeff, 69
Gorkhapātra, 103
Government of India Act, 1935,
29, 90
Government of Nepal Act, 1948,
90
Govind v. *State of Madhya Pradesh,*
48
Gracie v. *Wijeguna Wardene,*
208n73
Greek city-states, constitutions
of, 9
Greek law, 173
Griswold v. *Connecticut,* 53

Guha, Ranajit, 26
Guru, Gopal, 79

Habermas, Jürgen, 58
Hakim Khan v. *The State*, 226
Heidelberg's South Asia Institute,
    6
hereditary kingship
    of Bhutan, 29
    of Nepal, 29
Hindu law, 4
Hindu–Muslim relations on Asian
    subcontinent, 182
Hirschl, Ran, 13, 22
HIV/AIDS therapy and Section
    377, 56
Holocaust, 296
Holocaustian 'governance', 32
homosexuality
    analogy between sexual
        orientation and
        untouchability, 78–9
    Article 17 and, 80
    Blue Diamond Society (BDS)
        case, Nepal, 110
    criminalisation of, 76–7
Hoque, Ridwanul, 20, 22
Hossain, Kamal, 8
human rights in SAC, 30–2

Indian Constitution, 3
    analogy between sexual
        orientation and
        untouchability, 78–9
    Articles, 31, 48, 56, 73, 79,
        81, 156, 234
    contingencies of constitutional
        politics, 31–2
    Criminal Procedure Codes,
        Section 144, 278
    defense of constitutional
        identity, 183
    directive principles, 190, 202–3,
        208, 234, 307n17, 349

forms of governance, 29
freedom to criticize caste-based
    preferences, 298
fundamental rights, 31
fundamental right to
    'propagate' religion, 210
Indian Contracts Act, 1872,
    270
Indian Evidence Act, 1872,
    270
Native Marriages Act, 1872,
    270
'optimal constitutional design'
    (OCD) approaches, 32–3
political participation by
    'untouchables', 31
position to 'add' new heirs,
    222
Preamble, 156
principle of *sarva dharma
    sambhava*, 191, 217
principle of secularism, 156
process of inheritance, 222
religious-cum-legal reform,
    221–2
religious denominations, 190
religious freedom, 190
reservation system, 101
restrictions on a fundamental
    right in language, 284
right to assemble, 282
Right to Equality, 59–60, 71,
    73, 191n27
right to form associations and
    unions, 282
underlying themes, 75–6
Indian Constitution-making, 26
Indian jurisprudence, 20. *See also*
    Indian Penal Codes
anal intercourse, criminal
    prohibitions on, 52–4,
    73–5, 80
Babri Masjid (a mosque)
    demolition case, 190

basic structure, 182–3
Indian judges, 45, 78, 81, 181,
    188, 193n32, 292, 343–4,
    348, 357–8, 362
judicial borrowing of, 181
progressive conception of,
    modern times, 357–66
prohibition of Taslima Nasrin's
    Dwikhondito, 290, 298–9
public interest litigation (PIL)
    in, 8, 21, 347–55
Sarla Mudgal case, 206–7
Shah Bano case, 190, 207
Stainislaus judgment, 210–13
Stephen's contribution,
    268–74
vs Pakistan judiciary, 19
Indian Law Institute, 5
Indian Penal Codes, 274–5
    Section 95, 289
    Section 144, 286–9, 300–1
    Section 124(a), 285
    Section 153 (a) and 505(2),
        285
    Section 377, 15
India's indigenous village system,
    182n5
Indonesia, 5
Indo–Sri Lankan accord of 1987,
    196
In re Ram Kumari, 254n22
Interim Government of India
    Act, 92
Interim Government of Nepal
    Act, 1951, 91
International Covenant on Civil
    and Political Rights (ICCPR),
    148, 150, 155–6
international human rights, norms
    of, 148–51
    constitutional arrangements or
        forms of State structures,
        150
    equality, 148

non-discrimination, 148
    religious pluralism, 148
    rights of minorities, 149
    right to freedom of thought,
        conscience and religion,
        148–9
    South Asian experiences,
        151–6
    State religion, 150–1
international human rights
    norms, 19
intra-regional borrowing, 2
Introduction to Legal Systems, 4
Islam, principles of, 152
Islamic family law, 222
Islamic Republic of Pakistan, 152
    religious freedom, 152
    right to assemble, 283n73
    right to form associations or
        unions, 283n73
    right to freedom of speech and
        expression, and freedom of
        the press, 283n73
Iyer, V.R. Krishna, 350, 358

Jackson, Vicki, 186
Jacobsohn, Gary Jeffrey, 17, 21,
    118, 267
Janatha Vimukthi Peramuna
    (JVP), 196
Jathika Hela Urumaya, 171, 174
Jayawardene, President J.R., 163,
    196
Jeevakaran v. *Ratnasiri*
    Wickremanayake and Others,
    194n36
Jennings, Ivor, 3, 33, 93
    articulation of negative
        liberties, 4
    Ceylon *vs* India, 4
    dangers of communalism, 4
    Waynflete Lectures, 3
Jinnah, Governor-General
    Muhammad Ali, 152

declaration on Pakistan, 152
John Jiban Chandra Datta v.
  Abinash Chandra Sen, 248n3
Joint Action Council Kannur, 55
*The Journal of the Indian Law
  Institute,* 5
judges and lawyers, South Asian,
  5, 8, 10, 14–15, 36, 296, 310,
  370–1, 375
  'activist' judges, 346–7,
    358–66
  appellate, 8
  Bangladeshi, 304, 308–10,
    315–18, 327, 329–32, 334,
    338
  Bhutanese, 141
  Indian, 45, 78, 81, 181, 188,
    193n32, 292, 343–4, 348,
    357–8, 362
  Nepalese, 109
  opinions, and speeches of, 8
  Sri Lankan, 196, 203–5,
    211–12, 214, 217–18
judiciary, South Asian. *See also*
  Supreme Court
  Bangladesh, 20, 304, 304n6,
    308–13, 329–32
  Bhutan, 118, 134, 141
  India. *See* Indian jurisprudence
  Nepal, 88, 96, 109
jurisdictional studies, 6

Kalanjiam Ammal v. *Shanbagam,*
  255n30
Kamtapur Liberation
  Organisation (KLO), 128n28
Kaneez Fatima v. *Wali
  Mohammad,* 227
Katyal, Sonia, 55
Kazakhstan, 7
Kesavananda Bharati v. *State of
  Kerala,* 188, 188n21,
  200
Khaitan, Tarunabh, 49

Khan, General Mohammad Ayub,
  221, 224, 230
Khanal, Reabatti Raman, 103
Kharak Singh v. *State of Uttar
  Pradesh,* 48
Khosla, Madhav, 51, 55, 345
King Jr., Martin Luther, 38
King v. *Perumal,* 206, 208n73
Kodeswaran v. *Attorney General,*
  193n32
Kodikam Pillai v. *Mudanayake,*
  193n32
Koirala, Bishweshwar Prasad, 94
Koirala, Prime Minister Girjia
  Prasad, 106
Kokkinakis v. *Greece,* 173
Kommers, Donald, 11n40
Kriegler, Justice Johann, 65
Kudrat-E-Elahi Panir v.
  Bangladesh, 321–2
Kuenlay, Rongtong, 127
Kunwar, Jang Bahadur, 88
Kyi, Aung San Suu, 36

Lama, Dalai, 36, 120
Latham, John, 5
Lau, Martin, 261
Lawrence, Dudgeon, and *Norris* v.
  Ireland, 74
Lawrence v. *Texas,* 52
liberal democratic constitutional
  order, 13
liberal/libertarian forms of
  constitutionalism, 36
Liberation Tigers of Tamil Eelam
  (LTTE), 196
Lily Thomas v. *Union of India,*
  248n2

M. Asafuddowla and Others v.
  Bangladesh, 335
Macauley's Penal Code, 271
Madan, T.N., 154, 181
Malagodi, Mara, 15–16, 21

Maldives, 156
Mandal Commission Report, 101
Mandela, Nelson, 38
Maneka Gandhi v. *Union of India*, 49
Mansfield, John H., 19
margin of appreciation, notion of, 68
Marriage Act 1961, 373
Marriage Registration Ordinance, 205
Martha Samadhanam David v. *Sudha*, 255n28
martial law proclamation, 312
Massamat Farishta v. *Federation of Pakistan*, 226n12
Mathou, Thierry, 125
M.C. Mehta v. *Union of India*, 354
Md. Idrisrur Rahman v. *Bangladesh*, 336
Menski, Werner, 4
Menzingen judgment, 209, 214
methodological matrix of a national constitutional tradition, 70
military constitutionalisms, 30
Mill, John Stuart, 19, 268, 293
Millenium Development Goals, 164
Minerva Mills Ltd. v. *Union of India*, 188, 188n22, 200
Mitakshara School of law, 234
Monk Body of Bhutan, 124–8
and draft Constitution, 128–40
lopons (*lopon* means teacher) of, 129
moral full citizenship, 77
Moran, Mayo, 67, 291–2
Moyezuddin Sikder v. *State*, 333–4
Mrs A. Marthama v. *A. Munuswamy*, 255n29
Mst. Zarina v. *State*, 257

Mudanayake v. *Sivagnasunderam*, 193n32
Muhammad, Holy Prophet, 277
Muhammad Ismail Qureshi v. *Pakistan*, 261n58
Muralidhar, S., 8
Musharraf, General Pervez, 232
Muslim Marriage and Divorce Act, 206
Muslim personal law, 190, 226, 226n12, 227, 229–31, 238–9, 239n41, 240, 240n43, 260

N. Adithayan v. *Travancore Devaswom Bd.*, 263n64
Namgyal, Zhabdrung Ngawang, 119–21
Nandy, Ashis, 154, 181
Narayan, Jay Prakash, 36
Narmada Bachao Andolan v. *Union of India*, 354
Natalie Abeysundere v. *Christopher Abeysundere and Another*, 205, 256n32
National Coalition, 77–8
proceedings during, 78
National Coalition for Gay and Lesbian Equality v. *Minister of Justice*, 52
national constitutional traditions, 69
interpretive methods, 69
methodological distinctiveness of, 69–70
set of outcomes, 69
nation as 'charter of social revolution', 26
Naz Foundation v. *Union of India*, 15, 46–7, 187, 267, 374–5
application of Section 377 of IPC, 48
Article 17 interpretation, 79–81
Article 21 interpretation, 82

case of *Lawrence,* 52–4
comparative constitutional
    interpretation, 57–72
cultural nationalism in, 72–3
dialogical interpretation,
    63–82
doctrine politics of, 48–57
equality dimensions, 49–50
failure to use comparative
    materials, 52
Justice Verma's
    reinterpretation, 56–7
particularist conception,
    58–61, 72–3
prohibition based on sexual
    orientation, 72–3
right to privacy, 48–9
South African analogy, 65–7,
    77–8
universalist conception, 61–3,
    74
Voices Against 377, 54
Nazi speech, prohibitions in, 70
N.D. Dayal v. *Union of India,* 354
negative liberties, 4
Nehru, Jawaharlal, 75, 236
Nehru, Jawarharlal, 151
Nelson, Matthew J., 18
Nepal, 7
    Blue Diamond Society (BDS)
        case, 110
    Chanda Bajracarya case, 109
    Constituent Assembly (CA),
        87
    1990 Constitution, 98–110,
        155
    constitutional developments,
        86–7
    constitution-making and
        constitutional processes
        in, 21
    1990 Constitution-making
        process, 102–3
    Constitution Recommendation
        Commission (CRC), 98–9,
        101

degree of socio-cultural
    diversity, 101
Democratic establishment
    (1951-60), 91–4
elections for house of
    representatives, 113–14
electoral system, 100
forms of CN, 34
forms of governance, 29
freedom of worship and
    equality of citizens, 90
Fundamental Principles of
    Law, 92, 96
Gorkhali conquest and
    expansion, 87
Hinduism, 90, 107
Hindu kingship, notion of, 94
'Hindu' religious state
    (kingdom), 27
interpretation and
    implementation of the
    1990 Constitution, 104–10
Jan Āndolan (People's
    Movement), 97–8, 105
Jang Bahadur's reign (1846-
    77), 88
under King Mahendra, 92–4,
    97
language in constitutional text,
    107–8
massacre of King Birendra and
    his family, 104
Mira Dhungana case, 109
Muluki Ain (Law or Code of
    the Country), 88, 96, 109
Panchayat period (1960–90),
    94–7
Parbatiya caste structure, 87–8,
    106
post-1990 establishment, 97–8
post-2002 series of unelected
    governments, 114–15
pre-1990 legal developments
    in, 87–97
public interest litigation in, 8
Rana-Congress government, 91

Rana regime (1846–1951), 88–91

range of external legal concepts, 16

Reena Bajracharya case, 110

Right to Equality, 100–1

Right to Religion, 102, 107–9

Royal Palace Communiqué, 98n37

Shah period, 87, 101

Treaty of Sagauli, 1816, 87

Twelve-Point Agreement, 105

Uniform Civil Code, 92

Westminster model of Constitution, 93, 99

Nepal Janajati Mahasangh, 102

Nkrumah, Kwame, 36

non-establishment, principle of, 184

non-preferentialism, principle of, 66

Objective Resolution, 75

O'Dowd, T. John, 19–20

Official Secrets Act, 29

Okoth-Ogendo, H.W.O., 26

Olson, Mancur, 40

On Liberty, 269

optimal constitutional design, 38–42

'efficiency' matrix, 40

SIMS approach, 41–2

wealth-maximization perspective, 41

Pakistan, 5, 156. *See also* Islamic Republic of Pakistan; personal law reform in Pakistan

arrests of tribal people, 28–9

Codes of Criminal Procedure, 279

differences with Indian legislature, 220–2

directive principles, 223, 234

Enforcement of Shari'ah Act (1991), 231

Federal Shariat Court (FSC), 225–7

freedom of expression, 283

Hudood Ordinances, 232

'Islamization' campaign, 1979, 225, 231

under Mohammad Ayub Khan, 221, 224, 230

Muslim Family Laws Ordinance (MFLO), 223n6, 224, 226n12, 228

Muslim Personal Law (Shariat) Application Act, 1937, 223n6

Muttahida Majlis-e-Amal (MMA), 232

under Nawaz Sharif, 231–2

non-contiguous federalism, 30

Northwest Frontier Province Muslim Personal Law (Shariat) Application Act, 1950, 223n6

Pakistan Muslim League-Quaid-e-Azam or PML-Q, 232

Penal Code, 27, 277

perpetuation of 1901 Frontier Crimes Regulation (FCR), 28–9

under Pervez Musharraf, 232–3, 264

position to 'add' new heirs, 222

process of inheritance, 222, 228, 230

Punjab Muslim Personal Law (Shariat) Application (Amendment) Act, 1951, 223n6

Qur'anic heirs, 222, 224, 229

religious-cum-legal reform, 221–2

religious freedom in, 265

sedition (with adaptations), deliberate and malicious acts, 276

special constitutional amendment (Article 260), 230
State-based Islamic laws, 220
status as an 'Islamic' State, 219
substantive religious-cum-legal reform, 19
terms of 'religious' personal law, 220, 223–33
West Punjab Muslim Personal Law (Shariat) Application Act, 1948, 223n6
Zila Nazim (District Mayor), role of, 279
under Zulfiqar Ali Bhutto, 225, 230
Pakistan Federal Shariat Court, 19
Pakistan People's Party, 230
Parashar, Archana, 236
Pareto 'theorems', 40
parliamentary government, 5
Pasayat, Justice Arijit, 287
passive nihilism, 34
personal law reform in India
'a usufructuary right of maintenance', 234
Commission of *Sati* (Prevention) Act, 1987, 241
Criminal Procedure Code (Section 125), 238–9
equal-opportunity 'reform', 234
'equal status' provisions, 233–4
Hindu 'coparcenary' law, 237–8
Hindu Law Committee, role of, 235
Hindu Law Committee report, 1941, 235n30
Hindu Law of Inheritance (Amendment) Act, 1929, 235n29

Hindu Marriage (Amendment) Act, 1964, 241
Hindu Succession Act, 1956, 236
Hindu Succession (Amendment) Act, 2005, 241, 246
Hindu Women's Right to Property Act (The Deshmukh Act), 235n29
Kerala Joint Hindu Family System (Abolition) Act, 1975, 237n37
'limited' lifetime estate, 234, 237n35
maintenance of divorced wives, 239–40, 239n41
Marriage Laws (Amendment) Act, 1976, 241, 241n46
Muslim Women's (Protection of Rights on Divorce) Act, 1986, 239, 240n43, 240n45
religious personal law, 234
Shah Bano decision, 239
single-party majority, 242–3
status of women, 234–5
'substantive' religious-cum-legal reform, 233, 238, 241
personal law reform in Pakistan, 223–33. *See also* Pakistan
Commission on Marriage and Family Laws, 224n8
Council of Islamic Ideology, role of, 223–5
Dr Mahmood-ur-Rahman Faisal case, 227–8
Enforcement of Shari'ah Act (1991), 231
exclusion principle, 227
Farishta case, 226, 226n12
First Schedule, 225, 225n9
Hudood Ordinances, 232
intra-sect mobilization, 228

Muslim Family Laws
Ordinance (MFLO),
223n6, 224, 226n12, 228
Objectives Resolution, 223
process of inheritance, 222,
228, 230
Protection of Women (Criminal
Laws Amendment) Act,
2006, 232
right of representation under
Muslim law, 224n7
Shariat Appellate Bench, role
of, 225, 227
'substantive' religious-cum-
legal reform, 230–1
Pirjada Syed Shariatullah v.
Bangladesh, 323
Piyatissa, Sinhala King Devanam,
158
Planned Parenthood v. *Casey*, 53
Politics, 9
polygamy, 205
Posner, Richard, 41, 185
postcolonial constitutional form
(PCF), 35
postcolonial state formation, 35
Premalal Perera v. *Weerasuriya*,
195n40
presidential form of governance, 42
Provincial Councils Bill, 196, 198
*Public Interest Litigation in South
Asia*, 7–8
public interest litigation (PIL), 20
in Bangladesh, 8, 310, 325–8
descriptive argument, 342
in India, 21, 347–55
in Nepal, 100
normative argument, 342
progressive conception of,
modern times, 357–66

Queen Victoria's 1858
Proclamation, 28
Qur'anic heirs, 222, 224, 229

Raghavan, Vikram, 48
Rahman, President Ziaur, 152
Rajasinghe, King Kirti Sri, 158
Rakeya Bibi v. *Anil Kumar
Mukherji*, 254n22
Ralung monastery, 119
Ram Prasad v. *State of U.P.*,
189n24
Rana, Jang Bahadur, 88–9
Rana, Prime Minister Padma
Shamsher, 90–1
Rayamajhi, Keshar Jung, 103
Razzaque, Jona, 8
reasoning by analogy in
comparative constitutionalism,
71–2
Redding, Jeffrey A., 226
regional economic integration of
South Asia, 2
Regmi, Mahesh C., 89
Reid v. *Reid*, 255–6
religious conversion, India
anti-*Sarla* cases, 251n12, 253
Caste Disabilities Removal
Act, 1850, 256
Converts' Marriage
Dissolution Act, 1866,
256–7, 257n35
David case, 255
decisions post-Independence,
255
for dissolution of marriage,
253–4
early period, 250
husbands' conversions and
second marriages, legal
consequences, 248
issue of divorce, 250
issues if both spouses convert,
252–3
legitimacy of children of the
second marriage, 250, 252
pro-*Sarla* cases, 251n12
rights of maintenance, 252

under Special Marriage Act,
253
writ petition process, 252
religious conversion, Pakistan
under Blasphemy Laws, 261
Caste Disabilities Removal
Act, 1850, 260
Dissolution of Muslim
Marriages Act, 260
Hudood Ordinances, 258, 264
from Islam to the Ahmadiyya
faith, 261
Mst. Zarina case, 257–60
Special Marriage Act, 259
religious conversion, prohibition of
in comparative context, 262–6
conversion, issues related to,
209–15
Greece, 173
Sri Lanka, 171–4
religious pluralism, 147
in Kerala, 154
'rent-seeking' self-interest
maximizers (SIMS), 41
Rev. Stainislaus v. *The State of
Madhya Pradesh*, 169
rights-based constitutionalism, 13
Right to Equality (Article 15),
31, 49, 49n14, 59–60, 71, 73,
77, 93, 100, 148, 171, 174,
191n27
right to life, 48
Right to Privacy (Article 21),
48–9, 73–5
rioting and associated offences,
276
Robasa Khanum v. *Khodadad
Bomanji Irani*, 254n22
Roe v. *Wade*, 53
*The Role of the Judiciary in Plural
Societies* (*ROJ*), 20–1, 341–3,
358, 367
themes and conclusions,
343–7

S.R. Bommai v. *Union of India*,
191n26, 198
Sarla Mudgal v. *Union of India*,
190, 191n25, 206–7, 247,
249–52
sarva dharma sambhava, principle
of, 191, 217
Sayeda Khatoon v. *M. Obadiah*,
254n22
Scheduled Castes and Scheduled
Tribes Act, 1989, 79
Schmitt, Carl, 37
School of Oriental and African
Studies (SOAS), 4
secularism, 18, 27, 117–18,
134–6, 140, 147, 151–4, 156,
176–7, 180, 183–4, 186,
189–96, 204–5, 216, 233,
267, 287, 296–7
secular constitutional
development, 181
in India, 134, 183–4, 188–91
in Sri Lanka, 191–6
Seervai, H.M., 169–70
Selvi v. *Karnataka*, 49
Sen, Amartya, 154
sepulchral constitutionalisms, 27
sexual orientation, 51
National Coalition between
and caste, 77–8
Shah, King Prithvi Narayan,
87–8, 93
Shaha, Rishikesh, 94
Shankar, Shylashri, 17, 21, 118,
267
Shari'a-based constitutionalisms
in South Asia, 27
Sharif, Prime Minister Nawaz,
231
Sharvananda, Chief Justice,
198–9, 202
Silva, Colvin R. de, 162
Singapore, 14
Singh, Justice Kuldip, 206

Singh, Ram Ugra, 91
Sinhalese–Tamil ethnic
    relationship, 196
Sorabjee, Soli, 8
Soulbury Constitution of
    Sri Lanka, 4n10, 146, 160. *See
    also* Sri Lanka
    Article 29(2), 160
    Article 29(3), 161
    Buddha Sasana, 194, 201, 212,
        214
    'Buddhism Clause' (Article 6),
        161–2, 161n46, 164
    Clause 9(3) (of the Bill), 174
    de Silva's views, 162
    equality before the law,
        194n37
    ethnic divide, 161
    freedom of religion and
        worship, 195
    'freedom of religion clause'
        (Article 18(1)(b)), 162
    freedom of thought, freedom
        of worship, and free
        expression, 194–5
    fundamental right to
        'propagate' religion, 211
    higher education, 164
    judicial review of legislation,
        162–3
    minority rights, 163
    power to repeal and replace the
        Constitution, 195
    Preamble, 194
    prevention of judicial review,
        195
    propagation of the *Buddha
        Dhamma*', 164, 194
    State religion, adoption of
        (Article 9), 164
South Africa, 7
    Bill of Rights, 65
    Christianity in public policy,
        66–7
    Establishment Clause, 66
    Justice Albie Sachs' judgment
        in *State v. Solberg*, 66, 77–8
    Treatment Action Campaign
        (TAC), 368
South Asia
    adoption of a State religion,
        152–3
    'constitutional common sense',
        9
    constitutionalism in, 2, 372
    cultures of, 1
    defined, 24–5
    degree of constitutional and
        legal kinship, 2
    intra-regional borrowing, 2
    judiciaries, present times, 21
    modern constitutional schemes
        of, 154–5
    Orientalist accounts of, 1
    principle of secularism, 156
    regional economic integration
        of, 2
    religious freedom, 147–56
    as a source of extremist
        ideology and terrorism, 1
    as 'the illegitimate children of
        the Anglo-American legal/
        political tradition', 3
South Asian Association for
    Regional Co-operation in Law
    ('SAARCLAW'), 8n28
South Asian Association for
    Regional Cooperation
    (SAARC), 2
South Asian constitutions (SAC),
    23–4
    approaches to, 25–6
    balance of class forces, 25
    civilian and military
        relationships influence/
        condition, 25
    'civil society'-based
        persecution, 27

colonial 'constitutionalism',
27–9
constitutional nihilisms, 33–6
constitutional toleration for
religion, 27
constitutions as governance
machines, 28–9
constructions of 'ethnicity', 25
contingency/necessity in, 26
forms of governance, 29–30
founding choices, 27
framing categories of juristic
and judicial understanding,
37
histories of movements of
independence, 25
human rights in, 30–2
human social/cultural plurality,
27
imageries of constitutions and
constitutionalism, 32–3
metaphor of 'charter of
revolution', 32
metaphysics of power and
domination, 25–6
optimal constitutional design,
38–42
political participation by
'untouchables', 31
processes of decision-making,
25
right to equality, 31
social exclusion, 27, 31
in terms of governance,
development, justice, and
human rights, 36–8
in terms of parliamentary
sovereignty, 38
typology of fours 'Cs', 37–8
South Asian law, 4
Sri Lanka, 17
alliance between Buddhist and
Hindu groups, 160

application of Indian secularism
jurisprudence in, 18
Buddhism in, 18, 161, 192
Christian Sahanaye Doratuwa
Prayer Centre, case of,
165–6
Citizenship Act of 1948, 193
civil war through
constitutionalism, 7
colonial powers ruled over, 157
comparative constitutionalism,
field of, 176–9
comparative constitutional
reflection on India, 183
confusing treatment of
religious diversity in, 17
constitutional freedom, 159–64
constitutional jurisprudence,
165–76
Constitution of Sri Lanka
(1978), 155
destructive and debilitating
ethnic conflict, 183
Dharmavijaya Foundation Act
No. 62 of 1979, 167
Dravidian settlers, 158
ethno-nationalist identity, 160
ethno-religious identities, 157
forms of CN, 34
Franchise Legislation of 1949,
193
incorporation of a religious
institution, cases of, 165–71
Independence Constitution
(the Soulbury
Constitution). See Soulbury
Constitution of Sri Lanka
Jathika Hela Urumaya, 160
Kandyan Kingdom, 158
Mahavamsa account of, 157–9
majority–minority struggle, 193
'Nineteenth Amendment to
the Constitution', 174–5

obligations under the ICCPR,
169
Official Language Act of 1956,
193
politics of religion, 157–9
population characteristics, 157
'Prohibition of Forcible
Conversion of Religion',
171–4
Republican Constitutions of,
146
as a secular state, 175–6
Sinhala identity *vs* Tamil
'otherness', 159
Sinhala nationalism, 192
'Sisters of Saint Francis of
Menzingen' case, 168–9
Tamil minority, 18
Tiruchelvam's insights, 7
Sri Lankan society, 17
Stainislaus v. *State of Madhya
Pradesh,* 210–11
State of Bombay v. *Appa,* 189n24
State–religion nexus, 150–1
in Pakistan, 152
State v. *Solberg,* 66
State v. *Sukur Ali,* 324
Stephen, James Fitzjames, 19,
268, 270–4, 292, 301–2
Subhash Chandra v. *Delhi
Subordinate Services Selection
Board,* 50
Supreme Court
of Bangladesh, 20, 153, 304,
306–7, 330–1, 333–4, 337
of Bhutan, 118, 134, 141
of Canada, 293
of Canada and the European
Court of Human Rights,
293
of India, 6, 19, 36, 53, 156,
182–3, 188, 190, 206, 210,
234, 247, 249, 256–7, 262,
269–70, 284–6, 290–1,
294, 328, 345, 347–8,
350–9, 363, 375
of Pakistan, 36, 43, 225–7,
240, 338
of Sri Lanka, 146, 165, 167,
169–71, 173–4, 176–7,
184, 196, 206, 209, 255,
262n60

Taliban 'constitutionalisms', 27
Tamil United Liberation Front
(TLF), 35
*Tata Housing Development
Company* v. *Goa Foundation,*
354
Thakur v. *Union of India,* 50
Thirteenth Amendment case, 18
Thapa, Prime Minister Surya
Bahadur, 107
Thero, Reverend Omalpe
Sobhitha, 171
Thero, Ven. Ellawala
Medhananda, 174
Thirteenth Amendment,
196–205, 209
Thiruvengadam, Arun, 20–1, 55,
337
Tilakawardane, Justice, 175
Tiruchelvam, Neelan, 7–8, 20,
154, 341
on South Asian
constitutionalism, 7
Tobgye, Lyonpo Sonam, 128
Togadia, Praveen Bhai, 287
transformative constitutionalism,
38
Tripathi, P.K., 185
Tullock, Gordon, 38
Tushnet, Mark, 13, 70

Udagama, Deepika, 7, 17
unanimity rule of decision, 38

UN Declaration on the Elimination of All Forms of Intolerance and of Discrimination Based on Religion/Belief, 148

UN Declaration on the Rights of Persons Belonging to National, Ethnic, Religious and Linguistic Minorities, 148

United Liberation Front of Assam (ULFA), 128n28

United States Supreme Court, 51

universal adult suffrage, principle of, 31

Universal Declaration of Human Rights (UDHR), 30, 147–8

unnatural sex, ban on, 51

Upadhyaya, Chief Justice Bishwa Nath, 98, 103

Upadhyaya, Home Minister Yog Prasad, 103

Upadhyaya, Surya Nath, 99

US constitutional doctrine, 151

US First Amendment cases, 269, 292

Venugopal, K. K., 118, 129

Vishaka v. *State of Rajasthan*, 328

Voices Against 377, 54

'wall of separation' theory, 151

Wanasundera, Justice, 201–2

Wangchuck, His Majesty Jigme Khesar Namgyal, 116

Wangchuck, king Jigme Dorji, 121, 127

Wangpo, Mipham, 120

Waynflete Lectures, 3

Weerasuriya, Justice T.B., 175

Weimar Constitution, 6

Welikala, Asanga, 193

Western democracies as reference points, 3

Whitecross, Richard W., 15–16, 21, 88

Wickramanayake, Prime Minister Ratnasiri, 174

Zia-ul-Haq, General, 152, 225

Editors and Contributors

EDITORS

Sunil Khilnani is Avantha Professor and Director, King's India Institute, London, England, UK. He was educated at Trinity Hall, Cambridge, where he took a first in Social and Political Sciences, and at King's College, Cambridge, where he gained his doctorate in Social and Political Sciences. Khilnani's research interests lie at the intersection of various fields: intellectual history and the study of political thought, the history of modern India, democratic theory in relation to its recent non-Western experiences, the politics of contemporary India, and strategic thought in the definition of India's place in the world. He is the author of *The Idea of India* (1999) and is completing a book on India's global role and prospects, while he continues with his research studies of Jawaharlal Nehru and the history of democracy in India—two of his long-term projects.

Vikram Raghavan is Lead Counsel, Legal Vice-Presidency, World Bank, Washington, DC, USA, where he works in two different practice groups. As a member of the East Asia and South Asia group, he is 'country lawyer' for the World Bank's operations in India, Myanmar, and Korea. Raghavan is presently co-writing a textbook on comparative constitutional law in five democracies. His longer-term research project focuses on how India became a republic after the Raj. He created and contributes to a much visited blog on Indian constitutional law and governance: www.lawandotherthings. blogspot.com.

Arun K. Thiruvengadam is Associate Professor, School of Policy and Governance, Azim Premji University, Bengaluru, India. Previously, he was Assistant Professor, Faculty of Law, National University of Singapore, and Visiting Fellow, National University of Juridical Sciences, Kolkata. He holds degrees in law from the National Law School, Bangalore and New York University. He served as a law clerk to Chief Justice A.M. Ahmadi (1995–7) and practised before the High Court of Delhi and the Supreme Court of India (1997–9). Thiruvengadam teaches, researches, and writes in the areas of Indian constitutional and administrative law, comparative constitutional law and theory, legal theory, legal education, and law and development. Among his recent publications is a co-edited volume, *Emergency Powers in Asia* (2010).

CONTRIBUTORS

Upendra Baxi is Emeritus Professor, Universities of Warwick and Delhi. He was educated at Rajkot; the University of Bombay; and the Law School (Boalt Hall), University of California at Berkeley, where he received his LLM and JSD degrees. Baxi's areas of expertise in teaching and research include comparative constitutionalism, social theory of human rights, human rights responsibilities in corporate governance and business conduct, and materiality of globalization. His publications include *The Future of Human Rights*, 3rd Edition (2008) and *Human Rights in a Posthuman World: Critical Essays* (2009).

Sujit Choudhry is Cecilia Goetz Professor of Law, School of Law, New York University. He holds law degrees from the Universities of Oxford, Toronto, and Harvard, was a Rhodes Scholar, served as a law clerk to Chief Justice Antonio Lamer of the Supreme Court of Canada, and was Graduate Fellow at the Harvard University Center for Ethics and the Professions. Choudhry has written widely on comparative constitutional law and comparative constitutional development with a particular focus on Canada, South Africa, India, and the United States. His edited collections include *Constitutional Design for Divided Societies* (2008) and *The Migration of Constitutional Ideas* (2006).

Ridwanul Hoque is Associate Professor of Law, University of Dhaka. He studied law at the University of Chittagong in Bangladesh, obtained an LLM from the University of Cambridge, and completed his doctorate in comparative public law at the School of Oriental and African Studies (SOAS), University of London. Hoque's areas of interest include comparative public law, judicial behaviour studies, human rights (especially of the 'marginalized'), law and society, population movement, and Muslim personal law. He has been consulted by government and international agencies on issues related to human trafficking, access to justice, child rights, child labour, and immigration. His recently published book is *Judicial Activism in Bangladesh: A Golden Mean Approach* (2011).

Gary J. Jacobsohn is H. Malcolm MacDonald Professor of Constitutional and Comparative Law, Department of Government, University of Texas at Austin. His interests and work involve constitutional theory and comparative constitutionalism. Among his writings are *Constitutional Identity* (2010), *The Wheel of Law: India's Secularism in Comparative Constitutional Context* (2003), *Apple of Gold: Constitutionalism in Israel and the United States* (1993), *The Supreme Court and the Decline of Constitutional Aspiration* (1986), and *Pragmatism, Statesmanship, and the Supreme Court* (1977).

Mara Malagodi is British Academy Postdoctoral Fellow, Department of Law, London School of Economics and Political Science. She obtained her PhD from SOAS with the thesis 'Constitutional Nationalism and Legal Exclusion in Nepal (1990–2007)'. She holds a BA (Hon.) from SOAS in Nepali and Politics, a Laurea Degree from the University of Trieste in International Relations, an MA from SOAS in South Asian Area Studies, and a Graduate Diploma in Law. Her research interests encompass the historico-political and legal developments of South Asian jurisdictions—especially Nepal, India, and Pakistan. Her published works include articles in *Studies in Ethnicity and Nationalism* and the *European Bulletin of Himalayan Research*, and a chapter on Nepal in the edited volume *Rights in Divided Societies* (2012).

John H. Mansfield is John H. Watson Emeritus Chair of Law, Harvard Law School. He has a long history of engagement with South Asian laws and has written extensively about personal laws, religious speech, and the possibility of a Uniform Civil Code in India.

Matthew J. Nelson is in the Department of Politics, SOAS, University of London. He completed his PhD from Columbia University. Before

SOAS, he held faculty positions at the University of California at Santa Cruz, Bates College, and at Yale University. He focuses on the politics of Islam in South Asia. Nelson's first book, *In the Shadow of Shari'ah: Islam, Islamic Law, and Democracy in Pakistan* (2011), concerns the relationship between Islamic law and democratic politics in Pakistan. His current work concerns the politics of doctrinal diversity in the context of Islamic education.

T. John O'Dowd studied law at University College Dublin (UCD) and the University of Oxford (Wolfson College) and has been a member of UCD Faculty of Law (now School of Law) since 1991. His particular research interests are Irish constitutional law, European human rights law, economic, social, and cultural rights, comparative constitutional law, right to freedom of expression, and media law. O'Dowd has published articles in journals and books on differents aspects of each of these. He is an active member of the European Group of Public Law since 2000 and was for several years a member of the executive body of the Irish Council for Civil Liberties and of the council of the Irish Association of Law Teachers.

Shylashri Shankar is Senior Fellow at the Centre for Policy Research, New Delhi. She has held academic positions at the University of Texas at Austin and the Center on Religion and Democracy, University of Virginia. She was also a Bellagio Fellow at the Rockefeller Centre in Bellagio, Italy. Shankar has degrees from Columbia University, the London School of Economics and Political Science, the University of Cambridge, and the University of Delhi. Her interests include constitutionalism, judicial politics in India, and the political economy of anti-poverty initiatives. She is the author *of Scaling Justice: India's Supreme Court, Anti-Terror Laws and Social Rights* (2009) and the co-author of *Battling Corruption: Making Governments Responsive to the Poor* (forthcoming).

Deepika Udagama is Head, Department of Law, University of Peradeniya. She was Founding Director, Centre for the Study of Human Rights, Faculty of Law, University of Colombo (2001–7) and has served on human rights bodies both in Sri Lanka and in the United Nations. She has published on various dimensions of human rights issues in Sri Lanka with a focus on the interplay between international law and constitutional law. Her most recent essay, 'The Sri Lankan Legal Complex and the Liberal Project', is a contribution to the volume *Fates of Political Liberalism in the British Post-Colony* (2012).

Richard W. Whitecross holds degress in history, law and social anthropology. His doctoral thesis, The 'Zhabdrung's Legacy: Law, State and Social Transformation in Contemporary Bhutan', was the first anthropological work to examine law in everyday life and the role of law in the process of social and political development of Bhutan. In 2007, he moved from the University of Edinburgh to join the Scottish government as a senior researcher in its Justice Directorate. He remains an Honorary Fellow in Social Anthropology at the University of Edinburgh. His publications include 'Intimacy, Loyalty and State Formation: The Spectre of the "Anti-National"' in *Traitors: Suspicion, Intimacy and the Ethics of State Building* (2009) and '"Keeping the Stream of Justice Pure": The Buddhicisation of Bhutanese law?' in *Law and Anthropology in a Trans-national World* (2009).